T0364786

THE BIG ASIAN BOOK OF LAND SCAPE ARCHI TECTURE

THE BIG ASIAN BOOK OF LAND SCAPE ARCHI TECTURE

Heike Rahmann
Jillian Walliss
(Eds.)

jovis

Form is no other than emptiness,
Emptiness no other than form.
Form is only emptiness,
Emptiness only form.
...
So, in emptiness, no form,
No feeling, thought, or choice,
Nor is there consciousness.
No eye, ear, nose, tongue, body, mind;
No colour, sound, smell, taste, touch,
Or what the mind takes hold of,
Nor even act of sensing.[1]

To Marieluise. We hope to have found
some answers to your last question ...

What is an Asian practice?

Speed

Preface

I recall the day when I went to the University of Melbourne as part of my overseas study in architecture after gaining some years of architectural work experience in Singapore's public housing sector. Intrigued by how landscape architecture in Asia has influenced a positive change to the built environment, I went on to pursue a master's degree in landscape architecture in the same campus, hoping my degrees could complement each other and make me a better designer. Nearly twenty years on, the request from my alma mater to write the preface for this book seems like a déjà vu where my involvement in this profession seems to have gone a full circle.

The privilege to be part of Singapore's greening effort in the public service for more than seventeen years, coupled with my past presidential roles in the Asia-Pacific region under the International Federation of Landscape Architects (IFLA) and Singapore Institute of Landscape Architects (SILA) for many years, provided me the opportunities to experience, explore, and engage Asian landscape architecture practice in many different ways. I have exchanged conversations with diverse people and communities across geographical borders in the Asian region. I have insights into the challenges and design solutions that landscape architects proudly share and have been fortunate to see this work close up.

And as landscape architects in Asia, we are blessed to do what we do. It can energise and inspire not only us, but also the people who experience our projects. The continuous discovery of good landscape architecture and the brilliant people behind it is astounding. How I wish that such exchanges of knowledge and insights might be widely shared. The lack of awareness of excellent projects and innovative design practices in Asia is partly due to the absence of a consolidated platform that celebrates and communicates the scope of Asian landscape architecture. Even if we are well-travelled and well-informed, or are engaged in projects across the region, it is not possible to fully apprehend the spirit behind Asian landscape architecture and distil the complex thinking behind its materiality, design process, impact, and other key influences that shape project outcomes. These projects represent a diverse array of cultures and a tapestry of landscape architecture traditions in Asia. They also reflect the breadth of cultural, environmental, and socio-political issues faced in different countries, underlined by diverse contexts and constraints, shaped by distinctive parameters.

Given the need for greater awareness in landscape architecture in the Asia-Pacific region, the IFLA Asia-Pacific Landscape Architecture awards were rebranded in 2017 with a stronger partnership from the international community to provide a push for the recognition of the landscape fraternity in the region. The IFLA AAPME awards–Resilience by Design was initiated in 2018 with support from IFLA Africa and the Middle East regions to reflect the urgency of nature-based solution in the era of climate change and resilience-building through design. These awards also aim to heighten recognition for landscape architecture practised in this lesser known region. These two award schemes have received overwhelming responses and continue in subsequent iterations.

Now in 2020, the time for this book's publication has never been more timely to spur the motivation for Asian landscape architecture to combat climate change and join forces with the other design professions for greater urban innovation. Mooted back in 2019, I hope that *The Big Asian Book of Landscape Architecture* will mark the importance of the landscape architect's role in Asia and expand the possibilities for what Asian landscape architecture can bring to the global community. I sincerely thank Jillian Walliss from the University of Melbourne and Heike Rahmann from RMIT University for the tremendous energy and efforts that has gone into the making of this book. With great enthusiasm and perseverance, they have produced a valuable book with insights and voices from designers, academics, developers, and other experts. From breadth to depth, you will be intrigued by some of the thinking and sharing from the landscape architects and professionals of Asia.

I hope you find this book a refreshing read, and that it is able to renew your mind to the achievements and potentials of Asian landscape architecture.

Damian Tang
Immediate Past President
of IFLA Asia-Pacific

Heike Rahmann/Jillian Walliss

Introduction

What do we really know about contemporary Asian landscape architecture? From outside Asia, knowledge is sporadic, gleaned from project descriptions on websites such as dezeen or the rare presentation from an Asian academic or designer at a conference. Within Asia, there has been limited exchange, complicated by the relative youth of the discipline, along with the fact that a collective notion of an Asian identity is new. With so many Asian designers and academics studying and training overseas, there is a tendency to look to international influences for validation or inspiration over Asian peers. As a consequence Asian knowledge is often conceived relative to North American or European perspectives, which can cloud what is particular or unique to Asian landscape practice.

Given this, why are two Australia-based academics editing this book? As an Asian-Pacific nation, Australia has a very close economic and cultural relationship to Asia. Sydney and Melbourne for instance are now considered Euro-Asian cities. This position has seeded our interest in the region, which we have explored in previous research projects and through extensive travel and professional exchange. Our related but distant relationship to Asia provides an important objective oversight for conceiving content, while our experience in publishing research, which spans practice and academia, is valuable for a book targeting equally professionals, students, and academics.

The catalyst for this book can be traced to our experience editing a special themed edition of *Landscape Architecture Australia* titled 'Embracing the Asian Century'. This project revealed just how little had been published about Asian landscape architecture in English and laid the foundations for this more ambitious book project. However, to do this we needed to extend our network of Asian designers and academics. In a twenty-minute chance meeting with Kongjian Yu in Melbourne in 2018, we declared our intention, along with the desire to run a workshop in Asia (albeit we had no funding). Generously, Kongjian offered to host a two-day workshop in Beijing, although participants would need to fund their own travel. This was planned for January 2019 and we set about inviting a practitioner and academic from different Asian contexts to attend the 'The Big Asian Book' workshop. To some participants we were unknown, so travelling to a self-funded workshop was a generous leap of faith.

Unaware of it at the time, this workshop unfolded with a distinctly Asian sensibility. We offered no framing beyond an invitation for each designer or academic to prepare short presentations discussing landscape architecture from their cultural perspective and to nominate three influential contemporary Asian projects. Looking back, it is surprising that such busy practitioners and academic leaders came to Beijing with the promise of so little. We had after all had no money, no book contract, and no articulated agenda. Participants crossed generations and geographies and featured Yoon-Jin Park (PARKKIM) and Professor Jeong-Hann Pae (Seoul National University), Jeffrey Hou (University of Washington), Stanislaus Fung (Chinese University of Hong Kong), Huai-yan Chang and four other designers from Salad Dressing (Singapore), Prapan Napawongdee and Yossapon Boonsom from Shma (Thailand), Kongjian Yu from Turenscape, Ricky Ray Ricardo (former editor of *Landscape Architecture Australia*), Dorothy Tang (University of Hong Kong, now MIT), Miki Mitsuta from Overlap (Japan), Yazid Ninsalam (formerly Singapore ETH Centre Future Cities Laboratory, now RMIT University), Sidh Sintusingha (formerly Thailand, now University of Melbourne), Alban Mannisi (formerly Korea, now RMIT University), Zhifang Wang from Peking University, and Dong Zhang and Huicheng Zhong from the Chinese design practices of Z+T Studio and Lab D+H.

During the process of developing this book, a colleague used the following analogy to explain a fundamental difference between doing business in Asian and Western contexts. In Asia, someone might offer an invitation to get in a boat. You take up the invitation without knowing anything more. During the journey, more information may (or may not) be revealed—where the boat is heading, how long the journey will take, why you are in the boat, and who else is getting in the boat. The critical point is the invitation, and its potential to develop into something, which is unknown at the point of embarking. Whether the information is forthcoming will depend on how your relationship unfolds. Your trip might be over quickly, or it could end up being a lifelong connection.

In an Australian, European, or North American mindset, without knowledge of the organisers, and a clear understanding of workshop's structure, intent, and outcome, participants would simply not come, especially to a self-funded conference. In an Asian context, the workshop operated as a first step, as an invitation.

Over Chinese banquets, breakfasts, smoke breaks, and discussion sessions, people got to talk and know each other. We set up exercises as a catalyst for establishing the book's major framings. These included understanding their nominated projects without relying on Western classifications and typologies of space and exploring the diverse terminologies and concepts related to 'landscape' in different Asian languages. What quickly became apparent was that these designers and academics rarely get a chance to talk to each other. Conferences are increasingly popular in Asia; however these are avenues to *present* ideas, rather than to discuss. Further these conferences often privilege international keynote speakers offering perspectives of questionable relevance to the Asian region. Designers, in particular, talk to clients, government, or developers but have limited avenues to debate ideas with their peers. And in a surprising conclusion to the two days, many participants stated that before the workshop they did not see themselves as 'Asian' designers but now they were 'proud' to take on this title.

We left the workshop with still no clear book structure. However we had a far more valuable commodity—relationships. Hopping on the high-speed train back to Hong Kong, we spent the next ten hours establishing the book's ambition and scope, fresh from our discussions and notes.

Through the framing of 'Asia as Method', this book aims to document an emerging, diverse, and adventurous contemporary landscape practice (post 2000). Importantly, it establishes Asia as multiple and overlapping framings and ideas rather than defining knowledge and design approaches by geographies. As we established at our first workshop dinner, defining Asia is an impossibility and inspires endless debate. Consequently, our book is not conceived as a national catalogue or record of 'Asian' design projects. Instead it aims to build a picture of what it means to design, do business, and think about nature, space, and urbanism with an Asian sensibility.

Through the tripartite structure of *Continuum*, *Interruption*, and *Speed*, we develop ways for conceiving design through characteristics that simultaneously influence an Asian practice. There is no hierarchy to these influences; readers can start at any section.

Continuum establishes some of the shared cultural and philosophical understandings of space, time, and nature that cross the Asian region and explores how these are interpreted within contemporary design practice. While the discipline of landscape architecture is new, this knowledge is many centuries old and supports the adoption of 'Inter Asia referencing' as a method for deepening understandings of Asian landscape architecture through grounded knowledge.

Interruption explores the impact of modernity and economic growth on Asia. Urbanisation shaped by complex relationships between government, developers, international and local investment, and citizens underpins the introduction of new open space typologies and the emergence of landscape architecture as a discipline. Even though these typologies may resemble Western models they defy classifications such as public and private space, instead operating distinctly in Asian economic, cultural, and political contexts.

Speed examines how governments and designers are responding to the boom and bust cycles of economic development, the imbalance of rural and urban processes, and the density of the Asian city. Rather than being viewed as a hinderance, speed can be considered a mechanism for innovation and change, acting as a catalyst for fast and slow design practice as Asian societies transition into a new phase of development.

Each section begins with a positioning essay, which has an unapologetically wide scope. However the purpose of these essays is not in the detail. Too often discussions of Asia in English retreat into problematic binaries such as tradition and modern; the West and the East; and local and global. Therefore, these opening essays introduce ways for escaping these limitations, introducing new framings and ideas emerging from Asian scholarship, which are relevant to landscape architecture. Their aim is to offer theoretical, cultural, and political contextualisation for the more focused academic writing, shorter reflections, practice interviews, and design projects which comprise each section.

The book is designed to encourage readers to 'dip' into content. Academic essays and critical reflections from original workshop participants are expanded with contributions from Kelly Shannon, Bruno De Meulder, Fumiaki Takano, Damian Tang, Charles Anderson, Eiki Danzuka, Nirmal Kishnani, Akiko Okabe, Kyung-Jin Zoh, Ziying Tang, Jungyoon Kim, and Zhongwei Zhu. Featured design projects were selected from an open project call distributed through Asian landscape professional bodies and are weighted to showcase the most recent and innovative work. Over eighty design projects are included, presented either as standalone or discussed as part of academic essays. Projects from Japan, Korea, mainland China, and Singapore dominated the project call, reflective of the different stages of professional and economic development in the region. We have tried to offer the widest possible representation of projects (but not at the expense of merit) and have limited work produced by international designers to that which demonstrates ideas of significance to Asian understandings.

A special thanks to Ricky Ray Ricardo who provided the initial invitation to guest edit the Asian-themed edition of *Landscape Architecture Australia* and to Gary Xujie Fang and Lily Yue Gu who provided invaluable support in running the Beijing workshop, along with tracing contacts and offering translation. We did eventually get money for the book production from the Ellis Stones Memorial fund from the University of Melbourne and the SRIC fund from RMIT University's School of Architecture and Urban Design.

And finally, a word on the title. We never came up with a better title than the workshop name *The Big Asian Book*. It stuck. Over time the unusual word order has made more sense. We believe this is the first book to document emerging design and theoretical directions for contemporary Asian landscape architecture. It is a book written for the next generation of Asian designers offering much needed culturally specific theory, along with a celebration of an extraordinary body of design work, which is largely unknown to a wider English-speaking audience. This is why the emphasis is on 'Big' as a celebration of the diversity and complexity of ideas and 'Asian' in recognition of this new collectiveness of 'Asia'. We hope you find the ideas, concepts, and projects in *The Big Asian Book* as inspiring as we do.

CONTINUUM

Think Like a King

Act Like a Peasant

Where Is This Place Called Asia?

In 1583, Italian Jesuit missionary Matteo Ricci (1552–1610) travelled to China, bringing with him a map of the world. Constructed using recent advancements in European cartography such as oval projection, this map shocked the Sinocentric world view of the Chinese who 'believed that China contained almost the whole world and that there could not possibly be other equivalent civilisations outside of China.'[1] Instead, this map depicted China as part of a continent described as Asia—a term traced to the Ancient Greek historian Herodotus (440 BCE) who used the Greek word Ασία to refer to the Anatolia peninsula (part of present-day Turkey).[2]

A scientist, linguist, and scholar, Ricci was subsequently commissioned in 1602 by the court of Emperor Wanli to develop a new map, titled *Kunyu Wanguo Quantu* 坤輿萬國全圖 (*Complete Map of Ten Thousand Countries of the World*).[3] In collaboration with Chinese scholars, this map placed China—represented as Middle Kingdom—in the centre of six panels and introduced new scientific and religious perspectives to the Chinese. By 1603, the *Complete Map of Ten Thousand Countries of the World* arrived in Japan where it was widely reproduced using woodblock prints.[4] This Western-style map dramatically challenged Japanese conceptions of space and geography, which up until this point were based on the Buddhist understanding of the cosmos and earth.

Arriving via Korea in the sixth century, Buddhism described a world comprised of the Three Sacred Countries: Tenjiku 天竺 (India), Shintan 震旦 (China), and Honcho 本朝 (Japan). Japan was depicted as a satellite island to a world centred on India. The arrival of Ricci's map was a sensation, confronting the teachings of Buddhist cosmology and inspiring intense debate within Japanese intellectuals and religious leaders.[5] The impact of the *Complete Map of Ten Thousand Countries of the World* on Japan offers just a glimpse of the complexity inherent in engaging with this place described as Asia. It highlights Asia's origins as a European concept, constructed by European knowledge and colonial and missionary expansion. To consider Asia is to engage with far more than geographic boundaries. As Hui Wang comments: 'The issue of Asia is not simply an Asian issue,

Heike Rahmann
Jillian Walliss

but rather a matter of 'world history'.[6] He continues: 'The idea is at once colonialist and anti-colonist, conservative and revolutionary, nationalist and internationalist, originating in Europe and, alternatively, shaping Europe's image of itself.'[7]

The map's influence highlights the complex and intertwining relationship between China and Japan, which continues today. While sharing cultural and spiritual similarities following the introduction of Confucianism, Buddhism, and the Chinese writing system during the Yamato period (between the second and the fifth century CE), Ricci's map inspired intellectuals and scientists to break from Buddhist spatial concepts, which held Japan in a dependent and inferior position to India and China and to construct its own place in the world.[8] Japan's subsequent spatial and cultural repositioning is just one example of the fluidity in which Asian countries have reconfigured their relationship with their neighbours. Over centuries, relationships have been redefined and adjusted based on political, economic, and cultural advantages.

Consequently, contemporary Asian scholars and intellectuals encourage an understanding of Asia as an elastic concept, rather than in terms of nation-states. Amitav Acharya comments further:

> Asia is not 'one' and there is no singular idea of Asia. Asia is of multiple (although not always mutually exclusive) conceptions, some drawing on material forces, such as economic growth, interdependence, and physical power, and others have ideational foundations, such as civilizational linkages and normative aspirations. Some of these varied conceptions of Asia have shaped in meaningful ways the destinies of states and peoples. Moreover, they have underpinned different forms of regionalism, which, in turn, has ensured that Asia, despite its fuzziness and incoherence, has remained a durable, if essentially contested, notion.[9]

17

Drawing on the contemporary discourse on region and regionalism this essay explores this elastic idea of Asia, highlighting the dynamic and complex flows and mobilities of people, economies, culture, and religion that cross national boundaries. This is followed by the introduction of 'Asia as Method', which offers a valuable framing for deepening understandings of Asian perspectives of nature, space, and time. In contrast to the fluid definitions of Asia, these philosophically grounded concepts provide consistency of actions, relationships, and thoughts, independent from dynamic political and economic shifts. Further, these ideas form the basis for conceiving an Asian 'mood' or 'inclination', which continues to influence vernacular and contemporary landscape practice.

An Elastic Asia

In his 2010 essay 'Asia Redux: Conceptualizing a Region for Our Times,' historian Prasenjit Duara highlights how for much of the twentieth century, social space was conceived through understandings of 'the territorial nation-state under conditions of global capitalist production and exchange.'[10] Alternatively, he calls for the return to pre-modern constructs, which emphasise regions and processes of regionalism rather than nation-states. Within this framing, a region is defined as a social construction, which is constantly remade through social, economic, political, cultural interactions and interdependence, while regionalism is viewed as the 'deliberate act of forging a common platform, such as intergovernmental and transnational objectives to deal with common issues and advance a common identity.'[11] This departure from nation-states is particularly appropriate in the Asian context given that many countries did not gain independence from European powers until the latter half of the twentieth century.[12] Independence led to new nations shifting alliances from European colonisers to explore economic, trade, and cultural links within their region. As the following discussion reveals, considering the flows and networks beyond national borders 'brings the notion of Asia alive.'[13]

Connections forged for economic gain offer the clearest demonstration of processes of Asian regionalism. The Southeast Asian nations, for example, were amongst the last to gain their independence, and from the 1960s began to explore the advantages of regional alignment. In 1967, the Association of Southeast Asian Nations (ASEAN) was established by Indonesia, Malaysia, the Philippines, Singapore, and Thailand, with memberships subsequently expanded to include Brunei, Myanmar (formerly Burma), Cambodia, Laos, and Vietnam. ASEAN aims to address 'intra-regional tensions' whilst raising the profiles of Southeast Asian nations in the wider region.[14] Looking to more recent developments, the Belt and Road Initiative, announced by Chinese president Xi Jinping in 2013, can be considered a further strategy of regionalism. This ambitious vision funded by the Chinese government aims to inject new vitality into the ancient silk road trading routes through a large-scale development policy connecting Asia, Europe, and Africa. Framed around building 'a community of shared interests, destiny and responsibility' the strategy requires 'mutual political trust, economic integration and cultural inclusiveness.'[15]

Flows of migration between Asian countries parallel economic connections, creating geographically dispersed populations linked by ethnicity. It is estimated that between thirty and forty-five million people of Chinese ethnicity or ancestry live outside greater China, including as many as twenty-five million in Southeast Asia.[16] With a strong history of maritime trade, Chinese people have moved throughout the Asian region for centuries, with significant populations emigrating from mainland China during the twentieth century. Many emigrants maintain economic links with China, conducting business across national boundaries. However, this extensive diaspora raises questions of identity, as reflected in the many terms used to define this population such as Han ethnic (*Han ren* 汉人), Hua overseas person (*Hua ren* 华人), or Chinese national (*Zhongguo ren* 中国人).[17]

In considering economic migration, it is important to distinguish between the experiences of elite professionals moving to major cities and the working class servicing labour shortages in growing economies such as Singapore, Hong Kong, Japan, Korea, Taiwan, Malaysia, and Thailand.[18] This group of migrant workers, mostly from Southeast Asia but also India, Bangladesh, and Pakistan, are often trapped within a permanent second-class status, reflecting a minority Asia within a wealthy Asian country.[19] Given this complexity, many scholars warn against using Western theories of multiculturalism to describe these ethnically diverse Asian societies, arguing that the term does not reflect the geopolitics and cultural history of the region.[20] For example, Malaysia, shaped by migration from the Indo-China continent and the Malay Sundaland, is considered a particularly pluralist nation, as celebrated in a widely publicised touristic claim 'Malaysia [is] Truly Asia'.[21] However, applying Western framings of multiculturalism to ethnically diverse nations such as Malaysia and Singapore is problematic as they overlook inequitable relationships evident in these societies.

Networks of cosmological thinking and religion introduce a further way for envisaging Asia. Diversity of religions is cited as one of Asia's biggest differences to Europe. While Europe is equally diverse in terms of language, it is considered far more homogenous due to the largely Christian-influenced culture.[22] Across Asia, Hinduism dominates the Indian subcontinent; Islam is found in Malaysia, Bangladesh, and Indonesia (which is considered to host the world's largest Muslim population); Buddhism is dominant across Indochina, Thailand, Bhutan, Burma, Laos, Cambodia, and Sri Lanka; Shintoism is Japan's ethnic religion and is practised alongside Buddhism; Korea has communities of Buddhism, Confucianist doctrines, and Christianity; Christianity dominates in the Philippines; and China has a mix of Buddhist, Confucian, and Taoist communities. In a further complexity, Taoism, Confucianism, Shintoism, and Buddhism are also defined as philosophies, and in some cases, religions are mixed depending on life events. For instance, in Japan, the saying 'born Shinto, die Buddhist' reflects the cyclical ideas of life where Shintoism is generally associated with more positive events such as celebrating birth, child growth, marriage, harvest, and prosperity, while Buddhism is drawn upon for more serious events such as death, the afterlife, and ancestral lineage.[23]

Tracing economic, migration, and religious connections and networks demonstrate just a few ways for conceptualising an 'elastic' Asia and also accounts for the region's cultural and religious diversity. But given this complexity, is there merit in the idea of shared 'Asian values'?

In 1917, Rabinindranath Tagore published *Nationalism*, which challenged the concept of a state-centric nationalism to propose a 'common bond of spiritualism' that unites Asian people.[24] A poet, musician, and polymath from India, Tagore promoted the idea that Asian people shared 'spiritual and civilizational affinities'.[25] These concepts were advocated by other Asian contemporaries, including Japanese thinker Okakura Kakuzo (1862–1913) and Chinese intellectual Zhang Taiyan (1869–1936).

Beginning in the 1970s, this notion of shared Asian values experienced a resurgence, adopted by political leaders such as Singapore's founding prime minister Lee Kuan Yew and Malaysia's long-serving prime minister Mahathir bin Mohamad to explain the region's rapid industrial growth.[26] Lee Kuan Yew was particularly vocal, linking economic performance with cultural traits and habit. Initially, his argument revolved around the idea of 'Confucian values', which emphasises work ethics, along with the importance of social obligations.[27] However, this evolved into the broader idea of 'Asian values', which stressed 'hard work, thrift, an emphasis on education, consensus, national teamwork and respect for authority.'[28] His position was controversial, viewed by some as an argument for governments to maintain an authoritarian position and not progress into more open democracies. Others claim that the notion of 'Asian values' was co-opted as a tool for integration, offering a sense of cohesiveness in multi-ethnic Asian societies.[29]

Shared Asian values are, therefore, a topic of much debate, especially given the cultural and religious diversity of the region. At the same time, it is acknowledged that many Asian belief systems play a significant role in shaping a collectivistic Asian society. Emphasis on group harmony over individuality, the avoidance of open conflict, indirect communication, and loyalty to an extended family and community are all commonly attributed to Asian society. However, scholars warn about the reductive assumption that Christianity encourages an individual presence in the world in contrast to the collective nature of Asia, highlighting, for instance, that both Hinduism and Buddhism include theories of an 'inner self'.[30]

The concept of 'Asia as Method' offers an alternative interpretation, based not on the identification of similar values, but on gaining knowledge from an understanding of similar historical experiences. Despite this concept having particular relevance to the contextually driven practice of landscape architecture, to date it has had far more influence on architecture. But as we argue in the remainder of this essay, Asia as Method has an important role in strengthening understandings of an Asian practice of landscape architecture.

Asia as Method
In a 1960 lecture, Japanese philosopher Yoshimi Takeuchi advocated breaking from binary framings such as progress and tradition, or the East and West. Agonising over Japan's role during the Second World War, Takeuchi argued that it was unproductive and inadequate to turn to Europe or North America for explanations of where and why Japanese history had gone astray. While Asia's intellectual elite in their pursuit of modernisation tried to emulate the West, Takeuchi reflected on the hierarchical relationship between the West and Asia resulting from the 'different stages of modernisation'[31] stating that 'If one went to Europe or the United States, there would be a sense that people there are superior to or better than oneself.'[32] Instead, he suggested 'inter-referencing places' that share similar historical experiences to produce grounded knowledge.[33]

As such, Asia as Method has found a concrete intellectual agenda that 'enables research to be placed in its specific historical context without the epistemological and ontological burden of catching up with the West.'[34] Importantly, Takeuchi argues that Asianism is not an objective concept or one that can be '"narrativized" into a history of a single trend of thought', which is organised around an innate 'cultural essence'.[35] Alternatively, he describes Asianism as method or means—'a mood' or an inclination.[36]

Asia as Method is particularly valuable for considering ideas of landscape in the Asian context, which have strong links to philosophy and religion. For centuries, Indian, Japanese, and Chinese intellectuals have meditated on the philosophy of nature, time, and space, which shaped a holistic understanding of the human and non-human environment. Unlike Western classical thought, which was interrupted by the rational thinking of the Enlightenment (for instance establishing the binary framings of nature and culture), these

19

philosophies continue to have a direct influence on contemporary culture. Consequently, many Asian cultures have maintained an interconnectedness between nature and humans, which provides the foundation for consistency of actions, relationships, and thoughts, independent from dynamic political and economic shifts.

While spatial concepts such as the Chinese *feng shui* or the Japanese *ma* have been introduced to non-Asian cultures, it is questionable whether their true meaning can be understood by those engaging outside deeper philosophical and cosmological understandings. The relevance of semantics and cultural contexts are important factors to consider in the construct of concepts, even in widely used terms such as landscape. Geographer and sociologist Olaf Kühne highlights that 'Outside of the Germanic languages family the word "Landscape" has hardly any every current day and secular equivalent'.[37] He continues that 'While most Europeans may describe much of what they perceive in their environment as landscape, Chinese, Japanese and Thai people use, in order to convey similar meanings, a great number of different words with very specific content'.[38]

The introduction of the word landscape into Asian languages in the late twentieth century has problematically interrupted concepts, as is well demonstrated by the Japanese experience. For example, the Japanese language uses the indigenous word *keshiki* alongside *fukei* and the newer term *keikan*. With Buddhism's arrival in Japan, the term *fukei* was introduced as a Buddhist impression of the world. Written in the Chinese characters 風 *fu* (wind) and 景 *kei* (scenery), *fukei* was adopted within literature and the arts in reference to the perceptible environment.[39] In the contemporary Japanese language, *fukei* is used interchangeably with the older word *keshiki* (景色, using the characters for scenery and colour). Nevertheless, as Japanese art scholar Ken-ichi Sasaki highlights, there are subtle semantic distinctions between these terms. Referring to *waka* poetry, Sasaki states that

> in the twenty-one royal anthologies of waka (905–1439), we find as vocable only keshiki. This means that the word fūkei was never used in waka, i.e. in purely Japanese poetry, and that whereas fūkei was accepted as a Chinese word, keshiki was considered Japanese. So fūkei was considered suitable for translating the Western word 'landscape.'[40]

During the Meiji Restoration (from 1868) European scientific concepts from natural science and engineering were introduced to Japan. The German word *Landschaft* was interpreted into a new Japanese word *keikan* (景観, using the Chinese characters for scenery and appearance). Some consider *keikan* a more 'objective' view of the environment associated with civil engineering, while *fukei* reflects a more subjective understanding of the landscape.[41] However, there is far more fluidity in these terms than many English translations suggest.

In a further complexity, the term landscape was introduced as a loan word—meaning a word adopted from a foreign language with little or no modification, as reflected in the Japanese Katakana syllabary ランドスケープ (pronounced as landoskepu). The loanword is used today to describe the landscape architectural profession. Despite not being widely understood by Japanese people, it was seen as an appropriate term to differentiate contemporary landscape practice from traditional garden design, while also aligning the definition of landscape in Japanese practice with the European Landscape Convention, which defines landscape as 'an area, perceived by people, whose character is the result of the action and interaction of natural and/or human factors'.[42] Foregrounding a systems approach, this definition misses the subtle nuances and cultural connotations embedded in the traditional readings of landscape.

Similar complexities arise with the introduction of other spatial terms with cultural references commonly used in landscape architecture and urban design, such as private, public, and place. The misconception of these terms is not merely related to linguistic issues or challenges of translation but points to unfamiliarity with and understanding of 'conceptions of the original terms.'[43] For example, in Thai the perception of place is conceptualised by two terms, one that is 'explicit, readily identifiable and describable' and another that is 'more ambivalent, less describable'.[44] Thai architecture scholar Cuttaleeya Jiraprasertkun argues that 'The merging or interweaving phenomenon of these two notions results in contrasting characteristics in the conceptual, social, and political realms of Thai place.'[45] In other words, the meaning of foreign terms with little or no reference to the socio-economic make-up of Asian cultures is defied by their disassociation with the everyday lived environment.

This story illustrates not only the compounding problems of translation but also the impossibility of overlaying European concepts into the Asian context. It offers clear evidence for why Takeuchi was inspired to challenge Japan's adoption of European concepts rather than looking to 'inter-Asia' framings. Instead of adopting landscape as a loan word, is it not possible to develop a landscape 'inclination' that comes from Asian perspectives of nature, space and time?

Time, Space, and Nature

Arguably, an Asian inclination towards landscape leads directly to Taoism or Daoism (道教, literally: Teachings of the Way). Viewed as a religion and a philosophy linked to Chinese philosopher and writer Laozi, Taoism is considered one of the most influential bodies of thoughts for understanding the true natural order of the world and universe and can be found in Confucianism and Buddhism. Tao offers guidance for living in harmony with nature, including principles for leading a life of selflessness and simplicity, and for expressing the essence of spontaneity.[46] Under Taosim, the universe is defined according to a 'tripartite structure' consisting of the two poles of heaven (天) and earth (地) with man or humanity (人) occupying the middle realm.[47] The universe is considered to be under constant transformation, with the connecting power of *qi* (氣) flowing through everything as essential energy of existence and action.[48]

This concept of universal energy as life energy is not limited to Taoism, evident for instance in the Sanskrit word of *prana* used in Hindu philosophy. Further, *qi* or *prana* not only relates to the metaphysical conception of relationships in space but also provides an understanding of an actual physical presence, which can be perceived through the body, such as in the mood, spirit, or atmosphere of places or things. For example, Japanese people refer to positive experiences as *kimochi ga ii* (気持ちがいい, literally: possessing good energy) and negative as *kimochi ga warui* (気持ちが悪い, literally: possessing bad energy). Importantly, these concepts refer to a holistic idea of the universe, where the energy flows through the human body, connecting man with heaven and earth, as studied in yoga or many Asian martial arts.

Reflecting on the relationship between body and space in Asian culture, Cheryl Stock highlights the concept of 'the middle way' as one the most crucial aspects of Taoist and Buddhist philosophy.[49] This notion of a 'betweenness' offers a critical passage for the creative energy flow of *qi* to move between being and non-being and presents one of the most challenging concepts for those outside of Asian cultures to comprehend.[50] The Japanese concept of *ma* (間) provides a further example. Extremely difficult to translate into English, *ma* is defined variously as gap, space, pause, emptiness, or blankness. A critical component is an 'awareness in everyday life' or 'state of mind'[51] that is present in every aspect of Japanese culture, from theatre to music, art, language, and architecture.[52]

In spatial terms, *ma* can be understood through multiple dimensions. For example, in a one-dimensional definition, it denotes not only a straight-line distance between two points in space but in addition a simultaneous awareness of both poles as individual units.[53] Unlike in Western architecture, which describes space mostly by objects, poles, or boundaries that give space physical presence and dimensions, the Japanese concept of space starts with the void. Importantly, *ma* refers to space as 'felt experience for the viewer or listener to pass through; the quintessential experience of what lies between the words, the steps, the notes or the images of the work'.[54] As Japanese architect Arata Isozaki states:

Space could never be perceived independently of the element of time [and] time was not abstracted as a regulated

21

homogeneous flow, but rather was believed to exist only in relation to movements in space.[55]

While metaphysical and cosmic concepts of time, space, and nature are not unique to Asian cultures, for example, evident in many Indigenous cultures, what is important to our discussion is that this knowledge continues to influence agricultural and ecological practices and designed landscapes and gardens. Over the past fifty years, Asia has experienced rapid processes of modernisation and urbanisation (as discussed in *Interruption*). Yet these concepts have not been relegated to the position of history or tradition but are increasingly being explored as a means for producing more sustainable outcomes for contemporary situations. An intent to balance energies within a dynamic world can, therefore, be considered a major philosophy shaping an Asian perspective of landscape. However, the goal is not to achieve a balanced state, but focuses on the challenge of occupying a world in a continuing state of impermanence.

The Pursuit of Balance in a State of Impermanence

In their 2009 essay, Xiangqiang Chen and Jianguo Wu highlight the value of Taoism and its underlying ambition to harmonise with the rhythms of nature as the foundations for developing a sustainable approach to landscape architecture.[56] Philosophies derived from Taoism such as yin-yang dualism, the five-element theory, the eight-trigram theory, and the sixty-four hexagram of the *I-Ching*, which all inform *feng shui* theory, are influential in many Asian countries.[57] However, translations of these concepts into English has led to misrepresentations. For example, Stanislaus Fung highlights how the concept of *yin* and *yang* is often read as an oppositional relationship (light and dark, male and female, nature and culture) with each conceived as complementary to make a whole. He maintains that

such terms are not dialectical. Unlike dialectic relationships, polar relationships are not involved in an oppositional play moving from contradiction through synthesis to sublation. Rather, yin is becoming-yang, and vice versa. Further, yin and yang refer to the relationships of unique particulars and express: ... the mutuality, interdependence, diversity, and creative efficacy of the dynamic relationships that are deemed immanent in and valorise the world.[58]

Fung elaborates further on the dynamic relationship between *yin* and *yang* by introducing the Chinese notion of propensity (*qi*). With origins in Chinese discussions of politics and military strategy, *qi* has been influential in history, painting, and landscape and refers to the oscillation 'between the static and the dynamic points of view; in any given configuration there is an inherent propensity for the unfolding of events.'[59] Fung writes:

> Like the water surging from a breach in the wall that had previous held it back, bringing everything tumbling downward with it, or like a crossbow, stretched to its limit, that can release a fatal effect from a distance, the skillful general achieves maximal effect with minimal effort from a distance by exploiting the strategic factors in play. The field of propensity is charged with tension of forces (water held back by a wall, crossbow stretched to the limit).[60]

Thus, in considering these balancing forces, we can argue that the 'basic premise' of the 'continual balancing of opposites through a duality' in *yin* and *yang* is 'ternary rather than binary.'[61] Geomancy practices of *feng shui* (風水, literally: wind and water) offer clear evidence of how an ambition for continual balance influences landscape practices. Geomancy has been used across Asia for reading the land and natural forces in both a concrete and metaphysical way, including 'geophysical factors—geographical landforms, climate, magnetic fields—and astral phenomena—movements of the stars, solstices, lunar phases—[and] the psychosomatic welfare of the human being.'[62]

Working with a vast collection of rules, a geomancer defines the ideal location and configuration of houses, burial grounds, villages, and even entire capital cities in harmony with the complex configurations of nature that already exist or are man-made.[63] Sometimes described as a scientific model due to its systematic approach of evaluating morphologic features, *feng shui* is equally open to superstition, as the location and configuration, in particular of graveyards, would decide on the luck and prosperity of a family. A geomancer offers a reading of the existing morphological features relative to the heavenly body and draws on principles of *feng shui*, including balancing *qi* on the earth's surface, to reshape the landscape for maximum advantage.[64]

For centuries, these theories and practices have been applied in China 'to probe the landscape and to discern from the irregularity and asymmetry of mountains and waters appropriate locations for specific human occupancy'.[65] But how can this knowledge inform a contemporary practice of landscape architecture? This question lies at the heart of Kongjian Yu's 2020 book *Ideal Landscapes and the Deep Meaning of Feng-Shui*, which traces and unpacks the origins and meaning of this philosophy. Wary of *feng shui* being considered a 'low-class cultural phenomenon', a superstition linked to predetermined ancestral lineage, or a science based on strict rules,[66] Yu instead discusses its principles in relation to landscape perception and ecological experience. He states:

> I firmly believe that the ecological experience of Chinese culture, especially the ecological experience of the culture-forming period, has played a key role in the formation of our landscape-perception relating to good or bad fortune and the models of ideal landscapes.[67]

Focusing on the biological and cultural patterns relating to the ecological experience, Yu uncovers a new conceptualisation of *feng shui* that provides insight for contemporary landscape design and planning. Doing so, Yu joins other Chinese scholars in their endeavour to find answers to the current environmental crisis by revisiting Taoist philosophies and the rules that formulate the relation between human and nature.[68] Similarly, Japanese landscape architect Fumiaki Takano sees value in the *feng shui* philosophy, arguing that 'land rich in biodiversity is also full of ki' from a perspective of *feng shui*.[69] While the Western science-based concept of ecology evaluates the 'potential of the land' through a series of natural factors, *feng shui* 'reads the power of the land represented in ki.' Thus, Takano concludes that *feng shui* 'is an Asian concept of ecology.'[70]

Feng shui practices continue to be applied in Japan and Korea to establish agriculture and villages, and to manage ecological systems. In Japan, the concept of *satoyama* (里山, literally: village mountain) describes an important perimeter of nature, 'enriched by human intervention' that has traditionally been designed on the edge of rural villages.[71] First recorded in 1759 in a book entitled *Miscellaneous Stories of Kiso Mountain*, *satoyama* contains the terraces of paddy fields, along with other important resources such as pines for fuel and edible wild plants.[72] Similarly, the newer concept of *satoumi* (里海, literally: village sea) responds to the relationship between communities and the coastal ecosystem. Often reduced to a particular appearance of or signature features in the landscape, these archetypes, in fact, embody a deeper meaning that extends to general principles of living in such environments including sustainable land management practices. Thus, *satoyama* and *satoumi* reflect a holistic understanding of the human co-existence with nature and since the late 1970s have begun to influence conservation laws and practices.[73]

Looking to Southeast Asia, century-old water structures of canals continue to be adopted by farmers and villages. In the case of Thailand, networks of irrigated *quanat* units offer 'micro-scale, community-based water management' in contrast to larger-scale royal infrastructure water management projects.[74] Moving further south to Bali, the *subak* system of weirs and canals, first developed in the ninth century, remains central to Balinese rice production.[75] This system is underpinned by the Tri Hita Karana philosophy, which originates from India. Based on the integration of the human, nature, and the spiritual, Tri Hita Karana considers rice as a gift from god. Consequently, the *subak* system is closely tied to temple culture, with the irrigation system integrated with the village's Bale Banjar community centre and Balinese temples and the priests responsible for water management.[76]

The continuation of these vernacular techniques and practices for managing landscapes for cultural, spiritual, and economic advantage demonstrates their enduring value in connecting communities to wider cycles of life and nature. For example, Japanese philosopher Watsuji Tetsuro (1889–1960) has suggested that the shared conditions of the monsoon have significantly shaped the cultures of China, Japan, India, and Southeast Asia. Watsuji believes that 'moisture' is the symbol of 'life', and that people living in the monsoon regions must acquire tolerance and active ways of living with this climatic phenomenon.[77] Increasingly Asian designers are exploring how these vernacular practices, together with cultural concepts of time, space, and nature, can shape a contemporary Asian practice of landscape architecture that operates as a mix of philosophies and ecologies.

'Inter Asia Referencing' in Landscape Architecture

The voices of Asian designers who share the formative influences on their design practices are an important feature of this book. For example, Singapore-based Huai-yan Chang highlights the value of *satori* (悟り), a Japanese Buddhist concept for awakening, or *lingwu* (领悟) in Chinese, for guiding his approach, while Korean practice PARKKIM point to the value of *sansu* (山水) in conceiving an urban paradigm responsive to an era of climate change. Eiki Danzuka of the Japanese practice EARTHSCAPE highlights the influence of Shinto in positioning landscape design within a flow connecting the past and future, the human world and the natural world and the world of gods, while Chinese designer Pang Wei proposes a return to *bao shou* (保守) to construct a landscape architecture of care which focuses on the intimate lived experience of people in specific places.

In showcasing these diverse design voices, alongside design projects from across the Asian region, this book demonstrates the value of 'Inter Asia referencing' for landscape architecture. For over one hundred years scholars and thinkers across Asia have been exploring the potential of a more integrated idea of Asia as a means for gaining autonomy from the West.[78] This is not without controversies, raising debates over who is included and excluded, along with issues over which parts of Asia (i.e., East Asia) are more dominant in discourse and debate.[79] However, in the context of deepening an understanding of contemporary landscape architecture practice its value is immense. Asia as Method does not propose the searching for 'the roots of knowledge' but focuses on producing grounded knowledge sensitive to cultural context.[80] This is extremely important given that so many Asian designers and academics have gained their professional qualifications in Western countries where they have been drilled in the English-language discourse of nature, culture, ecology, and landscape.

Throughout this book, we have tried as much as possible to privilege culturally specific terminologies and practices, along with encouraging authors to position their ideas against Asian scholarship rather than Western landscape theory. We encourage readers of *Continuum* to focus on the culturally based descriptions of concepts and practices that begin to build an Asian 'mood' or 'inclination' towards landscape architecture. ∎

Artificial
Nature

Bruno De Meulder
Kelly Shannon

Throughout Asia, there is an emerging wave of water urbanism practices together with a plethora of projects that attempt to reverse the detrimental effects of excessively hard engineering and environmental degradation. A cocktail of nostalgia and ecological concerns is catapulting water back onto the scene of urbanism. On the one hand, water is surely on the marketing menu of many urban management programmes of beautification, including the uncovering of rivers, usually with adjacent pathways or biking trails. New waterfronts revalue the economic, social, and environmental potential of such landscapes. On the other hand, there are a host of projects that specifically aim to increase biodiversity, create recreational opportunities, connect people to 'nature', and revitalise settlements.

The 5.8-kilometre-long Cheonggyecheon Restoration Project/linear park in Seoul (2003–5) is emblematic of a beautification and 'branding' project for Korea's burgeoning capital city. The highly celebrated project sought to restore an ancient stream that was replaced by an elevated expressway. Although the project is not a restoration project, since it simulates a natural river landscape above a concrete channel, it has proven an incredibly popular urban park. It has also been credited with spurring economic growth in the northern area of the city and reducing small-particle air pollution. In Japan, there has been a huge resurgence of river restoration projects. The country boosts a River Law enacted in 1896, during the Meiji Restoration, when many foreign experts contributed to modernising the country following the samurai era and immediately after a series of damaging floods.[1] Between 1990 and 2004, more than 23,000 *ta shizen gata kawa zukuri* (nature-oriented river works) were initiated throughout Japan.[2] Straight and concrete channelled rivers have had their beds excavated and native species are again flourishing. There is a holistic restoration process, which also includes lakes, headwater management, and coastal ecologies. In parts of Japan, countless 'fishermen's forests' acknowledge an essential link between forests and water.

In China, numerous landscape architects such as Kongjian Yu/Turenscape, DLC (Design Land Collaborative), and Beijing Tsinghua Urban Planning & Design Institute, amongst many others have made it their mission to reverse China's ubiquitous channelisation of rivers in urbanised areas. Projects in quite different localities and with correspondingly varied responses reveal the possibilities to not only ecologically restore, but also imbue, a rich public realm into urban riversides. Other projects emerge from the 'sponge city' government programme that since 2013 has subsidised sixteen cities (including Wuhan, Chongqing, Xiamen, and others). This programme focuses on the creation of city structures, which absorb, capture, and recycle rainwater—a form of sustainable urban drainage. This way, at least 70 per cent of rainwater would be absorbed underground instead of being discharged into the nearest rivers and lakes. By 2030, 80 per cent of cities in China should have state of the art drainage systems and infrastructures that allow for efficient infiltration of rainwater.[3]

Moreover, other Asian countries are promoting 'performative' water landscapes that address water storage, recycling, and flooding. Since 2006, Singapore has been developing the ABC (active, beautiful, clean) Waters Programme to counter its drinking water dependence on Malaysia (which is due to expire in 2061). A holistic water management includes a comprehensive new blue-green infrastructure, which coordinates housing, road, and park departments. The initiative seeks to transform Singapore's drains, canals, and reservoirs beyond their utilitarian functions of drainage, etc., into beautiful streams, rivers, and lakes integrated with their surroundings. The resulting water landscapes include waterway parks, constructed wetlands, rain gardens, and detention ponds.[4] In Vietnam, planning projects are emerging, such as the Mekong Delta Regional Development Plan, in which the water structure is taken as the register for the spatial development of whole regions and which includes large new monsoon reservoirs. They reconnect and adapt to the historically transmitted strategies of domesticating the territory while providing water downstream during times of drought.[5]

The growing catalogue of contemporary Asian landscape architecture projects that include water as a primary component should come as no surprise. Throughout the region's history, water was invariably an essential component of worldviews. The resurgence of water elements in designed landscapes not only harks back to history but also addresses the consequences of challenges related to accelerated climate change.

Deep Form Water Landscapes

Bruno De Meulder

Kelly Shannon

Water has been of fundamental importance in the history of Asia; it once held a privileged position, symbolically and physically. Complex water management not only intertwined social-cultural and political organisation but also afforded the settling with water—literally the construction of settlement as well as settling with, as in dealing with water's very unpredictable nature. Throughout the region, various settlement morphologies developed—from centres to peripheries and lowlands to mountains—all, in their various ways, closely related to water flows. Settlement, in cities or villages, requires water sources be tapped, distributed, maintained, and managed. The control of water required the mastery of topography and the precise effects of gravity in water flows. The primitive logic of 'cut-and-fill' and differences in microtopography were powerful tools in lowland and valley conditions. Levels of inundation determined distinct land use, and therefore defining component parts of the land mosaic in terms of wet/dry, productive/inhabited, and safe/unsafe was considered essential. Water management methods simultaneously addressed pragmatism, urbanism, and symbolism with innovative engineering and an understanding of topography, hydrology, soil types, and seasonal weather patterns.

There is evidence from early history for the deep-seated relation of water to settlement and various productive and cultural landscapes. Many of the region's great contributions to landscape architecture stemmed from both ingenious water management and site-specific designs of territories, cities, and gardens in relation to water. They have had enduring impacts as they imprinted some of Asia's 'deep form water landscapes', but they also form the base of enduring practices of settling with water. As such, they articulate Asian water urbanisms and encompass the fundamental issues of settling with water. Evidently, technological development was a force driving innovation, particularly in colonial settings and self-inflicted modernisation processes. The iterative adaptations and restructuring of Asian water urbanisms have always been embedded within an enduring belief system, which placed water and water gods in an essentialist and symbiotic relation with mountains and mountain gods. However, since the 1950s until recently, the socio-cultural aspect has largely succumbed to economic prerogatives. It is only since the 2000s that there has been an emerging revival of deep form water landscapes. This essay briefly highlights the legacy of Asian water urbanisms, the eternal re-articulations of its practices in relation to worldview and belief systems, and the recent re-creation of deep form water landscapes.

As evinced in Asian cartography, water, and specifically rivers, are of paramount importance. The first known map of China (1137 CE), from the Song dynasty (960–1279 CE), depicts only one of the eighty rivers in the country that King Yu (founder of the Xia dynasty) was given credit for taming. He dredged riverbeds and enriched livelihoods by constructing extensive irrigation networks. In contemporary times, Yu the Great, as he has become known, is mythologically idolised by hydraulic engineers, irrigation experts, and water conservancy workers. Another classic map of China, believed to have appeared before the first century BCE, brings in another important element of ancient Asian cartography, namely that of mountains. The *Shan Hai Jing* (Classic of mountains and rivers) recorded mountains, rivers, animals, vegetation, and legends in different parts of China. It was considered more representative of ancient tradition, and perhaps magical and ritualistic rather than geographical—'something of an imagined world concerning man's relationship to mountains, rivers, and the sea'.[1] Nonetheless, the coupling of mountains, rivers, and the sea is inextricably bound to the common-sense understanding of their ecosystems' interdependence as well to various Asian worldviews (which elevate this understanding to a symbolic level). Traces of the Chinese cartographic traditions can clearly be found in Vietnam, Korea, and Japan.[2]

At the same time, everywhere in Asia, indigenous water spirits and deities were considered territorial guardians, and they continue to dominate myths and legends. In Asia's rich cultural heritage, water continues to hold a revered role. In many parts of Asia the prominent figure of the *naga* ('serpent' in Sanskrit), is believed to be closely connected to water and rainfall. *Nagas* represent cosmic power and are considered the protectors of springs, wells, and rivers.[3] Water is considered purifying, life-giving, and sustaining. It is linked to fertility and extraordinary events, and its tutelary spirits are both celebrated for life-giving, healing, and transformative powers and feared for malevolent, belligerent, and calamitous forces.[4] Both spirits and ancestors derive from lakes, rivers, and seas and are linked to various rituals. The sacred nature of water is expressed in diverse beliefs and religions of Asia, including Hinduism, Islam, and Buddhism.

The Origins of Asian Water Urbanisms

Many regions in Asia developed wet rice cultivation on vast lowland expanses. This, in turn, demanded a precise system of water management and control. In the 1950s, Karl Wittfogel, an influential Sinologist, coined the term 'hydraulic civilization', which implied a strongly hierarchic society and elaborate bureaucracy.[5] Irrigation required a precise preparation of the ground and implied a sophisticated interaction of settlement, terrain, labour, and water.

Society was predominantly rural. Systemic irrigation and water management went hand in hand with a dense and stable occupation of the land (as required for wet rice cultivation). The legitimacy of such a strong bureaucratic rule is dependent on its performance. As long as it results in food security for all—providing minimal welfare—the stability of the system is safeguarded. The centralisation of bureaucracy allowed for a massive mobilisation of labour. Building dykes along the Yellow River in 1351, for example, required a workforce of not less than 100,000.[6]

Urban water control in Asia reveals highly structured rural and urban territorial systems that are physically and symbolically linked to technologies, religious beliefs, cultural and social practices, and power structures—all strongly related to water. However, water management is not always permanent and not necessarily state controlled. Today, the northern Thailand highlands have long hosted a peculiar human ecology. The mountainous terrain provides safe haven for tribal groups that practice what James C. Scott, an influential anthropologist with expertise in Southeast Asia, labelled the 'art of not being governed'[7], which includes a form of 'escape agriculture'. This uses the landscape literally as infrastructure and adapts accordingly to crops that grow fast and are easily harvested. Even the stationary agriculture practised in the region by other groups, such as the Lanna people, remains flexible and natural. Their communal irrigation systems for rice cultivation—*muang* (canal) and *fai* (weirs)—have been in operation for more than 1000 years. 'In the *muang fai* system, villagers work collectively to build enormous weirs across the major rivers at the start of the rainy season, diverting water to major irrigation canals several kilometres long, which in turn feed village-based tributaries. The top of the bamboo and mud weirs wash away once the paddies fill.'[8]

Many of Asia's earliest cities and settlements had a close relationship with and relied upon rivers, coast, and deltas; they developed in tandem with the dynamics of floodplains. Settlement locality statistics show that almost all historic cities in China were located along or beside water bodies. According to recent research, all the ancient national and provincial capitals were located along main rivers, and this was also usually the case for local cities.[9] The efficient use of water resources was a decisive factor in the survival or demise of settlements. Agricultural land was a binding element between city-states, and the mastery of water resources was the single most important development deciding which civilisation would be dominant and which subservient. Territories were crisscrossed by vast yet intricate networks of irrigation canals, small levees, and rivulets, creating a mesmerising geometric mosaic of mathematically correlated precision. Such water bodies and waterways were important for transportation, defence, and livelihoods; they also demanded respect. They were the centres of public life and simultaneously represented profit, power, and danger.

In Asia's tropical monsoon belt, huge water infrastructure projects supported the region's thriving wet-paddy rice civilisations for millennia. Low-tech rational logics using the dynamics of erosion and sedimentation led to the efficient use of seasonal watercourses and storage of monsoon rains for use in dry seasons. Building methods were adapted to flooding. Extensive irrigation frameworks not only gave structure to overall landscapes but also facilitated the transport and exchange of goods. However, over time, there have been fundamental shifts in territorial

The tidal mudflats and mangrove forests of Ca Mau Cape are important and dynamic ecosystems that are progressively being reclaimed for aquaculture and industrial development. The Mekong Delta Region Plan proposes a coastal mangrove 'necklace' which operates as an afforestation strategy to protect against storm surges and to create a healthier brackish water environment. Integrated shrimp and fish farming, in addition to renewable energy production in mangroves, is encouraged, as opposed to monocultural shrimp farming. Restoration of the coastal mangrove belt includes the planting of numerous native species, amongst which are many medicinal plants.

The Mekong Delta Region Plan (2030–2050) was co-developed by RUA (Research Urbanism Architecture) at KU Leuven and the Southern Institute for Strategic Planning (SISP), Ho Chi Minh City. Development is realigned to take advantage of climate change and the vulnerabilities of the landscape. The delta is optimised as a productive landscape and new territorial and settlement morphologies and typologies work with character of the delta's six agro-ecological zones. The plan re-establishes a robust landscape structure in order to embed urbanisation, which responds to increased incidence of numerous phenomena including flooding, drought, and subsidence.

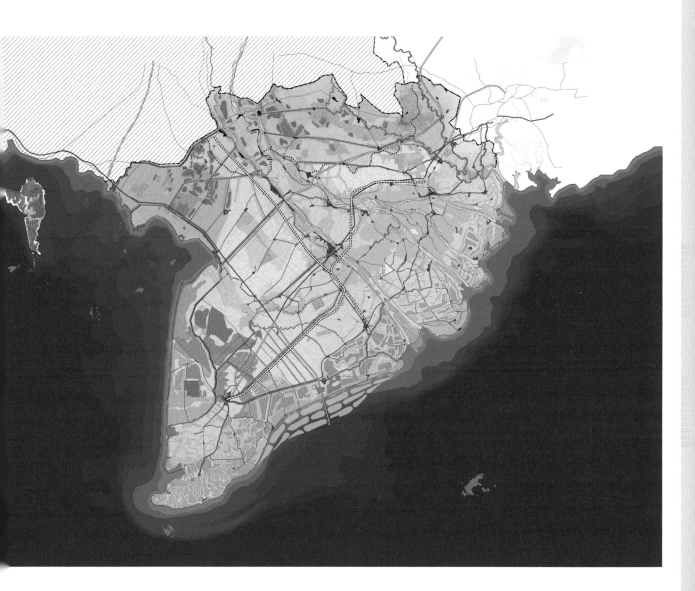

land management and living with floods, and inter-connected canal systems are no longer as evident as they once were. The domestication and colonisation of the landscape led to the shift from a gradual transition between water and land towards a categorical division between wet and dry. Over time, gradients were largely eliminated through the introduction of linear elements such as canals, dykes, ditches, and other irrigation/drainage means. Territories transformed from dynamic mud plains with softly undulating topography and gradients of wetness, to assemblages of low/wet and dry/high components (where high remains a relative notion).

Similar to the tropical monsoon water management systems, the techniques employed for dry environments required a certain degree of centralised control and design together with collective maintenance. In the region's arid and semi-arid landscapes, a number of state-of-the-art systems were developed to both cleverly tap into groundwater sources (qanats or kariz in western China and stepwells in South Asia) and harvest rainwater (tanks in South Asia and Indo-Islamic garden waterworks). Qanats, underground water transfer supply systems, were precisely engineered, gravity-fed horizontal wells that extracted water from aquifers and delivered it through systems of underground, almost horizontal tunnels to distant settlements and agricultural fields.[10] Tanks are deep reservoirs to combat evaporation and to harvest and preserve rainwater and water from streams, while stepwells are dug deep into the ground to reach groundwater. Both tanks and stepwells were important not only for drinking, bathing, washing, irrigation, and fishing; they also served a host of social, cultural, and religious purposes.[11] These practices are anchored to water infrastructures. In qanats, tanks, and stepwells, novel public spaces developed, both formal and informal. Each of these techniques went hand-in-hand with particular water management practices, including, for example, the sophisticated community distribution of water rights and obligations concerning maintenance in the qanats.

The Influence of Feng Shui
Feng shui, the science of 'wind and waters' which was already recognised by the beginning of the Han dynasty in 206 BCE,[12] is the art of adjusting the features of the cultural landscape to minimise adverse influences and derive maximum advantage from favourable conjunctions of settlement. Geomancers were figures endowed with the ability to read the dynamic powers of the genius loci's specific topological features and their relation to heavenly bodies. Gardens, tomb landscapes, and even some cities themselves were designed according to feng shui, including proximity to an upstream flowing river course (supplying clean water, minerals, fish, and prosperity through transportation and communication links); protection from cold northerly winds and malignant spirits (by way of mountains, hills, or trees); and a south-facing platform or high ground (to have ample access to light and air and provide protection from flooding). Needham himself recognised geomancy's connection with hydraulic engineering works and water control.[13]

Feng shui principles and its regional variations are widespread in Asia. Applications are omnipresent. The imperial city Hue is a good example. Its construction started in 1804 during the reign of Nguyen Phuc Tran. Almost simultaneously with the construction of the citadel on the west bank of the Perfume River, the Royal Canal (Ngu Ha) was built, diverting the flow across the east bank. Hue's citadel, a complex earth and water sculpture, is often characterised as a power symbol rather than a defence structure.[14] The citadel iterates dialectically between working with the existing water structures and plugging in a new, alien water machinery. As such, it is a synthesis and can be considered as an archetype of how to settle with water, where water is simultaneously understood as a condition and as a tool, and settling is conceived as a colonisation, an occupation of territory, and at the same time as dealing with an issue (in this case water) and as a coming to terms by opposing parties (in this case water and city or in general terms nature and culture).[15] Water and earth remain closely intertwined within and around the majestic earth and water sculpture that constitutes the citadel, but they are first of all turned into two distinct categories. They are no longer intermingled as on the original flood plain with its ever-changing proportions, where they are rhythmically defined by seasons and weather patterns. At the same time, the canals around the citadel and the Royal Canal function as a pinwheel, redistributing the river flow over a range of canals in addition to the main riverbed. This deviation and redistribution of flows evidently decreases the water pressure on the citadel. It enhances its protection and simultaneously spreads water flows in various directions over the territory. As such it opened up the whole plain between it and the majestic Tam Giang-Cau Hai Lagoon (to the east) for irrigation, bringing a vast natural environment into the space of culture. The provision of water (fertility), once tamed, becomes an instrument of culture. Mastering water is the gateway to colonisation, transforming natural environments (wild, untamed, primitive) into cultured ones.

The scale and sophistication of Hue is nothing compared to the historically much earlier territorial mastering of water and land on the Angkor plain by the Khmers in Cambodia. The land-based Khmer Empire built one of the region's most renowned sacred landscapes in the midst of productive paddy in the fertile alluvial plain. The legendary Hindu city of Angkor (802–1432 CE), is not only renowned for its astonishing collection of unrivalled and monumental temple precincts, but also for its complex irrigation system—connecting the Angkor plain to the Kulen Hills in the north and to the great Tonle Sap Lake (connected to the dynamic rhythms of the Mekong River). The highly engineered landscape at such an enormous scale is without parallel in the preindustrial world.[16] Already by the thirteenth century, the urban core of Angkor encompassed thirty-five square kilometres while the extensive urban complex stretched over 1000 square kilometres.[17] The ingenious water system formed the backbone of the agro-urban landscape, in which forestry also played a role since, except for the religious buildings, all construction including even the royal palaces was in wood or thatch (and thus did not survive). The Khmer's development of a carefully engineered network of canals, dams, *barays* (artificial reservoirs connected to the natural river regime made by embankments or dykes that were a means of both irrigation and transport), and *trapeang* (excavated ponds for collecting rainwater used by households for drinking, bathing, watering animals, small-scale hydro-agriculture, etc.). A series of Temple Mountains were built (sometimes as islands within the *barays*) to honour gods and ancestors, serve as mausoleums for the various kings, and display the Khmer Empire's omnipotence. It is believed that the king, priests, army, and bureaucrats lived within the moats and walls of the various monuments. Urban space however continued far beyond the moated precincts of the temples, and rectilinear grids encompassed intramural as well as extramural areas.[18] In its heyday, the urban landscape of Angkor may have supported a population approaching 750,000.

The spatial concept of the Khmer agro-urban landscape was defined over centuries, but always as a highly engineered system with a strong geometrical order. This strongly contrasts with Sri Lanka's system of tanks following natural contours. It is tempting to think of both as categorically different, in line with the opposition Colin Rowe articulated between engineering and bricolage,[19] or the dichotomy of political versus vernacular landscape proposed by Jackson.[20] Either way, the Khmer or Singhalese examples both work on a breathtaking systematic level and both are shaped by the particular context.

The first planned settlements in Sri Lanka date from 1000 BCE and were located in the nation's dry zone where watercourses are seasonal. Ingeniously constructed water retention reservoirs made it possible to support life. The construction of small storage reservoirs in the narrow linear valleys characteristic of the landscape gradually evolved into a comprehensive system of planned river basin development. Potentially irrigable land was either in narrow ribbons in tributary valleys (where dam sites were difficult because of relatively low water flows) or on the coastal plains (where land was abundant, but dam sites were rare). Tanks offered a solution. Large scale irrigation networks began crisscrossing the parched landscape as early as the first century CE. By the end of the eighth century, irrigation systems had allowed the Singhalese to 'bring in culture' by irrigating extensive tracts of land. The tanks were complemented by larger dams with broad bases able to withstand heavy pressure. These dams also modulated main river flows with valves, an invention by Singhalese engineers which antedated equivalent European inventions by 1,500 years.[21] Larger reservoirs were required in the downstream courses of rivers to deal with the force of flooding and to irrigate the plains. Surveyors mastered topographic levelling skills, allowing the construction of thirty-kilometre-long canals, and these structures (acting as controlled inlets), together with masonry weirs, made the larger reservoirs manageable. Eventually, entire river basins were modified by interdependent systems of large and small reservoirs, redirected streams and connective canals. Many rivers in what is now labelled as the country's vast 'dry zone' carry water for less than two months a year, during the rainy season—hence the importance of reservoirs and their integration into a system covering large areas. Spill water from one reservoir was collected at a reservoir lower down and this system was repeated over and over again to form a regional network of canals and reservoirs in which cities were an integral component. The landscape of the city was inseparable from its larger territory. Early royal cities integrated ingenious systems of water management for both pragmatic purposes and as exquisite pleasure gardens. The reflective and recreational aspects of the pleasure gardens accentuated the majesty of the landscape. Ponds made of carved stones, within the gardens and canals built to connect them, exemplify the artistic, architectural, and craft skills and engineering ingenuity of the Singhalese.

Many of the pre-colonial water management systems installed over time in Asia, ranging from the antique times in Sri Lanka until relatively recent eighteenth-century interventions in Hue (or nineteenth-century interventions in the Mekong Delta), have not only the massive investment they required in common, but also their fundamental and long-lasting spatial impact. They did not merely leave a fingerprint but marked an imprint. One could argue that they also function as a blueprint, since they forcefully give direction to future development. They often structure areas for centuries. Their lifespan transcends regimes, and life cycles of buildings and even cities. Even after decay or erasure after centuries of function, their imprint remains so striking and apparent that often-used metaphors such as palimpsest become rather inadequate. The archaeology of Angor to the Sri Lanka's ponds, reservoirs, and gardens to the vast irrigation systems in Vietnam and elsewhere remain remarkable remains of deep form water landscapes.

As they have an enduring impact, they inevitably intertwine with colonial hydraulic endeavours that, in turn, were also often accompanied with a discourse of innovation and technological advancement. More often than not, colonial 'hydraulic interventions ... altered radically a vast spectrum of pre-colonial hydraulic relationships that had defined and sustained complex equations between land and water.'[22]

The dramatically misfitting Dutch plans for water cities like Batavia, nowadays Jakarta, belong to the earliest wave of European colonial hydraulic projects in the region. The plan of Batavia, based on a water city model developed by mathematician Simon Stevin for the lowlands of the Maas Schelde Delta in western Europe, was not at all adapted to the tropical river regime of the Ciliwung and the local geographical conditions, which were the root of enduring public health issues.[23] It is not without reason that the Dutch colonial government withdrew its own population to higher ground (the Dutch colonial 'Weltevreden' area), without ever solving the water-related problems of the city. It has since proven impossible to turn around an originally ill-conceived interplay between water and urban system. The water-centred problems of the city endure and are amplified by climate change. Large parts of Jakarta are sinking into the vast mud plain which the city occupied. Regular floods have devastating effects. Regardless, the contemporary Dutch industrial water engineering complex, backed by the Dutch government and savvy salesmanship, continue to export their equally generic and massive hard engineering models—to the city, as well as countless other locations throughout Asia.

Hydraulic Engineering in Overdrive

The increase of technological capacities and subsequent waves of modernisation since the eighteenth and nineteenth century, and surely in the post-1945 era, led to an overdrive in hydraulic engineering, not least in Asia. Modernisation and the introduction of Western technology and management are often a product of colonialism, but just as often they are the result self-inflicted processes of modernisation, as in Japan (during the Meiji era in the second half of nineteenth century) and in China. Sun Yat-Sen, regularly referred to as the 'father of the nation',[24] simultaneously envisioned a new China that combined political independence (making it anti-imperialist) with radical technological modernisation. His programme, 'international development of China',[25] contained five major (predominantly infrastructural) components. Not surprisingly, water-related works are omnipresent, in addition to those for railway networks, telephone systems, etc. Dams for 'water power development', 'irrigational work on the largest scale in Mongolia and Sinkiang', 'ports', 'improving existing canals and building new ones', and 'regulating the embankments' of an endless list of rivers were cornerstones in the 'international' development scheme.

The 'international' component refers to both investment and taking advantage of the latest Western technology. Sun Yat Sen considered both to be key in launching a great leap forward. Nation (re)building (after the stagnation of the nineteenth century) required leap-frogging. As such, water works belong to a long Chinese tradition. Sun Yat Sen advocated a systematic approach across the entire territory and a dramatic shift of scales made possible by technological advances. As technological possibilities steered his revolutionary vision, attitudes towards water (and nature in general) also shifted. The new northern international port on the Gulf of Pechili—to be 'as large as New York and developed in a reasonable limit of time'[26]—was decoupled from any river 'which might carry silt to fill up the approach of the harbor'.[27] For Sun Yat-Sen, who was driven by an urge for instant modernisation of the nation, river conservancy meant first-and-foremost regulating embankments. The vast works he supported for the Yangtze River Delta were all about taming and regularising the river regime. Natural forces are exchanged for engineering schemes. In retrospect, Sun Yat-Sen's modernisation programme was a clear precursor for even more categorical changes.

The post-1945 overdrive of hard engineering works was predicated by a fundamental shift in ideology led by China's strongman Mao Zedong, who insisted that 'man must conquer nature'—rather than the earlier national dictum of 'harmony between heaven and humans'[28] or the often-quoted Chinese fundamental axiom to 'be in tune with nature'.[29] It is a common threat of Communist regimes that the instant construction of a fair world for all humans requires the radical appropriation, transformation, and exploitation of nature. Meanwhile, in Japan, the motto was 'develop now, clean up later'.[30] Water progressively disappeared from urbanism. Rivers were straightjacketed into canals or piped underground. They became backsides and often served as sewers and garbage dumps. All the previous centuries of reverence for water bodies vanished in the drive towards 'progress'. In densely inhabited floodplains, new irrigation and embankment techniques converted ever-larger swaths of territory into productive landscapes—at first paddy and, later, vast areas of aquaculture. This process entailed the near erasure of riparian forests. River diversion projects both changed the fundamental geography of landscape and increased 'water wars'. Higher and stronger levees were constructed to protect settlements and productive land from unwanted water.

At the same time there was the unmatched and colossal flagship of global modernisation, namely, dams and reservoirs. At great economic and environmental cost, water was harnessed and tamed so that its unpredictable rhythms no longer threatened development. A number of technological developments allowed for a decade-by-decade dramatic increase in the volume and number of dams and reservoirs. These became the fundamental infrastructures for the water and energy supply to region's ever-larger populations. As such, dams and reservoirs were, and still often are, considered symbols of modernisation. By regulating the wild and irregular natural forces, they turn potential into an assured promise of development and progress. Tested and perfected in the industrial world, dams and reservoirs quickly spread throughout Asia and, in a tangible way, supported globalisation. The Three Gorges Dam—larger than any before it—is merely only one of the testimonies to the resolute belief in dams as an instrument of development and the expectation of affluence thought to automatically follow in its wake. As no other construction, dams and reservoirs illustrate the etymological meaning of infrastructure: the basis of a system (of development).

However, dams and reservoirs are also highly contested due to their enormous ecological and environmental impacts, as well as the often dramatic social and economic consequences for resettled populations and their painfully unfulfilled expectations of development. These structures have a devastating impact on riparian ecologies and their associated economies—a disastrous impact that extends to large territories. In the close vicinity of dams, the removal of vegetation from riverbanks and deforestation in watersheds triggers flooding, enhances runoff rates, reduces aquifer recharge, depletes wetland, and changes the natural character of watercourses and estuaries, including increasing the variability of water flows. Further downstream, it is not only livelihoods severely affected by the decrease of water flows (and increasingly by drought), but also riverine and marine ecologies shift due to the decrease in nutrients and minerals disgorged by rivers. Finally, there are as well as radical shifts in sediment loads that alter river courses and coastline processes. During recent years, with effects of climate change manifesting more prominently, an ever-greater number of reservoirs have suffered from water shortage, which in turn obstructs hydropower generation.

New Challenges as the Foundation for Water Design

Asia's 'hydraulic civilisation' worldviews resulted in complex water management that not only intertwined social-cultural and political organisation but also afforded the settling with water—literally, in the sense of constructing settlement, as well as in the sense of settling with, dealing with, the very unpredictable nature of water. The historical geography of urban water control in Asia reveals highly structured rural and urban territorial systems that are physically and symbolically linked to technologies, religious beliefs, cultural and social practices, and power structures—all strongly related to water. Today, Asia is in a period of resettling and redefining the terms constructing settlement. When the industrial revolution spread through Asia, it also pushed water aside, outside of the social and cultural imagineering of progress. Nature evidently took revenge for this (attempted) submission in the form of climate change and many other

manifestations, and today it obliges societies to adjust their attitudes. In this process, water is regaining a primary, structural role in the conception of settlement.

Asia's continued modernisation and urbanisation has had an exponentially devastating impact on ecosystems. It is often stated that nearly two-fifths of the world's population lives within 100 kilometres of a coastline. In Asia, the proportion of those in coastal areas is much greater and the region will bear a disproportionately large share of global warming consequences—particularly related to sea level rise and more frequent and severe typhoons. Vulnerable coastlines (and rivers) are where social inequality and ecological disruptions are most visible and require urgent attention. At the same time, droughts and temperature rise are leading to more serious attention focused on food and water security. And as Indian strategic thinker Brahma Chellaney has written:

> [W]ater scarcity is set to become Asia's defining crisis by midcentury, creating obstacles in its path of continued rapid economic growth and stroking new interstate tensions over shared basin resources … The linkage between water and peace is particularly striking in Asia, where the per capita availability of freshwater is less than half of the world average.[31]

At the policy level, there is a focus on water governance, transboundary water management, the water-energy-food nexus, and water economics. 'Water stress', domestic water supply, and sanitation are high on national agendas. There are specific policies and projects developed for integrated water resource management (IWRM), integrated flood management (IFM), and integrated drought management (IDM), all of which are highly contested fields with complex, multi-scalar, and multi-sectorial issues. Only in very rare instances are urbanism and design thinking a part of dealing with the water issue. This is notably a vast new arena for urbanists and landscape architects. ∎

Jurong Lake Gardens

Singapore

Project Name: **Jurong Lake Gardens**
Landscape Architect: **Ramboll Studio Dreiseitl**
Location: **Jurong Lake, Singapore**
Client: **National Parks Board**
Completion Year: **2019**
Text: based on information from Ramboll Studio Dreiseitl

A new undulating topography
of streams and swales.

Jurong Lake Gardens will be the first national gardens in Singapore's heartland. It will complement two existing world-class national gardens—Singapore Botanic Gardens and Gardens by the Bay. The fifty-three-hectare park aims to restore the landscape heritage of the swamp and forest as a canvas for a people's garden, accessible to all segments of the community. Large-scale nature playgrounds and more formal recreational facilities are mixed with grasslands and fresh water swamps to offer a wide range of ecological habitats and recreational experiences.

    The site's gentle topography and high water table created major issues with waterlogging and water stagnation. As part of the Active, Beautiful and Clean Waters (ABC Waters) Programme, vegetated and gravel swales were developed to improve drainage. This included the demolition of 12,000 metres of concrete drain and the construction of 4,750 metres of swales and streams. The introduction of the Neram Streams is a major feature of this water strategy, replacing a straight concrete drain that previously led from Yuan Ching Road to Jurong Lake. The channel has been transformed into almost 900 metres of braided waterways, which meander around islands of trees.

Ramboll Studio Dreiseitl developed an undulating topography while retaining the existing banyan trees along the original concrete canal. Excavations of up to six metres required the precise engineering of stream banks using various bioengineering techniques to ensure slope stability. The banks of the Neram Streams are planted with collections of tree species commonly found in tropical riverine forests, such as the *Dillenia*, *Syzygium*, *Diospyros*, *Saraca*, and *Barringtonia* species. Clusters of neram trees (*Dipterocarpus oblongifolius*) can also be found along the streams' bends.

    Closer to the edge of Jurong Lake is the meandering 300-metre barrier-free Rasau Walk, which offers visitors the opportunity to get up close with nature along the shoreline. Winding around islands of special palm collection and existing trees, moments of the tranquil grasslands and serene lakeside scenery are uncovered at various viewing spots. With a carefully engineered slope edge, the boardwalk sits within the transitional tidal edge that has varying water depths. Plants along Rasau Walk such as the sealing wax palms and nibong palms are adapted to cope with constant inundation. In the evening, the curvatures of the meandering boardwalk are illuminated with a soft glow along the edge.

37

Meishe River Greenway and Fengxiang Park

Haikou

Fengxiang Park's terraced wetland.

Project Name: **Meishe River Greenway and Fengxiang Park**
Project Location: **Haikou, Hainan Province, China**
Landscape Architect: **Turenscape**
Client: **Haikou City Government**
Completion Year: **2017**
Text: based on information from Turenscape

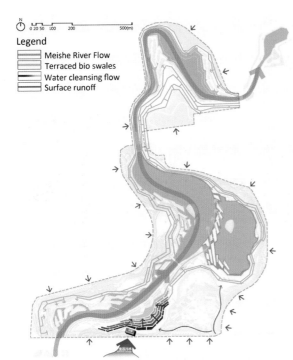

Legend
- Meishe River Flow
- Terraced bio swales
- Water cleansing flow
- Surface runoff

The tourist city of Haikou is located in South China's tropical monsoonal zone. Decades of urban growth has unfolded with little consideration of urban water infrastructure, leaving the Meishe River (meaning the 'beautiful mother river'), which runs through the city, as a lifeless concrete channel. In 2016, the Haikou government commissioned Turenscape to recover the health of the river. Their proposal recast thirteen kilometres of the river running through the dense urban area into a green infrastructure corridor, featuring the eighty-hectare Fengxiang Park.

Three water strategies were adopted. First, a green infrastructure corridor was designed to separate the stormwater from the sewage and integrate the river, its tributaries, and wetlands. An interconnected pedestrian and recreational network was also embedded in the corridor. Second, wherever possible, concrete flood walls were replaced by eco-friendly river banks and green space. Blocked waterways were reconnected to the ocean allowing tides to again enter the city, wetlands, and shallow shores along the river. Third, interconnected terraces of constructed subsurface flow wetlands were built along the riverbank, formerly occupied by a concrete flood wall and garbage dump. These terraces cleanse nutrient-rich pollution water runoff, along with the sewage from the local urban villages that is unable to access the centralised sewage treatment system.

This terraced wetland forms a major feature of Fengxiang Park. After the smell of the sewage is removed through the upper terraces, water is exposed in the lower level terraced wetlands, where wetland plants remove nutrients from the contaminated water. The public can walk amongst a geometric landscape of lush tropical vegetation and water ponds. Amazingly, this wetland can clean up to 6000 tons of urban runoff daily, transforming it from grade V to III (which is swimmable). The biomass from the wetland is also harvested and decomposed for use as fertilizer for the park.

Lupin Research Park
Pune

The farm-inspired terrace provides edible
plants and long lunch communal tables.

Project Name: **Lupin Research Park**
Project Location: **Pune, Maharashtra, India**
Landscape Architect: **Shma**
Client: **Lupin Limited**
Completion Year: **2017**
Text: based on information from Shma

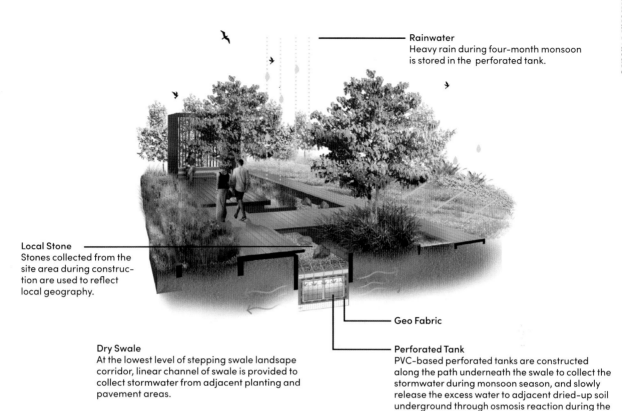

Rainwater
Heavy rain during four-month monsoon is stored in the perforated tank.

Local Stone
Stones collected from the site area during construction are used to reflect local geography.

Geo Fabric

Dry Swale
At the lowest level of stepping swale landsape corridor, linear channel of swale is provided to collect stormwater from adjacent planting and pavement areas.

Perforated Tank
PVC-based perforated tanks are constructed along the path underneath the swale to collect the stormwater during monsoon season, and slowly release the excess water to adjacent dried-up soil underground through osmosis reaction during the dry season.

Located 150 kilometres inland from Mumbai, Pune and its locale are well known for extreme weather conditions—cycling yearly from a drastically dry season to heavy monsoons. Thai-based landscape architects Shma were challenged to develop a sustainable campus landscape for the biotechnology company Lupin that responds to this fluctuating semi-arid climate. They looked to local farmer's wisdom and natural forest ecological formation to inform their sustainable landscape strategies.

Capturing water for use during the dry season was critical to their scheme. A dense layer of trees, of varied size and species, was designed along the site boundary to create a forest-like backdrop and to operate as a rain garden corridor for controlling large amounts of water within the campus. In order to sustain the dense greenery with limited water, the area was graded lower to capture the site's rainwater runoff, including the roof drainage from the building. PVC-based perforated tanks were constructed along the path to collect water during the monsoon season and slowly release excess water underground through osmosis during the dry season. In addition to its ecological function, the forest offers a

restful experience incorporating walking paths and a timber cabana.

Closer to the research centre, a series of spaces were carefully inserted to provide workers the rare opportunity to relax and work within a lush landscaped setting and comfortable microclimate. A farm-inspired terrace, crafted to reflect local agricultural patterns, was designed next to the canteen. Edible plants and trees are interspersed amongst the lunch communal tables inviting people to share quality time amidst lush vegetation. Surrounded by buildings on three sides, the forest courtyard is well protected from the harsh sunlight and wind, making it an ideal place for resting all day. Pocket sitting spaces designed among trees, reflective ponds, and interactive fountains can be adjusted for different moods, promoting a comfortable microclimate during the drier months. The Lupin Terrace, a large green lawn in front of the grand meeting room, offers a more formal space, which can accommodate mass gatherings and major events. To negotiate the steep level change between the road and the research centre, a slow ramp was inserted into a stepped slope. Framed by tree groves and shrubs of local species, this hardscape provides a solid tectonic base for the research centre.

Chulalongkorn University Centenary Park

Bangkok

Project Name: **Chulalongkorn University Centenary Park**
Project Location: **Bangkok, Thailand**
Landscape Architects: **LANDPROCESS**
Architects: **N7A Architects**
Engineers: **(CASE) Civil and Structural Engineers**
Client: **Chulalongkorn University Property**
Completion Year: **2017**
Text: based on information from LANDPROCESS

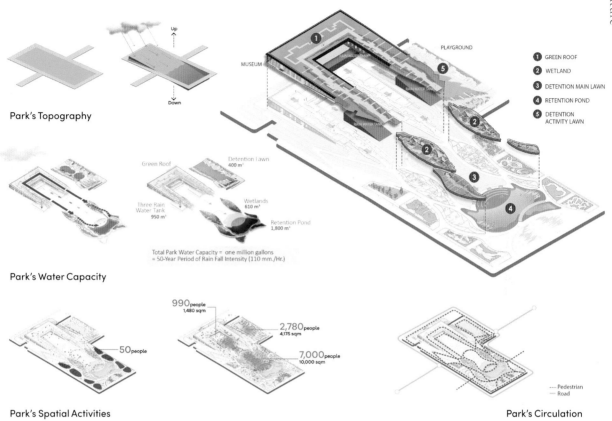

Park's Topography

Park's Water Capacity

Total Park Water Capacity = one million gallons
= 50-Year Period of Rain Fall Intensity (110 mm./Hr.)

Green Roof

Detention Lawn
400 m³

Three Rain
Water Tank
950 m³

Wetlands
610 m³

Retention Pond
1,800 m³

1 GREEN ROOF
2 WETLAND
3 DETENTION MAIN LAWN
4 RETENTION POND
5 DETENTION ACTIVITY LAWN

MUSEUM

PLAYGROUND

Park's Spatial Activities

50 people

990 people
1,480 sqm

2,780 people
4,175 sqm

7,000 people
10,000 sqm

Park's Circulation

···· Pedestrian
— Road

Considered the first major piece of green infrastructure for Bangkok, Chulalongkorn University Centenary Park is located in central Bangkok, close to residential, entertainment, and major retail facilities. The park celebrates the foundation of the university one hundred years ago, by King Chulalongkorn (Rama V), and contributes much-needed public space to Bangkok. The rain tree, the symbol of Chulalongkorn University, informs the concept for the designed ecology, with the park conceived to absorb water like tree roots and provide a natural system for the city.

The entire park is inclined to operate as a container for water. At its highest point is Thailand's largest green roof (at the time of construction). The programs under this roof include a gallery, museum, and parking. The water treatment system and outdoor spaces run along the inclined plane culminating in a retention 'container' created by depressing the plane below grade.

The main lawn acts a detention area to increase ground water infiltration and allow space for flooding (accommodating fifty to hundred-year floods) and retention pond overflow. Storage tanks throughout the park collect and distribute to the water treatment system for zero water discharge. A separate detention lawn adjacent to the main lawn collects water in periods of heavy rainfall for use during drier months. This space can be explained by the Thai phrase 'monkey cheek', a reference from King Bhumibol (Rama IX) as a monkey stores its food in its cheek to 'eat' later.

Constructed wetlands along the inclined plane are fed from the green roof rainwater tank overflow and runoff from the park lawn. The wetlands step through a series of weirs and plant-filled ponds, until reaching the final retention pond. Eight landscape rooms, each with a distinct program such as herb garden, amphitheatre, meditation walk, and reading area, are adjacent to the wetlands. The retention pond completes the water circulation system: in the dry season, water is pumped from the retention pond to the top of the wetlands. At the edge of the pond are interactive water treatment bikes, which visitors can ride to create movement and introduce more oxygen into the water. The park also collects water from the surrounding neighbourhood, integrating wider urban runoff into the park's filtration system for treatment.

Interactive water treatment bikes for aerating water. These are small versions of the Chaipattana Water Aerator, which was invented by King Bhumibol (Rama IX), who developed many technological devices for improving the environment and people's living conditions.

Flood and Mud

Jillian Walliss

Despite the fact that many Asian cities have long histories as aquatic cultures, rapid urban development has often been accompanied by engineering approaches to water based on control and risk management. Asian landscape architects have played a critical role in advocating for more ecologically and socially resilient design directions. However, as a design community, we tend to focus on design outcomes and pay less attention to the tactics used by landscape architects to advocate for this change. This essay explores the characteristics of Asian design agency, examining how three designers in China, Thailand, and Korea engage with their political and cultural contexts to achieve alternatives to the hard engineering of water systems.

This discussion highlights how different governance structures and cultural contexts influence the tactics adopted: a direct professional to political leader dialogue in top-down China; an activist approach in Bangkok where designers work as part of an emerging public consciousness to empower communities to express their views; and a competition in Seoul which provided the platform for innovation developed through a strategic collaboration with engineers. All of these examples reveal that, despite the relative youth of landscape architecture in these contexts, Asian designers are not afraid of being political to achieve better ecological and social futures for their cities. Significantly, their political engagement should not be viewed as oppositional, but instead as highly tactical, in that it seeks to find opportunities to influence their distinctive governance contexts through engagement, rather than dissent.

Appealing to the Leaders

Kongjian Yu is arguably one of the most overtly political landscape architects in Asia. Since his return to China from his international studies in 1997, Yu has advocated for ecological approaches to resource management and urban development. Internationally, he is synonymous with the 'sponge city approach', which was adopted by the Chinese Central Government in 2014. Sponge city's emphasis on floods may mistakenly give the sense that China has too much water. In fact, water is a scarce resource. However, China's mid-twentieth-century development under Chairman Mao was shaped by the belief that the path to modernity and industrial growth would be achieved regardless of limited resources such as water. Instead, it was believed that the combination of human power, socialist ideology, and technology could overcome the limits of resources.[1]

Chairman Mao's position inspired many monumental technologically driven water projects, such as the South-North Water Diversion Project. Speaking in 1952, Mao stated: 'The South has lots of water, the North has less, if it were possible, it could borrow a little.'[2] This statement inspired the construction of a 1200-kilometre water canal system connecting Yangtze and Beijing, which is considered one of the world's most expensive infrastructures.

In 2012, the Chinese government announced a profound shift in its development approach, declaring an 'ecological civilization' at the 18th National Congress of the Communist Party of China. After decades of rapid urban development, environmental concerns were now elevated to the level of national policy.[3] This political recognition of a more ecologically responsive economic development was driven by extensive scientific research and debates during the previous decade.

In his dual role as an academic leader and the head of China's first registered landscape architecture firm Turenscape (1998), Yu has been influential in the reshaping of the Chinese government's development trajectory. Through books, conference papers, design projects, and advocacy to local, regional, and national government departments and leaders, Yu has argued for the recognition of national ecological security patterns, the protection of cultural and heritage landscapes, and more resilient approaches to engineering infrastructure. A critical part of his strategy is to find 'loopholes' or opportunities for change, which has included writing letters directly to national leaders.[4]

What is particularly interesting, and perhaps a characteristic of Chinese politics, is the content and tone of Yu's letters.[5] Whether he is writing to Xi Jinping, president of the People's Republic of China, or a more regional mayor, his language is direct and critical, suggesting new design strategies to replace government development approaches. For those reading the letters from outside China, this approach is surprising. However, in the Chinese context, change comes from the top, hence his targeting of the most senior leaders of the nation.

To the Honourable Secretary Guo:

Rainwater is a blessing, not a disaster. However, in recent years, stormwater runoff has presented disturbing problems that threaten people's lives and property. Rather than constructing a costly network of drainpipes, an economic and highly effective solution would be to build a green stormwater capture and storage system. Such a system could simultaneously meet goals of flood mitigation, rainwater utilization, groundwater replenishment, and environmental improvement.

...A simple, highly effective way to deal with stormwater runoff is to build a green-sponge system that retains rainwater, purifies it, and replenishes the groundwater table. Specific strategies to achieve this include restoring floodplains, building stormwater parks, lowering the elevation of green space in existing parks, constructing artificial swales, and installing community stormwater collection facilities.

Excerpt from a letter to Guo Jinlong, the Secretary of Beijing Municipal CPC Committee (2012)[6]

To the Honourable President Xi:

It's indeed a brilliant act for the Party Central Committee and the State Council to propose a grand vision of an Ecological Civilization and 'Beautiful China'. The motto of citizens' enjoying the view of mountains and rivers and being reminded of their hometowns evokes a simple yet wonderful expectation for our people. However, insofar as we are boarding a Hydraulic-Engineering-Projects-Run-Rampant train, we will stray far from this vision. I've travelled thousands of miles across China, talking to local villagers and conscientious grassroots cadres. Reflecting upon those experiences and professional lessons I've learned, I feel very much obliged to advocate through you to China's top decision-making body: Please put an end to the brutalist hydraulic engineering projects that are now rampant in both rural and urban areas, especially channelizing and damming waterways. The ultimate solution to water security and related environmental problems should lie in ecological ideas and practices, and specifically in hydrological infrastructure.

Excerpt from a letter to Xi Jinping, president of the People's Republic of China (2014), containing suggestions on 'Curbing Brutal Hydraulic Engineering Projects and Building Hydro-Ecological Infrastructure'

Empowering the Community

Shifting to Thailand: the Bangkok-based firm Shma offers a radically different model to Yu's appeal to the national leaders. Instead, Shma position themselves as activists whose role is to mobilise and empower the community to express their voice in campaigns of change. This approach emerged as part of Shma's efforts to stop the government's plan for an elevated promenade along Bangkok's Chao Phraya River. The city of Bangkok is known for its historic water-based urbanism, which has increasingly come under threat due to development and flooding. In 2014, the government proposed the construction of a raised promenade on both sides of the Chao Phraya River to provide new public space and uninterrupted bike and pedestrian paths.

Stage one was a seven-kilometre stretch (on both sides of the river) from the Rama VII Bridge in Nonthaburi to the Pin Klao Bridge. This included the construction of a 3.7-metre-high floodwall alongside the promenade.[7] Because the project was deemed to be recreational in purpose, the Bangkok Metropolitan Authority was not required to submit an environmental impact assessment.[8] Shma director Yossapon Boonsom was deeply troubled by this proposal, which would cut off the surrounding communities from the river, require the relocation of twelve communities, significantly narrow the river, and shatter important Thai cultural connections between people, sacred spaces, and the river. Speaking in 2015, he commented that

'The Chao Phraya River is a precious gem. If we polish it and look after it, it will be worth a fortune. We can't make any more mistakes.'[9]

Working with his design friends, Boonsom established the not for profit Friends of the River (FoR). Conceived as a social platform, FoR offered a means for providing information to the community and for opening up the discussion. Through workshops, exhibitions, performance, and installations, FoR gathered views and diverse perspectives to begin a dialogue with the government.

Currently, Thai citizens have little say in the formal delivery of public spaces, which generally emerge from either a bureaucratic top-down approach or through privately owned public open space. A major part of FoR's initiative was to demonstrate an alternative development potential for the river that involved the entire district, not just the promenade. Working with the local communities, FoR sought to understand the existing assets and potentials and to develop a co-creation model that reconnected the physical and social to the river. Their process encouraged the community 'to exercise their creativity' and interact with 'people of similar or opposing views'.[10] Workshops with students, business owners, residents, state employees, and academics

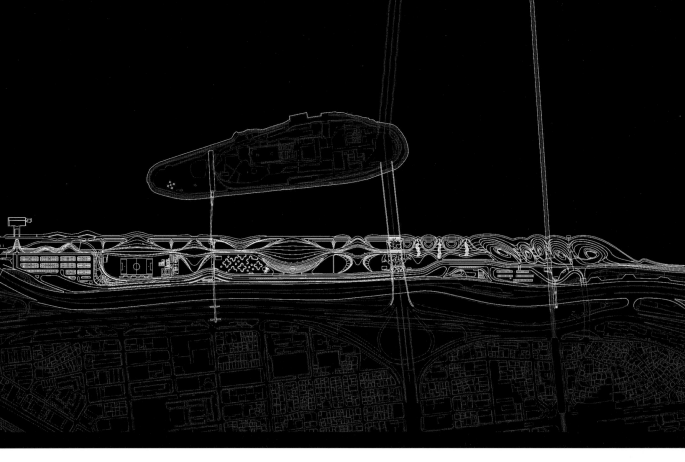

led to the identification of community-responsive development approaches, such as providing recreation along the public waterfront, new urban pocket landscapes, the adaptive reuse of vacant shop houses, and improving connections along local alleys. FoR's efforts have been successful in slowing progress on the promenade proposal. In 2019, they submitted their case to the administrative court that put the project on hold due to the government not carrying out the project according to the law.[11]

With little public policy in place to guide the development of public space in Bangkok, Shma has positioned themselves as a middleman between the government and private development, working to negotiate new opportunities for public space and to protect important cultural and ecological assets such as the Chao Phraya River. This commitment was formalised by the creation of Shma Soen in 2014, which focuses exclusively on the research and development of public space in the public and private sectors.[12] Working with various agencies, they use exhibitions, films, workshops, and design to cultivate innovative ideas for spaces of social and ecological value.

Collaborating for Change

Sometimes the power of an innovative design idea is enough to initiate change. A well-run design competition can offer the opportunity for landscape architects to present new approaches. However, for new ideas to be implemented, it is necessary to gain the backing of the professional 'gatekeepers', which in the case of water projects tend to be the engineers. Since the 1960s, engineers have constructed large concrete levees on the banks of the Han River to protect Seoul from the powerful monsoon flood. Daily tidal fluctuations and high rainfall during the monsoon season transform the shallow waters and extensive mudflats of the river into deep and dangerous currents. Concentrations of silt and grit deposits, built-up from soil erosion in the mountainous areas further upstream, create extensive mud deposits along riverbanks, on parking lots, along highways, and in parks.[13]

After an extensive consultation process (from 2012 to 2013) the Han River Renaissance programme was announced. In a first for Korea, the programme invited landscape architects to conceptually lead the renewal of major infrastructure, launching a design competition to transform a section of the highly en-

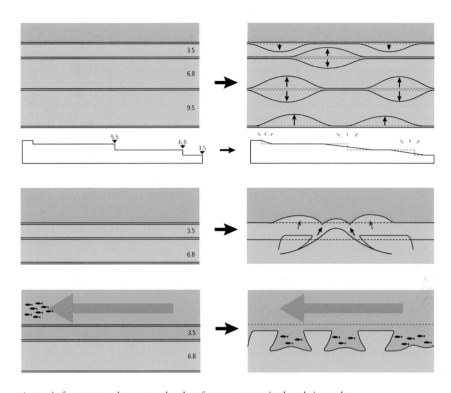

A new infrastructural topography that features an articulated river edge.

gineered river embankment into a new public park. Despite this, the winning scheme by PARKKIM was the only entry to challenge the engineering status quo of concrete levees.

Their design, Mud Infrastructure, emerged from an inspiring collaboration with engineers. Technical engineering knowledge was folded into their landscape systems approach to develop an innovative approach to flooding and sedimentation. This collaboration was critical to the scheme's success. As PARKKIM state, given their 'control over Seoul's infrastructure, engineers cannot be treated as enemies if we are to achieve our design intentions.'[14]

Addressing the existing concrete terraced levee structure along the two-kilometre embankment was the major design issue. While the structure successfully controlled floods, its stepped configuration led to the accumulation of mud and silt up to 1.5 metres deep. PARKKIM felt that by significantly reconfiguring the topography, it would be possible to encourage a more resilient management strategy, increase biodiversity, and offer new recreational and spatial experiences.

Working closely with a hydraulic engineer, PARKKIM conducted extensive topographic studies

to establish a landform which would encourage the tidal mud to flow back into the river once flood water receded. Informed by this knowledge, the embankment was transformed into a series of gentle slopes, ranging from 4 per cent to 13 per cent grade.[15] An articulated rip rap edge adjacent to the river offers sheltered spaces for fish and other species, while the deposited mud encourages a novel ecology of plants. A series of promenades at different levels delineate the landforms, offers easy access to the river, and most importantly maintains movement through the park during times of flood.

The new topography divides the park into activation zones, including a plateau, a riverine theatre overlooking the river and adjacent Seonyudo Island, and a series of undulating wild hills that form an entrance into the ecological area. Since its completion in 2011, the park's annual maintenance budget is 80 per cent less than nearby riverfront parks and it has become popular for walking, picnicking, open-air events, and fishing. Even more importantly, the 'engineered urban wild' of Mud Infrastructure has re-established a spatial and ecological relationship between water and land, and between people and the Han River.[16] ■

Wan-Nian Creek Watershed Revival Plan
Pingtung

Project Name: **Wan-Nian Creek Watershed Revival Plan**
Project Location: **Pingtung, South Taiwan Region**
Landscape Architect: **Golden Park Landscape Architecture, Environmental Planning & Design**
Client: **Pingtung County Government**
Completion Year: **2014**
Text: based on information from Golden Park Landscape Architecture, Environmental Planning & Design

Recycled columns were transformed into gabions to support an aquatic eco-habitat.

Wan-Nian Creek runs diagonally through downtown Pingtung, a tropical city located in southern Taiwan. For over one hundred years, the residents of Pingtung have been nourished by this creek. Known for its weeping willows, bamboo groves, suspension bridges, boating, and fishing, the creek's beauty has been lauded in songs, poems, and paintings. However, rapid urbanisation led to the creek's channels being narrowed by the construction of factories, houses, and roads. Many water sources were cut and buried, leading to the deterioration of water quality to the point that no aquatic life could survive.

In 1994 the government planned to 'hide' the problem by entirely covering up the creek. Willows were removed and the embankment redeveloped into a concrete canal. A double row of concrete pillars was erected for almost 3.5 kilometres in the centre of the creek. On observing these dramatic changes, residents began to protest, leading to the first civil movement in Pingtung. However, over 185 metres of the canal had already been covered, and the creek was functioning only for stormwater discharge.

In 2007, Golden Park Landscape Architects were commissioned to remediate the creek and for seven years worked on a comprehensive revival plan for 4.5 kilometres of the creek, including the renovation of Millennium Park located upstream. Ecological engineering methods focused on recycling material to save money and achieve zero waste. The monumental concrete pillars were cut down and ground into fill for gabions, which were used as underwater planting beds for aquatic plants to purify the water. Concrete edges were transformed into riprap creek beds for aquatic habitats while the banks of the few remaining natural waterways were protected.

Millennium Park, one of the rare natural waterfront spaces on Wan-Nian Creek, was transformed from a lost gloomy area into a bright open space offering accessible grass slopes and a suspension footbridge as a salute to the creek's cultural history. Stonemasonry techniques were used to fix the creek banks and create an ecological island, riprap methods restored habitat for fishes and amphibians, and new ecological ponds were established for irrigation, water purification, and flood retention.

Changchun Water Culture Ecological Park

Sunken rain garden.

Project name: **Changchun Water Culture Ecological Park**
Project Location: **Changchun City, Jilin Province, China**
Architect & Landscape Architect: **SHUISHI**
Cooperation Landscape Architect: **Zonbong Landscape**
Client: **Changchun Urban and Rural Construction
Committee, Changchun Construction Investment Company**
Completion Year: **2018**
Text: based on information from SHUISHI

Water reservoir transformed into an
ecological and recreational wetland.

For eighty years, the former Changchun No. 1 Water Treatment Plant built during the Manchukuo Regime supplied domestic water for Changchun City. Following the relocation of the plant in 2015, the thirty-two-hectare site was transformed through an urban regeneration project into a vibrant cultural, creative, and recreational precinct. Art centres, a museum, exhibition halls, and cultural and creative offices were incorporated into the industrial buildings, while the purification infrastructure constructed over the site's thirty-five-metre drop was imaginatively redesigned as rainwater gardens, multi-function spaces, and recreational wetlands. The entire site operates as an open-air museum educating the public on water purification processes.

A sunken rain garden was inserted into the previously closed water sedimentation tanks. With the top of the structure removed, a series of walkways and staircases of steel grilles weave down through the industrial infrastructure and along former ventilation corridors. The pool is dissected into two spaces: a rain garden and water purification facilities and an artistic space for art installations and events. Traces and relics of the sedimentation tanks and walls are featured.

At the core of the park is a multi-function activity space, which focuses on a large lawn constructed on top of the old sedimentation tanks. Renovated buildings and the lawn offer spaces for art installations, exhibitions, and concerts. The transformation of the iconic water reservoir into an ecological wetland provides a further recreational experience. The open sedimentation tank restores the water storage function and integrates aquatic plants and hydrophilic platforms to create an ecologically functioning wetland. This adaption of the water infrastructure, along with the careful capture of the surface runoff along gullies, creates a self-purification system for the entire park.

Working imaginatively with the historical infrastructure, the park offers a comprehensive experience of culture and environment, maximising the original site features and adding new recreational, cultural, and creative opportunities.

Enabling Village

Project Name: **Enabling Village**
Location: **Redhill, Singapore**
Architect: **WOHA Architects**
Landscape Architects: **Salad Dressing**
Softscape Contractor (Native Plant Hunter):
Plantwerkz
Client: **SG Enable**
Completion Year: **2015**
Text: based on information from WOHA
and Salad Dressing

The extensive water system
introduces a *kampung* feel.

Enabling Village is a demonstration of heartland rejuvenation and community building. Through careful site planning and the adaptive reuse of the Bukit Merah Vocational Institute built in the 1970s, the public housing estate was repurposed as the Enabling Village—an inclusive space that integrates education, work, training, retail, and lifestyle, connecting people with disabilities and the society.

The landscape is curated as an immersive tropical forest garden, featuring an extensive water system that interweaves amongst the architecture and walkways to offer a *kampung* feel. Operating through a phytoremediation process, the system stores excess water during the monsoon wet and provides moisture during hotter months. Key buildings are orientated to major ponds, while verandas and cabanas extend into outdoor spaces and frame views of the dense tropical forest.

The use of natural succession and native species was a major design principle, allowing plants to mature, evolve, and adapt over time. Over 75 per cent of the 140 different plant species are from the Malesia region. Ironwood species of *Cyrtophyllum fragrans*

and peat swamp marginal trees like *Alstonia spatulata* and *Dillenia reticulata* soar skywards; *Rhaphidophora* climb trunks, and creepers and climbers tangle and entwine, while epiphytic ferns and orchids adorn the branches. Closer to the ponds are edible plants such as pandan, lemon grass, and banana.

The addition of native fish is an important aspect. Apex predator *Channa striata* were released to tackle the African cichlids and red-eared terrapins; territorial puffer *Tetraodon nigroviridis*; benthic nocturnal kuhli loaches, and labyrinth gilled *Trichopodus trichopterus* were also introduced.

Over time the layering composition of the biodiversified planting has intensified, with each part of the composition gaining equal status. Similar to Henri Rousseau's painting *The Dream*, the absence of depth in midst of greens presents a peculiar chaos that lacks of hierarchy, giving a sense of calmness. The utopian forest garden is still far from perfection; hardly a retreat for any wildlife. Only on rare occasions will a pair of hornbills visit during their crepuscular return.

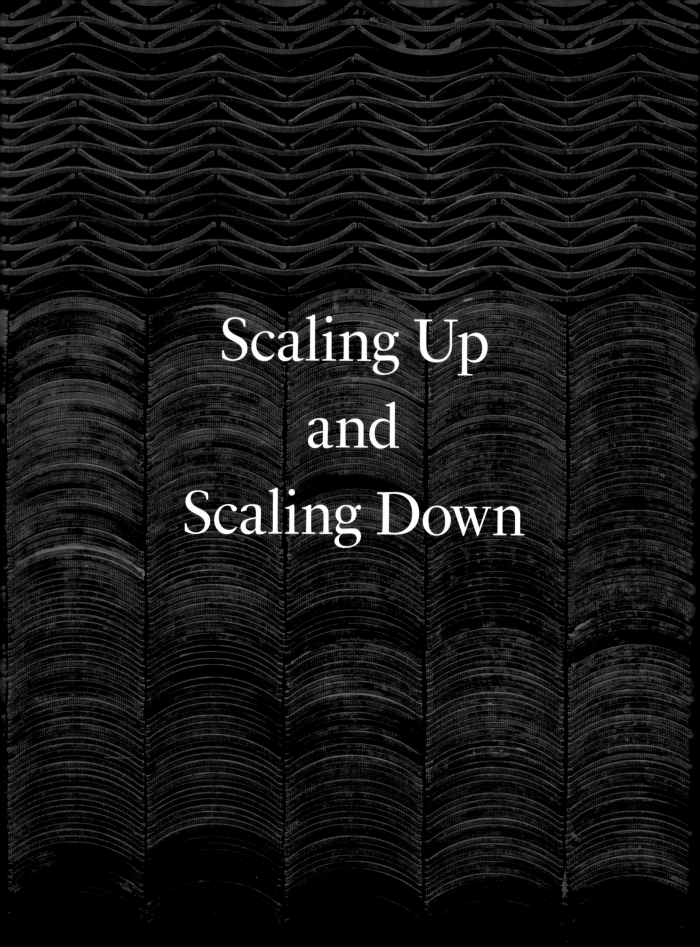

Scaling Up
and
Scaling Down

Heike Rahmann
Jillian Walliss

Across Asia designers have a vast repertoire of symbols, patterns, and philosophies to look to for aesthetic, spatial, and material inspiration. Dragons, tigers, turtles, and elephants are commonly found in traditional garden design with reference to religious gods and cosmological figures. The challenge for the contemporary designer is how to interpret and adapt this rich cultural legacy rather than just replicate historic form and imagery. The spread of religion across Asia means that many places share cultural and philosophical references. For example the 'bamboo civilisations' of Korea, Japan, and China all share an understanding of 山水 (*shanshui* in China, *sansu* in Korea, and *sansui* in Japan). Literally translating as mountain (山) and water (水), the composite is broadly translated as landscape; however, the term has a deeper 'conceptual and visual differentiation' as it denotes the 'polarity of mountain and water.'[1]

For those outside of Asia, *shanshui* is perhaps best understood for its reference to landscape paintings, less in terms of an actual rendering of a real landscape than as a creation that connects the individual to the world through carefully crafted visual compositions. Yet, in the Chinese context *shanshui* culture is expansive, encompassing ancient religious and philosophical knowledge offering guidance on virtue, beauty, human spiritual enlightenment, and 'the pursuit of an ideal natural environment for human habitat', including ideal city form.[2] Japan as an island nation and Korea's peninsula share similarities, with 70 per cent of the land covered by mountains, which gave rise to a symbolic referencing of the natural environment and people's relationship to nature. Mountains in Japan are also intrinsically linked to the Japanese construction of society. As the country has little physical space, mountains have historically been considered the only place where a person could withdraw from the wider community. With no word for privacy, Japanese people are always conceived in relationship with others and educated to not have an individual ego.[3] The mountain therefore offers a rare occasion for withdrawal from society.

The concept of *sansui* in Japan is predominantly associated with *karesansui* gardens, which emerged during the Muromachi period (1333–1568). These dry landscape gardens intricately arrange rocks and gravel as a stylised representation of the world. Japanese garden designer Mirei Shigemori was the first to adapt the highly formalised principles of these gardens into a modern design language offering an opportunity to 'explores what *karesansui* garden can be in the context of twentieth-century Japan while remaining close to its cultural roots.'[4]

Increasingly Chinese architects and landscape architects are exploring *shanshui*'s application in contemporary urbanism. During the 1990s, discussions around the future of the Chinese city highlighted the potential of the *shanshui* city.[5] Chinese scientist Qian Xuesen (1911–2009) is considered to have been particularly influential, writing letters to architects describing a modern city that felt connected to nature, designed with principles from classical garden design, Chinese poetry, and landscape ink painting.[6]

Ma Yansong from MAD Architects references *shanshui* in his exploration of high-rise alternatives to generic residential buildings. Ma rejects the commercial mass production of residential blocks, along with other rationalist approaches such as MVRDV's urban strategies based on 'calculation, efficiency, and operation'.[7] Instead he aims to imbue urbanism with human spirit and emotion, stating:

> a garden can be culture asset because it embeds spiritual elements in it. Since we can have small-scaled objects involving emotional elements, from a plant to a city, why cannot the larger-scaled? the dense cites? this is the key problem today.[8]

Yizhao Yang and Jie Hu comment that unlike 'anthropocentric' framings which emphasis nature as pragmatic or utilitarian and eco-centric perspectives that equate naturalness with wildness, *shanshui* embraces the idea that an 'ideal human settlement is a combined work of nature and of men.'[9] Ideas of nature are therefore 'always filtered through culture' which explains why *shanshui* is so valuable for design exploration.[10] Beijing Olympic Park is considered one of the first contemporary landscape projects to be designed according to *shanshui* urbanism principles,[11] while there is growing interest in developing new towns or eco-city projects that are aligned with the traditional Chinese *shanshui* city.[12]

Drawing on Prasenjit Duara's theory of superscription, Jesse Rodenbiker highlights how this translation of the classical notions of *shanshui* into a contemporary model of sustainable urbanism generates a 'new imaginary of teleological urban modernity.'[13] This layering of new meanings is therefore premised on 'simultaneous elements of continuity and discontinuity.'[14] Increasingly, Asian designers are developing confidence in working between continuity and discontinuity moving from the strict replication of symbols and detailing into a contemporary design language. This includes exploring new uses for traditional material either through the application of new technologies or by drawing on the expertise of craftsmen to produce innovative material applications. Most importantly, these new applications are still grounded in cultural stories, yet in ways that defy a simple reduction to symbolic gestures, instead lifting the narratives into the contemporary realm of spatial typologies and aesthetic outcomes.

Hoshinoya Kyoto

The featured *hojyo* garden uses moss, roof tiles, and small pebbles to create waving ground patterns similar to traditional *karesansui* gardens. Trees in the background are drawn into the garden as *shakkei* (or borrowed scenery), a design move that is further extended by the geometric hole pattern in the steel fence.

Project Name: **Hoshinoya Kyoto**
Project Location: **Kyoto, Kyoto Prefecture, Japan**
Landscape Architects: **studio on site**
Architects (Renovation & Interior): **Azuma Architect & Associates**
Client: **Hoshino Resorts**
Completion Year: **2009**
Text: based on information from studio on site

This renovation project for the luxury hotel chain Hoshinoya offered studio on site the opportunity to rediscover the value of landscape on the steep slopes of Arashiyama, Kyoto. A former retreat for nobles, the site has been a great platform for cherishing the grand view across the Oigawa (Oi River). The challenge for studio on site was how to turn an exterior space hidden behind a building into a significant garden. Separated from the major cultural attractions, this space had been left as simple passage, with a little bit of Japanese style. Visitors would never pause in this space—hence the challenge to transform this hidden treasure into a valuable spatial experience for this upscale resort.

Tradition represents the power of this unique place in Kyoto. Collaborating closely with traditional Japanese gardeners, the designers sought to breathe new life into the site by proposing new spatial and cultural relationships. The contrast between geometrical forms and natural shapes, along with the variety of materials, are some of the key features of the traditional Japanese garden. Stones, plants, bamboo fences: all have their own expression of how they wish to be in the world. Together designer and gardeners must try and find a sensitive balance between an intention to create forms and their material existence.

It was necessary to retain the simple arrangement of the buildings and circulation pattern, along with vehicular and pedestrian access through the space, to surrounding lounges and gardens. A series of spaces such as a pond, path, and garden were created. These spaces were not separated by boundary objects or buildings, but rather defined through their unique scale and the character carefully assigned within the design. Changes in spatial density further develop the atmosphere of each area. Each guest room features newly designed gardens on one side and the splendid view of the valley on the other. Thus, Hoshinoya Kyoto ultimately embodies the vision of the Hoshino resort; disembarking from a gondola, guests find themselves in an authentic Japanese retreat. This is a place to enjoy the view of Arashiyama and to spend a relaxing time away from the hustle and bustle of life.

Yongqing Fang

Guangzhou

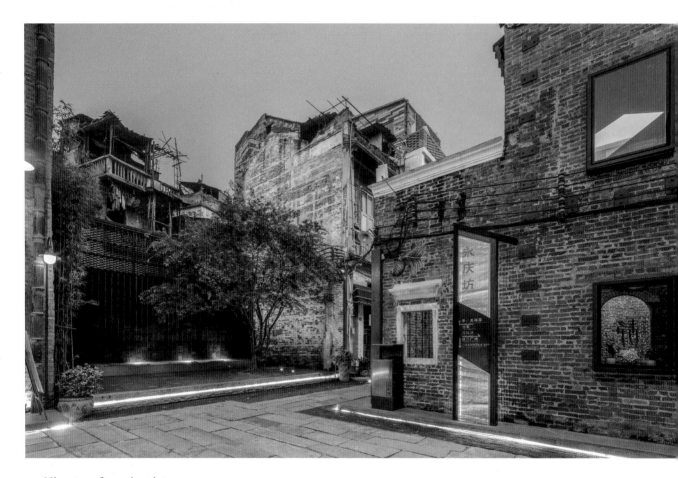

Micro-transformations into
the urban fabric.

Project Name: **Yongqing Fang Landscape Design**
Project Location: **Guangzhou, Guangdong Province, China**
Landscape Architects: **Lab D+H**
Client: **Guangzhou Vanke**
Completion Year: **2017**
Text: based on information from Lab D+H _____

A generous staircase
inserts public space.

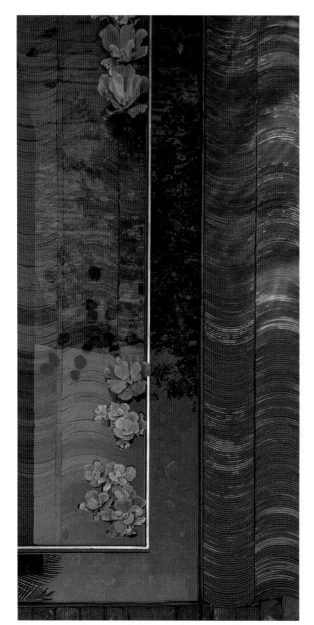

Sitting in the heart of Guangzhou old town, Yongqing Fang is an inner-city renewal project that offers an alternative to the rapid urban transformation of modern everyday life. This project aims to improve the quality of life for all residents and focuses on the renewal of buildings and the strengthening of place attachment by preserving the historic neighbourhood fabric. Lab D+H's design strategy demonstrates a micro-renovation approach developed through precise site-specific measures which rejuvenate and activate the urban fabric.

Residential houses, commercial shops, and a combination of historic and modern buildings make up the crowded urban fabric of Yongqing Fang. To unify the diverse styles and retain the historical context, a series of micro-transformations were developed. At the beginning of the renovation, most of the dwellings in Yonqing Fang were abandoned. A comprehensive site inventory formed the starting point for intensive discussions with stakeholders. This led to a classification of buildings into the five renovation categories of restoration, façade redesign, structural reinforcement, partial rebuilding, and new construction. Rather than adopting a unified measure, an organic approach was taken, which embraced the co-existence of a wide range of different building types and styles, while combining restoration with the injection of a new urban program.

An environmentally sustainable and low-impact approach to rehabilitation was applied, using the original materials of the site such as tiles, brick, natural stone, and wood. These materials were adaptively transformed into landscape elements, producing key moments such as a large section of a wall 'falling' into the water, a feature timber staircase for festivals and recreation, roof gardens, small pausing moments, and an entrance garden to Bruce Lee's ancestral home. These expansions and reconnections of public space offer new creative possibilities for outdoor activities, while respecting the local culture and rejuvenating the historic neighbourhood of Yongqing Fang.

Recycling of bricks and slate tiles.

Restroom in the Mountains
Yantai

A flexible modular approach, which responds to varied topographic conditions.

Project Name: **Restroom in the Mountains**
Project Location: **Yantai, Shandong Province, China**
Landscape Architect: **Lab D+H**
Client: **Kunyu Mountain National Park Management Committee**
Completion Year: **2018**
Text: based on information from Lab D+H

Interlinked pavilions, terraces,
and stairs provide a place of rest
and utility.

Walls of twig and sanded glass offer privacy and a unique diffuse light.

Two types of screens are juxtaposed to identify different functioning areas: rough-finished spruce and fine-finished merbau. Weathering (one year after construction) blends the two contrasting screens into harmony.

In 2017, Kunyu Mountain National Park began upgrading facilities in its fifty-square-kilometre nature preserve. The management committee invited Lab D+H to design a pilot public toilet, which would serve as the new public facility model for the national park. Given the client had not decided on the toilet's location, Lab D+H proposed a modular system which could be adapted based on different topographic conditions. This site-specific strategy was greatly appreciated by the client, and together the designers and client selected a terraced site within the alpine botanical garden located at the edge of the forest.

In English-speaking societies, a toilet is often referred to as a 'restroom', suggesting a place for rest. Therefore, instead of designing a toilet building, Lab D+H created a graceful and restful place in dialogue with nature, within this environmentally sensitive place. Through the adaptation and organisation of the modules, a central courtyard garden was created and wrapped by a canopied corridor running up and down the slope. This corridor threads the courtyard's two parts: the rest area and restroom area. The rest area provides a waiting place and offers a spectacular view towards the mountain. The restroom area is divided into a men's room, a women's room, and a family room, while two hand washing points at the edge of courtyard charge water directly to the ground after being filtered from the gravel basin. After assembling the module, the diagonally pitched roof units form a geometric silhouette, generating a dialogue with the rolling mountain ridge.

From site selection, design strategy, and materiality through to construction method, Lab D+H offer an innovative low-impact design approach. This modular system proved easily adaptable for facility upgrades throughout the national park. Lab D+H are currently working on two more restrooms in other locations, based on this modular approach, which accommodates different topographic conditions.

Sansujeonlyag Strategy for Mountain and Water

Jungyoon Kim and Yoon-Jin Park
of PARKKIM

Sansu (山水) from Korea, compared to *shanshui* (山水) from China and *sansui* (山水) from Japan,[1] suggests an unvarnished relationship with nature, arguably due to the abundance of mountains and waters in the Korean peninsula, about seventy per cent of its surface. After fifty years of drastic economic development, during which Korea soared from one of the world's poorest nations to one of the top twelve global economies, the country has lost its inherent culture of nature. PARKKIM's idea of *sansujeonlyag* (山水戰略, literally: strategy for mountain and water) stems from a self-reflection on Korea's modernity. How do we bring back its forgotten *sansu* culture, which has deteriorated because of such brutal urbanisation? Or, if some of the spirit of *sansu* has managed to survive this chaotic modernism, what alternative forms does it take? Finally, and ultimately, can this spirit and its 'spatialisation' invite a new paradigm for how a city works in an era of daunting climate change?

Looking back at these past years, PARKKIM's practice has been a process of self-questioning. Considering our built and unbuilt projects as evidence, we can summarise our self-reflection into three speculative agendas.

Sansujeonlyak and Lost Nature

At the beginning of a project, we always identify the status of nature in the context of the site—what nature looked like in the past, what was deformed, and what remains. Through research and interviews, we confirm how a lost nature is being remembered by society. For inspiration, we stroll in museums and stand in front of paintings, such as seventeenth-century *sansuhwa* (山水畵), which are landscape paintings from the Joseon dynasty. Unlike the Japanese and Chinese landscape paintings of a similar age, *sansuhwa* reveal the then-contemporary culture of nature and depict its reality without exaggeration or distortion.

The meandering sand shore of the Han River in Jeong Seon's *Yanghwa Hwando* (Calling back the boat from Yanghwa) inspired us while fabricating the mud dynamics of the Yanghwa Riverfront. The depiction of the foggy and arcane landscape of the Seoul region of *Inwang jesaekdo* (Clearing after rain on Mount Inwang) brought us back to a time when the city of Uijeongbu was still surrounded by mountains and intersected by a network of watercourses. This inspired us to design the plaza of the Provincial Office in the city with a pattern of contours to present a set of micro-topographies corresponding to the hydrological morphology.

Based on this inspiration from *sansu*, we bring engineering and technology into our projects. The engineers who have control over Seoul's infrastructure cannot be treated as enemies if we are to achieve our design intentions. Engineers and PARKKIM inspire each other, and engineers become our strategic comrades who make our inspiration a reality. *Sansujeonlyak* is thus a design strategy based on inspiration from the seventeenth-century Korean peninsula and made possible by our collaboration with engineers.

Alternative Nature and Artefacts

If we consider the factors that make Park Ave in Manhattan and Kensington St in London the most expensive residential areas, it is quite hard to understand why the houses in the Gangnam area of Seoul are also in that price range. Without the presence of a park system, this area still maintains the highest real estate value in Seoul. This observation inspired PARKKIM to search for alternative ways of having an experience of nature without the help of parks. What possibilities could an alternative nature offer the residents of Gangnam in their everyday life? In our essay *Gangnam Alternative Nature*, PARKKIM identified five ways of replacing parks: revealed nature, spot nature, memory of nature, interiorised nature, and distancing nature.[2] These concepts extend beyond the binary thinking of 'natural vs. artificial', enabling landscape to reposition itself from something considered 'natural' and liberating PARKKIM's practice in a more speculative direction. The restoration of lost experience has been tested on diverse scales, from gardens to corporate headquarters, especially through the use of materials not often used as landscape materials, or by unusual combinations of common materials. We try to recreate ephemeral moments that would normally be encountered in our contact with nature.

New Wilderness and the Function of Nature

In the territory south of the DMZ (Demilitarised Zone) there is no wilderness left in the conventional sense. Considering that excessive human manipulation of the earth is the major cause of the current climate crisis, we noticed the immanent role of wilderness as an undisturbed status of things. A wider look around the Korean peninsula identifies Siberia, the DMZ, and the Gobi Desert as wilderness. However, if there are places that can be redefined as wildernesses in neighbouring areas could we not find a new function of nature there? This kind of effort could not become real by separating spectators and actors in the landscape. Since alternative nature does not desire one ideal form of nature, PARKKIM believes in searching for a multiplicity of natures from a redefined wilderness. Can a wilderness be designed? It does not seem impossible to imagine a fabricated urban wilderness through a highly engineered approach.[3]

Humanity has taken up a common challenge: zero greenhouse gas (GHG) emissions by 2050. Currently, human beings live in urban structures where daily life creates large carbon footprints and emits GHG even unknowingly. As professionals, we recognise that this threat can become an opportunity if we can succeed in spatialising the speculative agenda. Notably, the tradition and ideology of nature that East Asians share through *sansu, sansui,* and *shanshui* may suggest a compelling future for an Asian landscape practice in the era of global environmental crisis and extend its influence to a more universal value. ■

Blossom Park   Gwanggyo

The new sculptural slope of
Only One Garden.

Project Name: **Blossom Park, CJ Research
& Development Centre**
Project Location: **Gwanggyo, Gyeonggi
Province, Korea**
Landscape Architect: **PARKKIM**
Client: **CJ Group**
Completion Year: **2017**
Text: based on information from PARKKIM

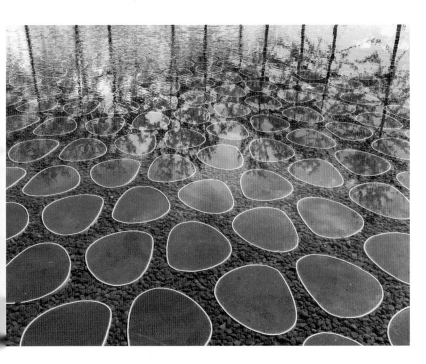

Black polished granite modules
are set within aluminium frames.
The reflectiveness of the two
materials maintains the pond's
visual effect, even when the water
is drained during winter.

The CJ Group, one of the Korean conglomerates that is famous for its K-culture leadership, has diversified into a business encompassing chemistry, food, agriculture, and medicine. This new research and development complex merges the labs and offices of these different disciplines into three mid-rise buildings that resemble the company's logo.

Due to the mountainous nature of the Korean peninsula, urban development has necessitated cutting into topography. The client asked PARKKIM to remove an ugly civil-engineered retaining wall at the border between the complex and the adjacent mountain, which is also a public park. This was not only a visual disconnect but meant that citizens were strolling in the mountain park adjacent to a steep cliff. A major part of their design approach was to conceive a seamless spatial transition along this property line, which included regrading the slope to a maximum of 1:3 to allow for planting.

White stone blades were embedded into this slope to visually blend the space into the mountain and merge the border between the complex and the park. Named Only One Garden, the area provides an open resting space for daily use, while the undulating blades contribute to slope stabilisation (even turning into a cascade during rainfall) and symbolise the mountainous character of Gwanggyo City, of which 60 per cent is green space.

Closer to the research complex, PARKKIM explored alternative ways for simulating the experience of nature, such as solitude, reflection, vastness, and undulation, while offering spaces for researchers to relax and be inspired. On the roof garden of the complex, a sculptural wavy landscape offers a place for small gatherings and solitude. At the main entrance, a reflection pond provides the ambience of a body of water all year round, even in winter, when the pond is empty.

In comparison to many vast and soulless research campuses of the United States, PARKKIM's design provides an inspiring landscape within a tight city space. The gentle slope with the stone blades, undulating roof garden, and reflection pond with unique materiality combine to offer alternative ways of creating the experience of nature.

69

Triple Street

Songdo

Mockups (1:1) of paving patterns were installed on site so that the designers and the clients could examine the visual effect from the surrounding lower buildings and the high-rise towers nearby.

Project Name: **Triple Street**
Project Location: **Songdo, Incheon Metropolitan City, Korea**
Architect and Landscape Architect: **PARKKIM**
Client: **SD Frontier**
Completion Year: **2017**
Text: based on information from PARKKIM

Five instagramable plazas break up a monumental shopping mall.

Triple Street is a 540-metre-long shopping mall in Songdo, a newly developed city within the Incheon Free Economic Zone. A lack of public open space in modern Korea means that commercial venues often play the role that parks do in the Western world. Young couples can spend the whole day in a shopping mall: starting with a cup of coffee, watching a movie, strolling in an exhibition, having lunch and dinner in between, and even sunbathing in an open space. For younger families with strollers, this kind of private-public space is a great alternative to picnicking in a park, with convenient parking spaces and universal circulation. Public space as a commercial commodity is an undeniable fact.

Triple Street comprises five open space plazas, which can be utilised as gathering and resting spaces without having to purchase a thing. The most critical design concern was to provide a pedestrian-friendly landscape that is also highly instagramable in competition with neighbouring shopping areas. Given only twelve centimetres of depth was available between the finished ground floor level and the top of the slab (meaning no planting was possible), PARKKIM seized the opportunity to intensively design the ground plane of the shopping street, without relying on greenery. Different patterns of paving and furniture create a variety of outdoor venues suitable for a contemporary urban lifestyle.

A range of paving materials, from the most conventional to the most unprecedented, were tested both in three-dimensional renderings and mock-up tests on site. While granite pavers are normally considered classy in Korea due to cost and durability (and their associations with Korean palaces), PARKKIM felt the material too conventional and rigid, restricting their ability to play with various patterns and colours.

Instead ceramic pavers were chosen. Initially the client and the city questioned their possible slipperiness and durability, since they had rarely been used as outdoor pavers in Korea. Strength tests for multiple thicknesses determined the thinnest pavers possible while maintaining optimal durability. Four different patterns were designed with the same triangulated modules to create a dynamic backdrop both in reality and in the world of Social Network Service. The matching of black and white diffuses a neutral yet elegant atmosphere.

Fragmented Nature, Delighted Experience

Dong Zhang and Ziying Tang   of Z+T Studio

Before we started Z+T Studio in 2009 in Shanghai, we went to graduate school and worked in the United States for five years. Due to our experience practising both in the United States and China, we realised just how much the vernacular landscape is deeply rooted in people's everyday life and is differentiated by regions and culture. Human beings have modified their environment based on particular territories and conditions of topography, vegetation, or weather conditions. Perception and appreciation of the environment are correspondingly different and embedded deeply in particular cultural traditions. It's intractable and inappropriate to transplant the same design strategy or philosophy from one to another.

China, as one of the ancient civilisations, has a long history of garden making that has produced an important contribution to the landscape architecture profession of the world. However, in the twentieth century, China has been undertaking an unprecedented social-economic reform. Its economic development based on universal processes of manufacturing and infrastructure reduces its unique social and cultural identity at the same time. After coming back to China, we have focused our designs on understanding the current situation deeply by looking back to local histories and studying the regional culture of landscape.

In classical Chinese gardens, miniature landscape brings an extraordinary experience of wilderness to ordinary inhabitants of the city, often as an escape from desolate reality. Landscape elements such as water, rock, plants, and structures were often symbolised to tell a bigger story of an imaginary experience with wild nature. When designing a landscape in modern China, we try to celebrate this tradition in contemporary ways and reconnect people with nature in an urban setting. Instead of rebuilding a 'nature', which is nearly impossible, we bring the experience of nature into the city. Sunlight, fog, rain, creeks, waterfalls, cascades, ponds, riverfront, beaches, oceans, cliffs, woods, grasslands, wildflowers, and meadows—all these natural attributes, elements, or phenomena can be creatively transformed and experienced in the city environment.

The fragments of nature for different cultures often have different symbolic meanings. For instance, water is a symbol of wisdom in Chinese culture, indicating how to work around obstacles and find ways to the destination, while rock, representing mountains in the garden, is a symbol of kindheartedness. Partly due to its symbolic meaning, China has a long history of engagement with water landscapes. There is a beautiful story from the Jin dynasty. A group of artists and poets gather to have a party. They sit along a creek and let a wine cup flow in the water. Wherever the cup would stop, someone would drink and make a poem. This well-documented event not only influences Chinese classic garden design and creates a symbolic landscape feature but also highlights an intimacy and interactivity between people with nature.

The design of Yueyuan Courtyard was inspired by this story. It is a small project located in a residential community centre in the new town of Suzhou, a famous UNESCO heritage garden site. To build a connection between the new and the old, we borrowed the spirit of meandering water and re-interpreted it through a modern design language. A sculptural creek forms the central feature in the courtyard. It intertwines the outdoor spaces with the architectural interior and brings closer together the creek garden and the lake garden, which were separated by the architectural layout. Made from monolithic granite, the 'creek' artfully simulates the natural hydrological process—how the cut contour lines indicate runoff water rushing over the earth's surface, transforming land into river valleys over millions of years. Time is interpreted both horizontally as a linear shape flowing and vertically as a historic record. When filled with water, the creek becomes a curved reflecting pool. It reflects the building, sky, cloud, and moon in a meandering frame. We balanced the details between simplicity and complexity and re-interpreted traditional craftsmanship with modern technology.

There is a statement suggestive of minimalism written by the Chinese philosopher Lao Tzu around 2000 years ago:

The five colours blind the eye.
The five tones deafen the ear.
The five flavours dull the taste.
Racing and hunting madden the mind.
Precious things lead one astray.
Therefore the sage is guided by what he feels
and not by what he sees.
He lets go of that and chooses this.

This philosophy explains that the more natural elements are mixed, the less they are recognisable. By simplifying design elements and focusing on single natural phenomena, we use craftsmanship of details to establish intimacy and a sense of curiosity between people and the environment.

The environmental issues we are facing right now are complicated. There are many reasons why we have got to this point. One reason, we believe, is that people are more and more removed from nature either physically by infrastructures or mentally by digital devices. In 2050, it is projected that 68 per cent of the world population will live in urban areas (increasing from 55 per cent in 2019). Precious clean air, sunlight, rain, and plants are more and more invisible for people. In the densely populated cities of the future, especially in Asian cities with limited access to nature and open space, landscape architecture can contribute to the improvement of the quality of life by creating a better connection and healthy relationship between people and the environment.

The work of Z+T Studio looks for distinct landscape features as a way to bring delightful experiences into people's everyday life and to raise public awareness and appreciation of our environment. Designs with strong associations with history and culture will build stronger bonds between human habitation and the wilderness of nature. ∎

Yueyuan Courtyard

Suzhou

Project Name: **Yueyuan Courtyard**
Project Location: **Suzhou, Jiangsu Province, China**
Landscape Architects: **Z+T Studio**
Installation: **Z+T Art Studio**
Client: **Suhang Real Estate**
Completion Year: **2016**
Text: based on information from Z+T Studio

The Yueyuan Courtyard showcases a modern landscape reflective of China's rich culture and history in classical garden making. Though inspired by the local Suzhou classical garden, the design does not employ simplistic representations, instead abstracting elements from cultural traditions and nature. Z+T Studio creates a simple yet complex experience in a small natural space. In contrast to Suzhou's famous classical gardens, Yueyuan Courtyard's palate of plants and stones is minimal, expressing a distillation of materiality and the contemporary artistic mind.

The sculptural water feature is the most innovative design element, integrating artfully into the landscape and serving as a tribute to the region's distinctive natural characteristics along with its tradition of fine craftsmanship. The water feature connects the two parts of the courtyard—the creek garden and the lake garden—structuring the visitor's journey as they move between the two. The meandering pool reflects the environment and frames artful images on the water. The effect created by this sculptural water feature is a metaphor for scenery-borrowing which, along with an ever-changing sky, offers a poetic description of the Yangtze River. As the light pours into the central garden and the day passes, people experience the moving shadow and the sound of the water flowing through the creek, generating a tranquil and meditative atmosphere. At the end of the creek, the water flows into another pool in the lake garden.

Embedding a sculptural water feature with a complex geometry into the courtyard was technically challenging. A collaboration between landscape architects and the craftsmen from the Z+T Studios' art workshop, the sculpture was completed in segments which were fabricated individually and then carefully installed on site. This design and construction process relies on a series of highly precise movements, offering a modern interpretation of more traditional Chinese garden-making techniques.

The prefabricated runnels were carefully adjusted on site before the laying of the paving stones.

75

Yan'guilai Courtyard Park

Suzhou

Project Name: **Yan'guilai Courtyard Park**
Project Location: **Suzhou, Jiangsu Province, China**
Landscape Architects: **Z+T Studio**
Installation: **Z+T Art Studio**
Client: **CIFI Group**
Completion Year: **2018**
Text: based on information from Z+T Studio

Stormwater is channelled through an
interactive contemporary water feature.

Dusk view toward Taihu Lake.

Yan'guilai Courtyard Park forms part of a greenway on
the edge of Taihu Lake, the third biggest of China's five
freshwater lakes. The greenway acts as a freshwater
buffer zone, as well as providing outdoor recreation
for a newly developed residential community. Culturally and historically, the visual qualities of the lake's
landscape have inspired literature, art, and garden
design. The extremely windy weather creates unique
landscape tectonics and soil and vegetation conditions,
including a grassy 'wildness' along the water's edge.

Z+T Studio sought to capture this spectacular
natural phenomenon and interpret the landscape
qualities through exaggerated landforms and native
grass planting. An interactive fountain enclosed by a
landform compensates for the limited recreational
opportunities in the 'water-view-only' lake park. Alongside the lakeside walkway, places for sitting, lying, or
running are created. Set against the background of a
setting sun or star constellation, these spaces suggest
a harmonious meeting between man-made landscape
and natural wildness.

Initially Z+T Studio struggled with the density of
the proposed housing project, which is typical of large-
scale housing developments on the outskirt of China's
metropolises. The project offered a chance to rethink
the adaption process between humans and nature and
their position as designers on this divide: how much
could they cross over, when should they retreat, and
what would happen if they manipulated more or less?

The spatial organisation of the housing is based
on Chinese traditional garden philosophy with connect
ing corridors, borrowed views, and designed interactions between internal and external space. The design
strategies within the residential community contrast
with the organic spatial organisation along the lakeside, creating a transition from artificial to natural. At
the centre of the housing, stormwater infrastructure is
transformed into a series of runnels and ponds through
the application of a modern design language. Running
parallel to a series of steps is an interactive fountain,
designed to encourage kids to walk along the 'creek.'

Small granite pavers (10 x 10 cm) create a dynamic
and non-slippery surface for the undulating surface,
which also acts to aerate the water.

Landscapes as Microcosm of the World

Eiki Danzuka

of EARTHSCAPE

Every traditional Japanese design has meaning. The Japanese view of religion has had great influence on shaping this understanding. Since ancient times, Japan has been a Shinto country that worships over eight million gods or spirits. The basis of Shinto (神道, literally: philosophical path of spirits) is the idea that 'God lives in everything'; from the rocks in the mountains to the grass on the roadside—God is everywhere. Throughout history, this philosophy has been a part of Japanese life and become deeply ingrained in the Japanese psyche. At the same time, Japan has the philosophy that 'everything flows'. The idea is that individual things in nature are continually generated and change like the flow of a river, yet the whole of nature itself is eternal and remains unchanged.

Many Japanese patterns are drawn to symbolise the shapes of worshiped natural things. Since for the Japanese nature *is* God, in praising God people express various feelings of gratitude and reverence for what is alive in nature. The heightened sensations are expressed, for example, aloud by singing songs, spelled out in brush writings, or danced and articulated through the body, through the sounds of instruments, and in paintings; and they have given rise to a variety of unique Japanese art forms and garden designs.

The traditional *karesansui* garden (枯山水庭園, literally: dry mountain water garden) is a particular garden style made only of rocks and sand. The scenery of mountains and flowing water (without actually using water) expresses a microcosm of the natural world with minimal materials and patterns. In addition, it is an expression of the Zen view of the world and the universe—a place for training to confront the nature in its greatness, to become 'nothing' by unifying with one's own existence and developing a self-reflective state of mind. The patterns and materials that make up our Motorcycle Parking Karesansui Park are designed in the same way as these traditional gardens. Patterns drawn on the ground represent the flow of water. The raw materials of asphalt and paint are also natural materials, such as gravel and crude oil, and the motorcycles, arranged in the same way as rocks, are made from minerals originally occurring in the natural world—only the formation has changed.

I often talk about landscape as art. We aim to develop a new genre of Japanese landscape design and to consciously create landscapes that did not exist before. Having trained as a sculptor under world-renowned sculptor Nobuo Sekine, I became interested in larger forms of art—in using landscape as a means of creation and composition. An influential moment for me was visiting Moerenuma Park in Hokkaido designed by Isamu Noguchi. The sculptural park includes a large hill, and I remember when climbing that hill, I thought this might be close to what I wanted to do. Later I visited Gaudi's Casa Mila in Barcelona. Standing on its undulated roof, which is much like a distorted swell, I felt the feeling of nature—the real earth—transmitting through my ankles. This feeling was clearly different from standing on usual asphalt and concrete surfaces. I thought at that time that, depending on the form, one could create the sense of nature even with concrete.

Enjoyment and fun are probably the most fundamental human feelings, almost like primal sensations. Creating exciting and unexpected spaces that achieve these feelings is a major challenge. At Urban Dock Lala Port, a shopping complex in the new town of Toyosu in the Tokyo Bay area, the challenge was to think about the kind of landscape design that is available to make this facility enjoyable for families. How does one design a park for children in a shopping mall development without using play equipment? A landscape that would create a chance for discovery and encounters at all levels was considered ideal for this project. With the iconic history of the site as a former shipyard and the panoramic views of the bay, the plaza was conceived around the idea of the 'great voyage'; the pond represents the vast sea, while the undulated surface resembles the flow of the waves and the seating reflects corals. It was a well-constructed landscape design, and we were able to create a worldview in Japan's commercial landscape that had not been realised until then.

Topography is ever-present in the Japanese landscape. Mountains and volcanoes cover about 70 per cent of the archipelago. Our work usually starts with reference to topography. In traditional Japanese gardens, mountains, ponds, and rivers were created as a microcosm or an abstract form of nature. Although this project refers to the sea, the topography here is an epitome of the natural world. As such, it mirrors the way of thinking applied in traditional Japanese garden design.

In Japan, economic growth led to an increase in urban development that eradicated the historic *satoyama* environment (里山, literally: village mountain), an archetype associated with small-scale agricultural and forestry landscapes symbolising the sentiment of people's co-existence with nature. In addition, we have witnessed everyday landscapes literally washed away overnight, as the consequences of natural phenomena such as large tsunamis, typhoons, and river flooding caused by weather fluctuations due to climate change. Human beings' tiny existence is at the mercy of the flow of time and the power of nature in its greatness. The landscapes we design, if seen in the long history of the earth, exist only for a moment. They have a fleeting fate that flows and changes, and in the next moment, the place in which we live and its shape will have transformed. Landscape design in Japan is about connecting people, and at the same time, it is work that connects the past and future, the human world and the natural world, and the world of gods. ∎

Karesansui Park   Tokyo

Through the re-interpretation of cultural patterns and materials, EARTHSCAPE offer small insertions into the urban fabric which combine Japanese beauty, history, and humour in a contemporary design response.

Project Name: **Karesansui Park**
Project Location: **Tokyo, Japan**
Designers: **EARTHSCAPE**
Client: **None**
Completion Year: **2012**
Text: based on information from EARTHSCAPE

The *karesansui* concept has been interpreted in the design of a parking lot for motorbike enthusiasts in Tokyo. A rider parks their bike, recalling the urban scenery through which they have ridden all day, and places a cover to protect their bike from the rain. It is at this moment, when the bike transforms visually into a 'natural' stone, that a modern *karesansui* garden suddenly emerges.

Bancho no Niwa
Tokyo

Bancho is a community development common which offers a fresh look at lifestyle, culture, and history. The name Bancho dates back the Edo period when the direct retainers of the shogun were settled in the Yonbancho area to protect Edo Castle. The town's division from this period remains to this day, offering a bridge between history and the future. The buildings and garden of Bancho no Niwa follow the structure of the original samurai residence, while the garden is decorated with the *shippo*, or seven treasures, pattern. Typical of the Edo era, this pattern of unending chains of circles expand in all directions, symbolising eternal prosperity. EARTHSCAPE hopes that this place of circles will connect people and offer richness to the urban landscape.

Project Name: **Bancho no Niwa**
Project Location: **Tokyo, Japan**
Designers: **EARTHSCAPE**
Client: **Nippon Television Network Corporation**
Completion Year: **2017**
Text: based on information from EARTHSCAPE

Contradiction, Complementarity, and Continuity

Charles Anderson

In the *Tao Te Ching*, all things come in pairs and these pairs exist as inseparable, contradictory, and seemingly paradoxical opposites. As twinned pairs, they attract and complement each other with neither pole being superior to the other. This ever-changing relationship between the two poles is responsible for the constant flux experienced in the Cosmos and in life in general. A 'correct' balance, or a 'naturally' drawn distinction, between the two poles is the achievement of harmony and the performance of virtuosity.[1]

It is tempting to portray the two offices of Turenscape in this Taoist framework. For Turenscape can be seen to be fashioned in the dynamic of differing yet complementary practices. Certainly, Kongjian Yu and Pang Wei regard each other's practices as being the complementary opposite of the other. Kongjian Yu, globally recognised, bestrides the world advocating for fundamental change in thinking—demonstrating how 'things can be done better'—through large terrestrial manipulations, pedagogical reform, and advocacy at the highest levels of government. In contrast, the lesser-known Pang Wei, working from the smaller Guangzhou office, participates in the world through a commitment to a more intimate, place-based approach. If Kongjian Yu is expressly interventionist, Pang Wei is perhaps more light-handed, process-based, and embracing of chance.

But is this framing too simplistic? With a focus on Pang Wei, this essay focuses on the philosophy and design approach of Turenscape's lesser-known Guangzhou office and uncovers what can be understood as a landscape architecture of care, a practice inflected by Taoism and a particularly nuanced usage of the Chinese word 保守 (*bao shou*), which translates literally as 'conservative'.[2]

The Tiger and the Mouse

Kongjian Yu and Pang Wei exemplify two contrasting yet complimentary energies and skillsets. Pang describes this relationship to be 'like the Tiger and the Mouse': he, Pang Wei, is the Mouse and

Kongjian Yu is the Tiger. They will never have the same path, he says, but this is as it should be because 'we are all different species'. Indeed, Pang admires Kongjian because Kongjian can take the large-scale ecological perspective and has the ability to persuade higher officials 'to do the big things'.

From Kongjian's perspective, Pang is 'different from normal architects'; he possesses exemplary 'artistic thinking and artistic ability' and is someone who is able to deliver definitively 'non-standard' projects.[3] As Pang observes, this difference is 'not about good or bad.' As he puts it: 'I am I. I follow my heart.' Indeed, Pang admits to 'a kind of Taoist complex'. Certainly, this is revealed in his attitude to life, design, and business, which demonstrates an overarching approach to excellence through an attuning to 'the unplanned rhythms of the universe'. Pursuing 'the way' or Dao, Pang's method, emphasising naturalness, spontaneity, and action without intention, embodies a Taoist ethic expressed in the Three Treasures of Laozi: simplicity, patience, and compassion.[4] Indeed, in contradiction to his very own name—which means Big Grand or Big Huge—Pang thinks that if a thing is too grand, or too large, it means that it will be 'ugly or fake'.

From their first project together, the two offices have taken divergent yet complementary paths.[5] From the beginning, the Beijing office grew extremely quickly, in contrast to the Guangzhou office. As Kongjian puts it, due to Pang's, 'artistic personality' and his intention to 'keep things small', the Guangzhou office did not undertake big projects, focusing instead on 'artistic', small to mid-scale projects. Pang muses that he didn't have the vision of Kongjian. Or rather, his was a different vision. He deliberately kept the company small. At the beginning, there were just a handful of employees, and this grew to—at the most—around fifty employees.[6]

This differentiation in practice is reflected in the location of the two offices. For Kongjian, it was important to locate the Beijing office in direct relationship to a major teaching and research university and adjacent to political power, as would best suit an enterprise with explicit ambitions for national and globally recognised design research impact. As such, the Turenscape office in Beijing can be understood as a case study in enterprise, entrepreneurial energy, intellectual ambition, and global reach and influence.

By contrast, the Turenscape office in Guangzhou is located in a residential estate ten kilometres to the south of the new central business district of Guangzhou.[7] Pang chose this place because it situated him directly in the milieu of contemporary China and the emergent complex relationships between urban expansion, with new housing estates and urban villages. Importantly for Pang, it was in the immediate proximity of a living community and not a place where he would be 'surrounded by designers'. In this way, the Guangzhou office is the embodiment of a situated landscape architecture practice that prioritises place-based knowledge in a globalised world.

Twinned Endeavours: Ecology and Culture

As the very name suggests, ecology and culture sit at the heart of the Turenscape enterprise (土 *tu*, literally: the earth + 人, *ren*, literally: man or mankind). Always championing a landscape architectural approach to urban development (now formalised globally as ecological urbanism), Turenscape proposes a less anthropocentric and more inclusive model of environmental design for human and non-human habitats. Kongjian and Pang have developed this shared idea through accomplished built design projects, albeit achieved via divergent paths.

Kongjian continues his advocacy at all levels of government and the global design industry and delivers territorial-scale projects involving the deployment of advanced digital spatial analytical tools, major terraforming, and manipulation of environmental systems. In contrast, Pang has become less and less interventionist. Often characterised by an explicitly hands-off approach, his projects provide glimpses of open-ended, emergent natural environments as a landscape architectural project. Inspired by the work of Aldo Leopold, Pang has partly abandoned the notion of people-orientated design and instead embraces an 'every-being orientated design', considering humans as only one part of this whole system. Accordingly, in pioneering projects such as the Memorial Park of the Botanical Congress, Shenzhen, Pang removes human intervention, instead allowing natural processes to self-organise, to literally 'take place' and evolve into novel environments, with human participation transformed into acts of custodianship. As Pang puts it, when human beings 'do nothing' then 'this is when nature comes and stays'.[8]

Culture is embedded in the ecological thinking of both Kongjian and Pang. However, their particular engagement with local histories and heritage is shaped by their divergent readings of site. Kongjian, with his perhaps more materialist understanding of site, conceives it as a complex layering of landscape systems of which culture is but one element. In this schema, site

offers itself to the designer as an object to be manipulated. In contrast, Pang conceives of site as constituted by lived stories. Such a heuristic engagement with site is not surprising, given that Pang is very much a philosopher-poet.[9]

A writer, artist, designer, and skilled calligrapher, Pang draws a very particular relation between writing and landscape design, coining the term 'landscape writing', which (with reference to the Surrealist painter Salvador Dalí) conceives of landscape as 'the appearance of the soul'. Powerfully, this notion of landscape writing suggests that the act of making place is akin to writing place, and it posits a relation between the act of writing, particularly that of poetic speech, and the creation of landscape. Even more profoundly, by extension, it suggests that there is an active, direct, and reciprocal relationship between 'human-soul' and 'landscape-soul'.[10] To explicate this idea, Pang refers to Li Yu, known as Li Liweng (1610–1680) a scholar, writer, and actor from the Qing dynasty who considered the landscape to be the 'talent of nature', and located the 'talent' that is the landscape in the human heart. Here, 'talent' is more associated with the notion of the gift and gifting. This posits an interconnected or reciprocal relationship between humans and the environment—each in the role of and responsible for gifting to each other.

保守 (*bao shou*)—A Landscape Architecture of Care

For Pang, the new China is defined by 'demolition'.[11] In his eyes, China's rapid urban development and the seemingly magical appearance of instant cities created by government fiat has meant the erasure of the past and the imposition of the grand narratives of modernisation—economic reform, development, progress—promulgated in government policy as well as in popular myth-making. This has induced what he calls a 'great forgetting' in China. Accordingly, Pang explicitly stages places of remembering, creating landscapes of sociological memory generated from the situated, intimate stories that constitute the local.

Because he no longer believes in globalisation or the advancement of technology, Pang thinks that all generations since the Second World War have 'become lost'. Perhaps it is a reaction to the Chinese experience of unparalleled rapid change and, as he reflects, perhaps because he is getting 'older and older', Pang says he feels closer, or more attached, to what he calls old things, and to what in Chinese the word 保守 (*bao shou*) relates to: the enduring aspect of things. As for landscape design, he thinks it's time to keep it relatively 'conservative'. Again, he uses the meaning of this word in Chinese to refer to the aspect of things that are 'softer, more gentle and closer to people in the world'.

This 'conservatism' is difficult to define. It has a very rich range of associative meanings in Chinese, and Pang does not use it in the common way.[12] Pang describes himself as 'conservative' in the sense that he 'goes back' to or seeks to engage with local cultures, or more specifically, to land and nature in the way the ancient Chinese would. He sees this not necessarily as a nostalgic return to things as they may or may not have originally been but as an engagement with the intimate lived experience of people in specific places. This denotes relations of care, prudence, and maintenance with the world. Against what he describes as an 'external radicalism' in landscape design, he thinks that 'conservative' landscape design should make people *feel*, and feel closer to the earth. In some way, this kind of 'conservatism' can be understood as not being about the imposition of the will (of a landscape architect) but of bringing forth or 'holding up those everlasting things' which connect people and land.

In the following poem, Pang tries to capture some of this spirit.[13]

OLD

I like everything that is old
Am I old
Old things
Make me feel
That the world is like a hug.

I must admit that I'm tired
Let me sleep for a while
I like the light that does not shine too
    directly into my eyes
I like things with history (they have historic
    memories).

And I like some sort of conservatism
I have already passed the age to be
    aggressive
And I like someone calling me in a
    low voice
I look back and see that in late afternoon
The landscape in the setting sun
And the setting sun in the landscape.

I live in the old house
Listening to the old-fashioned
    record player
I look through the old dictionaries
And feel a yearning for the people
    around me.

Leaving anxious people
No more rushing, no more chasing
I spend time together with those people
    with a calm face
Reading the classics
Reading the starry sky
Reading ourselves
And each other.

Pang believes that the majority of Chinese people do not relate to or understand the word *bao shou* in this way anymore, for in China, modernisation, development, and advancement have become like a religion. People, he says, 'believe in those things' and expect and look forward to perpetual novelty. This unceasing and relentless progress brings about radical change at vast scales, but these large projects are far removed from our inner world. Indeed, echoing Latour, Pang sees in this relentless movement forward how the actual lived experience, the traditions and inheritances, of generations which could be said to have made such transformations possible are deliberately erased.[14] Consequently, Pang wants to point us in another direction—not so much to look backwards but to look at other forgotten or deliberately ignored things, to rediscover and remember the past, and by so doing to reconnect with the land itself, to become closer to each other, our inner selves, and to our ancestors. Such a refocusing could be a way to rethink the local not necessarily as a static body of knowledge but as a 'creative potentiality'.[15] ■

Interruption

ASIANS ARE VERY ACCEPTING OF SITUATIONS

The Economic Reterritorialisation of Asia

In 2012, Singapore's Gardens by the Bay opened to much acclaim, with its iconic super trees quickly adopted as a national symbol. In less than fifty years after independence, Singapore had transformed into an exemplar of Asian modernity, positioned as a cosmopolitan and technologically advanced nation, underpinned by a global flow of knowledge and information.[1] Speaking at his 1997 National Day rally speech, Prime Minister Goh Chok Tong described his vision to attract a highly educated global community, stating that 'in the information age, human talent, not physical resources or financial capital is the key factor for economic competitiveness and success.'[2] Twenty years later, Singapore's foreign workforce had grown substantially, and its rapid economic growth was mirrored in other Asian tiger economies of Hong Kong, Korea, and Taiwan, who had similarly opened their markets to global opportunities.

Many accounts of Asia's modernisation emphasise the homogenising effects of industrialisation, globalisation, and urbanisation, highlighting the loss of traditional culture, forms, and practices. However, contemporary Asian scholars dispute this position, arguing instead that modernity and modernisation do not equate to Westernisation, and further, that Asian societies do not necessarily wish to emulate the West. Korean sociologist Kyung-Sup Chang, for example, observes that while Korea 'has undergone full-scale capitalist industrialization, economic growth, urbanization, proletarianization ... and democratization within unprecedentedly short periods' the country 'still manifests distinctly traditional and/or indigenous characteristics in many aspects of personal, social, and political life.'[3] Similarly, Singapore's economic reform was achieved while maintaining a government model of 'Asian authoritarianism' or one-party rule.[4]

Asia's transformation through processes of modernity and modernisation, therefore, represents a complex intertwining of continuity and interruption. Accordingly, scholars such as Weiming Tu argue that the three 'prevalent but outmoded exclusive dichotomies: the traditional—modern, the West—the rest and

Jillian Walliss

the local—global' are of little value for understanding this transformation.[5] In light of Tu's argument, this essay explores some specifics of an Asian experience of modernity, before turning to processes of modernisation and urbanisation. This discussion establishes the link between economic development and the emergence of the discipline of landscape architecture, along with the introduction of new open space typologies. Importantly, while these typologies may appear to be similar to Western concepts, in an Asian economic, political, and cultural context they operate very differently.

Multiple Modernities

Writing in 2000, Israeli sociologist Shmuel Eisenstadt argued that the idea of multiple modernities was the most appropriate framing for understanding the contemporary world. While non-Western contexts have taken on some aspects of modernity, they have also rejected many, which, Eisenstadt highlights, has led to diverse transformations 'shaped in each society by the combined impact of their respective histor-ical traditions and the different ways in which they became incorporated into the new modern world system.'[6] Consequently, he claims that the history of modernity should be written 'as a story of continual constitution and reconstitution of a multiplicity of cultural programs.'[7]

Eisenstadt's position challenges a Eurocentric concept of modernity, which adopts the development of the West 'as a reference point to guide the political, economic and cultural developments of the entire human society.' [8] This construction has led to the assumption that 'all cultures should be made in the image of the West.'[9] In contrast, multiple modernities recognise the continuation of traditions and values as distinct from suggesting a break from tradition in the pursuit of modernity (mirroring the West).

In considering Asian experiences of modernity, it is important to not equate modernity with modernisation. Whereas modernisation can be understood as a structural process of industrialisation and economic development, modernity is culturally and historically specific and refers to a process orientated towards the future—a questioning of the present.[10] In the West, modernity and modernisation overlap; however, this is not the case in the Asian context.

Continuum, the first section of our book, has already touched on the characteristics of multiple modernities, highlighting how contemporary Asian cultures continue to evolve from a rich foundation of cultural and philosophical understandings of nature, time, and space.

One clear example is the enduring influence of Confucian humanism in shaping the modern East Asian political economy.[11] From Western perspectives, it is often assumed that such thoughts are tied to feudal times and no longer relevant. However, Confucian teaching resurfaced in the 1960s and in the contemporary context shapes diverse values ranging from political ideology to the role of the family.

Confucian humanism is influential in many contexts including China, Japan, Hong Kong, Korea, and Vietnam. Tu highlights that 'As the demarcation between the capitalist and socialist East Asia begins to blur the cultural form that cuts across the great divide becomes distinctly Confucian in character.'[12] Some governance characteristics shaped by Confucian tradition include

- government leadership in a market economy taking responsibility for public needs;
- positioning civil society as an interplay between the public and the private (as distinct from operating autonomously above the family and beyond the state);
- considering the family as the basic unit of society from which core values are communicated; and
- the framing of education as a civil religion (character building), with such self-cultivation critical to society.[13]

Multiple modernities, therefore, recognises diverse experiences of Asian modernity reflective of specific economic, cultural, and political influences. For example, Korea is known for its 'compressed modernity', an idea that emerges from Chang's work examining the social consequences of Korea's twentieth-century economic growth. Chang explores the ramification of this intense period of national and individual advancement, shaped by the adoption of Western-style institutions and policies introduced from the American occupation, accelerated by the IT industry and forces of globalisation in the 1990s. While this was a time of unprecedented change, other parts of Korean culture and society were 'stubbornly resistant to change.'[14] He highlights how the 'dynamic coexistence of mutually disparate historical and social elements' produces 'a highly complex and fluid social system' which manifests at multiple levels of the individual, the family, urban space, civil society, and the nation.[15]

Hence compressed modernities acknowledge the extremely condensed manner (in terms of both time and space) in which political, economic, and social change has occurred in the Asian context. As a concept, it is not specific to Korea, with attributes such as familialism evident in other Asian societies. Familialism, which describes the structuring and conceptualisation of companies and businesses as a family, is evident in many Asian countries. It was particularly important in Japan's post-war economic growth, and Korea's chaebols—family-controlled companies such as Hyundai, Samsung, and LG—continue to play a major role in the country's economic growth.[16]

As would be expected, China's experience of modernity is distinctive. Modernisation of China began with the establishment of the People's Republic of China in 1949. However, The Great Proletarian Cultural Revolution (1966–1976), along with subsequent rapid urbanisation and economic growth in the 1990s, resulted in major upheaval to Chinese culture and traditions. Some scholars point to the declaration of an 'ecological civilisation' which became part of the Chinese Communist Party Constitution in 2012 as a critical moment, offering evidence that China had 'accepted the necessity to respect, strengthen and integrate her evolving traditions and culture and post-socialist commitments in the development of her own contemporary modernity.'[17] Heidi Wang-Kaeding highlights how this commitment acts to 'sinicize' environmentalism, demonstrating to the West that this shift is driven by Chinese policies producing 'environmentalism with Chinese characteristics', rather than international pressure to address poor environmental outcomes.[18]

China's opening to the world, and subsequent influence on the world order, has provoked the conceptualisation of a Chinese modernity, which encompasses its growing international influence. In 2015, Jilin Xu proposed *xin tianxia zhuyi* (new *tianxia* principle) as a way to address China's political order from inside and outside its territory.[19] Xu argues against nationalist perspectives that encourage China to turn its back on the West to focus on China's uniqueness, wealth, and power as a nation-state. Instead, he claims that historically China's greatness was tied to openness, as evidenced by the notion of *tianxia* 天下 (all under heaven), understood as 'an ideal civilizational order, and a world spatial imaginary with China's central plains at the core.'[20] Traditionally, *tianxia* offered an 'open kind of universalism to which other Asian cultures could aspire.'[21]

This interpretation of 'Tianxia 2.0' presents a 'de-centered and non-hierarchical' China, where relationships with surrounding neighbours are based on shared *tianxia* values rather than 'interest-based alliances or antagonisms.'[22] The new *tianxia* principle thus offers a way for explaining China's position in the wider Asian region and the world order, realising 'one system, different modes' at the core, 'one state, different cultures' at the frontier, 'one civilization, different systems' in Hong Kong, Macao, and Taiwan, 'one region, different interests' in East Asia, and 'one world, different civilizations' in international society.[23]

While this Sinocentric concept may 'resolve the anxiety of identity for China' it is extremely challenging for peripheral countries, which view China's expansion as more threatening than sharing.[24] These concepts of 'compressed modernity' and 'the new *tianxia* principle' are just two examples of a distinctive Asian experience of modernity, which remain strongly informed by culture and tradition. As Tu argues, these diverse experiences render the simplistic binary framings of 'traditional—modern' and the 'local—global' obsolete.[25] However, what can be declared as common to an Asian construction of modernity is a projected future of shared prosperity.

Processes of Prosperity
During the mid- to late twentieth century Asia was in various states of economic development and political turmoil, recovering from the effects of war (Japan, Korea, Vietnam); colonisation (Singapore, Hong Kong, Indonesia, Malaysia, India); or widespread poverty (China). Subsequent economic advancements have occurred in cycles, beginning with the post-war development of Japan, followed closely by the emergence of the tiger economies of Hong Kong, Singapore, Korea, and Taiwan. The introduction of market reforms in China by Deng Xiaoping in 1978 set in motion the largest economic transformation in the region, not only shaping a new future for China but unsettling the world economic order. Most recently Southeast Asian nations have emerged as the new global centre for value-added manufacturing (particularly in electronics and precision engineering sectors), attracting extensive investment from other Asian nations. Guided by diverse government structures and development models, these economic transformations form an essential background for understanding resultant processes of urbanisation shaped by complex relationships between government, developers, international and local investment, and citizens. Importantly, these processes underpin the emergence of contemporary landscape architecture in Asia.

The industrial development of the Asian Tigers (also known as the Four Little Dragons or the Four Asian Dragons) was a key moment in the economic growth of the region. Beginning in the 1960s, Hong Kong, Singapore, Korea, and Taiwan prioritised interventionalist industrialisation to gain national development through economic growth.[26] Broadly speaking, the Asian Tigers adopted a growth-orientated modernisation, which featured rapid urbanisation, the allocation of state-led financial resources directly to select private corporations, and a top-down model of governance along with the expectation of a hard-working society. Urban development operated as an 'instrument of social and political control' central to accommodating rural to urban migrations and providing necessary labour for swiftly expanding industries.[27] While sharing a common development model, individually each Asian Tiger operated with its distinctive governance and characteristics.

Although Singapore was granted internal self-government in 1959, the Crown colony was not officially dissolved until 1963 when Singapore became a state of the Malaysian Federation. Two years later Singapore became a sovereign republic after withdrawing from the Federation. As Singapore was considered a resource-poor nation, the first prime minister Lee Kuan Yew instigated state-led processes of modernisation and industrialisation. This development model was driven by a single party that maximised power at the level of government agencies. Singapore is distinctive, in that it 'defies Western predictions that modernisation will inevitably lead to democracy', having become the 'only country in the region to achieve advanced economic industrialisation without undergoing substantial political liberalisation.'[28] Integral to this model is a close relationship between the government and the National Trade Union Congress (NTUC), which has served to minimise labour grievances, thereby creating a stable economy attractive to investors, along with extending business-friendly laws to multi-national corporations (MNCs) to invest and train the local workforce. With strong economic performance, and by providing citizens with extensive financial and social benefits such as housing and public facilities, Singapore has transformed into a stable administrative state where 'the country's once politically active citizens have become depoliticised over time.'[29]

In contrast, Korea and Taiwan developed into manufacturing centres driven by government partnerships with private developers.[30] Rebuilding after the Korean War, the government offered cheap loans and relief funds to the private sector that were committed to rebuilding the country, as well as offering local industries protection from foreign competition.[31] This led to the domination of the family-based *chaebols* such as Samsung and Hyundai who on some levels operate as private agents of the state by implementing government policy. Translated as *chae* (wealth) *bol* (clan), many *chaebols* are traced to the period of Japanese occupation and are modelled on the powerful *zaibatsu* of Japan—industrial and financial conglomerates.[32] For example, Samsung began in 1938 as a small food exporting company run by the Lee family, who according to Forbes is now the second wealthiest family in Asia.[33] *Chaebols* continue to dominate Korean business, although in 2017 President Moon Jae-In was elected with a mandate to break the *chaebol*-government nexus.[34]

These governance models establish very different relationships between political power citizens, developers, and business. Over time Korea has transitioned into a more democratic political structure, while Singapore has remained within its 'one-party rule'. Despite these differences, both have been equally successful in achieving economic wealth for their citizens. For example in 1960 the GDP per capita in Korea and Singapore was just USD 156 and USD 428 respectively. By 2014 this had risen to USD 27,9470 in Korea[35] and by 2015 to USD 52,888 in Singapore, making it one of the world's highest.[36]

China's population size, geographic scale, and distinctive political system make its late twentieth-century transition from agrarian to open market economy of international significance. This transition occurred in two phases, starting with reforms led by Deng Xiaoping in 1978. Before the reforms, China's modest economic growth was stagnating. In response, Communist party leadership instigated market-orientated reforms, beginning with decollectivisation of agriculture and the encouragement of foreign investment while maintaining state ownership of industry. The second phase was far more radical. From the late 1980s state-owned industry was privatised and protectionist policies lifted, stimulating an unprecedented growth of 9.6 per cent on average annually from 1978 to 2017.[37] The declaration of special economic zones (SEZs) was central to this reform. Commencing in 1979 with the coastal provinces of Guangdong and Fujian, the Chinese government declared strategic coastal cities and border zones as SEZs, which were developed for foreign trade and to attract foreign investment.[38] This growing list of cities inspired extensive urban migration and created a 'movement of labour and capital that is arguably unparalleled' in human history.[39] For example, during the 1980s over 80 per cent of the population lived in rural villages, yet by 2011 over 50 per cent had relocated to the city in pursuit of a brighter economic future.[40]

On one level, the economic development of Japan, the Asian Tigers, and China has been driven by top-down governance; however, this fails to acknowledge the critical role of family-run conglomerations or 'Confucian capitalism'. Considered 'the business backbone' of Asia, family-based conglomerations have developed extensive wealth and are widely influential in banking, shipping, real estate, and manufacturing. The centrality of family relationships, networks, and personal bonds to business dealings is reflected in the Chinese concept of guanxi 關係, which provide critical informal networks that sit alongside state institutions and offer a 'sense of network capitalism.'[41] These models encourage an entrepreneurial and opportunistic approach to business, unhindered by government rules and institutions. However, they can also foster a culture of corruption, as demonstrated in the political history of Korea, where the close relationship between chaebols and the government has led to many examples of corruption, bribery, and embezzlement.[42]

The 1997–8 Asian financial crisis was a major shock to the region, leading to stock market crashes, devaluing of currency, and in the case of Indonesia and Thailand political instability. Generally, the recovery was fast, and it did lead to some positive economic reform including the introduction of stronger corporate governance in Korea and Indonesia, along with reducing the influence of the 'bamboo network' (a term for overseas Chinese family-owned businesses) on Southeast Asia.[43] In a longer-term development, the financial crisis shifted investment patterns in the region, encouraging Korea, Japan, and China to invest in the new 'world factories' of Southeast Asia. Since 2001, more than half of the USD 510-billion foreign investment in Asia originates in the region.[44]

For example, Vietnam has emerged as the new star economic performer in Southeast Asia, shifting from one of the world's poorest countries (following twenty years of war) to a middle-income country. The introduction of political and economic reforms in 1986 known as doi moi (restoration) transformed Vietnam into a socialist-orientated market economy featuring trade liberalisation, deregulation, and public investment in physical and human capital.[45] Vietnam's economic growth of 6–7 per cent and extensive manufacturing now rival China.[46]

Added to the influence of family conglomerates and government-directed economic strategies are informal economies (also referred to as the shadow, black, or unofficial economy), which play an equally significant role in Asia's economic transition. In 2008 the Asian Development Bank reported that informal economies supplied 25 per cent of the gross national product in twenty-six Asian countries.[47] In many Asian cities, the informal sector is growing more quickly than the formal sector. A 2018 International Labor Report highlights that more than 68 per cent of the employed population in Asia works in the informal economy, averaging 71.4 per cent in the emerging economies of South and Southeast Asia and 21.7 per cent in developed Asian economies.[48] Almost 95 per cent of agricultural employment is informal, compared to 68.8 per cent in the industrial sector and 54 per cent in the services sector.[49] While poverty is considered both a cause and a consequence of informality, [50] it is important to acknowledge its value in creating jobs for individuals at the lowest end of society, along with the fact that many informal workers make a good income.

The presence of such a large informal economy, along with informal settlements, raises the issue of inequality in Asia. Since 1980, it is estimated that over one billion Asians have been lifted out of poverty, within just one generation.[51] This fast cycle of economic advancement has created some of the wealthiest citizens and companies in the world. At the same time, extreme inequalities are present, particularly in Southeast Asia. For example, in Mumbai, more than 40 per cent of the population of over twenty million continue to live in slums or squatter settlements.[52]

However, inequity is a complex issue. In his 2019 book, *The Future is Asian*, Parag Khanna argues that inequality is accepted within Asian contexts, considered 'an inevitable consequence of the tide that has lifted most boats.' He states that the debates within Asia are not 'about lowering the ceiling for the wealthy but about raising the floor for the masses.'[53] Similarly, Jean-Pierre Cling et al. highlight that given Asia's spectacular economic development 'the region's governments, more than elsewhere, have decided that there is no need to concern themselves' with the informal economy with the assumption that this will eventually 'fade away with growth.'[54] Khanna comments that these attitudes towards inequality are mirrored by an acceptance of globalisation, claiming that unlike the West 'Asian societies remain pro globalisation *because* their governments are actively steering it in their favour.' [55]

At this point, a reader may be wondering how this discussion of development models, economics, and wealth relates to the emergence of landscape architecture. The reasons are twofold. First, the introduction of public space and parks within cities is inherently linked to Asia's economic advancement, tied into investment and development strategies along with the growing lifestyle aspirations of an emerging Asian middle class. Second, the structural mix of the informal economy, government development models, family conglomerates, and international and local investment significantly influences the meaning and role of these designed spaces. As I discuss in the final part of this essay, the rapid economic growth and accompanying processes of urbanisation and modernisation result in the introduction of new open space typologies aligned with the West. However, these models operate very differently in these new economic and cultural contexts.

Landscape Reterritorialisation

The extraordinary economic transformation of Asia has resulted in cities of immense population and density. By 2025, it is projected that twenty-one of the forecast global thirty-nine megacities (over ten million) will be Asian, with the biggest population growth expected in South and East Asian meta cities (larger than twenty million).[56] Cities operate as the economic engine for growth, investment, and development. Before this urbanisation, there were few public squares or parks in Asian cities. Instead, open space was largely found in palaces or temple grounds, while publicness was enacted in markets or through street interactions.[57] The real estate boom, new housing demands, and the competition to attract global investment were a catalyst for the introduction of new types of spaces and roles for landscape. At face value, the ensuring introduction of parks, the shopping mall, urban squares, the pedestrianised streets, boulevards, and gated residential communities appear to mirror the urban spatial typologies of the West. While these typologies may visually seem similar, how these

spaces are produced and funded defy straightforward classifications such as public and private space.

The complexity of these new urban spaces is well demonstrated by the Chinese experience. A critical component of post-reform China was the transformation of land from common ownership to a commercial commodity. Understanding the economic mechanisms of Chinese cities is extremely complex, a mix of economic theory and cultural processes. In their book *China Constructing Capitalism: Economic Life and Urban Change*, Michael Keith et al. emphasis the relational manner in which China's economy is conceived as 'a web of economic life that surrounds economic action.'[58] In contrast to 'an ideal-typical Western cultural paradigm that is individualised and disembedded,' Chinese economic life and its accompanying form of urbanism (influenced by Taoism and Confucianism) remains relational and situated.[59] The *danwei* (the work unit) is the clearest demonstration of this concept. Until Deng Xiaoping's economic reforms in the 1980s and 90s, most of the urban population belonged to either a collective or state-owned *danwei*. In the post-reform era, many new institutions emerged 'around' *danwei* and can still be considered to underlie 'economic life and urban change as the fabric of the city.'[60]

A land leasing system, which separates land ownership from land use, without challenging the Communist Party's public ownership, is central to reform.[61] Technically there is no private property in China; however, leasing allows land to be purchased and sold. The state retains long-term rights of land ownership and offers a property model that operates as leasehold with real estate developed in exchange for rights that can range between forty and seventy years. This model had an unintended effect of decentralising power down to municipal and district governments.[62] This decentralisation is what has allowed the Chinese city to develop so quickly, and demonstrates that while Chinese governance may be top-down, the development model is far more entrepreneurial.

In her 2014 book, *Shanghai Future: Modernity Remade*, Anna Greenspan offers insight into the complex financing and governance model applied in the development of Pudong, Shanghai's financial district. This involved transitioning from the government as the major shareholder into the creation of subsidiaries and even smaller, specialised companies, which become 'the pre-eminent representatives of the front line of entrepreneurial Chinese local government.'[63] Operating at the scales of the city and district in a bottom–up capacity and working across numerous projects concurrently, these companies engage global and private influences, including drawing on tight webs of *guanxi* (connections) of overseas Chinese. Greenspan highlights how these processes shape 'Chinese capitalism with a flexible, risk-taking diasporic culture that is notoriously adept at operating outside state control.'[64]

This development model defies simple definition, presenting as an entanglement of public and private interests—a hybrid of state, public sectarian, and private interests.[65] Offering a unique intertwining of relationships, economics and urban development, these processes render binary concepts of public and private void. As Qingyun Ma from MADA s.p.a.m. observes 'you have to understand there is no such thing as public space in China—the notion of the separation of the civic realm from the state does not make sense conceptually.'[66]

The introduction of parks in China in the millennium is explicitly linked to this expanding real estate market. From outside China, the extensive discussion of sponge city projects can suggest that the widespread investment in parks was driven primarily by ecological concerns. However, Zhifang Wang highlights that the introduction of the park in China predates the declaration of an 'ecological civilisation'.[67] With an increased value being placed on society within the liberal market, designed open spaces and parks were considered critical mechanisms to increase the value of land and commercial development. Following the establishment of market mechanisms in 1992, monumental squares, plazas, and boulevards (referred to as the 'Big Road, Big Square' movement) were adopted as a way to enhance the city image and attracting foreign investment.[68] However from 2004, with the further opening of China, open space together with transportation and sewage systems were repositioned as 'engines for urban expansion'.[69] This was the catalyst for the investment in an urban park movement encompassing wetland parks, expo sites, forest parks, and greenways. These parks were often huge in scale and constructed on rural-urban interfaces. Beyond generating investment income, the construction and maintenance of parks also contributed to economic growth. However, as Wang notes, the parks often became a maintenance burden for local governments and, given their distance from the city centre, were not well used.[70]

The Chinese experience demonstrates how the first waves of open spaces were intrinsically tied to the market economy, central to unfolding real estate investment driving China's urbanisation processes. In contrast, Singapore's development model has been fuelled by financial investment along with the attraction of an elite international workforce. Whereas China has remained a distinctly Chinese population, the Singaporean government has actively reconfigured the city's population and spaces to reflect the 'cosmopolitan' and 'heartland'.[71]

With few natural resources and a small population, Singapore has developed into a city-state that straddles the local and the global. The first development phase focused on addressing poor housing conditions for the existing population, improving infrastructure, and attracting enterprise. In terms of land ownership, the Singaporean government had the reverse issue to China, requiring access to individually owned land in order to adopt a centralised approach to urban development. The Land Acquisition Act of 1966 provided the state 'the power to acquire and appropriate land that was privately owned on a compulsory basis for any public purpose', which led to the state becoming the largest landowner by the 1970s.[72]

A mass public housing scheme providing affordable public housing for up to 80 per cent of the population and contributed to a stable industrial workforce which was critical to attracting international investors.[73] Concerns quickly emerged over the negative effects of this urbanisation process, inspiring Singapore's first prime minister Lee Kuan Yew to begin a tree-planting campaign in 1963. Four years later, this initiative was formalised into a national project to transform Singapore into a Garden City. Open space networks, gardens, and extensive planting were now elevated to the importance of housing, transportation systems, and employment in providing a universal standard of living. Singapore's government structure of public agencies and statutory authorities strictly regulated the development approach. For example, The Parks and Recreation Department, (the predecessor of the National Parks Board) was formed within the Ministry of National Development to plan and implement garden city policies.

Singapore's development directions shifted significantly following the Asian financial crisis of 1997. Speaking in 1999, Prime Minister Goh Chok Tong described his vision for aggressively internationalising Singapore by attracting 'transnational elite' or 'cosmopolitans' 'who ha[ve] the skills that command good incomes, banking, global market, IT, engineering, science and technology.'[74] Singapore would provide a base for cosmopolitans 'to operate in the region'. In contrast, the 'heartlanders' would make their living within the country, offering local skills such as taxi drivers, stallholders, provision shop owners, production workers, and contractors and speaking Singlish. By 2017 this vision had been realised. With a substantial well-educated and foreign-born population, along with investment in internationally focused attractions such as Marina Bay, Singapore had transformed into a global cosmopolitan city.

In parallel, Singapore's garden city vision was revised to 'city in a garden'. Singapore's semi-authoritarian governance implemented wide-ranging environmental policies addressing waste and pollution and encouraging green infrastructure and open spaces, in what Heejin Han describes as an 'ecological modernisation'.[75] Singapore transformation into a biophilic city and established itself as an international benchmark, offering landscape architects and architects extraordinary design opportunities, along with a place for international design practices to establish their first Asian offices.

Moving further south, as real estate and industrial opportunities became increasingly more expensive in the developmental contexts of Korea, Singapore, Japan, and China, Asian developers and investors looked to the growing economies of Southeast Asia. New economic and industrial zones, along with large-scale transnational projects, have emerged across Indonesia, Malaysia, and Thailand, most notably Chinese investment through the Belt and Road Initiative.[76] This investment has generated mega-developments, new towns, and luxury housing estates. In these projects, landscape and green infrastructure underpins investment strategies for attracting an emerging middle-class elite, offering lifestyle alternatives to crowded Southeast Asian cities.

In 2013, Chinese president Xi Jinping announced the 21st Century Maritime Silk Road, which together with the Silk Road Economic Belt is collectively known as the Belt and Road Initiative.[77] This strategy has attracted extensive scrutiny considered variously as a further example of China's internationalisation, evidence of a 'new regional order', or reflective of a new geopolitics reminiscent of colonisation and imperialism.[78] Hong Liu and Guanie Lim highlight that much of this critique mistakenly positions the Southeast Asian nations as passive to Chinese investment, instead arguing that these transnational projects equally reflect the ambitions of Southeast Asian stakeholders driven by their own economic and political visions.[79]

In Malaysia, economic zones and new rail infrastructures have inspired a series of ambitious residential and commercial 'mega developments' such as Forest City. Designed and constructed by Country Garden Holdings, one of the largest property development companies in China, Forest City is located on Iskandar Malaysia and is considered the largest Chinese urban development outside of China.[80] Three times the size of Singapore, Iskandar Malaysia is the second of Malaysia's special economic zones (inspired by the Chinese model), and is envisaged 'to transform south Johor into a sort of Shenzhen.'[81]

Designed for 700,000 people, Forest City has a planned stop on the high-speed rail connection linking Singapore and Kuala Lumpur, which in the future will continue through mainland Southeast Asia to China. Forest City is designed with all of the characteristics of best green practice: car-free, pedestrian-friendly circulation, extensive green infrastructure, and a variety of residential models. In these investment models, landscape is tied to a planned and exclusive standard of living, extremely attractive to the Chinese elite who desire a more affordable standard of living close to the amenities of Singapore.[82] At a smaller scale, gated communities are increasingly found throughout Southeast Asia, driven by the same investment strategies underpinning Forest City. In the crowded and congested cities of Ho Chi Minh, Bangkok, Jakarta, and Manila, a walled off 'landscaped' luxury condominium offers a rising middle class a 'modern' lifestyle offering respite and protection from the poverty of the subaltern.[83]

Landscapes of Economy

This contextualisation of investment in designed open space and green infrastructure against the state-centric policies and economic transformations of Asia offers critical knowledge for understanding *why* the discipline of landscape architecture emerges so strongly in the early twenty-first century. The introduction of parks in China was tied closely to real estate mechanisms while in Singapore landscape is integral to modernisation—first in improving living standards, and more recently as part of the transition to the modern biophilic city. The economic growth of Southeast Asia aligns landscape with urban typologies that offer an emerging middle class an alternative to the dense and unplanned Southeast Asian urbanism. Landscape, and thereby landscape architecture, is implicated in a complex economic reterritorialisation of Asia, an integral part of urbanisation fuelled by rural migration; it is influential in repositioning the Asian city in a global sphere and as part of a wider Asian investment in the region.

Unapologetically, this essay has delved into topics rarely discussed in landscape architecture. Understanding the priorities of the development state—including their utilitarian focus on economic growth, the complexities of land ownership and real estate in socialist contexts, characteristics of Asian business, and economic development cycles—is critical to conceiving how contemporary landscape architecture develops in the region. Importantly, it reveals the redundancy of concepts such as Westernisation or globalisation in comprehending the complex processes of modernity and modernisation underpinning the Asian experience.

Included in *Interruption* are design projects and critical essays that demonstrate how some of the influences and ideas discussed in this essay have diminished in recent years. For example, as economic growth has slowed in the tiger economies, many governments have embraced more community participation and citizen voices in decision-making. Governance, business, and societies continue to transition into diverse models, leading to spaces and landscapes, which resist neat classifications such as public and private or bottom-up or top down production. Therefore, when exploring the design projects featured in *Interruption*, look beyond any resemblance to Western typologies and instead concentrate on the Asian sensibilities, which underpin the way projects are produced, funded, understood, and used. ■

Repositioning the Private Realm

Jillian Walliss

With no tradition of public space, and land at a premium in dense Asian cities, urban open spaces are emerging as new hybrid mixed-use typologies. Once 'placeless' commercial towers, shopping malls, and residential developments are being transformed into recreational, work, cultural, and lifestyle opportunities featuring privately-owned public space. The demand for space in cities such as Singapore, Hong Kong, Tokyo, and Shanghai has liberated development from the constraints of existing retail or urban typologies, offering opportunities for developers and government to explore and experiment with new approaches to mixed use.[1]

For many Asians, shopping is considered recreation. For instance, studies reveal that 49 per cent of Singaporeans view shopping a hobby.[2] In the modern Asian city, shopping malls have emerged as important recreational and commercial spaces. In dense tropical Southeast Asian cities such as Bangkok and Jakarta, the shopping mall offers welcome respite from the traffic, humidity, and crowded streets. More and more developers are integrating open space into shopping malls as demonstrated by ICONSIAM, one of the largest shopping malls in Asia, which opened in Bangkok in 2018.

However, the rise of e-commerce and its threats to 'bricks and mortar' real estate has challenged the relevance of the shopping mall planned entirely around securing commercial tenants. Developers are now adopting placemaking strategies and innovative mixes of recreational and cultural space to appeal to increasingly 'digitally-savvy consumers pursuing a quality of life in a creative and sustainable environment'.[3] Singapore-based developer CapitaLand is one of Asia's largest and most innovative mall developers. Their 2019 remodelling of Funan (see pp. 100–101) explores the potential of a 'phygital' mall, blending elements of living, working, and shopping, along with Singapore's embracement of smart technology, to create an all-encompassing lifestyle concept.[4]

Woods Bagot director Stephen Jones, one of the designers for Funan, comments that working with Asian developers such as CapitaLand can be particularly rewarding given their adventurous 'make it happen' entrepreneurial spirit.[5] He observes that the acceptance of high density encourages the mixing of programming vertically in a way that would be discouraged in other contexts such as North America or Australia. Asia's comfort with density allows for the exploration of new relationships between living, working, and commercial activities. For example, designed in the higher levels of Funan is a theatre, co-working places (including one targeting working mothers complete with childcare), and accommodation aimed at the millennial traveller. This approach demonstrates that developers are willing to hand over profitable tenanted commercial space for a 'non-financial' outcome. Gathering spaces are no longer limited to a crowded food court or a smattering of couches on each level. Instead Funan offers privately owned public gathering spaces and facilities not associated with retail, such as a generous amphitheatre of internal stairs for hanging out, a three-storey climbing wall, and Singapore's largest green roof and urban farm. Jones also highlights that a strong organisational alignment within Asian development companies is particularly satisfying for designers.[6] This means that, following construction, the same developers continue to manage the project, reducing the likelihood of major modification or management practices at odds with the design concept.

In Chengdu China, Sino-Ocean Taikoo Li developed by Swire Properties offers a further reinvention of the shopping mall typology, this time adopting a low-rise open plan model. Conceived as an urban retail and entertainment destination, a high-end shopping experience is mixed with the adaptive reuse of six heritage buildings and ancient lanes associated with the Daci Temple found at the development's heart.[7] Similar to Funan, significant commercial space is given over to open space and other cultural uses. The dual retail concept of a 'fast lane' showcasing luxury brands and a 'slow lane' comprising cafes, outdoor cafes, and lifestyles stores underpins a 'play fast, live slow' retail experience. Offering the commercial goods of the high-end mall, alongside the 'more intimate feel of a boutique-lined side streets', the shopper is provided with an experience far removed from the internal box of the traditional mall.[8]

Even in some of the world's most expensive real estate of Hong Kong Island, developers are introducing rare open space into commercial developments. For example, the HKD 15-billion Taikoo Place redevelopment project also by Swire Properties is firmly positioned as community building, rather than purely a commercial project.[9] On completion in 2021, Taikoo Place will feature two new office towers—One Taikoo Place and Two Taikoo Place, along with eight existing office towers, connected by sky walkways. The allocation ▶

▶ of over 6,400 square metres of open space, designed by London-based landscape architecture practice Gustafson Porter + Bowman, delivers a very different atmosphere to other Hong Kong commercial developments. However, the commitment to community extends beyond the insertion of publicly accessible open space. Instead the developers aim to have impact at three levels: investment (comprising hardware such as buildings, infrastructure, and public space, and software such as engagement and social initiatives), place (engaging with vibrancy, livelihood, well-being, and resilience), and the city (how a place affects city-wide citizens). [10]

Through these projects CapitaLand and Swire Properties demonstrate a commitment to city building, which exceeds the provision of commercial or retail tenancy. This motivation is increasingly evident in residential development, shifting from the 'gated' exclusionary model to mixed-use schemes more responsive to societal change and offering privately owned public space.

This approach is apparent in the Vanke Group, who have been a major residential developer in China since 1984. Over the past five years their development approach has transformed from an initial focus on 'good houses, good services, good community' to a vision as a 'city and town developer and service provider' who contributes 'to a beautiful life', a harmonious ecosystem, and the economy, along with exploring 'creative experimental fields'.[11] Their mixed-use developments include a significant investment in high quality open space. Vanke Tianfu Cloud City, for instance, designed for a new hi-tech and sci-tech development zone in Chengdu, features a central green axis of 54,000 square metres, which connects a mix of different programs and buildings in a park-like setting.[12] For the Chinese landscape firm Lab D+H, working with the Vanke Group offers the opportunity to experiment in the design of public space. Most of the large government-driven public work in China is done by design institutes or extremely large firms with the necessary licenses. Despite their considerable experience spanning North America, China and Korea, Lab D+H's size means they will never be considered for 'public' government work. However, Director Huicheng Zhong comments that unlike in the West, the notion of public space in China is not necessarily aligned with government projects.[13] Working with the Vanke group on mixed-use projects such as Guangzhou Vanke Cloud City (see pp. 108–109) has offered Lab D+H a platform to engage with community building in a way that could not be achieved through government public work.

Much has been made of the expansive riches to be made in the Asian property market. However, this discussion of just a few development companies demonstrates that their approaches are not entirely focused on profit but also form a critical component in the establishment of an emerging urban public domain. Clearly not all developers operate at the same level, and in contexts such as Singapore strong government policy also influences design approaches. But equally, many developers are recognising that an investment in high-quality privately owned public realm is good for business.

Publicness defies clear definition in Asia. In the world's densest cities, the idea of laying down a clearly delineated 'public' park as conceived within a Western context is an impossibility. In contrast, developers with their eyes on commercial and cultural trends are mixing living, working, and creating into new urban typologies. Defying simple binary classification of public and private, these projects are of international relevance for both their design possibilities and their investment model, which brings responsibility for community, place, and the city into the private financial realm. ■

Visual continuity between commercial lobbies and the external spaces.

Project Name: **Taikoo Place**
Location: **Quarry Bay, Hong Kong**
Landscape Architects: **Gustafson Porter + Bowman**
Architect: **Wong & Ouyang**
Client: **Swire Properties**
Completion Year: **expected 2021**
Text: based on information from Gustafson Porter + Bowman

Taikoo Place *Hong Kong*

Dense tropical plants framed by sculpture stonework foster a calm atmosphere.

99

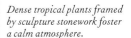

Despite its proximity to the natural world, Hong Kong Island has few high-quality green spaces which can temper the frenetic environment of the city. Taikoo Place, one of the city's largest privately owned business districts, will create an inclusive open space as part of a major urban transformation. The redevelopment of three older industrial buildings into two modern office towers with more open spaces and improved amenities will significantly enhance the public realm for office workers and the wider community.

Offering 0.64 hectares of open space, the design provides a sequence of spaces ranging from small intimate places around water to gather with friends and colleagues, to areas suitable for events such as jazz concerts and outdoor markets. The largest space, Taikoo Square, creates the impression of a series of terraces, featuring two large longitudinal pools connected by a cascade and a small water table. The water features include an interactive element, bringing movement and pleasant sounds to the Square whilst referencing the former Quays that once existed on the site. Shared surface areas and paving bands carry the aesthetics of Taikoo Place into the surrounding streetscape to deliver a continuous design that prioritises pedestrians.

In cities such as Hong Kong there is often a sharp contrast between the commercial interior of a building and its immediate outdoor space. The landscape architects challenged this delineation by continuing the same bands of granite and marble that define the dense lines of vegetation outside into the interior lobbies, creating a sense of movement which strengthens the concept of Taikoo Place as a destination.

To promote biodiversity and raise public awareness of Hong Kong's heritage of *feng shui* woodlands, fifty-three of the seventy trees at Taikoo Place are native species, grown specifically for the project. *Feng shui* woodlands are remnants of native woodlands, which are protected from agricultural clearances due to their spiritual significance. At Taikoo Place, these remnant species have found a new home and bring additional natural elements to an otherwise dense urban space. This unification of landscape and interior space embodies a genuinely whole solution, which enhances the public realm.

An intense interplay of work, recreation, retail, living, and entertainment.

A new civic precinct, which includes Singapore's largest rooftop urban garden.

101

Representing a new era in retail and mixed-use design, the redevelopment of CapitaLand's Funan has been designed as an innovative new civic hub for Singapore that blends retail, entertainment, leisure, wellness, dining, offices, co-working, and co-living environments. With the rise of online shopping, Woods Bagot's Hong Kong studio was challenged to maximise engagement for a new tech-savvy generation. They recommended the complete redevelopment of the formerly IT-focused mall and the construction of an integrated mixed-use development that maximises the site's prime downtown location at City Hall.

At the heart of the development is The Tree of Life, conceived as a habitat for creativity. This twenty-five-metre, six-storey wood and steel structure provides spaces for brands to showcase their products and crafts, and for entrepreneurs and design ateliers to conduct classes and workshops. The Tree's 'branches' offer environments for technology, fitness, dining, craft, shopping, and play areas. Co-working and co-living models are interwoven over the levels, introducing a new user to traditional retail focus. For example, lyf Funan (pronounced life Funan) provides a wide variety of accommodation targeted to the millennial market who favour connecting and collaborating within communities.

Spread throughout Funan are significant investments in public open space and recreational activities. A timber amphitheatre of steps connecting levels 1 and 2 provides an informal space to lounge. Opposite the amphitheatre, a central stage and video wall allows the transformation of the staircase into an event space seating up to 150 people. Green stairs, which nurture exercise and movement, lead from level 4 to level 7, which is home to Singapore's largest rooftop urban garden featuring a 16,000-square-metre food garden, Singapore's first fully unmanned futsal court and outdoor gardens. The Urban Farm operated by Edible Garden City showcases sustainable food production and technologies and offers a 'farm to table' experience for an adjacent restaurant.

In a major change to the internally focused shopping mall, Funan has been designed to connect to the city, accessible by pedestrians and bicycles. This includes linking to major tourist routes in the city—on foot and bicycle—as well as key landmarks in Singapore. In a particularly unique feature, cyclists can ride directly through the mall.

Project Name: **Funan**
Location: **City Hall, Singapore**
Architects: **Woods Bagot (Design Consultant), RSP Architects Planners & Engineers (Executive Architect)**
Landscape Architects: **Grant Associates**
Client: **CapitaLand Mall Trust**
Completion Year: **2019**
Text: based on information from Woods Bagot

Nihombashi Garden

Mitsukoshi

Tokyo

The original Mitsukoshi department store reflected in the pond.

Project Name: **Nihombashi Garden**
Location: **Tokyo, Japan**
Landscape Architects: **Landscape Plus**
Client: **Isetan Mitsukoshi**
Completion Year: **2019**
Text: *based on information from Landscape Plus*

The great roof offers a sheltered engagement with the garden.

103

Nihombasi Garden is located on the roof of Mitsukoshi, the flagship of Japan's oldest surviving chain of department stores, which was founded in 1673. Since the formation of the Tokugawa shogunate, Nihombashi, close to the palace of the shoguns, was the starting point of the Five Great Highways of Japan. This historical connection, along with the realisation that the roof of Mitsukoshi was at the same level as the Imperial Palace, inspired Landscape Plus to recreate the vegetation of the Imperial Palace in their new garden.

Located thirty-three metres above the streets of Nihombashi (a historic district in Tokyo) the garden is designed as a strolling pond garden, referencing the traditional Japanese concept of nature where the garden and the home are one. The designers refer to the rooftop greenery as *tsunagari no mori* or 'forest of connections', an acknowledgment of the verdant forest in the heart of Tokyo.

The garden features a large gabled open roof structure, a reflective pond, and native vegetation. This nostalgic landscape emphasises connections—providing a space to reconnect humans and nature, acknowledg-ing those that once lived and worked here, and offering the chance for visitors to learn of the Japanese lifestyle that matured at Nihombashi.

It was important that the design not stress the hundred-year-old building structure. The light metal-frame pillars of the new roof structure are fused with the existing building in order to distribute weight. The roof also incorporates a moveable awning that opens and closes according to an environmental sensor.

The square pond, the garden's symbol, is designed over the existing building's atrium, the weakest part of the structure. However, the use of lightweight FRP waterproofing allowed for a mirror surface pond just thirty millimetres deep. From the veranda's large eaves, the greenery reflects in the water day and night, not only allowing visitors to relax and enjoy the garden from under the great roof on a daily basis, but providing different and memorable backdrops through changing lighting. In summer, visitors can find refreshing coolness under the deep eaves, enjoying water amongst the shade from the trees. In winter, they can warm themselves as the sunlight dapples through the trees.

The Empty Garden

Busan

The empty garden borrows views of surrounding mountains.

Project Name: **The Empty Garden**
Project Location: **Busan Metropolitan City, Korea**
Landscape Architect: **PARKKIM**
Client: **Air Busan**
Completion Year: **2017**
Text: based on information from PARKKIM

Custom-made portable furniture offers maximum flexibility for the space.

The 'empty garden' forms part of the headquarters for the low-cost airline Air Busan, and consists of two parts: the rooftop garden available only for the employees and a ground level exterior space, which includes the surrounding streets. This is a rare example of PARKKIM undertaking a design-build project. With a strict budget and a limited time frame of just three months, they led the design and construction of all landscape elements including the pavilion and furniture.

On the ground level, the courtyard-like space is used mainly as a passageway by the occupants of two adjacent office buildings. The garden is also required to represent the company's identity since the space faces the street without a fence or wall. Bands of shrubs were aligned in the direction of flights' landing path along the runway of adjacent Gimhae International Airport. The triangular precast concrete module offered versatility to fit into the subtle undulation of the ground, in order to make a smooth hard surface that would help the flight attendants pull their suitcases.

The rooftop received more attention, requiring a shade structure and portable furniture, as well as conventional landscaping with planting. PARKKIM convinced the client to limit the planting to the periphery of the roof for efficient drainage and convenience of management. *Nandina domestica* (sacred bamboo) was planted for its fall foliage and winter interest. The space defined by the planting is expected to be empty when no events are planned. PARKKIM believe that a shade structure does not need to provide complete opaqueness since workers would rarely come up to the roof during extremely warm weather. An appropriate level of porosity allows users to enjoy natural breeze and sunlight during spring and fall. They thus designed a lightweight structure that offers stability through the tension between each element without requiring supporting columns or legs. This structure also resembles Korean traditional window gratings in the sense that both cast sublime shadows onto the ground. Thanks to the porous pavilion, users are exposed to the surrounding landscape of mountains and river, so the empty garden is full of other pleasures.

Vanke Research Centre

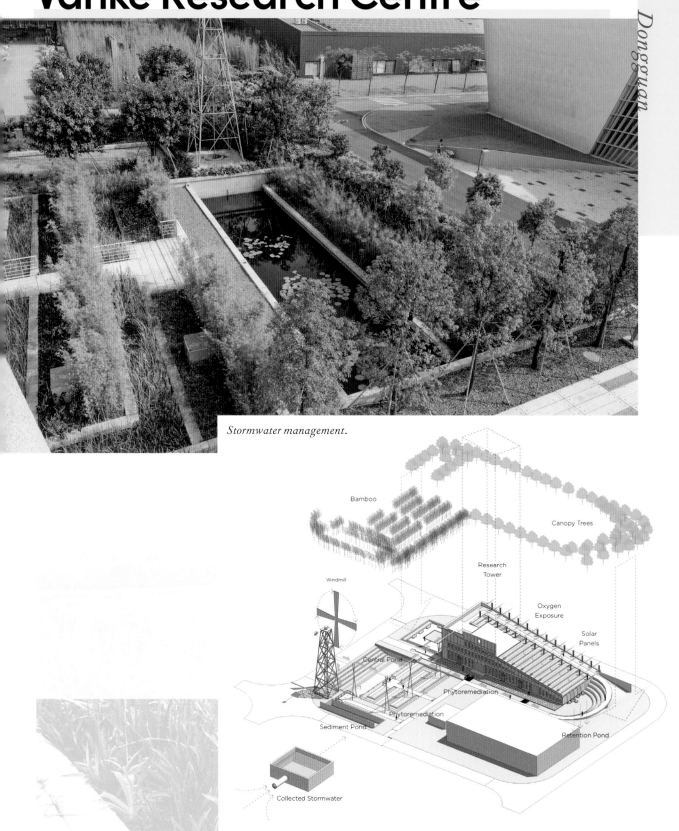

Stormwater management.

Bamboo

Canopy Trees

Research
Tower

Windmill

Oxygen
Exposure

Solar
Panels

Central Pond

Phytoremediation

Phytoremediation

Sediment Pond

Retention Pond

Collected Stormwater

Demonstrating how a rolling landform can slow down stormwater runoff and offer more time for infiltration.

Project Name: **Vanke Research Centre**
Project Location: **Dongguan, Guangdong Province, China**
Landscape Architects: **Z+T Studio**
Client: **Vanke Architecture**
Completion Year: **2012**
Text: based on information from Z+T Studio

The Vanke Research Centre is a campus dedicated to advanced architecture and construction research on residential buildings for the Vanke Group, one of the leading real estate developers in China. The campus houses research labs, workshops, testing labs, and service facilities. The research conducted at the centre focuses on sustainable building materials, energy-efficient design, low-carbon design, and overall sustainability. Z+T Studio was commissioned to design several sites on the campus. However, rather than adopting a regular design approach, they conceived their landscapes as a living lab to research low-cost and low-maintenance landscape design strategies and technologies suitable for China's ecological and economic environment.

Strategies for rainwater control and reuse, explorations of prefab concrete and eco-friendly materials, and the potentials of low-cost maintenance are integrated into their design response. As the project is positioned as research, it is ever-evolving, and can be scientifically observed, recorded, and analysed. The design offers the flexibility to be adjusted and modified as necessary. Z+T Studio have also considered the educational potentials of ecologically-responsible landscape design, encouraging user participation to bring awareness of the environment. The research centre is open to the public by appointment.

107

Tetris Square

Guangzhou

A modular design system offers flexibility and variety while controlling costs.

Project Name: **Tetris Square**
Project Location: **Guangzhou, Guangdong Province, China**
Landscape Architect: **Lab D+H**
Client: **Guangzhou Vanke**
Completion Year: **2019**
Text: based on information from Lab D+H

1 Free Island
Cave, Slide, Tree House

2 Family Pocket
Hammocks, Seat

3 Cloud Curtain
Seat, Shade Structure

4 Cloud Mount
Climbing Wall, Folding Deck

5 Sand Pool
Sand Pool, Seat

6 Cloud Pavillion
Seat, Shade Canopy

7 Amphitheatre
Seat, Theatre

A commercial plaza is transformed into a park.

Guangzhou Vanke Cloud City Phase 2 is a pioneering mixed-use development comprising of affordable housing, small apartments, incubator offices, a shopping mall, and a middle school. Lab D+H proposed a unified landscape framework for the new community based on a pixelated grid system which provides flexible space while maintaining a strong visual identity. In the northwest corner of the grid is Tetris Square, a name proposed by the landscape architects.

At over 6,000 square metres, Tetris Square transforms a commercial plaza into the largest public space for Cloud City and the surrounding communities. Playgrounds for different ages cater to the desires of its major users—the nuclear family. For example, the Family Pocket offers kids and parents an interaction with a series of hammocks, while the Free Island provides kids with spaces to explore in a three-dimensional play facility. Other design elements such as the Cloud Curtain, the Cloud Mountain, and the Cloud Pavilion offer further play possibilities.

An amphitheatre sited in front of the shopping mall provides an event space for commercial activities, as well as serving as an outdoor classroom for the middle school. Challenging the traditional design principles of a commercial plaza, which seek to optimise storefront views by minimising vegetation, Lab D+H strategically 'hid' a tree grove by integrating it into playgrounds. Moving from the sidewalks to the shopping mall, the trees are arranged in a dense-to-sparse gradient, with clear openings leading to the mall. Two mature shade trees frame the major corridor, enhancing the visual beauty of the space.

Lab D+H did not view the low construction budget for this project as a constraint; on the contrary, it was a driving force for the design vision. Two basic precast concrete modules were designed to be mixed, matched, and assembled into more than twenty different furniture combinations. Users can select the most comfortable furniture arrangement to meet their needs, a flexibility which appeals strongly to the younger user. The grid system of squares not only makes material fabrication and arrangement much cheaper but controls construction costs. This is especially important in China, where construction quality is often unpredictable. Precast concrete pavers were used for economic and environmental decisions, costing one third of the cost of natural stone, which is overexploited in China.

Private, Public, Commons, and the Challenge of Social Design in Japan

Akiko Okabe

An emphasis on social design is increasingly common in Japan. Social design can be defined as providing a solution to social problems through design outcomes and ensuring that the public interest is protected. Architects and designers now feel that a social value for their works is indispensable. The Great Eastern Japan Earthquake of 11 March 2011 played a significant role in re-orienting the practices of both architects and designers to become more 'socially focused'.[1] Japanese architects are progressively more aware that working in favour of the private interest of their clients does not necessarily contribute towards a better society, which is leading them to become more conscious of their social responsibility.

While social design is now booming in Japan, extending into all design sectors, this essay argues that it is too optimistic to believe that public interests are more respected and protected than in the past. For example, advertising agencies are expanding their business to incorporate social design, taking on a new role in this market. Advertising agencies are coordinating social design projects for the reconstruction of areas affected by disasters and regeneration of remote rural aging and shrinking areas.[2] Thus, social design is now considered an avenue for private companies to make revenue, with some companies building profitable business around social design projects. This development establishes a problematic contradiction given that social design emerges from the premise that private interests are not aligned with the public interest. Where does this leave a Japanese understanding of the concepts of public and private in these important social design projects?

The Public, Private, and the 'Official Common'
The dichotomy between the concepts of public and private is not obvious in Japan. This relates to the understanding and definition of public. The word 'public' is tricky in the Japanese language.[3] Translated as *kokyo* (公共), the word is composed of the two compounds: 公 (*ko*), meaning 'public', and 共 (*kyo*) meaning 'common'. Therefore, 公共 (*kokyo*) literally means public-common and does not precisely share a Western understanding of the term public.

This reading is reflected in the cultural classification of urban spaces. Japanese cities have not had a tradition of public spaces in the Western sense. Instead, in Japanese cities the socio-cultural role of space is reflected in traditional small-scale common spaces such as in the extensive network of narrow alleys, cutting through neighbourhoods of tiny wooden townhouses.[4] These alleys provided the opportunity for people to meet and for children to play. However, there is a crucial difference between the notion of common and public space, which is the prioritisation of common benefits for the exclusion of others. For example, while the alleys are not physically closed, they project a local identity that creates strong psychological barriers between neighbourhoods.

An additional complexity in defining the notion of 'public' is that 公 (*ko*) is generally interpreted as official or governmental, associated with top-down initiatives. Public space in Japan is therefore perceived as a new urban functional space implemented with modernisation by governmental-public works. Thus, both concepts (common and official) have the danger of prioritising collective benefits and sacrificing individual freedom. Therefore, in the original Japanese 公共 (*kokyo*) space, there is no scope for the Western idea of public interpreted as open to others, conditioned by inclusiveness, and respecting individual freedom and diversity.

In Japanese cities, these values are further undercut by the increasing privatisation of urban spaces exemplified in the enormous redevelopment projects being constructed in Tokyo's urban nodes such as Shibuya and Shinjuku.[5] Private initiatives lead these projects, framing whole districts as monstrous commercial shopping malls. The public is obliged to consume, spending money on shopping, drinking, or eating, to enjoy and feel comfortable in the spaces. Curiously, there is scarce criticism in Japan of the explicit commercialisation of public spaces. This differs from the extensive debate over the neoliberal trend to privatise and commercialise public spaces in European cities.[6] Moreover, in Japan, these approaches are appreciated as good practices of public-private partnership. However, given that 'public' in Japanese is not heteronymous of private and synonymous with

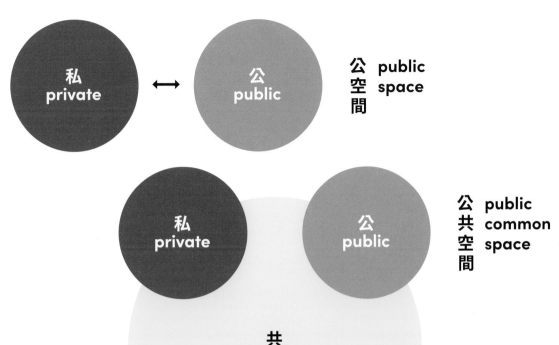

私 private ↔ 公 public

公空間 public space

私 private

公 public

公共空間 public common space

共 common

governmental, it is quite natural that there is no citizen's initiative to reclaim the public space.

Kokyo space is different from the space of solidarity to protest against the government. Historically, government authorities in Japan have used *kokyo* space, grounded on the association of common space and neighbourhood identity, as a means to align the whole nation towards a common purpose at the national level. In this context, Hannah Arendt's definition of society might provide a useful framework to reveal the tensions and challenges in dealing with public space and interest.

The Camouflaging of Social Design

In her 1958 book, *The Human Condition*, the philosopher and political theorist Hannah Arendt discusses the private and public realm and their relationship to society.[7] Taking recourse to the premise that the public and private are incompatible, Arendt argues that 'the rise of society brought about the simultaneous decline of the public as well as the private realm.'[8] She writes that 'A man who lived only a private life ... was not permitted to enter the public realm.'[9] Arendt uses the word 'society' in a very peculiar way. Her use of 'society' has a negative notion and could be considered to be close to the Japanese notion of 'the official-common realm' or 公共 (*kokyo*).

If we adopt Arendt's framework of public, private, and social interest in the Japanese context (where public interest might be confused with social interest), public interest can be interpreted as 'common interest for all' and thus can invade into the private realm as well. Such hidden threats can be observed in Japan, where corporate interest in social design projects (especially in the disaster recovery process) can easily be disguised as interest for all, or pseudo-public interest, by appealing to the sympathy of all Japanese. Social design that follows these principles can be equated with what Naomi Klein describes as 'disaster capitalism'.[10] As designers we need to be aware of these characteristics of capitalism that exclude or ignore outcomes unfavourable to the market. Social design is not always in conflict with commercial market activities but it should be used strategically to complement these commercial forces by representing the true public interest reflective of openness, diversity, and inclusiveness. ■

Politics, Citizenship, and The Making of Seoul's Urban Parks

Kyung-Jin Zoh

Throughout history, parks have operated as a mirror for civic values, social meaning, and political aspirations. This is particularly true of the urban park in Seoul, which has been political from its very inception. Since parks were introduced in the late nineteenth century to modernise the early city, they have been intertwined with the turbulent political changes that have shaped Korea. Working with the idea of 'governmentality,' this essay explores the links between shifting government ambitions and the rise of the contemporary urban park, with a focus on Seoul's much acclaimed 'urban park renaissance'.[1] The transition to citizen-elected mayors in 1995 led to successive mayors recognising the value of parks for improving the urban quality of life, attracting tourists, branding Seoul as a global city, and, most importantly, offering tangible election-winning evidence of their political achievements. The resultant suite of projects such as the Cheonggyecheon Restoration Project, Seonyudo Park and Yanghwa Riverside Park are celebrated internationally as part of Seoul's remarkable investment in urban parks. But arguably of even more importance is the parallel transformation of planning policies and political aspiration in the city, which has transitioned over time from top-down governance to the recognition and empowerment of citizens in the making and management of Seoul's parks.

Parks as Nationalistic Ideology

In 1392, during the Joseon dynasty, Seoul was designated as the capital city. The site was considered ideal from a *feng shui* point of view, with winding rivers and streams surrounded by many rugged mountains. These beautiful landscapes form an important part of the cityscape in Korea, presenting a reciprocal co-existence between people and nature. Before the formal planning of urban parks, there was no comparable space within the city boundaries. However, hiking through the mountains and valleys was a popular leisure activity. In his book *The Passing of Korea* (1896), H. B. Hulbert, a delegate from the U.S. government, commented on these leisure activities, observing that 'Korea has no notion of parks or other places of public ornament or recreation, and yet they are fond of wandering about hills, finding picturesque nooks, and enjoying the beauties nature.'[2] With mountains and valleys spread widely throughout the city, offering citizens easy access to the natural environment, there was little need to create urban parks within the city boundary.

Park culture was first imported into Korea in the late nineteenth century, during the age of Japanese colonialism (1910–1945). Kil-Chun Yu, one of the intellectual leaders of the Independence Association, introduced the idea of European and American urban parks in his text *Seoyugyonmun* (서유견문, 西遊見聞) in 1895.[3] Parks were considered a civilising institution of the modern industrial city and a source of social enlightenment. In 1896, Jaipol Soh, also a leader of the Independence Association, advocated for constructing urban parks to reform sanitary conditions and improve the urban landscape.

In the same year, King Gojong initiated an urban restructuring project, which included the construction of public parks for citizens. Tapgol Park, regarded as Korea's first urban park, was built on the site of the former Buddhist temple, Wongaksa. It was instigated by John McLeary Brown, the British financial advisor to King Gojong.[4] Brown was the chief commissioner of customs in Korea and was involved in diverse matters including park making. Opened in 1902 to celebrate the fortieth anniversary of the coronation ceremony, the park held public gatherings, including free concerts, as well as operating as a symbolic place for civic virtues and civil education.[5]

In contrast to these early Korean-led parks, which were driven by the desire to modernise the city, the Japanese occupational forces used the introduction of citizen parks as a tactic to weaken a Korean sense of place and its spiritual values. This included the repositioning of the royal palaces and gardens. For example, Changgyeonggung, the palace located at the heart of the city, was transformed from its role as a royal residence into an outdoor pleasure garden, including the clearing buildings to distort its powerfully symbolic spatial structure. From 1909 to 1912, a zoo, botanical garden, and museum were added. Japanese cherry blossom trees, the unofficial national flower of Japan, were planted in the palace, along with the initiation of a cherry blossom festival, which remained a popular event until the 1980s. Other sacred Korean places such as Jangchung-dan and Sajik-dan were also redesigned as public parks.

The history of Namsan, one of the major mountains and the most sacred place within Seoul, highlights how significant natural features were also politicised. The Japanese government, along with Japanese residents, developed several urban parks on Namsan. In addition, Japanese landscape architecture professor Seiroku Honda prepared a master plan for the Naman Forest Park in 1917.[6] Although this plan was never realised, it represents the first vision for modern park planning on a site of major Korean significance.

In 1925, a Japanese shrine was built on the mountain, designed with a straight-line spatial structure to emphasise its monumentality. The shrine was used for rituals and diverse festivals, including a site for compulsory shrine worship in the 1930s. Following Korea's independence from Japan in 1945, this shrine was dismantled, and in 1956, a statue of the first president of the Republic of Korea was erected on Namsan. This was demolished during the student revolution of 1961, and replaced six years later with a statue of Jung-Geun Ahn, a liberation fighter hero from the military resistance against Japan. This strategy of recreating public space to legitimise the political regime was therefore shared by the Japanese and the post-liberation Korean governments.[7]

This brief discussion of Seoul's oldest parks demonstrates their contested role in being co-opted by different political regimes as symbolic nationalistic sites. Alternating between political constructions of citizenship and celebrations of nationalistic moments, parks operated as sites of political inscription. This link between parks and political ambition is re-established in the late twentieth century. However, in this case, political influence shifts from the national level to that of successive city mayors, who actively construct relationships between citizens and public parks as a means to further their own political advantage.

An Urban Park Renaissance

In a significant political change, the adoption of a local autonomy system in 1995 allowed citizens to vote for mayors directly. Mayors quickly realised the multiple values of new parks as offering a medium for improving the urban quality of life (and thereby providing tangible evidence of political achievements), attracting tourism, and contributing to the branding of Seoul as part a global design city.[8] Seoul's contemporary open spaces have been shaped by consecutive mayoral vision, leading to what is now considered an 'urban park renaissance'. Underpinned by increased budgets for parks and open spaces as well as a heightened role for planning and design expertise, new urban open space opportunities emerged through the release of redundant land (landfills, factory sites, and water purification facilities) following the industrial restructuring of the city.

In addition, changes in lifestyle and technological innovation increased the importance of public spaces and parks. For example, the prevalence of the digital image galvanised street life and public spaces as people looked for interesting locations to take a picture. At the same time, increased concerns about health and well-being led many to reclaim the culture of walking and strolling. But most significantly, an increase in people's leisure time following the shortening of the working week created a demand for more parks. For much of the twentieth century, Korea as a developing country had much higher working hours than other countries. It was only in 2004 that a five-day workweek was institutionalised, offering citizens free time on weekends to visit riverside parks and nature parks. Concurrent to these changes, Korea experienced an influx of Western tourists, while the number of Koreans travelling abroad increased significantly. This exposure to Western lifestyles and urban culture inspired people to seek public and street space in both the public and private sectors.

Together these factors have combined over the past twenty-five years to produce a wide variety of urban parks. Since these public spaces were tied to political time schedules, the parks emerged at a rapid pace, thereby restricting community engagement and often negatively affecting the quality of construction achieved. Opened in 1999, Yeouido Park is a particularly significant project. A monumental concrete paved square, used as a makeshift air runway in the 1970s, was transformed into a large green space. Initially, the venue was used for large-scale events, such as religious rallies, a military parade, or a place for people to bike or skate. Transforming the open plaza into a large green parkland was a major symbolic gesture, signalling the beginning of Seoul's embrace of green urbanism. Seonyudo Park, Korea's first post-industrial park, was completed in 2002 and offers a further influential example.[9] Located on Seonyu Island in the Han River, a former water purification facility was transformed into an award-winning ecological park that is regularly nominated as Seoul's best urban park.

Myung-Bak Lee, the mayor of Seoul from 2002 to 2005, was very influential in shaping Seoul's new open space. He was responsible for the Cheonggyecheon Restoration Project, one of the grandest and most internationally acclaimed public projects in Korea.[10] Originally a stream that ran through the city centre, Cheonggyecheon was buried under an intercity high-way in the 1970s. Lee's audacious vision to demolish the highway and restore the stream was completed in just three years, including the negotiation process with stakeholders. Since its opening in 2005, the project has received positive responses from local and international communities. However, there has been formidable criticism of the project given that the 'artificial' stream did not achieve the principles of ecological restora-tion. Despite this shortcoming, the Cheonggyecheon Restoration Project introduced a six-kilometre green spine for Seoul. Also, it provided Lee with a valuable political asset in his successful campaign to become the president of the Republic of Korea by delivering a large-scale urban infrastructure project.

The Han River Renaissance, another major park initiative, was initiated under the mayorship of Se-hoon Oh, who held office from 2006 to 2011. Guided by the concepts of restoration and creation, this project fo-cused on water as a catalyst for improving the quality of city life and promoting urban regeneration. A compre-hensive socio-economic strategy was prepared around the river, including the successful remodelling of eight riverside parks. These included the Yanghwa Riverside Park, which was designed by Korean firm PARKKIM following a design competition.[11] Mayor Oh introduced the concept of city marketing for Seoul, developing a wide spectrum of public projects to market Seoul as a globally relevant design city. For example, in 2010 Seoul was designated as the World Design Capital, launching the city into a global network and enticing many inter-national tourists. The use of international designers to market Seoul (and its leaders) to the outside world has also been an important strategy.

In 2005, a conceptual design competition was held for Sejong City, setting a precedent for the use of international design competitions for public spaces nationwide. Invited competitions have been used to recruit renowned designers, as demonstrated by the design competition for Dongdaemun Design Plaza (DDP) which was envisaged as a new cultural complex for promoting the design industry, including a nearby fashion cluster. The majority of schemes submitted by the invited Korean architects responded to the exist-ing urban fabric and the site's historical significance, such as a part of a city wall structure built during the Joseon dynasty buried under the site. In contrast, the winning design by star architect Zaha Hadid featured a uniquely shaped building that had little to do with the local context. Instead, it was more like a spaceship landing in downtown Seoul. Many Korean designers had mixed feelings about the final design, which also led to an almost doubling of construction costs. Local architects criticised the winning scheme as brutal and cold given it did not address the local issues, while others complained that the voices of citizens and local vendors were not incorporated in the planning process.[12] However, since its opening in 2014, the public response has generally been favourable, largely due to its iconic design which brands Seoul's image as a dynamic and future-looking global capital.

The 2015 international design competition for Seoullo 7017, an elevated highway that connects across Seoul Station, was influenced by the success of the New York High Line. Constructed in 1970, the structure was particularly dilapidated and required complete reconstruction. Mayor Won-Soon Park, who came to office in 2011, wanted to explore the possibility of reus-ing this infrastructure as a linear park for pedestrians. In the beginning, there was little communication with residents and merchants who were against this project. However, the project was only able to proceed after extensive negotiations between the city government and residents. The international firm MVRDV won the competition with a scheme that featured a botanical bridge that orders plants according to the Korean alphabet. Some local landscape architects viewed this planting scheme as absurd and awkward, criticis-ing it for not being ecologically sound or aesthetically beautiful. Despite this, the original planting design was realised, and the project opened in 2017. Seoullo 7017 has become a major tourist destination in Seoul, no doubt aided by the star factor of the international designers. New urban regeneration projects have since emerged around Seoul Station, leveraging from the success of the project.

While Seoul's impressive new portfolio of con-temporary open space was primarily driven by top-down political ambitions, looking more closely at park governance from the early millennium onwards reveals the emergence of increased community participation in what could be considered a more civic-focused urbanism.

The Emergence of a Civic Urbanism

The establishment of the NGO Seoul Green Trust (SGT) in 2003 represents a critical moment in the re-shaping of the relationship between citizens and gov-ernment in urban park practices in Korea. Aiming to promote green space and culture in Seoul City, the SGT proposed a new park project to then-mayor, Myung-Bak Lee, for a site originally intended for a mixed-use development. The transformation of the site into what is now known as the Seoul Forest Park was conceived through close cooperation between the city govern-ment and the SGT.

Drawing inspiration from the Central Park Conservancy, the SGT established the Seoul Forest

Management Centre and actively contribute to the management, volunteer coordination, and funding support for planting trees and expanding green space. Through this accumulation of knowledge and experience in park planning and management, the SGT has become a creative hub for transmitting knowledge and skills in park governance guiding, for example, the development of the Busan and Suwon Green Trusts.

This new emphasis on community participation was consolidated by mayor Park, who in his three terms from 2011 to 2020 instigated a major shift towards a people-driven development approach. Prior to becoming a mayor, he was a leader of two NGOs—Beautiful Foundation and Hope Factory—and had shown great interest in creative city-making processes. Park introduced more civic engagement in decision-making in urban policy and was part of a movement to suspend New Town projects planned by a previous government that would have destroyed the existing urban and social fabric. Adopting civic urbanism as an alternative to park creation and management, Mayor Park encouraged a new approach to park management and green space policy and appointed dozens of public landscape architects to advise and consult on park policy and planning.

Under his leadership, a Green City Declaration was issued in 2013, encouraging Seoul's transformation into a 'park city', which includes the active participation of citizens. This was followed in 2014 by the Green City Strategic Plan, which has led to the creation of a new type of target-oriented green space featuring social and civic values. New partnerships systems are emerging as alternatives to top-down governance models, improving the quality of urban parks and expanding funding sources. For instance, in 2016, the Seoul Green Trust signed a three-year contract with the Seoul Metropolitan Government to commission the management of the Seoul Forest Park. Stimulated by the success of this partnership, in 2019 the management of Seoullo 7017 was handed to the NGO Walk to Seoul.

In addition, community participation and management are increasingly being incorporated into planning processes. For example, the Mapo Culture Depot, which opened in 2017, is a new industrial park located on the site of a former oil depot. One of the most interesting aspects of this park is its innovative governance system for park management. A young creators' group promoting a green lifestyle was already operating on the site. After a negotiation process, the city government permitted them to stay, and they are now stakeholders in the park-making process. The governance committee, including city officials, young creators, and other consultants, are entrusted as the decision-makers for all critical matters related to park management.

This revised interest in the community has also led to the emergence of new typologies of open space, as demonstrated by the new Seoul Botanic Park. Originally, the site was proposed as a waterfront park, but due to cost and technical problems, the scheme was revised into a botanical park that merges an urban park with a botanic garden. The mission of Seoul Botanic Park is to foster an interest in botany in its citizens, emphasising the role of exhibition and education for disseminating a gardening culture to the wider community.[13] Since its opening in 2019, Seoul Botanic Park has successfully functioned in its dual roles as a tourist destination and neighbourhood park.

Co-creation in the broader Asian context

From the large-scale, top-down infrastructure of the Cheonggyecheon Restoration Project to the international star designer's interpretation of Korean culture in the Seoullo 7017 walkway through to the 120 hectares of Seoul Forest Park driven by an NGO, Seoul's celebrated urban park renaissance reflects dynamic political aspirations and constructions of citizenship. Added to these examples are the twentieth-century parks, which were monopolised by different political regimes as symbolic nationalistic sites.

As this essay has discussed, under mayor Park's leadership Seoul's urban planning approaches were reshaped into a partnership between government and citizens, with 'every citizen considered a mayor of Seoul'.[14] However, this shift away from state-driven redevelopment approaches to new models for co-creation and management of open space is not unique to Seoul but also evident in the other tiger economies.

The economic slow-down of the 'export-orientated Asian economies' of Korea, Singapore, Taiwan, and Hong Kong, along with recognition of social marginalisation and disruption that accompanied their rapid industrialisation, has led to significant political reform and the rise of civil society.[15] Community participation projects encompassing community gardening, urban agriculture, heritage conservation projects, residential projects, and temporary activated urban space are now common in these contexts. However, what does make the Seoul experience unique is the incorporation of these values at the level of the large urban park.[16] ∎

Ensembles

Jillian Walliss

The first waves of Asian urbanisation were driven by development models emphasising economic growth, globalisation, and market liberalisation. Strong, authoritarian states focused on building industrialised economies, attracting investment, and providing housing, jobs, and wealth for their citizens. However, reaction to the adverse effects of rapid urbanisation, along with a slowing of growth, particularly in the Asian tiger economies, has led to the emergence of new models for design, which engage directly with the community.

The Japanese *machizukuri* approach has been very influential. Emerging in Japan in the 1960s, this anti-establishment social movement was a reaction to Japan's rapid economic growth and advocated for more democratic processes and community participation in decision-making.[1] In particular, the movement was driven by concerns for increasing environmental pollution, the potential fire danger following Japan's frequent earthquakes in areas of high-density timber housing, and weak planning regulations and models.[2] Shigeru Satoh defines *machizukuri* as an ensemble of approaches and activities based on the resources existing in each local society, carried out by diverse actors in order to improve the quality of life and surrounding living environments.[3]

Satoh's use of the term ensembles is significant. There is a tendency in Western discourse to lump community-driven design practices under the generalised terms of 'bottom-up' or 'participatory' design. However, these terminologies do not adequately reflect the diversity of agents and practices involved, or, more importantly, how these practices reflect a transition towards more civic-orientated societies. Seoul's late mayor Won-Soon Park for example reshaped his governance into an explicit partnership between government and citizens, while Singapore's shift towards a post-developmental city has led to an increased role for citizens in co-creating spaces. This is clearly evident in the development of Our Tampines Hub, Singapore's first 'integrated community and lifestyle hub', which was underpinned by a year-long participatory design process engaging local residents, extensive government agencies, and grassroots organisations. Social media channels, newsletters, roadshows, workshops, focus group discussions, workshops, and neighbourhood parties were all used to develop a co-sharing and community-orientated outcome.[4]

In China and Japan partnerships between universities and communities offer important co-creation models. Researchers and academics from the Landscape Architecture Department at Tongji University, Shanghai, have worked extensively with surrounding neighbourhoods to develop community gardens.[5] Similarly, design labs in Japanese universities have a long history of engaging students with communities to explore real-life issues in rural and urban contexts. Since 2006, Rural Urban Framework, a non-profit research and design collaborative based at the University of Hong Kong, has provided design services to government organisations, charities, and NGOs to address issues facing China's rural villages.[6] Their projects of schools, hospitals, public spaces, connections, reading rooms, and community gardens are intended to contribute positively to social, economic, and spatial transformations.[7] These important partnerships between universities and communities have been strengthened by the Pacific Rim Community Design Network.[8] Established in 1998, this network provides a series of conferences and publications disseminating practice and research and regularly features projects from Taiwan, Hong Kong, Korea, and Japan.

In some instances, designers step outside their business model to contribute pro bono work. Thai-based designers Shma for example created the separate company Shma Soen in order to explore more participatory community based projects. Working together, government, NGOs, charities, designers, communities, and universities are all contributing to the development of new types of space, which reflect a greater commitment to the diversity of community voices and needs. From large-scale facilities such as Our Tampines Hub to community gardens and ephemeral events, this ensemble of approaches and activities reflect an important transformation in the Asian city, transitioning from economic engines to include places that respond to everyday life, community connections, and needs.

Emerging Spaces of Citizenship

Jeffrey Hou

Against a background of colonial pasts and long-standing political suppression, a growing movement in East Asian societies is changing the way citizens and communities are engaged in the shaping of the built environment. Over the last few decades, political liberalisation coupled with the decentralisation of administrative responsibilities has gradually brought a shift to the model of top-down governance in parts of East Asia. Community demand and shifting professional doctrines have led to the introduction of public engagement into planning and design practices. Where institutional responses were slow or absent, ordinary citizens have taken matters into their own hands, sometimes with help from design professionals.

From informal and ephemeral acts to organised efforts by citizens and civil society groups, a growing collection of projects in East Asia demonstrate distinct forms of collective agency. In short, they manifest the power of citizens and engaged citizenships in transforming the built landscapes. Rather than just users or consumers, communities and organised groups are leading the transformation through a variety of initiatives. More than just amenities or scenic backdrops, these projects serve a vehicle for organising, networking, and formation of engaged citizenship. Beyond the typical design projects with sole authorship, these projects and processes involve collaboration and partnership, often among ensembles of actors from all walks of life, spanning different sectors in society.

Together, political openings and the rising capacity of a variety of actors, including citizens and designers, are shaping how contemporary landscapes in East Asia are produced politically, socially, and professionally. Mirroring the rise of civil society in the region, these projects represent spaces of emerging citizenships in the cultural and political context of the region, which has long emphasised loyalty to the state rather than the active engagement of the demos.[1]

The Rise of Citizen Design in East Asia

How did this movement of emerging citizenship come about in East Asia? What are the specific historical and social contexts of such emergence? Despite fundamental differences, there are remarkable parallels within the region in terms of context and shared pathways, as well as the impacts of specific events.

Starting with contexts, much of the civic activism in East Asia has been sparked by major social and environmental challenges. In Japan, citizen voices against top-down decision-making first emerged in the 1960s and 1970s, in a period of rapid economic growth accompanied by environmental degradation and urbanisation.[2] Labour movements, housing activism, and protests against environmental pollution in Taiwan also led the way in demands for government accountability. Similarly, citizen demands for participation in Korea emerged as a response to the large-scale construction of monolithic housing blocks, or 'block attack', along with forced evictions in the 1980s.[3] The rise of civil society in both Taiwan and Korea has paralleled the paths to democratisation since the early 1990s.

In Hong Kong, without the kind of major political reforms experienced elsewhere, coupled with the continued dominance of pro-development interest, citizen movements have emerged through self-organised resistance against the demolition of historic landmarks and the eviction of communities due to proposed redevelopment and infrastructure projects.[4] In mainland China, where the party-state maintains paramount control at all levels of society, some forms of community ment has since had a strong influence throughout the region. For example in Taiwan, focusing on community building and local cultural and economic development, a *machizukuri*-style community development policy was introduced by the government to strengthen civic engagement in local affairs.[9] Similarly, in Korea, the introduction of *machizukuri*-style community design from Japan helped inform the development of local practices.[10] By the late 1990s, community building or *maeul mandeulgi* has become a movement with the engagement of civil society groups in Korea.[11]

In Hong Kong, the protest against the demolition of the Star Ferry terminal followed by Occupy Queen's Pier coincided with the growing local identity after the handover to China[12] and an attempt to reclaim public space.[13] The restoration of Blue House, a historic tenement building in Wan Chai, represents a rare success story even as the rest of the district becomes gentrified. Starting with a focus on preserving local history in the city centre, the movement has since spread to rural communities through resistance against evictions by proposed developments. Besides the context of resistance, community engagement in Hong Kong has been developing through the work of charity organisations, with support from planning and design professionals.

119

engagements have occurred in selected cities and rural villages. Most notably, participatory budgeting was introduced at the local level, in part to curb corruption, improve administrative efficiency, and enhance state capacity.[5]

The specificity of these contexts notwithstanding, there are some shared pathways in how these movements materialise in actual practices across the region. They include the establishment of legal frameworks, the rise of local consciousness, and economic shifts. In terms of legal frameworks, in Japan, starting with protests and confrontations, the public quickly turned to demands for participation in the planning process which led to the establishment of relevant ordinances, requirements for public hearings, and the introduction of district plans with required approval by local communities, experts, and planners. The emergence of an urban conservation movement in Taiwan led by civil society groups resulted in the introduction of laws to protect historic properties from unchecked urban development. In 1996, the Taipei City government introduced a programme that encouraged ordinary citizens, including those without professional training, to apply for grants to undertake neighbourhood improvements.[6] Citizen participation in planning and design in Korea emerged during the 1990s as the public administration changed from strong centralisation to new local governance. Public participation became mandated by law in many projects.[7]

In the context of nation-(re)building and state developmentalism in the later part of the twentieth century, the rise of the local represents another shared pathway in the region. The need to engage the community and stakeholders at the local level in Japan led to the emergence of the *machizukuri* (community building or town-making) movement.[8] The *machizukuri* move-

Shifting economic circumstances and recovery from major disasters also played a role in creating important openings for citizen involvement within the typically rigid institutional framework in the region. The collapse of the bubble economy in Japan during the 1990s and tightening of government finances led to a positive re-evaluation of the power of community organisations, a view reinforced by community-based rebuilding efforts after the Awaji-Hanshin earthquake in 1995.[14] In Korea, the collapse of the housing market led to community-based projects emerging as an alternative to large-scale urban redevelopment.[15] In Shanghai, with the slowing down of large-scale redevelopment in the city centre, community engagement has been introduced through recent micro-regeneration projects.[16]

Similar to the recovery from the Great Awaji-Hanshin Earthquake in Japan, the rebuilding effort from the Chi-Chi earthquake in 1999 in Taiwan coincided with the growth of community engagement practices. In Chengdu, the rebuilding effort after the Wenchuan earthquake in 2008 also led to a recognition of the benefits of civil society organisations and the growth of participatory budgeting practice. With more than 40,000 projects in over 2,300 villages, it was found that participatory budgeting has introduced democratic changes at the local level through processes of deliberation and greater democratic autonomy for village residents.[17]

Today, the growing interest in community engagement and civic participation in East Asia is reshaping the urban and rural landscapes in a variety of ways. From small-scale site interventions to large-scale projects, the power of civic engagement is manifested in a wide range of projects and initiatives. Distinct from past design and development practices that were dictated by the state, the recent projects and initiatives have often been produced through a combination of efforts by citizens, civil society groups, and sometimes partnerships between public, private, and non-profit sectors. Using a typology of cases, the following provides a snapshot of these initiatives and their collective significance, including the range of actors involved in these projects, their impacts, and the issues that they address.[18]

Activating Urban Spaces

One of the most prominent types of community-focused landscapes in East Asia consists of small-scale placemaking projects initiated by citizen groups. Instead of large-scale, top-down redevelopment projects that displace existing urban communities, these small-scale projects provided opportunities for experimentation in community engagement and community-driven placemaking. Aside from activating urban spaces, these projects also provide opportunities to re-examine how publics spaces are programmed and developed. Rather than a top-down process, community-driven projects provided opportunities for public engagement and a sense of collective ownership.

The Hanpyeong Pocket Park Project launched by the Urban Action Network in Seoul in 2002 serves as one such example. Hanpyeong, or one *pyeong*, refers to the smallest unit of land (3.3 square metres) in Korea (and also Taiwan). With support from Seoul Agenda 21 and, until 2005, a local bank, the project was designed to provide community members with responsibility and the ability to shape neighbourhood public space. Initially focused on community participation only, the projects later shifted their emphasis toward supporting community building.[19] From 2002 to 2014, fifty parks were constructed.[20] The project changed the common perception that public space was the responsibility of the public administration only. Instead, citizens and communities can be involved in the making and management of these spaces, and the process can create 'public values' and build community relationships, leadership, and participation.[21]

In Taipei, a similar initiative emerged in 2009 and was formalised as the Open Green Matching Fund Programme in 2014. Designed to encourage community-based urban regeneration, the Open Green fund supports community initiatives to reuse, program, and activate vacant properties in neighbourhoods throughout the city.[22] The properties include both private lands as well as government-owned lands that were previously inaccessible to the public. Unlike previous community planning projects in the city, the funds are available to support project projects proposed by any citizens and citizen groups. From 2014 to 2017, a total of sixty-one projects were implemented throughout the city, including pocket parks, community makerspaces, nature trails, daylighting of streams, community gardens, rooftop gardens, street and alleyway improvements, and public art.[23]

ParkUp is a placemaking project supported by the Open Green Matching Fund Programme. The project began as an experimental response by a group of artists and young entrepreneurs who started Taipei's first co-working space called Hun Commune. Hun converted a vacant lot nearby its business in the Guting neighbourhood of Taipei into a community gathering space. With few gathering spaces in the city, the space attracted other social start-ups to use the space for events. On a typical day, neighbours also use it to dry blankets, taking advantage of the open space.

The successful transformation of the space, along with other opportunities, led the founders of Hun to form Plan b, which includes placemaking as part of its business portfolio. With support from the Open Green Programme, the team revisited the original site and developed a second iteration based on their observations of how the site has been used by its neighbours and other visitors. The design features nine steel horizontal bars that can be adapted for a variety of uses, ranging from planters, hanging swings, and hammocks for drying blankets and clothes. An event space at the rear of the site can be used for concerts, workshops, or outdoor cinemas. Visible from afar, the words '5.32 m²' were painted in large letters on the back wall as a reminder that the amount of park space per capita in Taiwan is only 5.32 square metres, lower than in many other cities around the world.[24]

The Magic Carpet Project in Hong Kong represents yet another model of placemaking with community involvement. Organised by faculty and students at the Chinese University of Hong Kong, the first Magic Carpet took place in Sai Ying Pun in 2013, a historic neighbourhood on the west side of Hong Kong Island. The project involved the participation of local secondary school students in researching the neighbourhood history and narratives through video interviews. The screening of the interviews on the street provided an opportunity to engage the neighbours and reclaim the street from vehicular traffic for community use.[25] With its initial success as an alternative mode of public participation and public space activation, the project has since been introduced to other neighbourhoods in Hong Kong.

In the case of the Magic Carpet Project, the continued collaboration with Caritas, a charity organisation, led to funding for a storefront space in 2017, the Magic Lanes, to initiate a community-based public space co-creation exercise focusing on the adjacent Sheung Fung Lane.[26] This organic, scaling-up process, which was also evident in the case of Taipei's Open Green Programme, suggests the power of such projects beyond the initial starting point. ▶

A simple modular design offers progamming flexibility and allows residents to appropriate the space for everyday use. 5.32 square metres refers to the limited open space per capita available in Taipei.

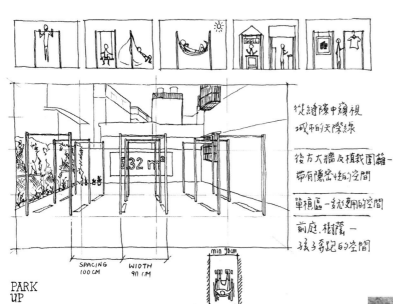

從縫隙中窺視
城市的天際線

後方大牆及積載圍籬-
帶有隱密性的空間

單植區-就於要的空間

前庭.樹蔭-
孩子等起的空間

SPACING 100 CM   WIDTH 90 CM

min 90cm

75 cm

PARK
UP

Designers: **Plan b**
Support: **Open Green Matching Fund Programme**
Location: **Guting, Taipei**
Date: **2017**

Parkup

Watching interviews on local history during the Moon Festival (Magic Carpet event).

The Magic Carpet Project

Collaborative placemaking strategies between faculty and students at the Chinese University of Hong Kong and local communities to activate public space.

Children and parents of the Sai Ying Pun community come together to play in Centre Street (Magic Tables event).

Designers: **Faculty and students of the Chinese University of Hong Kong (CHUK)**
Support: **Caritas and CUHK's Knowledge Transfer Fund**
Location: **Hong Kong**
Events: **Magic Carpet (2013) Centre Street, Sai Ying Pun (in collaboration with King's College, School of Architecture and School of Journalism and Communication, CUHK); Magic Tables (2015) Centre Street, Sai Ying Pun (in collaboration with BSSc in the Urban Studies Programme, CUHK)**

▶ **Making 'No Little Plans'**[27]

While most community-engaged projects in the region are relatively small in scale, there are also projects of much greater magnitude, which suggests that the emerging spaces of citizenship in East Asia are scalable, and that civic activism can contribute to and even lead the process of large-scale landscape transformation. One notable example is the creation and continued management of Seoul Forest Park, a 120-hectare urban park in Seoul opened in 2005. The park has been recognised as a model for citizen participation in Korea.[28] Between 2003 to 2005, more than 5,000 citizens and seventy companies participated in planting trees on the site led by Seoul Green Trust, an organisation founded by Forest for Life, a non-profit organisation. Following a public-private partnership model, the park has been managed by the Seoul Forest Park Conservancy (formerly Friends of Seoul Forest Park) since 2016. The park management involves the help of volunteers in maintenance and programming, including nature learning, community gardening, and a library, and through private donations. Since 2005, more than 50,000 volunteers have participated.[29]

Citizen participation in programming and management was also key to the development of Arima Fuji Park, a 175-hectare nature park in Hyogo, Japan. Due to the size of the park, management and programming became a major challenge. Instead of following a conventional model of institutional operation, more than thirty groups of citizens including non-profit organisations have received training to be involved in park management. Developed and organised by the citizen groups, activities include weekend excursions to terraced rice fields, workshops for observations of insects and animals, concerts, and kite flying. Administrative policy for park management has been handled by a committee of local citizens, staff, and scholars, with support from the firm studio-L. In 2009, 730 programs were offered in the park.[30]

Citizen involvement in large-scale landscape planning has occurred in other ways. In the case of Taijang National Park, a 4,905-hectare coastal site in Taiwan, the effort started as a protest movement against a proposed petrochemical and steel complex that would have decimated the local landscape, which supported a vibrant fishing industry and wildlife habitats for hundreds of species including the critically endangered black-faced spoonbill (*Platalea minor*). To fight against the development and to experiment with alternative economic development strategies, activists, local fishers, and researchers worked together to promote eco-tourism and ecological conservation. With the success of organised tours and small-scale business operations, the public perception of the region began to turn. What was once perceived as a backward and underdeveloped area has emerged as an ecologically and culturally rich coastal area. The process paved the way for the establishment of the National Park in 2009.

Heritage Activism

The development of the spaces of emerging citizenship in East Asia is represented at different scales and driven by specific issues at hand. Against the rapid urban development, heritage conservation has particularly been a common challenge facing many rapid growing cities in the region. As such, it has also been a source of citizen activism.

In Taipei, one of the most remarkable examples of heritage conservation was the case of Treasure Hill, a hillside informal settlement built by refugees from mainland China after 1949. Constructed over time on a public land zoned for parks, the community has evolved and endured through the city's rapid development till the 1990s when the city government planned to formally develop the site and evict the residents. Through several advocacy campaigns, the conservation and community activists successfully lobbied the city government to designate the settlement as a cultural landscape site. The non-profit Organization of Urban Re-s (OURs) developed the concept of a co-living commune that would support the co-existence of the existing community, together with a youth hostel and an artist-in-residence programme.[31] The site was reopened in 2010 following the renovation of existing structures.

The conservation of Treasure Hill was significant not only to Taipei but also to other similar efforts in the region, most notably the Pok Fu Lam Village, one of the last remaining indigenous villages on Hong Kong Island dating back to the seventeenth century. Crammed with low-rise, makeshift dwellings built by refugees from mainland China in the post-war era, the historic village has often been perceived mistakenly as a slum, a condition reinforced by the government's squatter control policy that provided residents with no incentives for improvement.[32] In 2009, the Pok Fu Lam Village Cultural Landscape Conservation Group (PFLV-CLCG) was established by the local villagers to study, document, and promote the conservation of cultural landscape in and around the village. The case of Treasure Hill has inspired the Pok Fu Lam villagers and organisers to consider conserving the entire village landscape.

Similar to Treasure Hill and Pok Fu Lam Village, Jangsu Village is also nestled on a hillside along the remnants of the historic Seoul City wall. Most of the low-rise buildings there were built by rural migrants after the Korean War (1950–1953) and during the 1960s.[33] The lack of sewage, water, gas, and other basic infrastructure has resulted in poor living conditions for the predominantly low-income residents who continued to stay because of the affordability of the area and also due to the hefty fines for illegal occupation upon leaving the site.[34] In 2004, the village was targeted for urban renewal that would have resulted in its demolition. In 2008, a volunteer group called the Alternative Regeneration Research Team and consisting of activists, architects,

123

and researchers began to work with the residents to repair their homes while resisting the redevelopment. It also created an alternative neighbourhood regeneration master plan.[35]

In 2009, residents in Jangsu Village voted to reject the redevelopment and began to gradually repair the community. To demonstrate the potential for renovation and how empty properties could be turned into useful community space, a small art gallery was first built on a vacant site and offered art classes for children. To facilitate building repair in a community with predominantly seniors, a 'community company' called Dong-nae Mok-Soo (community carpenter) was founded in 2011 with a grant from the government. The company began by hiring residents to remodel empty buildings and turn them into community spaces, including a café. In 2012, the repairs were expanded into the alleyways. The process has led to overall improvements in the physical and socio-economic conditions in the village.[36] In 2014, the Seoul government finally withdrew the urban renewal plan. The success of Jangsu has since inspired other villages along the City Wall to look for alternative approaches to neighbourhood regeneration.

From the Treasure Hill in Taipei, Pok Fu Lam Village in Hong Kong to Jangsu Village in Seoul, the informal landscapes built by villagers, migrants, and refugees are being recognised either as important cultural heritage sites or as sites of resistance against large-scale redevelopment. The spaces of emerging citizenship in East Asia, therefore, include not only new results of collective agency but also those that are already in existence.

Gardening the City

Community gardening and urban agriculture represent another growing movement in East Asia. Rooftop gardening, in particular, presents a common practice in densely populated Asian cities, with scarce land resources and high property prices.

Over 300 rooftop gardens of different forms and sizes are found throughout Hong Kong, including commercial, industrial, institutional, and residential buildings. They follow different organisational structures, ranging from commercial operations to those run by charity or non-profit organisations, educational institutions, hospitals, and individual owners and tenants.[37] Rooftop Republic, for example, is an urban gardening service start-up in Hong Kong with a mission to promote sharing and community building. More than just providing technical services such as design, installation, and management of gardens, Rooftop Republic actively recruits companies and organisations to share their privately-owned rooftops with communities for gardening and other activities.[38] From about twenty locations in 2015, the number of projects has expanded to over fifty sites, including rooftops of apartment buildings, company headquarters, schools, senior centres, and other public buildings.[39]

In Seoul, the Mullae Rooftop Garden was an early project established on top of a five-storey, mixed-use building in 2011 in Mullae-dong, one of the oldest industrial areas in the city, still dotted by small metal shops and hardware stores. The project was conceived by a group of local artists, a metal shop owner, a local resident, a designer, activists, and an NGO staff.[40] After a difficult start in finding an appropriate location for the garden and in getting permission from property owners, the garden was created, bringing people together from the nearby area who otherwise would have few opportunities for interactions.[41] The garden provided valuable learning activities for children and for neighbours to meet. It has also been used as a venue for a variety of workshops and provides organic vegetables for a local café.[42]

Rooftop spaces serve not only gardening but also growing activities in beekeeping. In Tokyo, the Ginza Honey Bee Project is a remarkable initiative founded in 2006 and located in Ginza, one of the city's main commercial centres and most expensive districts. With proximity to the Imperial Palace and several urban parks, Ginza turned out to be an appropriate place for bees to thrive. Perched on top of a nondescript office tower, the project is run by a group of volunteers that includes Ginza club workers, bartenders, landscape architects, art therapists, and school children.[43] The proximity to high-end department stores and businesses also provided opportunities to market the honey produced from the project.

Aside from individual cases, community gardening and urban agriculture in East Asia have been pursued as grassroots movements, leading to support from the local governments. In Seoul, advocated by the Seoul Green Trust, urban agriculture became the focus of the City's policy following the election of Mayor Woon-Soon Park. In 2012, the Seoul Metropolitan Government rolled out an Urban Agriculture Master Plan and set a goal to become a World Capital of Urban Agriculture.

In Taipei, a group of activists, community organisers, landscape architects, and scholars formed the Farming Urbanism Network in 2014 to begin advocating for urban gardening. The group took advantage of the mayoral election in the same year and succeeded in having the leading candidates adopt urban agriculture into their policy platforms. In 2015, with the election of Ko Wen-Je as the new mayor, the Taipei City Government rolled out the Garden City Initiative, and the entire government bureaucracy was mobilised to implement the initiative. Within four years, the number of gardens in Taipei grew to over 700, up from just a handful.[44] These include community gardens, school gardens, and rooftop gardens, in addition to the pre-existing citizen farms on the outskirts of the city. Citizen organisations also play an important role. For instance, Community University, a non-profit continuing education organisation with more than eighty campuses ▶

Treasure Hill

An informal settlement built by refugees from mainland China along the Hsintien River in Taipei, Treasure Hill has now been designated as a cultural landscape site.

Artists in residence and a youth hostel are mixed in with the local residents.

Designers: **NTU Building & Planning Research Foundation**
Support: **Organization of Urban Re–s (OURs)**
Location: **Taipei**

125

A community green space designed into the hillside.

Remnant land due to an underground pipeline was transformed into a community resource.

A community dinner where local residents gather to share food.

Knowledge and Innovation Community Gardens

Local government, developers, and businesses, together with local residents and the Clover Nature School, manage the KIC Garden to provide spaces for gardening, learning, and socialising.

The community seed bank.

Project Name: **Knowledge and Innovation Community Gardens (KICG)**
Location: **Wujiaochang Business District of Yangpu District of Shanghai**
Designers: **Pandscape & Clover Nature School**
Client: **SHUI ON group/Yangpu Science and Technology Innovation Group**
Completion Year: **2016**

▶ throughout Taiwan, including thirteen in Taipei, offers classes and workshops on gardening techniques and even beekeeping.

Urban agriculture and community gardening have been promoted in Shanghai by the non-profit Clover Nature School. Founded by Tongji University professor Yuelai Liu, the school has been building different types of community gardens since 2014 on sites including a vacant train track and other leftover urban spaces. These community gardens are envisioned as urban micro-spaces for nature conservation and social participation, turning fragmented land into productive spaces.[45] In four years, the school has completed over sixty gardens throughout the city. The Clover Nature School's signature project, Knowledge and Innovation Community Gardens (KICG), in particular, came about through a collaboration between the school, a private developer, and the local district government. KICG is open to the public year-round and combines garden plots, social spaces, demonstration sites, playgrounds, and an education centre. Based on the results so far, the organisation has an ambitious vision to create 2040 community gardens in the city by 2040.[46]

The growing movement in community gardening and urban farming in East Asia represents the latest chapter in the evolution of citizen engagement in transforming urban landscapes. Going beyond simple neighbourhood improvements and the development of civic open spaces, and by pursuing a variety of activities including environmental education, these sites further serve as spaces of ecological citizenship—reconnecting urban dwellers to natural cycles and processes and cultivating an ecological consciousness that has been undermined by the process of urbanisation.

Ensembles of Actors and Processes

Throughout East Asia, there are many more cases of bottom-up or community-driven placemaking than can be presented in this essay. They include not only projects made by civil society groups but also those produced through everyday activities, including transgressions and temporary appropriations of space. These include the weekly occupation of streets, sidewalks, and plaza spaces in Central, Hong Kong, by thousands of migrant workers that transform the financial district into a carnivalesque space of gathering and celebration.[47] Examples also include acts of protests that make creative use of streets, squares, and other forms of transportation or public infrastructure as vehicles of political expression and mobilising. These acts of appropriation, such as the Instagram Piers of Hong Kong (see pp. 142–143), have transformed underutilised sites into active social spaces at little cost.

By engaging ensembles of actors, including citizens, civil society groups, professionals, the private sector, and government institutions, the rise of citizen-driven placemaking in East Asia presents a model of community building and collaborative governance that

reflects the shifting state-society relationship in the region. These emerging spaces of citizenship in East Asia further serve as a vehicle for capacity building, a platform for creativity, and a means for re-imagining the social and political organisation of the society. These projects and initiatives may or may not have the iconic profile of their institutional or commercial counterparts. Instead, the source of their significance comes from the social and political transformations as embodied in the projects. Such profound and systemic changes in society are crucial to the future of the region and beyond.

As spaces of emerging citizenship, these projects contribute to the social and political processes that have significant implications for the continued evolution and transformation of society in Asia. Their collective significance far exceeds their formal presence and spatial footprints. As the cases in this essay demonstrate, many landscape planning and design professionals are already engaged in such transformation. Some play a supporting role to the community-driven efforts; others are engaged in building community capacity and serving to bridge between grassroots organising and institutional processes. There are also instances in which professionals have taken the lead in the movement and changing the way the built environment projects have typically been produced. Beyond building the emerging spaces of citizenship in East Asia, their continued engagement will also help redefine the practice of landscape architecture in the region. ∎

127

Acknowledgment

The author wishes to thank Hyein Chae for her support with translation and information on the cases from Seoul. A major part of the materials and sources comes from the collective work of the Pacific Rim Community Design Network, co-founded by the author in 1998.

Sidh Sintusingha

Designing Indigenous Modernity in Southeast Asia

Southeast Asian landscape architects have been receiving global and regional recognition predominantly for private projects. Why are public landscapes absent? A possible answer, often conspicuously ignored, is the prevalence of informal urbanism, catalysed by street commerce, or what this paper terms 'landscape architecture without landscape architects' in the public realm of these cities. In the cases where landscape architects are involved in public landscapes, they tacitly act as agents of formalisation which is synonymous with 'modernisation' towards the perceived condition of 'modernity'. Crucially 'modernisation' often manifests as a 'playing catch-up' with the West and developed economies of the East or as a phenomenon of 'internalised' Orientalism[1] consisting in a desire to conform or appeal to Western/Westernised gazes.[2] This is encapsulated in the Thai approximations of and desires for modernity, namely, *samaimai* (สมัยใหม่, 'new era') and *tansamai* (ทันสมัย, 'of the times'),[3] that manifest in elite practices of importing, interpreting, and adapting foreign forms and ways, while—subconsciously or not—culturally relegating pre-existing cultural practices. This partially explains the 'absence' of informality in media representations of Southeast Asian design—whether by locals who consider them obsolete forms or symbols of backwardness, or by others.[4] Yet this phenomenon reveals a fluid culture that is outward looking and open to changes that are negotiated or layered rather than imposed.

In economically developed cities wracked by decades of post-war zoning practices and car-oriented urbanisation that have caused socio-economical and spatial fragmentation, landscape architects self-define as advocates for the public realm. This manifests in the discipline's metanarratives of introducing nature in the city and of socially vibrant public realms that favour pedestrianisation and places for social co-presence and interactions. These could be categorised as 'informal' components (nature) and practices (people's recreation in and appropriation of public spaces). In effect, landscape architects are—or perceive themselves to be—purveyors of informalisation in highly formal urban contexts.[5] However, with the increased influence of neoliberal market-led urban development practices, the emergence of privately-owned public spaces (POPS) problematises this narrative, and spaces become depoliticised and highly choreographed, under constant surveillance, often favouring commercial interests and benefits.

In contemporaneous developing Southeast Asian cities, the urban context for the emergence of the discipline has been different. For decades, landscape architects have had limited influence in the public realm and have mainly designed gated, private spaces, whether commercial, residential, or for tourism developments oriented towards Western/Westernised gazes. Even in the design of public parks, whether as a colonial imposition or import, these spaces are in most cases gated and regulated with limited access. A large factor in this absence is the ubiquitous presence of rooted practices of informal urbanism. The urban 'public realm' has already been systematically occupied by heavy 'bottom-up' appropriations, mainly by street vendors, and the gates and walls are to keep them out and segregate parks for strictly regulated recreational activities, consistent with practices of their cultural origins. Landscape architecture is an imported novelty and seems less relevant in the intensively used public realm. It is mainly carried out in the service of the middle and upper classes, whose needs are met in the gated developments that, in an act of climatic self-colonisation, inhabit air-conditioned housing, malls, offices, and private vehicles. While there are moments of co-presence, their life is spatially segregated from street life.

In this context, any intrusion into the public realm becomes acts of formalisation of the informal rules encapsulated in Bangkok Metropolitan Administration's policy to *jad rabieb* (จัดระเบียบ) or 'bring order' to the streets. However, with expansion of the middle class and the proliferation of the Internet, and with these things, the influences of and desires for urban images from developed cities, such intrusions have increased and intensified. While this may be initially about cultural imagery,[6] the contestations have become more spatial with the increased urban density and urbanisation through rural-urban migration. Ironically, in cities like Bangkok, this could also be attributed to the introduction and expansion of the rail mass transit networks that, due to their synergy with pedestrians, by default forced the middle class back into the public realm and in direct conflicts with informal urbanism.[7] Here it is suggested that modernisation is a contested phenomenon.

Informal urbanism can be seen as a contemporaneous form of indigenous modernisation in these cities manifesting in street vendors that clustered at key districts and nodes, e.g., public bus and informal transportation networks, left behind by those who are more socially mobile, now patronised by the lower economic classes. Likewise, informal settlements, as part of rural-urban migrations, can be framed as bottom-up local modernisation practices. Often, the formal and informal realms manifest as hybridised systems serving the needs and desires of interlinked flows of economic transactions. As most major urban centres in Southeast Asia are embarking on mass transit infrastructure construction to redress years of underinvestment, this points to an emergent pattern or phenomenon across the region.

This essay discusses these issues and their manifestation in Southeast Asian urban landscapes through designed landscapes from Thailand and Indonesia, focusing on two main arenas in the spatial contestations between the formal and informal practices: streets (elevated spaces) and waterfronts.

Segregating Modernities through Elevation

A well-known attribute of many Asian megacities is their very high-density living coupled with a lack of public open spaces. These produce vertical urban forms whether commercial or residential and, at the street level, densely fluid, efficient, and innovative utilisation of spaces over the course of the day and night encapsulated by street vending practices. These are contributing factors to the emergence of elevated spaces, which by default discriminates between imported and indigenous modernities.

The first case, Siam 'sky-piazza', represents a depoliticised POPS. The sky-piazza is a new addition to and evolution of the expanding network of skywalks privately developed since the construction of the Bangkok Mass Transit System (BTS) Skytrain, Bangkok's first rail mass transit that began operating in 1999. The BTS and, since its opening in 2004, Metropolitan Rapid Transit (MRT) systems have driven private urban consolidation and intensification along their routes, with many shopping malls, high-rise residential and mixed-use developments funding skywalk links to stations. While their main purpose is to efficiently direct crowds of people from transportation nodes to businesses as raised pedestrian walkways, parts of the skywalk have been appropriated as public spaces and tacitly perform as regulated POPS.[8] ▶

129

BTB Siam Skywalk

A pedestrian platform floats above the busy traffic of cars and trains and allows people to move freely between major cultural, commercial, and retail activities. The vibrant green surface of the piazza references water lilies, while the lily pad-like structures provide shade and a canvas for street artists.

Project Name: **BTB Siam Skywalk**
Location: **Bangkok, Thailand**
Landscape Architect: **Martha Schwartz Partners**
Client: **Siam Piwat**
Completion Year: **2017**

▶ Opened in 2017, the sky-piazza is formally designed as an open space and is raised above one of Bangkok's major cultural and retail intersections (Pathumwan). The sky-piazza interfaces between the corner facilities of Siam Discovery mall in the northeast, Bangkok Art and Cultural Centre (BACC) in the northwest, Mabunkhrong (MBK) mall in the southwest and Siam youth-culture precinct in the southeast. As with the rest of the skywalk, businesses around it funded the construction and it marks the extension of the design-driven mall development approach of Siam Piwat (the developer of Siam Discovery) into the public realm. Inserted between the road level and the BTS sky-train above, the skywalk accentuates the dense, multi-level quality of Bangkok's urban thoroughfare. The piazza provides a buffer between commercial realms of the malls and the contested car-dominated streets—whether of everyday street vending or major political protests. In 2014, the intersection was one of the sites of the seven-month 'Shut-Down Bangkok' political protests against the government of the time, arguably representing a phenomenon of 'middle-class informality'. On 14 December 2019, the new-generation opposition party held a one-hour flash-mob protest at the fringes of but not in the sky-piazza itself, which is privately administered and, with a large oculus at the centre, is less suitable for mass gatherings. Socio-spatially, the sky-piazza and skywalks evade informality on the street level—a depoliticised first-world space hovering above the 'third-world' of Bangkok's footpath.

Moreover, as the Architecture Profession Act, B.E. 2508 (1965), prohibits foreign architects from working in Thailand, the project falls into an 'informal design' category with Martha Schwartz Partners providing design advice to the project without being able to be officially credited. This practice manifests the tension between the desire for 'world-class' facilities and post-colonial national pride and cultural autonomy that highlights and reinforces the role of local agents in the country's modernisation.[9]

Similar to the Siam sky-piazza, Teras Cihampelas in Bandung is an elevated, segregated open space but represents the contrasting practice of formalisation of informal street vendors. Compared to Bangkok, Bandung is a smaller centre and manifests a stronger presence of informality through its *desakota* 'village-city' characteristic—an informal-formal hybrid that sustains the contrasting Dutch colonial planning and architecture with the indigenous *kampungs* in its modernisation practices.

Opened in the same year as the Siam sky-piazza, the Cihampelas skywalk shares the legacy of the dominance of informal traders on the streets and the lack of public open spaces in Bandung's low-rise and high-density urban context. Teras Cihampelas is located on one of Bandung's major commercial-tourist strips, albeit one that forms a thin formal veneer, concealing informal *kampung* settlements beyond to the east (which are ironically exposed at the south end, by the raised skywalk) and planned former colonial areas to the west. The project, the brainchild of a political rising star and architect Ridwan Kamil when he was Bandung mayor (2013–2018), reflects the contested politicised image landscapes of the emergent middle classes and informal urban space. Indonesia has a unique tradition of designer-politicians begun by the first president Sukarno, with Ridwan Kamil inheriting the mantle, where design is utilised to both engage with and prune informal urbanism.

Crucially, this is a design that explicitly recognises—or at least proclaims to address—urban informality through the formalisation of street vendors and the improvisation of 'publicness'. This is achieved through the design of the spatially segregated raised platforms and vendor stalls, essentially an adornment of informal forms. In elevating vendors from the street and with only three main access points in its almost 450 metres of length, these platforms cut off vendors from the main flow and source of customers. Conversations with vendors confirm this predicament. Here, the design clearly harbours ambitions to be an urban destination in itself—conveying a sense of contemporary global public space (and one can't help making associations with New York's iconic High Line) with ample opportunities, apart from shopping and eating, to sit down and take selfies, evoking the resort cafe atmosphere for which the city is famous.[10] The design of the platform terraces down north to south following the topography, providing spatial variances and vantage points. The design also speculates that businesses on either side will further intensify, evidenced with a bridge link (not in operation in the author's first visit in 2017) to an adjoining building. In form and practice, Teras Cihampelas manifests the phenomenon of post-colonialism, modernisation, and gentrification, while acknowledging, engaging, and speculating with Bandung's informal urban conditions through design.

Critically, the space would have benefitted through direct linkages with the POPS in adjacent C-Walk, Bandung's most popular mall, created around large mature existing trees. However, it is the socio economic conditions associated with each that may have made the linkage unfeasible, despite the bridging of images in the design of Teras Cihampelas. At my second visit on October 2019, there are evidences of re-informalisation as vendors installed tarp canopies as practical protection from the elements and clothes sellers expand into the main thoroughfare. An extension southward, consistent with Ridwan's vision, is in the process of being built—but at the time of my visit construction seems to have stalled. On the other hand, formal private sector buy-in is crucial and the once-closed bridge link to the adjacent building has now opened into a restaurant with panoramic views of the *kampung*.

131

Teras Cihampelas, Bandung's 'Highline' for street vending.

Glocalising Public Spaces along *Khlongs* and *Kampungs*

Waterways were once integral to life in Southeast Asian settlements.[11] However, with the advent of modernity introduced by European colonisers, they have been superseded by roads. In the post-Second-World-War rapid urbanisation, waterways by default (and not design), served as open drainage and sewerage infrastructure and were often appropriated and settled by rural-urban migrants, whether in Bangkok's squatter settlements or Bandung's *kampungs*. Given emergent global environment and urban landscape values, the waterways are being contested in their rejuvenation and reintegration as part of the urban public realm.

The BanManKong project at Khlong Lardprao (known formally as 'BaanPracharat Rim Khlong Lardprao') represents the formalisation of informality. Bangkok was founded more than two centuries ago on the floodplains of the Chao Phraya River and *khlongs* (canals) traditionally formed the main transport network for the city. On contact with and under threat from 'civilised' European land-based culture in the nineteenth century, the city embarked on a cultural transformation where roads gradually replaced the canals. Further compromising the drainage functions, the now undesirable canals afforded space for squatter settlements that absorbed much of the post-Second-World-War rural-urban migration to the city. More recently, the rejuvenation of waterways was declared as a major objective and legacy for the new monarch's reign (from 2016), which has resulted in old market and settlement clearances in Old Bangkok. However, outside of the old centre, without formal historical baggage, the ap-proach to *khlong* rejuvenation has been far more benign and utilitarian. Here the government used Khlong Ladprao to the northeast of the old centre as a trial for an integrated flood mitigation and social housing for often-illegal occupants.

The approach builds on a two-decades-old practice of BanMankong slum upgrading where target communities are formed and/or strengthened through identifying natural leaders and establishing savings groups and community co-operations to leverage financial assets and secure housing loans. The practice is a synthesis of decades-old conflicts and negotiations between top-down public housing and bottom-up community engagement/empowerment.[12] Since in legal terms the strip of land by waterways is publicly owned, the government arranged long-term thirty-year leases with the community and provided subsidies for housing infrastructure. Through this process, the government is reclaiming the *khlong* side to build weirs (which enable canal dredging for effective stormwater drainage) and deliver social housing.

One crucial result has been the seemingly unintended creation of public *khlong*-side promenade where the community, now with secure tenure and houses oriented towards the canal, individually participate in decorating and beautifying the area, as landscape architecture without landscape architects. To some degree, the practice has led to a revival of the historic cultural relationship with the waterways through the transformation of their image. As the housing upgrading project runs along a twenty-two-kilometre section of the *khlong* (which includes 7069 households in fifty communities), the development will eventually result in the *khlong*-side promenade as an emergent landscape typology. This has become a model that will be up-scaled to Bangkok's canal network, including the historic Khlong Prem Prachakorn, about whose pollution level the current King Maha Vajiralongkorn had previously expressed concern.[13] This is a departure from previous practices of canal weir and pedestrian pathway construction, which were not able to redress the undesirable image of the canals.

In contrast, Teras Cikapundung riverside park in Bandung involved the displacement of informality for a formal public space. Opened to the public in 2015, the project is part of Ridwan Kamil's initiative to create new public open spaces in urban left-over spaces such as those created by large-scale infrastructure, but it also includes the evictions of *kampungs*. Teras Cikapundung is an example of the latter built on reclaimed land next to the Cikapundung River, the main river that runs north-south through Bandung. The practice represents the direct imposition of popular middle-class images and desires upon, and displacing of, indigenous patterns of settlements. Consistent with previous practices of formalisation down river at C-Walk mall or the Jardin Apartments, the open space is carved out of densely settled urban *kampungs*—but in a rare departure from such practices, there are no strong edges of walls to segregate the public space from the *kampungs*, which provide accessibility to the surrounding inhabitants.

The design builds upon the steep slopes of the riverside, inserting terraces of planter boxes and recreational spaces and creating a dramatic public landscape that 'celebrates' the river valley, in contrast to the adjacent *kampungs* that often treat the river akin

to 'no man's land' due to its boundary conditions. The resultant resort-like atmosphere consciously builds upon Bandung's reputation as a tourist city. As much due to the lack of public open space as to the investment in design, the park has been one of the most popular in Bandung (including for residents of the surrounding *kampungs*) and, along with the formal image-upgrading effect of the projects, successfully served the mayor's political agenda and ambitions (in 2018 he won the election to become governor of West Java Province). As an open park to the surrounding *kampungs*, it manifests a more inclusive message that the new, more elaborately designed parks are for everyone. On the other hand, the project creates a precedent for displacement and reinforces the undesirable image of *kampungs* as the barrier to urban modernisation, rendering them more vulnerable to eviction. This is expressed in the intention to replace the low-rise *kampungs* with architect-designed multi-storey social housing for existing and new residents and also at the broader scale of design upgrades to the city's pedestrian paths along major roads that displace and erect barriers to street vending.[14]

However, in the Bandung case studies, as public open space projects are commonly co-delivered through corporate social responsibility (CSR), the city government is struggling to maintain the spaces and evidences of re-informalisation and adaptation abound. At Teras Cikapundung, park shelters on the fringes of the park, across the river from the public entries on the main road, are being inhabited. Uphill into the wooded areas are traces of an informal market with a *kampung* just a short walk further north. Here, maintenance or formal government care is a critical determinant on which direction the spaces evolve.

At the other end of the socio-economic spectrum is Icon Siam, which represents the private sector's production of POPS and the aggressive gentrification of the Chao Phraya River (in collaboration with the state). In contrast to the *khlongs*, the Chao Phraya River, while experiencing neglect, retains its national cultural significance and has over time seen many public conceptions of imported images for the river. These range from the riverside highway proposed in the 1980s to the grand waterfront promenade proposed by the junta government in 2015, which met with strong resistance from the conservation, design, and planning community (with landscape architects Shma playing a prominent role). On the other hand, the river has been experiencing private gentrification of high-end hotels, residential towers, and tourist facilities that have repurposed old maritime warehouse structures. In 2012, the Asiatique open-air mall development, built on the historic East Asiatic Company's port, provided the first large-scale riverfront POPS.

Thai mall-makers have been central in the private production of 'public space' in Thailand—from the importation of the inverted public space model of giant-box air-conditioned mall interiors to the provision of urban courtyards and piazzas, segregated via fences and level/visual separation from the streets. Developed by Siam Piwat, the builder of the Pathumwan intersection sky-piazza, the 53-billion-baht Icon Siam provides another important vision in its ambition to shift the centre of retail gravity away from the downtown Siam-Sukhumvit areas to the traditionally less fashionable west bank of the Chao Phraya River. The orientation towards the river is another novelty, enhanced by the building of two large terraced riverside piazzas designed by local firm P Landscapes. At the centre of this extravagant architectural and landscape composition is the country's first Apple Store, occupying and serving as the main entry to the upper level piazza. Both Icon Siam and Apple share the vision and intensive ambition to be synonymous with the notion of 'public' and the symbol of national and global spaces respectively. Both manifest a purposeful blurring between private benefits and public life or publicness. The naming of the project and the design conception has been expressed in terms of national and cultural pride in the production of a world-class mall.[15]

Yet Icon Siam's riverside piazza treats the river similarly to how other Bangkok urban mall piazzas treats the road—as merely a backdrop, albeit one that is far more spectacular, as it is significantly raised above the water level and segregated from the everyday utility and informal practices of the river. Instead, the engagement with water occurs with a spectacular 400-metre 'ICONIC multi-media water feature' on the lower piazza, which is the longest fountain dance in Southeast Asia, according to Icon Siam's website.[16] On the other hand, the mall's transparent façade provides multiple public vantage viewing points of the river and Bangkok's skyline that were once reserved for tourists and residents in high-end hotel and condominium towers.

Reimaging Informal Urbanity as an Indigenous Modernisation

At the Big Asian Book workshop in Beijing in January 2019, in response to the author's research, Huai-yan Chang of Salad Dressing observed that, in Asia, inequality is an accepted fact of life. To elaborate further, key to its acceptance is the traditional patronage system that connects classes, formal to informal. This helps explain the resilience of informal urbanism, and despite formal top-down edicts and evictions, it is not possible to root this out, as it meets the needs and demands of vendors and their clients and is patronised/tolerated/cultivated by the lower tiers of government. Furthermore, informal urbanism's fine scale favours small entrepreneurs and provides a socio-spatial medium for social mobility or at least a means for lower socio-economic groups, such as rural-urban migrants, to establish footholds in the city. While the formal sector is failing to rein in inequality, the informal is sustaining its significant role in the city.[17] These specific characteristics are legacies of their own traditions, the conditions of post-colonialism, and desires for modernity.

The acceptance of inequality also explains why the terms 'public' and 'private' are problematic. In Southeast Asia, the practice of and/or desire for clear separations between the two realms as in advanced economies is less apparent. What is more commonplace is the blurring, the hybridisation of the realms—yet this sustains and exacerbates, through the forces of formalisation, social-spatial separations. Crucially, we have to note that informal urbanism is also a private appropriation of public open spaces—a point that detractors are eager to highlight. These issues are evident in the projects discussed: the interweaving of the practices of evading informality, formalisation of informality, and spatio-cultural gentrification. Yet they reveal opportunities and pathways forward for design and planning practice.

Asian landscape architects should decolonise their perception of and recognise informal urbanity as an indigenous modernisation phenomenon rather than practices to be evaded and/or evicted, and not only because of their omnipresence. It is argued that urban informality is not a 'problem' as often represented in the media—such as being the convenient scapegoat for traffic congestions or for polluted streets and canals. It should be viewed as part of the creative, 'participative' solutions that it already is in everyday practices. To create public spaces that truly benefit the broad socio-economic spectrum of Southeast Asian cities and mitigate urban inequity, landscape architects should endeavour to understand and meaningfully engage with the socio-spatial realities and innate creativity of their indigenous modernities. ∎

Tacit Negotiations and the Public Realm

On a typical Sunday morning, I stroll leisurely downhill along Robinson Road towards Central—Hong Kong's central business district. Heading east, I see luxury residential towers with multi-storey car parks and gilded gates occupying the left-side of the road while the right side is lined with concrete-reinforced slopes. As Robinson converges with Conduit Road, the view towards the city opens up as the sidewalk moves onto an elevated spiral flyover. A set of stairs leads down to a grove of trees below with some benches to rest. However, as I continue along the sidewalk I soon descend on an off-ramp underneath the elevated road and enter the lush green space of the Hong Kong Zoological and Botanical Gardens. To the far right, children are running around in a playground tucked underneath the shaded space of another flyover while in the Botanical Gardens they observe rare birds and other small mammals housed in cages larger than a typical Hong Kong flat. Continuing beyond a greenhouse filled with mainland Chinese tourists, a pedestrian footbridge crosses over the busy traffic of Garden Road and Cotton Tree Drive.

The sidewalk on the other side is quite narrow and wedged against a large podium tower, but there is some slight relief going down some stairs that lead to the Kennedy Road Playground nestled under the elevated road structure. Filipino domestic workers take advantage of the shade and are holding informal Sunday services. Their singing mingles with the noise of teenagers playing basketball in the adjacent court. At the bottom of the stairs, some construction workers rearrange bamboo scaffolding while others are smoking next to the public toilet. I pass a crowded bus stop before crossing the street and continuing downhill on Tramway Path, which is sandwiched between an open water drainage channel, the Peak Tram tracks,

and an elevated portion of Cotton Tree Drive. Underneath the flyover, the overflow queue area for the Peak Tram is bustling with impatient tourists. Across the street from the Peak Tram station, the U.S. Consulate is ominously quiet on a Sunday morning while churchgoers, tourists, and local residents struggle to find foothold on the crowded sidewalks as we wait for the traffic lights to turn.

Turning left into the car park of St John's Cathedral offers some relief from the crush and I hear faint music from the ongoing mass. On Battery Path, a few informal vendors are haggling with customers over handbags and backpacks adjacent to Norman Foster's famed HSBC building, where the ground floor plaza has been recently reconfigured with sculptures to prevent large group gatherings. A footbridge connects to the Standard Charter Bank Building and a much-needed blast of air-conditioning as I make my way through Hong Kong's network of polished marble corridors and elevated pedestrian bridges connecting luxury shopping malls and office buildings. This route bypasses the weekly gathering of Filipino domestic workers in Statue Square and the HSBC building plaza known as Little Manila, but the long lines to the bathrooms in the gleaming corridors of luxury malls is a clue of the primary demographic that occupies the CBD on Sundays. At the elevated walkway by Exchange Square mini-fortresses are built of cardboard boxes and blankets. Shoes line the threshold of these partitioned linear spaces as small groups of Filipino domestic helpers play cards, watch movies, share meals, or take naps. The rest of us pass through with purpose, passing by elderly sanitation workers who are manually picking up discarded trash. Soon, I reach the IFC mall for some ice cream and proceed to the roof garden. Many people are already picnicking in the 'public' roof garden—families, couples, teenagers, and even some domestic workers. I sit, enjoying the breeze and the views of the skyline across Victoria Harbour.

Hong Kong's Infrastructural Modernity

... infrastructures are largely responsible for the sense of stability of life in the developed world, the feeling that things work, and will go on working ... Among these is *systemic, society-wide control* over the variability inherent in the natural environment ... Infrastructures constitute an artificial environment, channeling and/or reproducing those properties of the natural environment that we find most useful and comfortable; providing others that the natural environment cannot; and eliminating features we find dangerous, uncomfortable, or merely inconvenient.[1]

Historian Paul Edwards describes infrastructure as a mediator between modernity and the natural environment; in turn, the natural environment shapes infrastructure and our experiences of modernity. This is an apt description of many Asian cities, especially Hong Kong. First impressions of Hong Kong often consist of the mass transit railway (MTR) system that brings people seamlessly from the baggage claim of the airport to the heart of the CBD in twenty-four minutes. The Airport Core project includes the new Chek Lap Kok Airport connected with a new highway system, MTR network, and multiple new urban developments along the coast of Lantau Island and the Kowloon Peninsula. It is considered one of the top ten construction projects in the twentieth century, along with the Hoover Dam and the Panama Canal, and acts as a seamless transect through Hong Kong's highly variable landscape.[2] The project was completed to universal fanfare in the territory. I remember visiting Hong Kong in late 1998 as a teenager and the sense of wonder riding the airport express to Central, passing through the rugged landscapes of Lantau, overlooking the vast container landscapes of the Tsing Yi Port terminals, and finally emerging in the glitzy new mall at IFC. The fare was so expensive that we only took the airport express once as a family, and in subsequent trips we always took the more affordable airport bus. On this initial trip, my uncle insisted on driving us back to the airport so we could experience the new tunnels and spectacular bridges along the way. The Airport Core project was considered evidence of Hong Kong's ability to overcome the limitations of its physical landscape and engineer its way into global modernity.

Starting with the construction boom in the 1970s, Hong Kong's identity is most visible in the myriad of transportation infrastructure projects that have effi-ciently produced a networked city—the punctual MTR system, modern airport, efficient port facilities, and massive arterial highways. Secondary networks of infrastructure such as pedestrian walkways, underpasses, and escalators blanket the city with such density that Hong Kong has been described by architects Adam Frampton, Jonathan Solomon, and Clara Wong as a 'city without ground'.[3] Indeed, these infrastructures not only obscure the ground plane, but also create ground through massive land reclamation projects that is the backbone of the city's economy. Therefore, Frampton et al. suggest, an analysis of Hong Kong's built environment defies traditional types of urban analysis such as the figure-ground diagram—since there is neither ground nor a clear figure. This valorisation of these engineering achievements coupled with a receding ground plane reinforces the notion that Hong Kong's infrastructural modernity is accomplished through highly efficient transportation spaces, ordered public facilities, and the active elimination of unregulated uses. This has also translated to a territorial-wide effort to regulate informal vendors that are common in most Asian cities, with the intention of eventually phasing out these aging entrepreneurs or relocating them to centralised facilities. The enforcement of such regulations has also become an important aspect of Hong Kong's modernity—its 'rule of law' and effective enforcement is an important distinction compared to its less modern neighbours of the region.

However, my weekly ramble from the Mid-Levels to the waterfront described in the preceding section depicts a different picture. I would argue that the inadequacy of the figure-ground diagram is not the lack of ground, but rather its amplified presence. Hong Kong's topography requires innovative engineering approaches to urban mobility, and the resulting roadway alignments are an index of its complexity. Hong Kong's unstable geology has been modified to accommodate roads and drainage, thus requiring extreme slope stabilisation techniques and maintenance for managing the risks of landslides. The same topographic constraints have motivated massive land reclamation projects to provide public space, infrastructure, and land supply. Rather than understanding Hong Kong's urban form as indifferent to its landscape, the specificities of the landscape are in fact driving these infrastructural solutions. In turn, these engineered strategies produce rich landscapes that defy conventional taxonomies or representation. I centre on the ground plane of Hong Kong, where its landscape shapes infrastructure but is in turn produced by infrastructure. Building on the work of two research projects located in overlooked urban landscapes, I question how the specificities of the terrain offer opportunities to redefine notions of the public realm and landscape architecture in the region.

This essay challenges two common assumptions about urban landscapes and uses Hong Kong as a case study to explore how landscape architects might reconceptualise our practices. The first project questions 'size'—how small is too small? Lu Xiaoxuan, Ivan Valin, and Susane Trumpf at the University of Hong Kong analyse *sitting out areas* formed by leftover spaces produced by infrastructure. Over 500 such landscapes are built and managed by the government and collectively play an important role in the public space network of the city. In *Interstitial Hong Kong*, a research project, exhibition, and tool for design outreach, the team asks whether 'largeness' is necessary for the planning and design of open space, and explores the potential that small interstitial spaces have ecologically and socially.

A second research effort in Benni Pong's master's thesis from Harvard's Graduate School of Design documents the public life of an industrial pier in real life and online. The Western District Public Cargo Working Area is a working waterfront by day and vibrant public space at night. There are also entire Instagram accounts dedicated to the space, and its social media presence creates a different temporal dimension. However, Pong demonstrates that the binary of formal and informal is inadequate in understanding the pier's role as a public space in Hong Kong, and suggests that we need to expand our concept of the public realm.

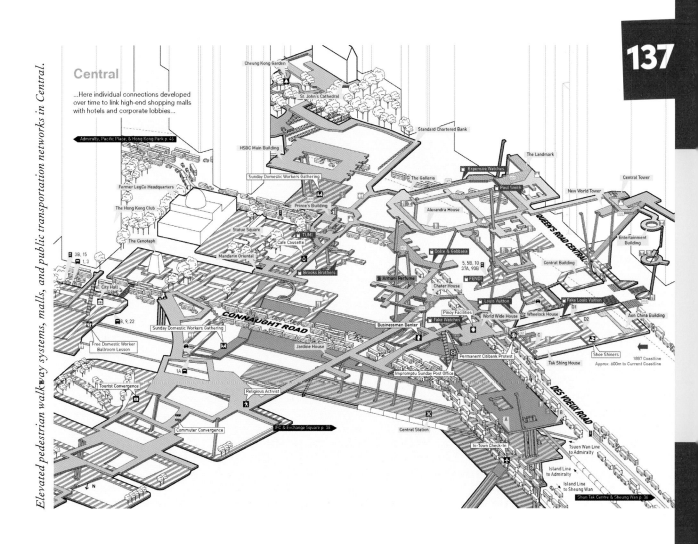

Elevated pedestrian walkway systems, malls, and public transportation networks in Central.

Interstitial Hong Kong

One of the enduring legacies of the North American theories of landscape urbanism is finding opportunities for design in interstitial spaces produced by processes of urbanisation and industrialisation. In a seminal piece advocating for landscape architects to reconsider how the post-industrial city informs a new practice, Alan Berger argues for finding value in 'drosscapes'—or what might conventionally be understood as wasted urban spaces.[4] Landscape practice, he suggests, must start by systematically analysing these drosscapes and designers must act as advocates—from the bottom-up—to incorporate these overlooked landscapes into the larger system of urban processes. However, this notion of a bottom-up approach to fully utilise interstitial spaces produced by infrastructure is irrelevant in the densely populated cities of Asia, and especially in Hong Kong. In fact, one finds that in Hong Kong there is already fierce competition for every scrap of open space in the city for both formal and informal uses. One example is the space underneath the Canal Road flyover in Causeway Bay. A large portion of the linear space is used as a major bus stop and transit interchange, while the other end of the space is built up with facilities such as public toilets. The remaining open space under the flyover is a known gathering space for traditional Chinese spiritualists and fortune tellers. Every inch of that landscape is fully utilised and supports a vibrant community with a wet market, and restaurants of varying size and fame.

Lu, Valin, and Trumpf explore a particular type of interstitial space that is produced in the 'cracks' of urban development, but that is also publicly managed. These sitting-out areas and rest gardens constitute the smallest unit of public open space that the Hong Kong government administers. Known colloquially as *saam kok see hang* (三角屎坑, 'three-cornered shit pit') in Cantonese, these landscapes are typically located at the intersections of transportation infrastructure and Hong Kong's steep terrain—land that is too small and too irregular for urban development or any form of revenue. Lu et. al. observe that these spaces

> oscillate between the exceptional and the mundane. In their abundance, the Sitting-out Areas are an exercise in repetition ... at the same time each Sitting-out Area fills a particular *interstice* in the city; each reflecting a unique solution to a specific adjacency, topography, microclimate, circulation, community, and history.[5]

Despite the standardised details and simplistic program of 'sitting and resting', each of these landscapes are an exercise in site specificity, and an index of its urban and landscape context.

The research team classifies these sitting out areas into five major categories: *rifts, misfits, gaps, lapses,* and *lacunas,* each contributing to Hong Kong's urbanism and ecology in specific ways. *Rifts* are found in geotechnically unstable areas that are prone to landslides and are intersected by massive drainage ways, engineered slopes, or other infrastructures to manage the ground. *Misfits* are the leftover spaces produced by Hong Kong's multi-layered infrastructure and act as connectors between the different infrastructure spaces. *Gaps* are incongruent spaces shaped by urban renewal processes and the drastic shifts in the scale of developments. *Lapses* are remnants of Hong Kong's historic heritage. And *lacunas* are intensely vegetated spaces that provide a burst of ecological energy in the city.

Understood collectively—all five categories and over 500 landscapes—Lu et al. suggest that these small invisible landscapes play an important role in the public life of Hong Kong. In contrast to the uneven distribution of larger public open spaces and the restricted access to privately owned public spaces in Hong Kong, these sitting-out areas are most widely and evenly distributed throughout the territory. As designated public spaces with dedicated maintenance, these interstitial spaces will endure despite constant urban evolution. They are mundane but also accessible; they have a simple program yet are extremely site specific; they offer a moment of pause in a city overwhelmed by its infrastructure; and as a network, they have the potential provide ecological value for a city that is known as *the* concrete jungle. As a research project and exhibition, Lu, Valin, and Trumpf propose a community process that would reclaim these valuable interstitial spaces and reimagine their role as instruments for spatial justice. The design potential of these formal public spaces as a network of 500 spaces, they argue, far surpasses the sixty urban parks, gardens, and squares that most landscape architects and planners consider as 'proper' open spaces in Hong Kong.[6]

Western District Public Cargo Working Area

In contrast to the tiny, overlooked, and mundane sitting-out areas distributed throughout Hong Kong, the Western District Public Cargo Working Area is a large open space with a spectacular view. It has a dedicated Instagram account by Italian photographer Pierfrancesco Celada (@insta_pier) and won the People Award from the Hong Kong Public Space Initiative's 2013 Public Space Awards programme.[7] The pier was in a *Transformers* movie, featured on the National Geographic website, and is a popular spot for wedding photos and tourists.[8] However, the Western District Public Cargo Working Area (a.k.a. the Instagram Pier) is *not* a public open space; in fact, it is literally a working pier with forklifts, trucks, and boats docking throughout the day. Public access to the pier is technically prohibited, and one enters the pier through an inconspicuous gate on the side—you might miss it if you weren't looking for it. And yet, in the evening hours, the pier is one of the most

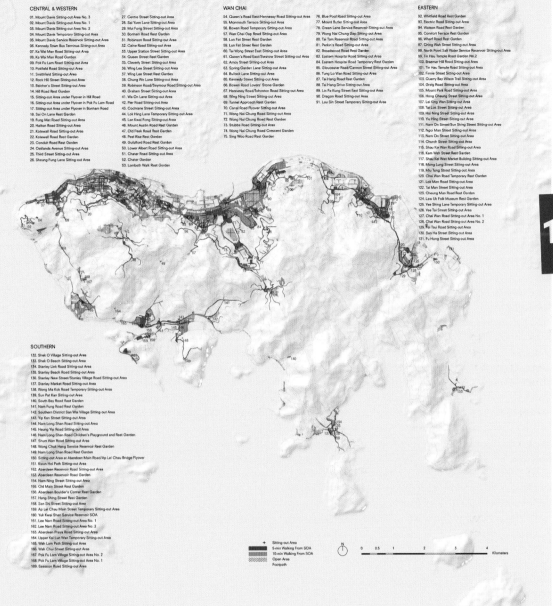

CENTRAL & WESTERN
01. Mount Davis Sitting-out Area No. 3
02. Mount Davis Sitting-out Area No. 1
03. Mount Davis Sitting-out Area No. 2
04. Mount Davis Temporary Sitting-out Area
05. Mount Davis Service Reservoir Sitting-out Area
06. Kennedy Town Bus Terminus Sitting-out Area
07. Ka Wai Man Road Sitting-out Area
08. Ka Wai Man Road Garden
09. Pok Fu Lam Road Sitting-out Area
10. Pokfield Road Sitting-out Area
11. Smithfield Sitting-out Area
12. Rock Hill Street Sitting-out Area
13. Belcher's Street Sitting-out Area
14. Hill Road Rest Garden
15. Sitting-out Area under Flyover in Hill Road
16. Sitting-out Area under Flyover in Pok Fu Lam Road
17. Sitting-out Area under Flyover in Bonham Road
18. Sai On Lane Rest Garden
19. Fung Mat Road Sitting-out Area
20. Hatton Road Sitting-out Area
21. Kotewall Road Sitting-out Area
22. Kotewall Road Rest Garden
23. Conduit Road Rest Garden
24. Oaklands Avenue Sitting-out Area
25. Third Street Sitting-out Area
26. Sheung Fung Lane Sitting-out Area

27. Centre Street Sitting-out Area
28. Sai Yuen Lane Sitting-out Area
29. Mui Fong Street Sitting-out Area
30. Bonham Road Rest Garden
31. Robinson Road Sitting-out Area
32. Caine Road Sitting-out Area
33. Upper Station Street Sitting-out Area
34. Queen Street Rest Garden
35. Cleverly Street Sitting-out Area
36. Wing Lee Street Sitting-out Area
37. Wing Lee Street Rest Garden
38. Chung Wo Lane Sitting-out Area
39. Robinson Road/Seymour Road Sitting-out Area
40. Graham Street Sitting-out Area
41. Wa On Lane Sitting-out Area
42. Pier Road Sitting-out Area
43. Cochrane Street Sitting-out Area
44. Lok Hing Lane Temporary Sitting-out Area
45. Lan Kwai Fong Sitting-out Area
46. Mount Austin Road Rest Garden
47. Old Peak Road Rest Garden
48. Peel Rise Rest Garden
49. Guildford Road Rest Garden
50. Lower Albert Road Rest Garden
51. Chater Road Sitting-out Area
52. Chater Garden
53. Lambeth Walk Rest Garden

WAN CHAI
54. Queen's Road East/Hennessy Road Sitting-out Area
55. Monmouth Terrace Sitting-out Area
56. Bowen Road Temporary Sitting-out Area
57. Wan Chai Gap Road Sitting-out Area
58. Lun Fat Street Rest Garden
59. Lun Fat Street Rest Garden
60. Tai Wong Street East Sitting-out Area
61. Queen's Road East/Swatow Street Sitting-out Area
62. Amoy Street Sitting-out Area
63. Spring Garden Lane Sitting-out Area
64. Bullock Lane Sitting-out Area
65. Kennedy Street Sitting-out Area
66. Bowen Road Lovers' Stone Garden
67. Hennessy Road/Johnston Road Sitting-out Area
68. Wing Ning Street Sitting-out Area
69. Tunnel Approach Rest Garden
70. Canal Road Flyover Sitting-out Area
71. Wong Nai Chung Road Sitting-out Area
72. Wong Nai Chung Road Rest Garden
73. Stubbs Road Sitting-out Area
74. Wong Nai Chung Road Crescent Garden
75. Sing Woo Road Rest Garden

76. Blue Pool Road Sitting-out Area
77. Mount Butler Sitting-out Area
78. Green Lane Service Reservoir Sitting-out Area
79. Wong Nai Chung Gap Sitting-out Area
80. Tai Tam Reservoir Road Sitting-out Area
81. Perkin's Road Sitting-out Area
82. Broadwood Road Rest Garden
83. Eastern Hospital Road Sitting-out Area
84. Eastern Hospital Road Temporary Rest Garden
85. Gloucester Road/Cannon Street Sitting-out Area
86. Tung Lo Wan Road Sitting-out Area
87. Tai Hang Road Rest Garden
88. Tai Hang Drive Sitting-out Area
89. Lin Fa Kung Street Sitting-out Area
90. Dragon Road Sitting-out Area
91. Lau Sin Street Temporary Sitting-out Area

EASTERN
92. Whitfield Road Rest Garden
93. Electric Road Sitting-out Area
94. Watson Road Rest Garden
95. Comfort Terrace Rest Garden
96. Wharf Road Rest Garden
97. Ching Wah Street Sitting-out Area
98. North Point Salt Water Service Reservoir Sitting-out Area
99. Tin Hau Temple Road Garden No.2
100. Braemar Hill Road Sitting-out Area
101. Tin Hau Temple Road Sitting-out Area
102. Finnie Street Sitting-out Area
103. Quarry Bay Wilson Trail Sitting-out Area
104. Greig Road Sitting-out Area
105. Mount Parker Road Sitting-out Area
106. Hong Cheung Street Sitting-out Area
107. Lei King Wan Sitting-out Area
108. Tai Lok Street Sitting-out Area
109. Hoi Ning Street Sitting-out Area
110. Yiu Hing Street Sitting-out Area
111. Nam On Street/Sun Shing Street Sitting-out Area
112. Ngoi Man Street Sitting-out Area
113. Nam On Street Sitting-out Area
114. Church Street Sitting-out Area
115. Shau Kei Wan Sitting-out Area
116. Kam Wah Street Rest Garden
117. Shau Kei Wan Market Building Sitting-out Area
118. Mong Lung Street Sitting-out Area
119. Miu Tung Street Sitting-out Area
120. Chai Wan Road Temporary Rest Garden
121. Lok Man Road Sitting-out Area
122. Tai Man Street Sitting-out Area
123. Cheung Man Road Rest Garden
124. Law Uk Folk Museum Rest Garden
125. Yee Shing Lane Temporary Sitting-out Area
126. Yee Tai Street Sitting-out Area
127. Chai Wan Road Sitting-out Area No. 1
128. Chai Wan Road Sitting-out Area No. 2
129. Fei Tsui Road Sitting-out Area
130. San Ha Street Sitting-out Area
131. Fu Hong Street Sitting-out Area

SOUTHERN
132. Shek O Village Sitting-out Area
133. Shek O Beach Sitting-out Area
134. Stanley Link Road Sitting-out Area
135. Stanley Beach Road Sitting-out Area
136. Stanley New Street/Stanley Village Road Sitting-out Area
137. Stanley Market Road Sitting-out Area
138. Wong Ma Kok Road Temporary Sitting-out Area
139. Sun Pat Kan Sitting-out Area
140. South Bay Road Rest Garden
141. Nam Fung Road Rest Garden
142. Southern District San Wai Village Sitting-out Area
143. Yip Kan Street Sitting-out Area
144. Nam Long Shan Road Sitting-out Area
145. Heung Yip Road Sitting-out Area
146. Nam Long Shan Road Children's Playground and Rest Garden
147. Shum Wan Road Sitting-out Area
148. Wong Chuk Hang Service Reservoir Rest Garden
149. Nam Long Shan Road Rest Garden
150. Sitting-out Area at Aberdeen Main Road/Ap Lei Chau Bridge Flyover
151. Kwun Hoi Path Sitting-out Area
152. Aberdeen Reservoir Road Sitting-out Area
153. Aberdeen Reservoir Road Garden
154. Nam Ning Street Sitting-out Area
155. Old Main Street Rest Garden
156. Aberdeen Boulder's Corner Rest Garden
157. Hung Shing Street Rest Garden
158. San Shi Street Sitting-out Area
159. Ap Lei Chau Main Street Temporary Sitting-out Area
160. Yuk Kwai Shan Service Reservoir SOA
161. Lee Nam Road Sitting-out Area No. 1
162. Lee Nam Road Sitting-out Area No. 2
163. Aberdeen Praya Road Sitting-out Area
164. Upper Kai Lun Wan Temporary Sitting-out Area
165. Wah Lam Path Sitting-out Area
166. Wah Chui Street Sitting-out Area
167. Pok Fu Lam Village Sitting-out Area No. 2
168. Pok Fu Lam Village Sitting-out Area No. 1
169. Sassoon Road Sitting-out Area

+ Sitting-out Area
5-min Walking From SOA
10-min Walking From SOA
Open Area
Footpath

0 0.5 1 2 3 4 Kilometers

Accessibility of sitting-out areas and rest gardens on Hong Kong Island.

interesting and vibrant public spaces in Hong Kong with skateboarders and BMXers testing tricks, group dancers competing for space, squid fishing during spring and summer, and over-excited dogs and their walkers racing along the waterfront.

In his ethnographic study of the pier, landscape architect Benni Pong analyses the paradox of how a working industrial pier with restricted access can co-exist as a leisure landscape with international appeal.[9] He arrives at a surprising conclusion that in fact this co-existance relies on clearly articulated warnings and disclaimers for public safety by the authorities that operate the pier and a self-regulating public with an understanding that public access is a privilege and not a right. A 'tacit agreement' of sorts emerges between the two entities where the authorities turn a blind eye to public access as long as there are no known illicit activities or dangerous actions that occur within the space. In turn, the public is careful not to create a nuisance for the operating authorities and despite the lack of railings along the pier's edge, has not experienced any major accidents. And thus, this spectacular space—which would not pass regulatory muster—persists as one of the most successful public landscapes in Hong Kong. Pong proposes that perhaps such 'unplanned' landscapes in the city have greater public value than the highly regulated and designed public open spaces maintained and operated by the government. It is also important to note that Pong's argument poses a challenge to the tropes of formal and informal urbanism—conventional notions of urban informality typically describe the extra-legal privatisation of public goods, but here we see a private space appropriated for public uses. In addition, the 'tacit agreement' requires a level of mutual trust between the management authorities and the public in how the pier continues to function.

The temporal arrangement between the 'working' times of the pier and its recreational function has not gone unnoticed. One of the greatest obstacles in designing a continuous waterfront landscape along Victoria Harbour is its vital function as a working waterfront. In 2013, the District Council received a large sum of money for a 'signature project scheme' and began work on a new waterfront park adjacent to the Western District Public Cargo Working Area. The plan repurposed four existing piers that serviced a major wholesale food market into a new public waterfront park with playgrounds, boat access, and references to its industrial past. However, one working pier was retained for the wholesale food market and through traffic is temporarily closed off to public access during designated times in the evening when goods are delivered by boat. The official layering of different temporal functions for this new waterfront landscape signals a breakthrough in how designers and planners conceive of flexible and multiple functions of space and a departure from rigid programming and the dilemma of managing 'incompatible' land uses that characterise modernist urban planning.

Forming a Tacit Public Realm

The temporal shifts and 'tacit agreements' observed at the Western District Public Cargo Working Area is not a unique phenomenon. One could argue that the Sunday gatherings of domestic helpers throughout public spaces in Hong Kong is also a form of tacit agreement, an unspoken social contract between the affluent residents of Hong Kong and their invisible counterparts. There are currently approximately 390,000 foreign domestic helpers in Hong Kong representing roughly 10 per cent of its working population.[10] According to government regulations, domestic helpers are entitled to time off on Sundays and other public holidays, thus leaving a large portion of Hong Kong's population seeking social spaces outside of their workplaces/homes. On Sundays, for example, Filipino domestic helpers congregate in Central while Indonesian helpers gather in Causeway Bay near Victoria Park. The locations of these gatherings are an index of sorts of the public spaces of Hong Kong. In Central, Filipinas occupy the shaded open space underneath the HSBC building since it is a designated privately-owned public open space while others appropriate the linear public footbridges that crisscross the central business district. Informal economies flourish on Sundays in these districts and the normally sombre and formal CBD is transformed, for one day a week, into a large living room for Filipino culture.

These 'tacit agreements' also blur the boundaries between formal and informal urban activities since they are contingent on clear rules and regulations and a social contract for selective enforcement. Architect Jonathan Solomon suggests the term 'aformal' as an alternative to describe the haphazard laisser-faire approach to elevated walkways in Central, since no master plan officially exists. The walkways are the result of opportunistic endeavours by both the public and the private sector, and to a certain extent these pedestrian networks are an unplanned collaboration between the two.[11] Similarly, the interstitial spaces that Lu, Valin, and Trumpf have documented are a pragmatic government attempt to utilise its land, and despite the fact that their own open space accounting does not include these small leftover spaces, they have

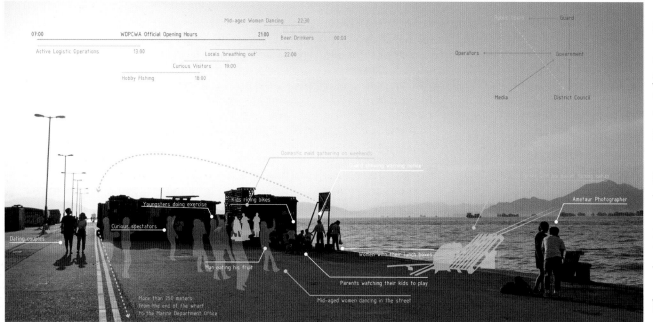

Observed activities on the Western District Public Cargo Pier.

unintentionally created a network of landscapes that service the public perhaps even more effectively. However, the concept of a 'tacit agreement'—an unspoken social contract—is a much more useful framework to understand the various landscape practices in Hong Kong. It draws attention to a relationship between the planned and unplanned public spaces of the city, and rather than dismissing the agency of design, it points to the opportunities designers could potentially utilise in negotiating the social dynamics and the production of the public realm.

At the time writing, the familiar scenes along my weekly stroll are no longer the same. The occupation of these infrastructural spaces has become important battlegrounds for the 2019/20 pro-democracy protests. In Hong Kong, linear processions from Victoria Park were the traditional realm of political protest instead of the nodal spaces that characterise other protests such as Tahrir Square in Cairo or Zuccotti Park in New York City. Organisers estimated upwards of two million people participated at the peak pro-democracy marches. The use of infrastructure space for protest is not unique to Hong Kong. The 2013/14 Thai protests in Bangkok constructed barricades and blocked traffic on major arterial roads to demand political reform, and in 2008 Bangkok's Suvarnabhumi Airport was also shut down.[12] However, one of the most significant turns in the 2019/20 Hong Kong protests was an erosion of trust in Hong Kong's public authorities from a mostly benevolent and law-abiding entity to one with sinister objectives[13]—the tacit agreement of how public spaces were governed and used was disrupted.

This loss of mutual trust resulted in a seismic shift in the political and symbolic meanings of Hong Kong's modern infrastructure and consequently produced a different form of 'infrastructural publics'. Protest tactics have shifted from organised marches to dispersed uprisings coordinated through encrypted social media platforms. Rather than a symbol of triumphant modernity, the Hong Kong International Airport is now understood as a site of state control and authority. In August 2019, protestors occupied the airport for two days and all departing flights were cancelled for a day. In addition, Airport express and vehicular traffic access to the airport were blocked by protestors. Arriving passengers walked five kilometres for alternative transportation into the city. Public sentiments towards the MTR system—the epitome of Hong Kong's efficiency and convenience—also changed drastically. For example, protestors stopped using the ubiquitous mass transit smart cards, in order to maintain anonymity, fearing that authorities would be able to use the data to track down participants. Further distrust in the MTR system was sowed with videos of the police storming the Prince Edward subway station spraying pepper spray in enclosed areas, and beating protestors with batons in late August. The MTR management exasperated this sentiment by bypassing certain stations on protest days. When the Hong Kong government decided to enforce a ban on face masks—a make-shift uniform for protestors—as part of an emergency law in early October, the MTR was firmly considered an instrument of the government and protestors began to vandalise MTR infrastructure throughout the territory. The MTR suspended all of its operations for the first time in its forty-year history and resumed limited services in the next few days.[14]

I returned to Hong Kong in January 2020 for a brief visit and encountered a vastly different city than what I have described in the opening paragraphs. From conversations with friends and family, I learned that many Hong Kongers now opt to take the bus instead of the MTR despite heavy traffic; a pregnant friend now avoids known protest areas and the MTR to minimise exposure to teargas residue; daily life is as usual on weekdays but most residents now avoid going out and about the city on weekends or holidays. However, perhaps one of the most pronounced shifts was the perception of what spaces were considered part of the public realm. With the MTR and other government-owned spaces under government control, privately-owned public spaces have emerged for a short time as an unlikely space of refuge for protestors, especially as they maintain their own privatised security forces and have refused police entry without legal grounds.[15] The vast domestic helper population has also had to seek out alternative public spaces for their weekly day off, and I observed much greater use of the overlooked sitting-out areas during my Sunday afternoon stroll around the city. Given the unpredictable nature of the weekend protests, the dispersed network of small spaces was a pragmatic alternative to travelling to centralised sites far from their employers' homes.

At this time, it is not feasible to generalise how recent protests have reshaped the infrastructural publics of Hong Kong with such fragmented observations and anecdotal evidence. Nor is it possible to predict the future of Hong Kong's public landscapes with the unresolved political conflicts. Rebuilding mutual respect amongst the various fractions in Hong Kong that would then transform into the types of productive 'tacit agreements' we have observed in the public realm will take an extraordinary amount of time and effort. However, it has become clear that the programmatic flexibility of landscapes of Hong Kong have in different times and circumstances served many social groups and functions of the city, and despite the political uncertainties, remain an important space of hope for the future of the city. ∎

141

Instagram Pier

The Western District Public Cargo Working Area is one of Hong Kong's most vibrant spaces. Public access is technically prohibited, yet this does not deter a wide range of activities from occurring around the actions of a working pier. The space is commonly referred to as Instagram Pier in reference to a dedicated Instagram account maintained by Italian photographer Pierfrancesco Celada (@insta_pier).

143

A Design Practice of Public Advocacy

Sidh Sintusingha

Escaping the economic downturn in Thailand resulting from the 1997 financial meltdown, the three Shma directors—Namchai Saensupha, Prapan Napawongdee, and Yossapon Boonsom, as fresh Chulalongkorn graduates—started their careers in Singapore.[1] This is a well-trodden path for Southeast Asian designers seeking international experience and better pay. The five to seven years spent working on mainly high-end residential and hospitality projects across Asia were critical formative years. This background accounts for the designers' outlook and confidence to operate internationally. Their careers overlapped for a time at Cicada Landscape Architects. Yossapon and Prapan were classmates who have worked together throughout (apart from when Yossapon undertook a master's degree at Domus), while Namchai is a couple of years their senior. They were particularly inspired and influenced by how Singapore developed from a Garden City to 'city in a garden'. Their exposure to Singaporean projects revealed how this green vision was achieved and integrated into urban developments through government regulations, policies, and incentives.

Shma was established and registered in 2007 when they were offered a project in Phuket by a Singaporean architect looking for landscape architects familiar with Singaporean ways of working, but with knowledge of the local culture and conditions. It was a timely opportunity as they had accumulated enough experience and 'always wanted to go home to help develop Thailand'. Yossapon was on his own at first to suss out the Thai market as, being away for a long time, they had no clients or connections. Shma was on firmer footing once they linked up with one of their undergraduate classmates who had joined a big local developer since, according to Yossapon, the Thai market is commercially dominated and it is only in the last decade that the government and private sector have begun to invest in public spaces.

There were a lot of adjustments as the Singaporean style of working is very efficient, very clearly 'a result-driven way of managing the project', while 'in Thailand one is not sure what is going to happen'. As the government has no clear visions, Shma found it 'harder to try something new as people were sceptical.

We needed to work harder to get the standard we want [to benefit society]', as Yossapon comments. While it was a steep learning curve, they found clients were willing to listen, to have dialogues and even lead on some issues. Yossapon and Prapan observe that 'we learnt from Singapore to be proactive—to question to [search] for new possibilities' and 'once we establish a mutual understanding [with the client] this can lead to a win-win situation for the developer, the public, and the environment'.

They noted that Thai policy is not supportive of public space creation but favours commercially driven developments, dominated by a few big players. Moreover, fees for government projects are very low. While the Shma directors would like the Thai government agencies to emulate their Singaporean counterpart, their objective to deliver comparable end-products but through bottom-up improvisations and explorative speculations often with private clients reveals an innovative, lateral thinking practice that demands a deeper engagement with Thai culture. When questioned on whether they were any particular watershed clients, projects, or events, Prapan replies that it was more about persistence, sticking to 'our beliefs to deliver the best outcome in each situation', and that media recognition was important encouragement. While Namchai notes that even today they struggle to get public projects, Shma have pushed the public and nature/social agenda since their early private projects such as Life@Ladprao 18 (published in *Landezine*).[2] From these small steps, and the fact they strategically set out to be an international firm, they have gained better opportunities and media exposure.

What is Shma's agenda? Ethically or socially? What drives their work?

This was not defined from the outset but as clients were drawn to Shma for their 'positivity' it has become more apparent. Yossapon notes it was not about 'standing out' adding that 'our projects merge into everyday life—we didn't want to force people into our way.' A sales gallery for Sansiri built in 2011 is a key project for setting Shma's 'tone'.[3] The clients wanted a little garden space but Shma questioned the limited landscape brief and instead proposed a green wall that envelops the building. 'We wanted a total environment and the client says yes ... A visual landmark would be beneficial to the building and city.' Here they broke disciplinary barriers to achieve 'what is best for the project'. Importantly, it was also one of their first projects to get international media exposure. Other important early work includes a shopping mall piazza at Chiang Rai,[4] a privately owned public space that expresses the local culture and natural landform, and their 'Bird Wave Bridge'[5] at Queen Sirikit Park in Bangkok (opened in 2016) which gained international recognition through an IFLA ASIA-PAC Award of Excellence.

Shma admits that it is hard to nominate their best project or specialisation. 'We don't believe in type. We think of ideas and problems and innovation in any job. Otherwise it will limit our thinking', comments Prapan. In other words, a type leads to the same approach. Hence Shma projects inform one another which lends to their characteristic pluralism.

Moreover, Shma is one of the first landscape architecture firms in Thailand to advocate for public agendas through direct communication with the public via workshops, lectures, and exhibitions. For example, since 2013 they have been campaigning for a park on ninety-six hectares of prime land at Makkasan owned by the State Railway of Thailand.[6] In effect, Shma play the role of public advocates, conversing with broader society. Filling a gap in Thai practice, this is a rare approach where a designer from the private sector has a strong public voice. This role allows Shma to 'chase their dreams'.

Is there a clear strategy on how to play this role? How is the firm specifically managed?

There's 'no smart strategy. We just do and say what we think is right', according to Namchai. Citing a very high benchmark (even for the standards of developed countries) for their practice, Namchai points out that Singapore 'has visions for the next fifty years ... in terms of green and public spaces' and hence, as designers, they know 'what can be done'. Elaborating further Yossapon states that in the beginning they 'were just responding to what the government does' but felt the need to move beyond that and to become relevant domestically and internationally. They entered competitions and when Thailand was hit with the catastrophic flood in 2011, Shma put together a vision for Ayutthaya and the Chao Phraya River floodplain.[7]

Shma's ongoing resistance to the government's Chao Phraya River Promenade project (see p. 47) attracted public attention to their role. Although working against the government could affect their business, they also found that it could lead to new possibilities such as the establishment of Shma Soen.

Shma Soen was strategically created as a separate company to address the demand in both public and private realms for community-based projects and participatory design process. Prapan adds: 'We wanted to make it a social enterprise but the government at that time did not have this category that pays less tax.' Hence they kept the firm size quite small so they can be more flexible. Yossapon notes that this arrangement allowed them to be more strategic in their public conversation and intervention, as they 'can't spend too much time as it affects our cash flow.'

Looking at their projects, Shma has an international outlook and language while Shma Soen is very local and engages with and extends Thai typologies and mines traditional practices. The temple ground renovation project is a perfect example.[8] Most Thais associate temple grounds as the original ubiquitous, multi-purpose open space in Thai settlements that, with modernisation, was reduced to hard-surface car parks. Their work here has potential to be up-scaled to the over 30,000 temples around the country. The unrealised Sathorn project for the Bangkok Metropolitan Administration is a robust synthesis of 'Thai' transport typologies from the past of *khlongs* to the present of Skytrains.[9] Together both firms are highly versatile with tactics of engagement and communication with different audiences and stakeholders, from local to international.

Moreover, Shma leverages with academic engagements or design week activities. They set aside a budget to seek funding, rather than just wait for clients, whether from public bodies like the Thai Health Promotion Foundation or through corporate social responsibility (CSR) projects with private clients. They teach at various Thai universities, involving students in community projects. Exploiting the new trend where developers who have a few projects in a neighbourhood are willing to improve public areas beyond their developments, Shma encourage less big walls and gates, pushing for careful transitions between public and private domains.

Yossapon and Prapan define this role as the 'middle platform' linking the private sector and government to spatially inform each other. 'Good things can happen in between' states Prapan. Perhaps this is the characteristic of their practice—a Thai way with lots of improvisation and learning on the go.

Are other landscape firms doing this?

'We are not successful yet!' replies Yossapon, laughing. Prapan adds: 'and no matter what, this kind of work will never get the kind of profit [as commercial work]—so you have to have your heart in it.' There's also more pressure and steps than conventional practice such as 'community intervention, workshops, exhibitions. We cannot control anything so we need other skills than normal practice.' Being active in the Friends of the River expanded their public network and reinforced their middle-platform role. Yossapon comments: 'Sometimes government is right, sometime wrong. Sometimes NGOs are right but can also be

145

wrong. Sometimes developers could be the good guys. We are in a good position to sit in between.'

As Thai public space is so fluid—always changing through multiple agents—Shma exploits and leverages their landscape architecture spatio-temporal skills, which suit the context quite well. There are precedents in the decades-old Thai community architecture movement, focused on social housing that has been successfully synthesised into the government-supported Baan Mankong project, a recognised international model.[10] This synergy with government seems to be what Shma seeks.

Opportunities to achieve that have emerged with Namchai elected as the president of Thai Association of Landscape Architects (TALA). Namchai states that every TALA president's agenda is to change the law, which is more difficult than advocating work. 'We know people in government who think like us but regulations are very restrictive and prevent change. For instance, the public park department of Bangkok cannot hire private designers and they have only two landscape architects.' According to Yossapon, more support from the government is needed to improve the whole landscape industry, especially for landscape architects' deeper involvement in infrastructure planning and development such as water management. The government needs to lead and set incentives for developers and the landscape industry will follow with research and innovation.

How supportive are the rest of the profession? The next generation?

'The previous generation have been [advocating] but in a different context as the profession barely existed.'[11] Yossapon adds that 'we are adding new tools but following the earlier generation.' Perhaps a critical gap is that there's no proper narrative on the profession in Thailand to define roles and direction. 'For the newer generation, they are interested in the public … People who join us want to do both private and public projects', observes Prapan.

'The timing is right, the arrival of social network. People see more things and are more aware of their rights', states Namchai. Prapan adds that 'green' stories can sell to the consumers. In condominium developments, developers no longer want to cut down trees and increasingly source their trees responsibly. Namchai credits TALA as being instrumental in the changing perception and practices of tree farms and nurseries, demonstrating that good practices are more profitable than transplanting or cutting down trees. In just the past five years there are shifts in values that prioritises landscape architecture, 'There are lots of talk about food security, urban farming, urban forests'.

Comments on the regional picture?

Regionally, Thai architects and landscape architects are quite well known. 'More overseas developers are contacting Thai designers, especially Chinese developers. They like the sensitivity in Thai design', states Prapan, adding that 'They come to visit us every month. We have projects in China which is important as their government understand the green issue following Singaporean ideas—so it is easy to push the agenda.' Shma recently won a competition in Singapore, have completed or are doing projects in India, Indonesia, and Hong Kong—in fact the proportion of overseas projects is growing, in the context of a sluggish Thai market.

Does the regional network, dialogue exist?

It exists through IFLA conferences—but there's a gap within practices on an everyday level. Yossapon notes that the Beijing meeting (to develop this book) was a rare moment outside of a conference to 'look back, look forward' about the regional: 'I want that conversation to keep growing.' They would like to collaborate with their Asian colleagues, as there are shared problems. 'We can improve the region and not just country or each city.' The collaboration needs to go beyond inspiring rhetoric and should 'trigger something' to effect changes.

Namchai notes that the conversation has to extend beyond the profession. In Singapore everyone is aware of the government's vision in the media, the news, entertainment; 'the taxi-driver is aware of the new jogging network.' Design competitions are part of the public conversation unlike in Thailand where 'the government seems concerned about what they don't want to have. We don't have the openness in our society and it's a reason why conversations about the landscape, not only in Thailand but in the region, are never spread out to society.'

In fact, Singapore shares the paternalistic government model with China and the relative higher public trust that the state will deliver urban green spaces. In the polarising (more) democratic Thai system, consensus is increasingly impossible. Given this, Shma isn't giving themselves enough credit in terms of the wickedness of the conditions that they are addressing in Thailand and the innovative resilience that their activities entail. What is also worth mentioning is that Shma's employee benefits are well beyond Thai legal requirements.[12] This continues a practice of Thai-style patronage and benevolent capitalism and reflects a consistency between the care of their own staff and of society at large. Shma is certainly a firm to keep an eye on, not only for their significant achievements and alternative practices but also their unrelenting ambitions for the landscape architecture discipline. ■

Reclaiming Bangkok's Open Space

The first floating park prototype.

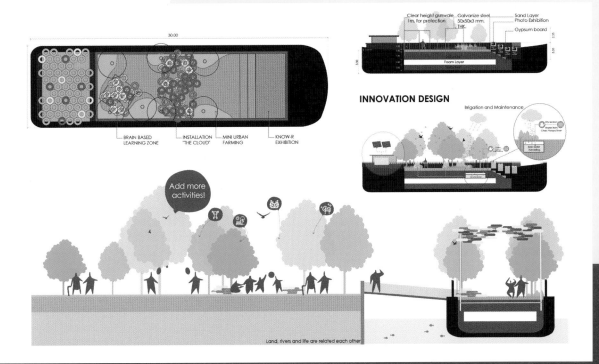

Currently Bangkok offers just six square metres of green space per person—far lower than the WHO's standard of nine square metres. With an absence of sustainable planning, Bangkok has developed with few open space networks. Expressways for cars, railway corridors, and canals dissect the city creating social and environmental issues and disconnecting important districts. Urban growth lacks connections with nature. Bangkok-based landscape architects Shma have developed a series of strategies and installations to demonstrate to government, developers, and communities how Bangkok's sustainability and citizens' quality of life can be improved through the insertion of new open space opportunities.

Floating Park

Rethinking the role of the Chao Phraya River, the precious ecological and cultural treasure of Bangkok, offers an important way to provide more green space. In the past, communities depended on the Chao Phraya River for transport and water agriculture. Now the river's value has been diminished, replaced by rapid modernisation, roads, and cars. The Floating Park aims to introduce public space along this large nature corridor, along with reconnecting people back to the river through activation activities such as a recreational waterfront park, playground, sports venue, and urban farming.

The first prototype was developed for Bangkok Design Week 2018. An ordinary sand barge boat was filled with top soil and trees to form a temporary floating park. Various festive activities were held in this new floating space including a brain-based learning playground for children, a mini urban farm that showcased food production, and art installations. In 2019, a second prototype, the Innovative Floating Park, was proposed for Bangkok Design Week, which involved a floating structure from SCG (Siam Cement Group) and the use of solar cells. This model returns green space back to the city while incorporating additional functions of electricity production and planting for water treatment.

A Ten-Kilometre Park

In 2019, Shma proposed the Bangkok Green Link, an ambitious vision to revitalise Bangkok's infrastructure through a linked green network connecting districts across the city. Shma mapped over fifty-eight kilometres of potentially networked public space emerging from the regeneration of canals and railway corridors, spaces under expressways and sky walkway corridors, and existing sidewalks. The ten-kilometre green corridor forms part of the outer ring strategy and cuts an almost straight line through the city. It relinks existing mass transit systems of car, boat, and rail, along with introducing alternative routes for cycling and walking to form an expansive urban promenade. New green ecological corridors link public parks while recreational activities are inserted into 'canal parks' proposed for abandoned space under highways. Shma hope that their interconnected vision will activate local economic growth, improve living standards, and act as a catalyst for community-based development.

149

Spaces under transport corridors come alive.

Transformative Forces

Heike Rahmann Asia's drive for modernity has dramatically transformed societies and places, exchanging agrarian traditions for urban-centred economies. Economic market pressures have been influential in shifting self-governing regions into an increasing global dependency and competitiveness. In this context, international designers arriving in Asia in the late twentieth century have contributed to the shaping of urban and rural landscapes under the prospects of modernity and globalisation. Conversely, in the twenty-first century Asian designers are beginning to introduce Asian conceptions of space and systems into the global realm. Simultaneously, government-driven large-scale infrastructure such as China's Belt and Road Initiative have national and trans-national impact, repositioning foreign policy and economic strategies across the region.

Yet, as sociologist Hartmut Rosa highlights in *Social Acceleration: A New Theory of Modernity*, other forces, beyond the control of governments and designers, also influence growth dynamics and transformative processes.[1] Rosa argues that as we set our world in motion, constantly shaping and reshaping our physical surroundings by changing the hardware and software, both the structure and culture of our institutions and practices are accompanied by the 'shrinking of the present', leading to an increasing disjunction between the rate of change and the experience of time. The drivers that inform this social acceleration are the modern (capitalist) society—which can only reproduce itself through growth, innovation, and speed—as well as the desynchronisation of nature and social life, politics, and economics. Modern society, Rosa argues, is anxious that the world will turn dead and silent, leading to alienation. As such he 'considers modernity in terms of a broken promise: the very technology and social revolutions that were supposed to lead to an increase in autonomy are now becoming increasingly oppressive.'[2]

This perspective is exemplified by Japan, where years of excessive growth has hollowed society leading to a lack of motivation and engagement in social activities, accompanied by social withdrawl, especially among young men. In its exteme form, the *hikikomori* (literally: pulling inward or shutting in, describing people who withdraw from society) emerged in the 1970s and is now considered a 'silent epidemic'.[3] Additionally, Japan's aging population and decreasing birth rate have slowly changed societal demographics over the past thirty years. Many scholars argue that Japan requires a new 'openness', to counter this withdrawl from international experiences, particularly amongst young people, shifting from a 'Tokukawa shogunate's policy of sakoku (or "closed country"),' to instead choose a new Meiji-era, outward-looking approach for engaging with the world.[4]

Natural disasters present a further powerful transformative force outside the control of the nation-state. The Asia-Pacific region is considered the most disaster-prone region in the world. Earthquakes, tsunamis, typhoons, flooding, landslides, volcanic eruption, and drought affect millions of people each year. Between 1970 and 2014, six billion people in Asia and the Pacific were affected by natural disasters, including 'the death of over 2 million people', which equates to 56.6 per cent of natural disaster fatalities globally.[5] The economic losses associated with natural disasters have long-term community impacts and highlight significant economic inequalities across the region, along with major discrepencies in disaster preparedness. A 2015 UN report stressed the importance of building disaster resilience as 'a necessary condition for protecting the region's growth prospects'.[6] It highlights how valuable infrastructure and assets 'are increasingly located on land exposed to hazards due to a lack of available space and rapid development', establishing considerible economic risk.[7]

The Great East Japan Earthquake in March 2011 and its catastrophic damage to the Fukushima Daiichi Nuclear Power Plant demonstrates this vulnerability, impacting on critical national infrastructure along with an already exposed Japanese society. As Dominic Barton, global managing director of McKinsey & Company observed, the disaster highlighted two 'emergencies' for Japan: first, rebuilding the disaster-struck Tohoku region, second, and less obvious, rebuilding the country's long-declining society and economy.[8] Many citizens remain sceptical about the ability of political leaders 'who have repeatedly failed' to address the weaknesses of Japanese society.[9] This fear was heightened by the national government's heavy-handed, engineering-led reconstruction, post March 2011, which centred on the construction of monumental seawalls. Concrete infrastructure, covering over four hundred kilometres of coastline (including sensitive national parks and fishing grounds) now separates communities from the ocean, disrupting cultural connections with the sea as well as necessary ecological water and nutient flows. Failing to acknowledge ecological or cultural engagement, this hard-engineering approach to recovery left little room for the valuable insights of landscape architects. ▶

▶ At the local level Asian communities have shown remarkable resilience in disaster recovery. Researchers studying the link between religion and mental health following the 2004 tsunami in Southeast Asia found that in countries where Buddhism is widely practised, such as Sri Lanka and Thailand, communities have developed valuable coping strategies for the multiple traumas inflicted by the natural disaster. These include accepting the events as reflections of transientness and change aligned with the Buddhist concept of impermanence, as well as the practice of mindfulness to deal with anxiety and compassion to deal with guilt.[10]

The acceptance of life cycles guided by natural forces that cannot be controlled by humans forms an important aspect in the lives of many communities, shaping a different relationship to convenience and technology. These perspectives were explored in the 2012 exhibition *Tema Hima: The Art of Living in Tohoku* presented by the 2121 Design Sight museum in Tokyo, which documented the creative practices and lifestyle of craftsmen, farmers, and studios, along with the attitudes, determination, and vernacular knowledge of people living and working in the disaster-struck region. *Tema hima* (literally: time and effort) introduced the 'process of making things with much care and time that contemporary society, with its tendency to be pragmatic, tends to forget'.[11] As industrial designer and curator Naoto Fukasawa reflects:

> All of these are the textures and the beating rhythm of life in Tohoku, woven together by nature and the working hands of man. These people build with gratitude on the powers of nature and the seasons as one of their efficient tools and store them as daily blessings. This gentle yet endless cycle defines the pace of the Tohoku people. This pace, honed through years of experience living in harmony with nature, synchronizes with their ecological ways without destruction. Making things through TEMA HIMA is a constant cycle of 'preparation.' There is never an end nor completion. However, the rhythm created by TEMA HIMA quietly soothes the pace of today's people who have started losing sight of the future. [12]

This insight into the notion of time and effort is a powerful reminder of the continuing relevance of cultural practices, particularly when contrasted with rigid 'engineered' responses which fail to acknowledge the life-affirming cycles of nature. The challenge for landscape architects is how to work between these two perspectives—how to draw on techniques that combine soft skills and hard technology while tapping into the vernacular knowledge of local cultures to transform social and ecological challenges into a more positive future. ■

Emerging Territories in Southeast Asia

Yazid Ninsalam

'Rust' colloquially refers to the de-industrialisation and resulting population decline in the US Midwest, which is largely attributable to the influence of new foreign policies and an economic shift away from the production of heavy industries. A similar post-industrial decline is now being experienced in northeastern China, in a region known as Dongbei. Established as an industrial centre during the Japanese occupation, Dongbei was China's premier industrial centre for most of the twentieth century and during the Cultural Revolution provided the oil, coal, and iron ore extraction to build Chairman Mao's China. In the 1980s President Deng Xiaoping introduced market-driven economic reform such as special economic zones (SEZs), which resulted in new outward-facing trade relationships. As a result, Dongbei entered into competition with China's southeastern coastline cities, which were offered different economic rules to the rest of China. Over one decade (2000–2010), two million people left the Dongbei region seeking better economic opportunities.

Dongbei's decline coincided with the 2007–2008 global financial crisis, which inspired a further restructuring of China's economy. A four-trillion-yuan (USD 586 billion) stimulus package was announced to help the domestic economy recover, allowing Chinese factories to now produce goods for domestic supply rather than for international consumers. By 2010, China had overtaken Japan as the world's second-largest economy, but at the same time, this stimulus produced an industrial oversupply, accompanied by slowing domestic demand in manufacturing sectors.

One of the most significant differences between the North American and Chinese experiences of industrial decline is the manner in which subsequent industrial reform influenced the foreign policies of the post-industrial nations. Policies such as the General Agreement on Tariff and Trade (1946) and the North American Free Trade Agreement (1994) resulted in the relocation of heavy industries from North America to the rapidly developing economies in Central America and an increasing reliance on material goods imported from Asia. This shift left former industrial areas such as the Midwest without productive use or any investment in public works or infrastructure to address these economic changes. More recently President Trump's protectionist trade policy stance has led to the introduction of tariffs on foreign goods (such as those from China) in order to direct domestic purchasing to local goods.

Conversely, the Chinese shift towards an outward-facing trade relationship through the SEZs aims to strengthen the nation by directing the flows of industrial excess overseas, into the urban-regional landscape.[1] Importantly, the SEZs serve as engines of economic growth for the rest of the nation. Using its newfound economic leverage, China's expansionist foreign policy seeks to internationalise its domestic strengths through the distribution and dispersion of resources at an unprecedented scale across Asia, Europe and Africa. This is most clearly evidenced by China's foreign policy known as the Belt and Road Initiative (BRI), which expands China's global presence through ambitious infrastructure projects.[2] These range from transnational railways stretching from Yiwu in coastal China to London, to networks of highways connecting eastern China to Pakistan's deep-water ports, and natural gas pipelines crossing Central Asia from Turkmenistan to the Chinese border.

These different national reactions to industrial reform provide an important background for understanding the new definition and role of infrastructure emerging in Asia. In contrast to increasingly insular North America, China conceives a geopolitics of transnational infrastructure which serves to position the country as a key player in Asia.[3] This essay explores this strategy through a discussion of two Chinese financed BRI projects—Forest City in Malaysia and Jakarta-Bandung high-speed rail in Indonesia. These projects highlight the motivations and potential mutual benefits between China and recipient BRI states, along with demonstrating how this infrastructure development facilitates capital and material flows in the region.

Capital and Material Flow: From China

Geographically, Southeast Asia is defined into two distinct regions, shaped by terrestrial and maritime geographies. The terrestrial (tellurocratic) empires, which are located from modern-day northern Thailand to the southern Malay Peninsula are nourished by major river systems and continuous continental holdings of extensive coastlines and port cities. Comparatively, the maritime (thalassocratic) empires, such as Indonesia, are derived from a 'patchwork of recurring land-sea patterns on widely dispersed islands and archipelagos'.[4] Indifferent to the ideals of territorial expansion, maritime empires deferred to relationships cultivated along the trade routes within the Indonesian archipelago.

Historically, the cities of Southeast Asia were located centrally to the Indian Ocean and South China Sea trading routes. Beginning in the 1500s and continuing from the mid-1940s onward colonisation was imposed over the region in successive waves by the Netherlands, Portugal, Spain, France, Great Britain, the United States, and Japan. Southeast Asia can, therefore, be considered as a catchment, wherein global forces flow and interact at varying speeds and concentrations. These forces have been driven by motives of territorial expansion, economic growth, and material exchange. Contemporarily, this model continues, now mediated by constructed dynamics of economic zones and trade agreements, among others. The actors may have changed but the broad motivation remains.

Today, China is one of the main actors in Southeast Asia. In 2013, President Xi Jinping enacted China's principal foreign policy through the One Belt, One Road project, which was subsequently rebranded to the Belt and Road Initiative (BRI) in 2017.[5] Through the BRI, Southeast Asia's geography is being transformed by transcontinental infrastructure projects in the form of roads, railways, oil and natural gas pipelines, telecommunications and electricity projects, ports, and other coastal infrastructure projects. As a result, China's foreign policies now shape the discourse of land transformation and urbanisation across many of Asia's terrestrial and maritime regions.

The main sources of funding for the bulk of BRI-participating projects are nine Chinese development banks and the Asian Infrastructure Investment Bank (AIIB). The AIIB was established in part to address the infrastructure and economic growth in the Indo-Pacific region advocated by China, which was not addressed by existing funding institutions under the Multilateral Development Bank (MDB) model.[6] China is the largest shareholder in the AIIB, followed by India and Russia. Developing countries were also moving away from the MDB model for infrastructure financing, because of the slow progression of projects and bureaucracy. The AIIB fills this gap, seeking to service Asian countries in need of financial investment for construction projects.

BRI projects in ASEAN countries presently amount to more than USD 739 billion. While Indonesia welcomes the highest BRI investment (USD 171 billion), countries such as Cambodia, Laos, and Brunei have received investments surpassing their gross domestic product (GDP) value for that same year. This increasing investment into infrastructure projects in Southeast Asia is shaping the economies and in turn, the landscapes of the ASEAN countries.

In the context of material flows, China intends to use the BRI to redirect the flow of industrial material production into the urban-regional landscape to address the 'deepening regional disparity as the country's economy modernises'.[7] A transnational infrastructure building programme can spur growth in China's underdeveloped hinterland and rustbelt, leveraging the BRI's development strategy and foreign policy to shift the country's chronic excess production. For example, Dongbei provincial governments are linked into two national strategies: the internationally targeted BRI, and the local Beijing-Tianjin-Hebei integration plan (known as the *jing-jin-ji*), which aims to create a world-class 'supercity'.[8] In doing so, China aims to share its developmental dividends with other developing economies, along with exporting China's technological and engineering standards, an aspect which Peter Cai observes is one of the least understood aspects of the BRI.[9]

To date, across Southeast Asia, the terms of engagement of the BRI are not yet well defined since bilateral funding agreements are still underway. However, the direct influence on major urban infrastructural design projects is evident through projects such as Malaysia's Forest City and Jakarta-Bandung high-speed rail.

Material Flow: Malaysia's Forest City

Malaysia, located in the middle of ASEAN, is home to 650 million people, including a growing middle class. Recognised for its strategic location in the global supply chain, Malaysia is one of several beneficiaries of China's BRI in Southeast Asia. The significant reorientation of global supply chain trade flows through the Pacific by the United States, and the Atlantic by the UK, has allowed Malaysia to access various economies and opened up a channel for Chinese-based exporters affected by the trade war.

Malaysia demonstrated its commitment to the BRI through the launch of the East Coast Rail Link (ECRL), with China Communications Construction Company as the lead contractor and Malaysia Rail Link as the local partner. The 648-kilometre railway will cut the travel time between Port Klang on the Straits of Malacca with the city of Kota Bharu in the northeast part of peninsular Malaysia from twelve hours to just a four-hour journey.[10] In addition to the original main tunnel, a total of forty-four tunnels and twenty-seven crossings will be needed for wildlife, in order to reduce the rail link's impact on forest fragmentation.

In November 2016, fourteen memorandums of understanding (MOUs) were signed between Malaysian and Chinese businesses. These cover a broad range of sectors from railways, ports, real estate, steel manufacturing, and finance to information technology.[11] Transportation infrastructure projects, which facilitate the transfer of goods,[12] were prioritised over real estate projects.[13] The Forest City project in Johor, Malaysia, which is located within a 3760-hectare Iskandar SEZ bordering Singapore, is the largest real estate project to date and is a 60/40 joint venture between two property development companies, originating from China and Malaysia.

The Forest City project is predominantly residential, occupying four human-made islands. Once completed it will house over 700,000 people on 1,386 hectares, an area four times the size of New York's Central Park.[14] With the project master plan designed by Sasaki, a multidisciplinary design firm based out of Boston and Shanghai, the development is set to be Southeast Asia's most extensive mixed-use green development. On the global scale, Forest City lies within a network of important shipping lanes and port developments along the Maritime Silk Road (a component of the BRI), which establish a strategic Chinese presence in the Southeast Asia maritime trade routes.[15] On the regional scale, Forest City is strategically located to service the Iskandar Malaysia SEZ and the island nation Singapore. At the local scale, the project is adjacent to the Port of Tanjung Pelepas in southwestern Johor and northwest of Singapore.

Forest City is an exemplary precedent for understanding infrastructure as a literal flow of territory—with sand the material of contention. Throughout Southeast Asia, coastal and riverine landscapes have been degraded through the mining of sand, an essential material for the building and expansion of infrastructure. The development of the Iskandar SEZ has caused extensive loss of natural capital. For example, aerial imaging has shown a 20 per cent decrease of mangrove swamp areas as a result of investment-driven fragmentation between 2006 and 2010.[16]

Despite Malaysia being a comparatively land-rich state, Forest City necessitates four new islands constructed through land reclamation, dredging works, and topside development over three decades. In general, land reclamation projects require two types of sand: sand from the sea, which is used as a filler into the ocean; and finer granular sand from rivers, which is used as an additive in concrete. These types of multilateral coastal earthwork projects test the limits of encroachment to sovereign neighbouring borders. Moreover, the large variance in official import-export figures of sand transaction within the region suggests a larger cause for concern regarding the undocumented extraction of sand from rivers and seas and its broader environmental impacts.[17] As a result, 'territory has acquired an unprecedented liquidity' through its ongoing transaction as a material commodity.[18]

The strategic reconfiguration of land-water relationships in projects such as Forest City is therefore not without conflict. The original Sasaki master plan sought to protect the delicate seagrass ecosystem essential for the local fishing industry and to re-establish mangroves, coves, and mudflats.[19] It is highly questionable that any remediation strategies can compensate for the level of environmental destruction required.[20] For example, the local fishing industry has expressed concerns over the reclamation and dredging work, which has degraded the seagrass bed causing loss of fishing grounds. At the present rate of development, despite adhering to mandated mitigation measures, the compounding effects of land transformation processes and the urbanisation of the coastline have demonstrated the measures to be ineffectual with significant socio-ecological impacts already felt.

The complexities of land transformation processes in the region are compounded by the speed of development, which is outpacing the environment's capacity to buffer changes. Project timelines are often influenced by political terms, with politicians keen to demonstrate progress and impact within a relatively short period of time. Opportunistic development at the expense of the environment has the potential to negatively affect existing local economies and escalate regional political tensions.[21]

While natural capital valuation is required prior to the commencement of such wide-reaching infrastructure projects, it currently does not extend beyond local territories to include impacts on the surrounding region (such as material resourcing and coastline ecology). Missing from regional negotiations is the consideration of *how* the geopolitics of transnational infrastructure are shaping new territories and, most importantly, at *what long-term and short-term cost*.

The Jakarta-Bandung high-speed rail provides an alternative example for considering the effects of capital flows, demonstrating how Chinese investment in transport infrastructure can have wider national infrastructural and investment benefits.

Capital Flow: Jakarta-Bandung High-Speed Rail

Indonesia is an archipelago nation with its population of over 267 million spread over 6000 islands. It is considered the largest economy in Southeast Asia and classified by the World Bank as an emerging lower middle-income country.[22] A historic lack of investment in infrastructure has manifest in traffic congestion, poor logistics performance, unreliable power supply, and inequitable access to clean water, sanitation, and other basic services. These compounding issues have 'seriously undermined productivity growth, competitiveness, poverty reduction efforts, and the health and well-being of the people'.[23] Indonesia's total infrastructure investment has remained unchanged at only 3 to 4 per cent of GDP for a decade, which is half of its level prior to the 1997 Asian financial crisis. This is in stark contrast to the 10 per cent and 7.5 per cent invested by China and India respectively in their own domestic infrastructure development.[24]

The Jakarta-Bandung high-speed rail (HSR) project is considered by current president Joko Widodo (Jokowi) as one of the priority projects for addressing this infrastructure deficit. Initial feasibility studies sought to connect 150 kilometres between Jakarta and Bandung, replacing the three-hour car commute with a forty-minute rail link. However, an estimated USD 450 billion is required for Indonesia's current infrastructure development plan, which along with rail includes roads, ports, and power plants.[25] Jokowi has looked to foreign investments, especially for infrastructure, to provide financing and boost Indonesia's economy more generally. Within the first year of his political term, Jokowi held several bilateral meetings with China and Japan to secure loans, seeking to use the presence of foreign investment to gain the confidence of local private companies to invest in state public work projects, which historically have suffered from a lack of regulatory transparency.

Both Japan and China expressed interest; however, the Chinese proposal was considered more favourable. The Japanese sought Indonesian state co-funding, whereas the Chinese proposed to wholly fund through a business-to-business partnership, led by a consortium of state-owned enterprises (SOEs) from both countries.[26] This financing model is similar to that employed in the Malaysian Forest City project and demonstrates China's strategic use of infrastructure to establish bilateral foreign relationships. Strategically the project offers China the opportunity to increase its regional presence by exporting industrial material surplus, technology, and engineering standards, along with providing a foundation for future involvement in Indonesian infrastructure projects, such as air and seaports in cities across Java, and light rail transit systems in the growing cities of Bandung and Surabaya. Moreover, since the Indonesian HSR project is the first in the region, this involvement places China in a favourable position to bid for upcoming HSR projects in nearby Singapore and Malaysia.[27]

Equally, the Indonesian government has taken advantage of shifting global finances to gain financial traction to deliver its own national infrastructure agenda. For example, Indonesia's coordinating minister for maritime affairs, Luhut B. Pandjaitan (one of Jokowi's trusted aides in Indonesia-China relations), declared that the two nations have become 'natural partners'.[28] While the HSR supports China's expansionist agenda, at the same time Chinese investment builds confidence in Indonesian businesses to invest in their own country. Pandjaitan observes that speed is an important virtue when dealing with international investment opportunities and will be cultivated into Jokowi's second presidential term. Returning to China's motivations for establishing the AIIB: this comment further demonstrates how developing nations' desire for quick progress is further reason for why the BRI offers an appealing model of investment and partnership for many ASEAN nations.

Trajectories of Territorial Expansion

The BRI offers a clear manifestation of how Chinese foreign policy is shifting and shaping the trajectory of territorial expansion of Southeast Asia. Bilateral funding provides investment for opportunistic development projects and much-needed infrastructure. In the case of Malaysia's Forest City, the strategic flow of material to develop islands at the southernmost tip of peninsular Malaysia (next to Singapore), physically creates 'the most advantageous located development within the Iskandar SEZ'.[29] However, this explicit geopolitical investment sanctioned by the state comes at the cost of local ecologies and related industries. Meanwhile, the flow of foreign capital required for the Indonesian HSR is being leveraged by the Indonesian government to add legitimacy to public infrastructure projects, including encouraging local investment to meet the needs of the nation. However, this fast injection of funding, along with the desire to develop infrastructure projects quickly, has also led to new deregulatory policies that conservationists, environmental activists, and indigenous rights defenders expect will have negative impacts on Indonesia's biodiversity, climate commitments, and vulnerable communities.[30]

These projects continue the historical development narrative of Southeast Asia as a catchment. Similar to earlier global forces such as colonisation that once shaped relationships within the region, China is yet another global actor within this catchment. At the same time, China's outreach into Southeast Asia should not be oversimplified as an imperialistic or neo-colonial act. Although China is painted as the driving force behind this regional territorial expansion these examples of infrastructure projects reveal that the motivation and benefits are not one-sided. ∎

After Landscape

The exposure to frequent natural disasters in Japan such as earthquakes, tsunamis, and typhoons means that Japanese people are used to living in a highly volatile landscape. Over centuries, attitudes to unpredictable natural forces have developed practices that accept the notion of constant change and rebuilding. The technological advancements in the second half of the twentieth century have allowed Japan to develop one of the most advanced systems for disaster preparedness in the world. While this has undoubtedly created safer communities the dependency on technology has come at a cost where large-scale infrastructure increasingly overwrites the vernacular knowledge, creating binaries between human and nature that divide communities. The After Landscape project, initiated by landscape academic Marieluise Jonas, focuses on the recovery process in Kesunnuma and Hashikami in Miyagi Prefecture after the 2011 Great East Japan Earthquake. It is one of many initiatives to reconnect people with landscape systems through small-scale community-based interventions, collaboration, education, and landscape advocacy.

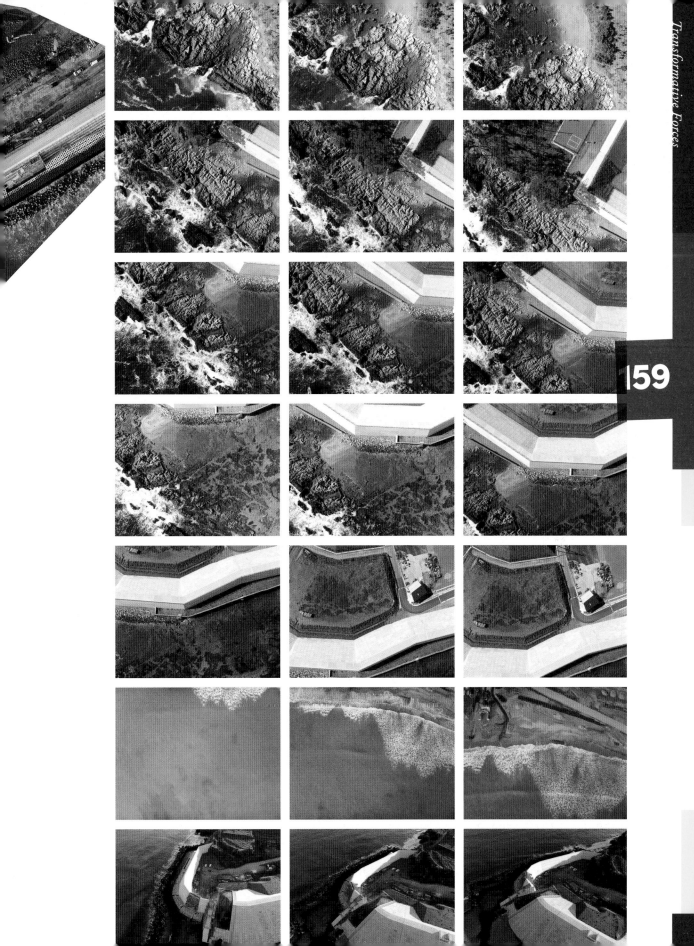

Doing Business in Asia

Ricky Ray Ricardo
Jillian Walliss

Since 2000, international designers have had an increased presence in the Asian region. Fuelled by the opening of China and the desire by Asian governments to develop globally recognised cities, international firms have been involved in major cultural and ecological projects, particularly in mainland China, Singapore, Hong Kong, and Korea. This engagement comes in a variety of models ranging from participation in design competitions from afar to the establishment of permanent Asia-based offices.

Beyond descriptions of the design projects disseminated on practice websites and professional journals, little has been written about the international experience of doing business in Asia. How do designers break into the Asian market? What are the cultural and business differences they encounter? Drawing on interviews and reflections with designers from Australia, North America, and Europe, this essay explores the challenges and opportunities presented by a professional encounter with Asia.

Filling the Gap
The earliest engagement of international landscape practices with Asia is tied to a perceived absence of professional skills and knowledge. With limited formal training and professional experience historically available in the region, government and developers looked to international expertise. The first wave focused on the former British colonies such as Singapore and Hong Kong as they transitioned into modern nation-states and territories. With a familiar language, and political and legal systems, Singapore and Hong Kong provided easy entry points for Australian and British designers. Projects tended to focus on government and corporate projects such as embassies, consulates, and corporate headquarters.

In the late 1970s, British-controlled Hong Kong's economy shifted from its industrial and manufacturing focus to one based on commercial and financial services, prospering as the conduit between China and the world.[1] This economic transformation, coinciding with large-scale protests concerning poor urban conditions, resulted in significant investment in urban development, which created work opportunities for landscape architects in Australia, North America, and the UK.

'The work was big and exciting—large-scale residential, land reclamations, infrastructure, heritage planning, and resorts', explains Catherin Bull, a founding partner in the Australian practice Edmond, Bull and Corkery, which established an office in Hong Kong in 1980. 'We felt we brought energy, creativity, and an inherent understanding of the kinds of issues at stake—especially the terrain, rainfall, hydrology, climate, and landscape ecosystems—to the projects.'[2]

The practice worked with contacts in Australia and North America, such as Tract Consultants from Melbourne and SWA from San Francisco, to develop the projects, using the local and in-house staff to complete the work. Edmond, Bull and Corkery completed many projects in Hong Kong through the 1980s, including Tuen Mun and Sha Tin New Towns, Ocean Park, and Gin Drinker's Bay, before it became part of Land Systems and later HASSELL, which still operates a Hong Kong–based studio.

The story of international practice in Singapore is particularly distinctive. Following independence, the Singaporean government actively encouraged the relocation of a highly educated global community to Singapore to guide its development. With government backing, many international architecture and landscape architecture design firms established permanent offices, and it has developed as a hub for international design practices.

Environment
This openness to foreign influence is not mirrored in all Asian contexts, especially where language and cultural barriers are more pronounced. This is particularly true of the two Asian nations that escaped colonisation, Thailand and Japan. Foreigners are excluded by the government from establishing design offices in Thailand. While Meiji-era Japan openly embraced Western knowledge in construction and design, this engagement with foreign practices shifted when the country started to develop its own architectural brand and design language, now appreciated around the world. The small size of the Japanese landscape profession and distinct

contracting conditions further contribute to the rare presence of foreign practices in Japan. The few landscape projects that involved international practitioners emerged effectively out of invitations to collaborate with local firms. For example, Peter Walker worked with Yoji Sasaki, his former student at the University of California at Berkeley, who established a practice in Osaka on his return to Japan. Their collaboration has led to a number of projects in the 1980s and 1990s, most notably the Keijaki Plaza in Saitama, which emerged from an open competition held in 1994. More recently, English landscape designer and horticulturalist Dan Pearson was invited to collaborate with Fumiaki Takano on a master plan and planting design for the Tokachi Millennium Forest on the northern island of Hokkaido.

Following its competition win for the Gardens by the Bay project, Grant Associates established a permanent presence in Singapore, bridging their Bath office, and the Asian region. The Singapore office provided convenience but more importantly the opportunity to be fully immersed in the local context and collaborate with local designers on the project. 'We decided to open an office in Singapore based on interest from local clients and the fact that on the back of the Gardens by the Bay site team, we had people in Singapore who had developed unique experience and expertise in delivering sophisticated landscape schemes in the tropics,' comments Keith French, director at Grant Associates.[3]

In 2008, Leonard Ng Keok Poh established a Singapore office of the international landscape architecture company Atelier Dreiseitl (which since 2013 has formed part of the Ramboll Group).[4] The much-awarded redesign of Bishan-Ang Mo Kio Park is one of the firm's earliest projects, introducing a new approach to blue and green infrastructure for Singapore's waterways. Permanent 'foreign' offices such as Atelier Dreiseitl and Grant Associates have significantly influenced the development of landscape architecture in Singapore and the Asian region more generally. Not only have they demonstrated innovative design approaches to government and developers, but they have contributed to capacity building, offering employment opportunities for emerging Asian landscape architects. As Keith French states: 'with a wide range of language, technical and design skills', he hopes that the Singapore office 'can set new standards for landscape architecture practice in the region.'[5]

A second model of international practice is associated with the economic and social development of Southeast Asia, such as Cambodia, Bangladesh, Laos, and Indonesia. Funded by schemes such as AusAid, various United Nations initiatives and the World Bank, international landscape architecture companies have collaborated with NGOs, communities, and governments on public health, education, or humanitarian projects.

For over twenty years, the Australian-based planning and landscape architecture practice Hansen Partnership has worked on aid-related projects in Southeast Asia. For example, in Vietnam, the practice has completed projects under the leadership and financial support of the Australian Federal Government's AusAid programme as well as projects led by the United Nations World Tourism Organization.[6] Director Craig Czarny comments that their earliest work focused mainly on capacity building of local authorities. With the maturing of local professionals and increased private interests, their work has evolved toward more sophisticated forms of active collaboration.

The opening up of China to global influences, accompanied by rapid urbanism, provided a boom for international practice. However, China's unique political and economic context establishes a very particular model of practice that restricts the scope of international designers and encourages a top-down design process. With strict rules governing professional certification and construction, international practices typically partner with a local design institute (LDI). The concept and schematic design are provided by the international practice and the remaining documentation and construction stages completed by the LDI. With all land held in public ownership, projects often develop at speed, without the more structured and linear design development and construction processes associated with Europe, North America, or Australia. Decisions are fast, and construction often commences while the project is still in the detail design phase.

161

'The challenge of a tight timeline is more logistical than intellectual,' comments Hong Zhou, principal at JCFO.[7] They often need to 'make things turn around' in a couple of days, generally during contract documentation phase 'when the construction has started and unexpected site discrepancies are found and need to be addressed right away.' Alex Breedon, who works for Gossamer, the international division of GVL Group, one of China's largest private LDIs, notes that while projects operate at speed, it was refreshing not to waste so much time with extensive and litigious project mobilisation, along with prolonged tender and construction processes that characterise his experience working in Australia and Europe.[8] Being positioned outside the Western litigious system means that trust is central to doing business in China. Alex comments that working in Australia, everything has to be negotiated from the start, whereas in China it is common to start with little formal agreement and contractual details to be negotiated progressively throughout the entirety of the project. He also highlights that in general fees are large incorporating 'a slack in case something goes wrong', meaning clients expect designers to accommodate any changes, without issuing any variations.

While design competitions in China can be high-paying for international designers, the separation between international practice and the LDIs often leads to frustration and limitations, even for those with international offices situated directly in China. On occasion an international practice may win a design competition but may not be invited to continue working with the LDI on the project. Yet despite this frustration, all practices agree that winning an international design competition in Asia is the fastest way to establish valuable connections and creditability.

Transitioning to an Embedded Practice

International design competitions for new entertainment and tourist precincts, major parks, museums, and cultural facilities have been a major way for Asian cities to brand themselves with a global identity. Shanghai, Hong Kong, Beijing, Taichung, Seoul, and Singapore have all used 'star' international designers to develop globally iconic places (and perhaps more importantly, images). Competitions play a valuable role in introducing international designers to key government figures, clients, and developers and can lead to the establishment of local offices or partnering with local firms (or in the case of China, LDIs). Such partnerships offer the opportunity for capacity building and the cross-fertilisation of ideas between local and international designers.

Winning a competition has contributed to many international practices establishing a local office. For JCFO this came with the Qianhi Water City competition in Shenzhen; for Grant Associates it was the Gardens by the Bay competition in Singapore; and for McGregor Coxall an international competition for a wetland bird sanctuary in Tianjin led to the establishment of a Shanghai studio. In all of these cases, the competition win provided the name recognition required to venture into a new business context.

However, the privileging of international designers over the local, especially for 'once in a generation' design opportunities, can lead to tension. Even in partnership, local designers often remain anonymous, with government typically championing the 'name', either directly or indirectly, in any local or international coverage. Tensions can also arise where highly reputable and skilled local designers are overlooked in favour of the 'branded' global designer. This is well demonstrated in the Seoullo 7017 competition for an elevated park on top of a disused roadway in central Seoul, which was won by MVRVD. This project created so much controversy that the professional journal *Landscape Architecture Korea* devoted two critical editions to the project.[9]

A tendency for international designers to present pan-Asian generalisation can be particularly frustrating. For example, in describing their approach to Seoullo 7017, Winy Mass, director of MVRDV, comments: 'In Asia, they want to dip their cities in this super green feeling that comes from science fiction, from movies like Avatar.'[10] While the scheme is considered successful, attracting many tourists and visitors, this shallow interpretation of Korean context and culture did not win favours from the local designers. As Jungyoon Kim from PARKKIM highlights, the issue is not necessarily about the designers being 'foreign' but rather that often the standard of the work is their second- or third-grade effort. She continues: 'If foreign designers succeed in carrying out outstanding design practice as they do in their own countries, I trust it would spur the improvement of Korean design culture and urban life.'[11]

This issue of foreignness raises the question of how to consider local designers when they return after an extensive international education and work experience. Are they local or international? After eight years away studying and working in North America and Europe, Jungyoon Kim and Yoon-Jin Park returned to Seoul to establish their firm. This international experience did set them apart from the local practices. They comment: 'We are certainly considered a "different" practice, but we try to "play" with this duality, rather than to promote ourselves for one fixed identity.'[12] Presently practicing from Boston and working at Harvard GSD, 'there is a certain expectation that their contribution is as Asian/Korean designers ... who practice internationally.' However, they don't consider themselves as specifically 'Korean designers' or 'regionalist'.

Increasingly international practices recognise the value of employing Asian landscape architects (local and internationally educated) within their Asian offices. For example, after fifteen years of experience working in SWA group's Texas studio, Taiwanese-born Shuyi Chang moved to Shanghai to establish a studio in 2009. Initially a small office, the SWA studio soon expanded to a full design studio of twenty staff with three principals and has completed numerous large-scale projects, including Ningbo East New Town Eco-Corridor, Changsha Baxizhou Island, and the Shanghai International Dance Studio.[13]

While Sasaki has had a periodic engagement with Asia since the 1960s, it wasn't until around 2000 when Sasaki alumni returned to China that the practice became more focused.[14] The employment of Chinese landscape architects offered the firm personal and professional ties that could not be established from North America. Their first project was in 1999, developing a masterplan for a large-scale new community for the developer Kingold Group.[15] Demonstrating 'some bold ideas and dynamic landscapes that were innovative at the time', the project opened the way for invitations for major design competitions throughout China.[16]

Asian projects are offering international designers different development opportunities and experiences. Woods Bagot director Stephen Jones, who has extensive architectural experience working in China, highlights that many developers in Asia have an adventurous spirit and are not constrained by rules, precedents, or particular urban or city typologies.[17] Instead, they have a 'make it happen' mentality, along with the capital and economic growth to support the projects.

For landscape architects, this has led to opportunities to lead development teams. Keith French of Grants Associates observes that 'Southeast Asian clients, both public and private developers, are more open to appointing a landscape architect to lead a team where the landscape is a defining part of the project.'[18] Similarly, according to JCFO principal Hong Zhou, 'landscape architects are often invited to join the team at the very early concept stage to help come up with a comprehensive solution, rather than "cleaning up" the leftover spaces.'[19] Many designers comment on the ability to test new ideas as a large scale. For example, McGregor Coxall director Adrian McGregor describes Asia as a laboratory, offering landscape architects the opportunity to engage with significant environment challenges 'from air quality to water pollution and food scarcity'.[20]

The increased presence of international firms practicing in Asia has also brought with it the desire to share experiences and develop platforms for a more focused discourse. For example, the bi-annual Shanghai Landscape Forum (SLF) was established in 2017 by several international practices including SWA Group, Sasaki, and AECOM. Its primary purpose is to share experiences of Western-led practices working in an Asian context and has grown to include HASSELL, ASPECT Studios, TLS, Gossamer, and SOM, among other smaller practices.

Despite this more embedded engagement, foreign designers and companies still suffer barriers in doing business in Asia where an intangible business culture is based on relationships rather than contracts. This is particularly true in engaging with *guanxi* (關係), which is central to doing business in China. Alex Breedon cites the difficulties of foreign companies achieving the 'level of Chinese-to-Chinese trust' as one of the reasons Gossamer was founded in partnership with the LDI GVL Group, to gain advantage of the decades of trust that GVL has earnt throughout China.[21] A further challenge is an increasingly skilled, experienced, and ambitious local practice. In just over three decades, the 'new' profession of landscape architecture in Asia has grown into a major presence, as evidenced in this book. International design practice has played a major role in this transformation, offering skills and experience, building capability in local designers, and helping to raise the profile of landscape architecture to government and client. However, questions are now arising over the continuing role of international practice in the region.

From a Deficit to an Exporter of Ideas

Landscape architecture in Asia is now entering a fresh phase where a new generation of local designers have developed considerable skill, experience, and ambition to direct their future. In one of the strongest indicators of this repositioning, international designers are now being employed directly within Chinese LDIs, which challenges the delineation between foreign and Chinese. Students are no longer required to go overseas to gain professional training, with esteemed master's programmes now available locally in Singapore, Hong Kong, Seoul, Bangkok, Shanghai, and Beijing. After years of providing professional education to Asian students, universities across North America, Europe, and Australia are readying themselves for a projected drop in student demand.

The unprecedented scale and range of projects found in Asia, along with their ecological and social innovation, has also produced a reversal of influence. As Stephen Jones observes, Asia has shifted from a deficit of ideas to an exporter of ideas that are of global relevance.[22] This is reflected in the increasing success of Asian designed projects in international design competitions. For example, the demonstration section of Yangpu Riverside Public Space (see pp. 192–195) designed by Original Design Studio received the 2019 World Architectural Festival-Landscape Urban Category: Landscape of the Year, along with Chulalongkorn University Centenary Park by LANDPROCESS (see pp. 42–44) receiving an Award of Excellence for Built Large-Scale. Asian designers, particularly the Chinese (Z+T Studio, Lab D+H, Turenscape, and numerous LDIs), are now regular award winners in the ASLA awards.

In a further trend, established Asian firms such as PARKKIM and Turenscape are beginning to work in North America and Europe. And looking more closely, there is also a 'new' take on international perspective as Asian firms increasingly work in other Asian contexts. For example, the Thai firm Shma is working in China, India, and Singapore; Singapore-based Salad Dressing practices in Indonesia, Malaysia, and Singapore; and Lab D+H has offices in Seoul, Shanghai, and Shenzhen. These developments reflect a major shift in how we might conceive of 'international', moving away from the assumption that international is aligned with the Western experience. In a further evolution of what might be considered an Asian practice of landscape architecture, Asian designers are now moving beyond local contexts to offer their expertise, energy, and innovation across their broader region. ∎

163

Speed

There is a Necessity for Retreat and Recalibration

Urbanism in a State of Impermanence

The Asian megacity occupies a particular place in the design imagination. Spatial constraints, population density, and rapid urbanisation, along with investors and governments keen to distinguish their developments in a global market, have inspired innovative explorations of urban typologies. Even more adventurous are the unbuilt speculations of design competitions and manifestos, which project towards a futuristic urbanism. For example, in 1960, Japanese futurists released *Metabolism/1960—The Proposal for New Urbanism*, a manifesto, which envisaged an organic city emerging through dynamic processes of change and renewal.

Sixty years after the Metabolism manifesto, eight of the world's ten largest megacities (all over twenty million inhabitants) can be found in Asia—Tokyo, Jakarta, Seoul, Guangzhou, Delhi, Shanghai, Karachi, and Manila.[1] Demographers identify 2019 as a particularly transformative moment, where for the first time the majority of the Asia and Pacific region became urban, comprising 54 per cent of all urbanites globally (exceeding 2.3 billion people).[2] Asian cities are amongst the world's densest, considered double the density of Latin American cities, triple that of Europe, and up to ten times denser than North American cities.[3]

The rise of the megacity in Asia has led to the paradoxical situation where many cities now struggle under the burden of population. Instead of providing better living conditions and health prospects, cities experience the environmental consequences of such fast and dense urban growth. Urban competitiveness is now measured in poor air quality, urban heat island effects, polluted water systems, and fractured ecological systems. Similar to cities around the world, these issues are being addressed through sustainability strategies such as ecological infrastructure, tree planting, and better waste management. But looking beyond these best-practice green solutions is it possible to discern a more contextually based approach to the challenges presented by rapid Asian urbanisation?

This essay explores how governments, designers and individuals are responding to the boom and bust cycles of economic development, the imbalance of rural

Heike Rahmann
Jillian Walliss

and urban processes, and the density of the Asian city. This discussion reveals how the intensity and temporality of these forces have created productive conditions for the recalibration of design practices across multiple scales. Ranging from Japan's deceleration after decades of unprecedented economic expansions to Singapore's developmental consistency and China's rediscovery of the rural, these diverse processes of urbanisation have been influential in inspiring innovative design approaches which reposition long-standing cultural and ecological practices, along with contemporary experiences of nature as complementary and necessary to urban life.

An Experimental Pursuit

In 1960, a group of seven young and ambitious Japanese architects and industrial and graphic designers developed a manifesto entitled *Metabolism/1960— The Proposal for New Urbanism*. Published at the World Design Congress, Japan's first large design conference held in Tokyo in the same year, the manifesto drew international attention for its ground-breaking ideas in architecture and urban design that would develop into one of the leading architecture movements of the twentieth century.

Influenced by modernist architect Kenzo Tange, the group envisioned a radical new future that would challenge the notion of Modernist housing and building typologies conceived as static, fixed, and machine-like. Critically, the Metabolists regarded their ideas as a departure from Japan's orientation toward the West. As founding member Kisho Kurokawa states: 'the end of the age of the machine is approaching simultaneously with the end of Eurocentrism.'[4] He continues:

The international architecture that became the prototype of modern architecture was also an expression of the models and norms of the age of the machine. The international style of modern architecture, created by the capitalists who manufactured those products and the middle class that used them.[5]

The avant-garde designers instead described architecture and cities as 'organic, growing through metabolic processes of change and renewal', and experimented with new forms of living and fabrication.[6] With only 30 per cent of Japan's landmass suitable for urban development, key concepts of the Metabolism movement included ideas around space and time efficiency, such as the development of three-dimensional 'artificial ground' for large public spaces and facilities, or 'prefabrication' methods to enable fast manufacturing and construction of factories and housing. As some explored the internal organisation and structure of the home and collective living experience, others envisioned radical urban design proposals with new modes of traffic and relationships to open space and agriculture.

While the Metabolists reacted to the rapid population growth and housing shortage in Japan after the Second World War, the 'grand vision' of Metabolist architecture and urban design in fact 'has its roots in pre-war proposals by Japanese designers for projects' in Japanese occupied territories of Korea, Taiwan, Manchuria, and Inner Mongolia.[7] Here, new forms of city planning and housing developments were explored such as the Plan for the Emigration Village in Manchuria 'produced in 1933 to facilitate the settlement of agricultural emigrants,'[8] or the 1939 Datong Project in Inner Mongolia. Developed 'in line with policy'[9] for the colonies, these plans were not only simple spatial explorations. Importantly, the schemes also represent social experiments relating to power, control, and new forms of society facilitated by physical form.

Responding to Japan's devastation and destruction after the Second World War, the explorations of the Metabolists were also seen as an opportunity for rebuilding the nation and transitioning from an agrarian to an information society through new urbanism grounded in technology and collective consumerism. As Japan scholar William Gardner outlines:

> In Japanese architecture and science fiction from the 1960s through the 1990s, there was a shift from bureaucratic attempts to implement the 'technopolis' through planning and economic guidance to a perception that the city itself was transforming through new media, new technology, and new patterns of consumption. In the first phase, the agent of change was understood to be the technocratic state in collusion with the national business sector; in the second phase, it was the consumer.[10]

These schemes were not limited to the major urban centres but extended into rural Japan as demonstrated by Kurokawa's Agricultural City Project, a 1960 proposal for the reconstruction of his hometown in Aichi Prefecture, after devastation by a typhoon.

Japan's fast-paced recovery continued to fuel experimental architecture and urban design through the 'bubble economy'. Cities were sprawling further into the hinterland and massive infrastructural work famously destroyed the pristine countryside and ecology well into the late 1990s.[11] For many landscape architects, however, these decades created hollow, consumer-driven outcomes, which chased international ideas that were perceived as 'fake' and lacking intellectual engagement to explore opportunities, which addressed the emerging societal and ecologic challenges provided by the rapid growth.[12] As Osaka-based landscape architect Yoji Sasaki reflects: 'There was no time for thinking deeply, it was very shallow.'[13]

In November 2011, the Mori Art Museum in Tokyo launched the retrospective Metabolism—The City of the Future, Dreams and Visions of Reconstruction in Postwar and Present-Day Japan. Delayed by eight months due to the Great East Japan Earthquake in March, the exhibition offered more than a comprehensive recollection of the Metabolism movement. Drawing parallels to the reconstruction efforts after the extensive destruction and devastation of war that gave rise to the movement, the Mori exhibition also reflected on possible contributions to the recovery process of disaster-affected areas.[14]

After the burst of the bubble economy, more than two decades of economic recession together with an aging and declining population gave rise to fears of social alienation and environmental destruction.[15] In this context, the triple disaster of the earthquake, tsunami, and nuclear meltdown seemed to have struck a nerve and further shattered Japanese confidence. Confronted by the devastation, many practitioners have since contemplated the significance and contribution of the design profession to address contemporary issues faced by rural as well as urban Japan.[16]

Referring less to the grand, utopian gestures of the Metabolist movement, Japan's recovery thus might ask for what Kurokawa defined as 'intermediary space', where 'opposing elements of a dualism … abide by common rules, to reach a common understanding.'[17] He continues that the 'Intermediary space does not exist as a definite thing. It is extremely tentative and dynamic. The presence of intermediate space makes possible a dynamic, vibrant symbiosis that incorporates opposition.'[18] In this context, some designers have started to re-envision their practice, slowing down to allow for creative experimentation, which invites dialogue to create new visions and dreams for a shared future.

These shifts are evident across all levels of practice, including a greater social, ecological and economic consciousness as designers search for new models of participatory design, which bridges the generational divide. Equally, slow-design approaches emerge, which explore natural processes as part of the project construction and maintenance. The recalibration of practice previously situated in an increasingly consumerist economy has similarly led to the redefinition of business models that work within the boundaries of sustainable growth. Drawing on traditional wisdom and customs provides a wealth of opportunities for these new creative experimentations. In his final years, Kurokawa shifted his attention from the utopian visions of the Metabolist movement without abandoning the underlying principles of life cycle and natural systems. Moving to politics and being 'instrumental in establishing the Green Party in Japan'[19] he became more and more critical of large-scale urban regeneration projects in Tokyo, advocating for soft urban qualities and sustainable design.

In comparison to Japan's economic and environmental volatility, Singapore's urbanism has been guided by a continuous and stable policy-led trajectory. Yet, this highly regulated developmental environment has not diminished opportunities for innovation, instead proving a playground for international and domestic architects and landscape architects to creatively explore green urbanism.

Located just one and a half degrees north of the Equator, Singapore's tropical environment has been influential in shaping an urbanism intertwining nature with the city. Beginning with colonisation, the British introduced the suburban bungalow housing typology, which reconstructed 'a piece of nature' and provided a 'calm and healthy environment' as distinct from the density of the inner-urban shop houses.[20] After leaving the Malaysian Federation in 1965, Singaporean government policies invested in apartment housing and encouraged the introduction of green infrastructure in the urban context. Starting with the 1967 garden city vision, which, in a demonstration of economic competitiveness, promoted Singapore as a 'tropical city of excellence', to the more recent 'city in the garden', legislation has supported population and economic growth, alongside investment in green space. From 1987 to 2007 Singapore's population increased by two million, while remarkably the rate of green space increased simultaneously from 36 per cent to 47 per cent.[21]

Recent endeavours have shifted to the conservation of natural biodiversity as a means to 'develop a "soul" for the city.'[22] Promoting ecosystems thinking, these policies together with the need for greater energy-efficient architecture adaptive to the tropical climate have given rise to creative explorations of biophilic designs. Addressing the innate affinity that humans have with nature, biophilic design has directed attention from the provision of green infrastructure at the individual building to the urban scale. Roads and buildings are now repositioned as part of a greater integrated network that connects habitats previously fragmented by urbanisation.

From an initial focus on the horizontal plane, Singapore's urban transformations have moved into the vertical realm with sky gardens, bridges, and courts integrated into the urban fabric, leading to the labelling of Singapore as the 'city in the sky'. For example, architecture practice WOHA is revisiting the twentieth-century Garden City, moving from the two-dimensional plan to a three-dimensional layered city.[23] Their vertical city explorations are accompanied by an innovative 'building rating system that measures indices of greenery, community, civic generosity, ecosystems, and self-sufficiency.'[24] For example, the Ecosystem Index ranges from 'a fully functioning ecosystem' that maintains 'a similar range of species to the biotope of the location' to a score of zero for no habitat or food,[25] while the Civic Generosity Index quantifies 'the extent to which a building encourages and facilitates the public life of a city.'[26]

Similar to the Metabolist group in the 1960s, WOHA used the ICSID World Design Congress 2009 to explore an idealistic self-sufficient city for Singapore in 2050. These ideas have since been expanded to produce 'a tangible and buildable blueprint for a new town master plan proposal in northern Jakarta.'[27] Clarifying their approach, Richard Hassell states that 'If you stop evaluating buildings on how little they harm the environment and start judging them by how much they enhance it, it could push green architecture towards the tipping point it needs to make a real difference.'[28]

What is particularly remarkable about Singapore's transition into a biophilic city is that its foundations were established decades before ideas of sustainability were politically accepted across the world. As early as 1992, Singapore announced its national goal to become an environmentally advanced nation by 2000.[29] Hence, the evolution of Singapore's urban and economic growth has been strategically intertwined with an evolving green vision responsive to best ecological practice. In the context of Asian urbanism, and international examples more widely, this process of urbanism is particularly unique and has produced a political environment supportive of design innovation. Working alongside government-driven initiatives, architects and landscape architects have been able to comprehensively explore the potentials of vertical green urbanism and challenge the intersection between ecological systems, technology, and architectural form.

Rural-Urban Reciprocity

Any consideration of Asia's fast urbanisation process requires equal acknowledgement of its reciprocal effect on rural areas. As John Lin and Joshua Bolchover observe, 'the rural is an active agent in this evolving process of urban transformation.'[30] This is particularly true of China. After lagging behind other countries for much of the twentieth century, China's urbanisation escalated from just 10 per cent in 1949 to 50 per cent in 2010 and is projected to hit 70 per cent (around 900 million people) by 2025.[31] Years of urban-biased government policy have significantly weakened rural areas,

169

leading in the last decade to a renewed concentration on the future of China's remaining 30 per cent.

While China's extraordinary urbanisation rates reflect immense speed and scale, its impact on people's lives only becomes apparent when contextualised against government policies. Until recently, people's movement has been highly regulated through a government-run *hukou* system based on people's place of birth. The introduction of Regulations on Household Registration on the People's Republic of China in 1958 assigned citizens a location and classification of either agriculture or non-agriculture.[32] Until the early 1970s, the *hukou* system operated as an 'invisible wall', dividing the urban and rural.[33] Rural people could not survive in cities given their *hukou* status made them ineligible for necessary housing, jobs, or state-sponsored benefits.

The opening up of China led to a demand for cheap labour, especially in the coastal cities, and encouraged a 'floating population' who do not live at their *hukou* location.[34] Despite lacking appropriate permits, these workers can survive through mechanisms such as the private market economy. In the early 1990s, some city governments began to sell 'blue stamp' *hukou* in cities such as Shanghai and Shenzhen to those who could invest or had desirable high skills.[35] By 2001, the system had been substantially reformed and rural citizens were permitted to come to the city if they had a permanent and legal place to stay, along with a stable income. However, *hukou* is still considered highly influential in impeding labour flow and establishing inequality between the rural and urban.

Understanding the influence of the *hukou* system is also critical for interpreting China's urbanisation statistics. Ruibo Han and Linna Wang highlight how during the 1980s China's national urbanisation policy was based on controlling the expansion of large cites and encouraging the growth of small cities.[36] Many towns were given city status, which registered as an increase in urban population given *hukou* registrations were reclassified to urban households. In the mid-1990s, government strategies moved from 'status designation to a newer, migration-based structure'.[37] Han and Wang observe that although urban population grew quickly between 1995 and 2005, the number of cities remained around 650, with growth registered as increased urban density.[38] It was during this period that the rural population diminished 'at a consistently rapid rate for the first time in China's history'.[39] This has resulted in devasting social and economic effects including the shattering of family structures as the elderly and children remained behind in villages as workers moved to the city and 'rural hollowing' which left many rural dwellings vacant and led to the 'lateral expansion' of settlement into valuable farmland.[40]

The decline of the rural village is not unique to China, evident in many Asian contexts such as Japan, Korea, Indonesia, the Philippines, Thailand, and Vietnam. After decades of investment in the potentials of the urban, governments, NGOs, universities, and designers have now turned their attention to the future of the village. Importantly, these approaches extend beyond the consideration of the economic livelihoods of communities to recognising the value of the cultural and ecological practices of the village to the broader cultural identity of the nation.

In 1961, the village of Oyama in the Oita Prefecture in southwest Japan initiated the NPC (New Plum and Chestnuts) Movement, which repositioned their agricultural production on these two products known to grow well in their region. This approach conflicted with Japan's post-war national agriculture policy, which encouraged the production of rice over local products.[41] This defiant move is considered one of the precedents for the One Village One Product (OVOP or PTOP) programme, which emerged in 1980 as a model for addressing the depopulation and the loss of industries in rural Japan. The OVOP programme has since been applied in China, Korea, Thailand, Vietnam, Cambodia, Philippines, Laos, and Indonesia.

The OVOP was developed under the leadership of Governor Morihiko Hiramatsu who was a former official in the Ministry of International Trade and Industry.[42] Importantly, this people-focused programme does not rely on government funding and aims to develop 'globally accepted products that reflect pride in the local culture', to foster self-reliance and empower communities with a challenging and creative spirit.[43] The use of the term 'product' therefore extends beyond physical goods to include the cultivation of capabilities and human resources. This includes the development of entrepreneurship-related 'academies' training future leaders of local industry. During the 1990s, the number of products registered under the OVOP movement grew to more than 300 representing revenue of over 100 billion yen.[44] Greenhouse mandarins, Shochu spirits, white spring onions, Sunqueen mandarins, kabosu, bungo beef, chestnuts, and enoki mushrooms are just some of the village specialties.[45]

Japan has actively promoted the OVOP to other developing nations through bilateral and multi-lateral cooperation frameworks, including working with the World Bank. It was first applied in China during the 1980s, beginning with the Shanghai city One Hamlet One Product and the Wuhan One Village, One Treasure projects. Other adaptations include The Philippines' One Barangay, One Product plan, Malaysia's Satu Kampung Satu Produk, and Indonesia's Back to Village.[46] As many researchers have highlighted, the governance applied in the adoption of OVOP varies considerably. At times it bears little resemblance to the original people-driven model, instead translated into government-led strategies for the manufacture of local specialities.[47] For example in 2001, Thailand implemented the national policy One Tambon One Product. Over 50,000 villages (*tambons*) received loans and grants in a scheme that formed part of then prime minister Thaksin Shinawatra's pro-countryside political agenda, appealing to his major electoral base of rural dwellers and addressing the national economic imbalance that favours Bangkok.[48]

By the early 2000s, the Chinese government began to address rural inequalities more comprehensively, acknowledging the importance of the countryside in the transition towards an 'ecological civilisation'. In 2002, the 16th National Congress of the Chinese Communist Party (CCP) declared the countryside as key to achieving the national goal of a 'moderately prosperous society'.[49] Their initial strategies involved applying 'standard quantitative urban-like models', but over the subsequent decade, these have transformed into more holistic approaches encompassing economic and social issues, cultural values, and environmental degradation.[50] The declaration of an 'ecological civilisation' and a Beautiful China as part of the 18th National Congress of the CCP was a turning point, recognising the significance of countryside in achieving wider ambitions to care for a common homeland. Junren Wan highlights the value of Beautiful China for introducing a shared obligation for future generations, stating:

> If we say that 'Beautiful China' should belong not only to us, but also to coming generations into the distant future, then caring for our beautiful homeland is not only a significant virtue for our generation, but also an embodiment of our feelings and sense of justice in relation to future generations.[51]

Programmes introduced to address rural China include a 'rural vitalisation' strategy, which features a 'beautiful village' scheme inviting planners, sociologists, designers, and artists to work together to improve living environments and offer new insights into the value and knowledge of rural communities.[52] In more remote and ethnically diverse regions, heritage tourism has been used to promote social and cultural development, though this has had mixed results given large-scale tourist investment has proven of limited value to the local people.[53] However, a renewed interest in villages has been influential in reshaping heritage practices from an emphasis on monuments and buildings to ac knowledge of the value of cultural practices such as hydraulic works, agricultural terracing, old postal and commercial routes, and construction technologies.[54]

Not-for-profit organisations are similarly making important contributions to the future of the Chinese village. Working from the University of Hong Kong, Joshua Bolchover and John Lin established Rural Urban Framework (RUF) in 2005 as a non-profit research and design collaborative. Their work highlights the 'in-between nature' of the Chinese countryside, situated amongst urban and rural processes, which result in diverse village typologies of the urban, factory, suburban, contested, and rural.[55] Beyond research, RUF provides design services to NGOS and charities working in Chinese villages and have developed a wide portfolio of constructed projects addressing social, economic, and ecological challenges.

Other design approaches emphasis the value of knowledge exchange between the urban and rural. In 2007, a collaboration between Studio TAO (the design research unit of Studio TEKTAO) and the College of Design and Innovation at Tongji University began a five-year programme on Chongming Island, an agricultural community close to Shanghai. Working with village communities, business, university partners, and government the programme 'set out to create an innovation network based on the philosophy of openness, connection and sharing.'[56] Design is positioned as a process rather than a product and builds on traditional values and practice to conceive new opportunities for socio-economic exchange.

This renewed attention on the knowledge and practices that shape village culture is mirrored in designers' rising interest in Chinese cultural concepts of sustainability. For example, Zizhao Yang and Jie Hu highlight the value of the environmental philosophy and aesthetics, which underpin the concept of *shanshui* (discussed in *Continuum*) as an urban sustainable model.[57] Yongqi Lou, founder of Studio TEKTAO and currently dean of the College of Design and Innovation at Tongji University, calls for a revisiting of the traditional notion of *she ji* (the Chinese word for design), which he thinks has been neglected following the establishment of modern design practice and education.[58] Lou highlights the military origins of *she ji*, which translates as 'to establish a strategy', while *ji* (which is the product of *she ji*) can be understood as a strategy or solution for guiding process and setting goals.[59]

In ancient China, the literati and the artisans were central to *she ji*. Guided by Tao (philosophy, ideology, morals, and ethics), the literati focused on military, political, social, and cultural purposes while the artisans working with *qi* (materiality and functionality) covered craft, technique, and implementation.[60] Lou highlights how the adoption of Western standards of design education led to *she ji* being considered 'too soft' and not 'sufficiently clear' while the knowledge and skills of craftsmen were marginalised.[61] He advocates for a renaissance of *she ji*, which he argues offers ways for addressing political, societal, cultural, and economic change, incorporating folk wisdom for a more sustainable life and guiding the redesign of a contemporary lifestyle without losing cultural essence.[62]

Importantly, Lou's position should not be viewed as nostalgic return to tradition. Similar to the Chinese government declaration of a Beautiful China, his views offer a further example of the recalibration of practice following the disruptive forces of modernisation and urbanisation. Expressed at the national and practice levels, these perspectives construct a new development direction for China which slow the previous 'speeding train' of social and economic transformation.[63] In the final part of our essay we demonstrate how this concept of recalibration extends beyond government strategies and design practice to the restoration and well-being of the individual.

A State of Equilibrium

The restorative qualities of living and being in nature are widely accepted throughout Asia. Ancient cosmological and religious conceptualisation of the world in which the human is an intrinsic part of nature are still very present in today's society. Many religious practices feature a withdrawal into nature for meditation and purification. For centuries, ascetic Buddhist monks such as the Thai *phra thudong* embarked on long pilgrimage journeys for wandering meditation.[64] The Hindu ashram offers a secluded retreat focusing on simplicity and meditation often in remote natural environments, while Shintoism encourages visits to sacred mountains and the practice of purification rituals such as *misogi*, also referred to as 'waterfall bathing', which involves meditation under running streams or waterfalls.[65]

Religious conceptions continue to play an integral role when considering contemporary ideas of health and well-being. Across Asia, 'the lines between the sacred and the secular are' often 'blurred', as in the example of Hinduism, which describes 'the vicissitudes of life not in medical, socioeconomic, and political terms, but in religious and supernatural language and in terms of karma.'[66] Similarly, in the context of Thailand, it is argued that the health care system cannot be understood without a reference to Buddhism, which defines health and disease in terms of the 'overall state of a human being' that is inseparable from the 'economics, education, social and cultural milieu'.[67] Grounded in Taoism and Confucianism, Chinese medicine embeds principles of *yin yang* and *qi* in the concept of *yangsheng* (養生, literally: nourishing life), a vernacular perspective on health and well-being that predates the modern medical system.

Central to these holistic approaches is an emphasis on the relationships to oneself, with others, and the environment to achieve an equilibrium between the mind and body plus the body-mind and nature to prevent and overcome disease.[68] The Chinese people refer to this as *tianren heyi* (天人合一, literally: unity of heaven and the human), which forms the underlying philosophy of *yangsheng*.[69] Achieving a healthy state that balances the 'forces between the body and its environment' is not limited to religious practices but is also expressed in daily routines of physical activity as well as meditative and dietary practices.[70] Routed in the conceptualisation of 'the law and order of nature' and 'the cyclical pattern of nature and dynamic balance and harmony that inform such a pattern', the five-element theory has found a particular focus in food therapy, widely practiced across China.[71] This relationship to food as an expression of natural energies and cycles has links to an Asian Deep Ecology, where 'rituals practiced in the urban context maintain significant agricultural and hence ecological meaning'.[72] As Christopher Key Chapple writes:

> In a Hindu context, deep ecology can be affirmed through reflection on traditional texts that proclaim a continuity between the human order and nature, through ritual activities, and through applying meditative techniques that foster a felt experience of one's relationship with the elements.[73]

However, the environmental degradation associated with rapid urbanisation and the rise of megacities exposes contradictions around Asian philosophies based on living in harmony with nature. Many scholars point to the environmental destruction and decline of Japanese society.[74] Similarly, Wei Guo and Peina Zhuang provide a critical view of the Confucian positioning of *tianren heyi*, tracing the historical linage of the term and the shifting relationship between humans and nature grounded in ecophobia and biophilia. They point to the inadequacy of *tianren heyi* to prevent the extensive ecological damage in China, arguing that 'it has actually blinded Chinese and other East Asian people to their own ecologically destructive behavior.'[75] Instead of simply defaulting to the concept, Guo and Zhuang reason for a deeper appreciation of its meaning and contribution to shift practice and attitude stating that *tianren heyi* 'could be helpful if it led humans to act like jazz musicians improvising harmonies in collaboration with nonhuman players.'[76]

Reconnecting urban populations to a rural experience and the restorative value of nature is an important step in addressing this imbalance. In rural areas of Southeast Asia, restoration is driven by community activation, for example in Thailand, where forest-dwelling monks engage in 'community development, forest ecology, and indigenous knowledge systems'.[77] In contrast, the stronger economies of Japan, China, Korea, and Singapore have generated a demand for eco, spa, and forest tourism, popular with urbanites who wish to temporarily escape the pressures of the city and enjoy the restorative qualities of the rural countryside. This has provided opportunities for landscape architects to work with developers such as the Japanese-based Hoshino Resorts to explore contemporary design practices of restoration.

In Japan, a return to domestic rural tourism began at the height of the bubble economy in the late 1980s, driven by nostalgic ideas of the countryside fuelled by the emerging idea of *furusato* (literally: a native place, or home) in politics and advertisement. The central government was instrumental in developing legislation to promote rural tourism. Recognising the issue of rural decline and marginalised communities,[78] which led to the Mountain Village Promotion Law in the 1970s, the government set incentives for investment in rural communities.[79] This included the 1987 Resort Development Law, which encouraged 'private sectors to invest in large-scale resort development'.[80] Targeting affluent urbanities, these developments promoted a short-term escape and romantic experience of the traditional Japanese countryside.

In 1992, following the burst of the bubble economy, along with further rural economic decline and depopulation, the government shifted strategies to support green tourism, aiming to encourage interaction between visitors and local communities through food and agriculture.[81] Developed by the Ministry of Agriculture, Forestry, and Fisheries and the Ministry of Land, Infrastructure, Transport and Tourism, these strategies expanded to include 'place-specific tourism (chakuchi-gata kanko) and nature-based tourism (shizen-gata kanko)', which emphasise 'the concept of "rural-urban interaction"'.[82] Agricultural experiences included farm stays and short-term joint projects 'between farmers and non-farmers'.[83] In addition, a new land tenure system was introduced, which encouraged 'non-farmers (predominantly city dwellers)' to 'engage in farming activities' as part of the 'urban-rural coalition'.[84] These initiatives not only allow urban residents to participate in rural life and reconnect with nature. Importantly, they contribute to the preservation of satoyama, the traditional cultural landscape (discussed in Continuum).[85] Other examples to revitalise rural communities include art-based tourism such as the Echigo Tsumari Art Triennial in Niigata Prefecture. Launched in 2000, the triennial comprises a regional outdoors art exhibition and the Satoyama Museum of Contemporary Art that display local and international artists. Similarly, The Hokkaido Garden Show was initiated in 2012 by Takano Landscape Planning to support the local construction and tourism industries.

Alongside these approaches, other strategies for rural revitalisation centre on the explicit improvement of health and well-being, especially in remote forested area that suffered from a declining forest industry. The concept of 'forest bathing' (shinrin yoku) first occurred in the 1980s as part of the government's health care plan to manage the effects of stress related to urban life, such as hypertension prominent in the elderly population. Increasingly popular outside Japan, the term 'forest bathing' is often used interchangeably with 'forest therapy', which is 'considered more advanced' and 'evidence-based'.[86] In 2004, the government-led Forest Agency and the Forest Product Research Institute introduced a certification programme where villages apply for funding to develop the infrastructure and systems to promote forest therapy programmes. These include either 'therapy roads' (as linear experiences) or 'therapy bases', where the therapeutic effects extend into a wider area.[87] As of 2015, fifty-five therapy bases and five therapy roads have been designated.[88] Reconnecting people with the natural environment, the Forest Therapy programme offers vital economic stimuli to marginalised communities. These programmes also provide designers an avenue to explore new infrastructural approaches, which place an ephemeral experience of nature at its core.

An Urban Sensibility

Any discussion of Asian urbanisation inevitably acknowledges the negative impact of speed, evident for example in the destruction of heritage, social dislocation, and environmental issues. By considering more closely the forces that shape Asian urbanisation, this essay demonstrates how these conditions have provoked a valuable readjustment of design practices across multiple scales. After a period of accelerated growth, Japan's deceleration has inspired designers to search for new participatory models encompassing a greater social, ecological, and economic consciousness. The Chinese government's declaration of a Beautiful China after decades of emphasis on the economic potential of the urban reflects a recalibration at a national scale, returning focus to the countryside and a revaluing of cultural capital. This repositioning has been accompanied by contemporary Chinese designers' re-engagement with Chinese sustainable practices such as shanshui and she ji which tap into cultural, technical, and philosophical knowledge highlighted in Continuum.

The Singaporean government's consistent urban agenda intertwining economic and urban growth with an evolving green vision has established optimum conditions for designers to explore innovative biophilic urbanism. Biophilic ideas and the necessity for retreat are deeply engrained in Asian cultures. Government-led tourism programmes in Japan's declining economy have utilised these links to health and well-being to provide economic opportunities and environmental restoration for declining rural communities. This investment has opened up new avenues for design practices that embrace a bodily experience of nature.

The projects and writing featured in Speed are therefore conceived in the context of slow and fast design practice and have emerged in direct response to the processes of urbanisation discussed as part of Interruption. Many of these ideas draw on cultural practices and philosophies introduced in Continuum, while others work at the edge of new technologies and materiality. Rather than viewed as a hindrance to design, speed can be considered as a mechanism for innovation and change, acting as a catalyst for new design practice as Asian societies transition into the next phase of economic development. ∎

173

Fast and Slow

Jillian Walliss China is known for its fast rate of construction, but how is design practice implicated in this speedy process? Understanding the role of design institutes is an important starting point. Design institutes emerged during the Mao era, when private design practices were incorporated into agents for state-driven central planning. All practices were transformed into *danwei*-based (working units) multi-disciplinary design institutes, which serviced different tiers of government and geographic regions. As China opened up to the market economy, government funding diminished, leading to the institutes diversifying and becoming more entrepreneurial.[1] In the early 2000s, the Chinese government shifted to a policy of 'maintaining the big and releasing the small', which led to the privatisation of smaller institutes and maintaining public ownership of the large.[2] Some of the most 'prestigious' design institutes have evolved into comprehensive state-owned groups, which are used in major interventions such as overseas construction aid, post-earthquake reconstruction, and other strategic projects.[3]

Encompassing a range of disciplines, design institutes often employ thousands of staff and form a critical component in China's design and construction processes, which require particular design certifications and licensing. For example international design practices are required to team up with design institutes for design development and documentation. As Feng Li comments, the models adopted by the design institutes are extremely complex and defy clear associations with ideas of public and private practice.[4] Some continue to be highly influenced by governmental policies, while others work between commercial interests and state demands or are driven more explicitly by market forces. Alex Breedon, who works for Gossamer, the international division of GVL Group, one of China's largest private landscape design institutes, comments that things happen at 'quadruple the pace' of an Australian design practice.[5] However he maintains that it is a misconception to assume that speed equals less time spent on design, highlighting just how much time is wasted in the preambles and administration of Western design projects, where negotiations over fees, the establishment of project teams, and extensive meetings cuts considerably into productive design time. To work in China at speed, Breedon argues 'is a fantastic thing to do' as it hones your skill as a designer.[6] It is also a fast way for young designers to build experience and design portfolios.

University-run design institutes are particularly unique, offering opportunities to combine production, teaching, and research (*chan xue yan*).[7] During the Great Leap Forward (1958), architecture professors and educators were encouraged to use their professional skills, including training students to engage with production by joining university-affiliated design institutes.[8] After the disruption of the Cultural Revolution, they remerged in the late 1970s and remain a major influence in the design market. For example Tongji Architectural Design Group (TJAD) (formerly the Architecture Design and Research Institute of Tongji University) was founded in 1958 and employs more than 3,000 people working across architecture, engineering, landscape architecture, heritage, and environmental protection.[9]

Incorporated into this large design group are smaller academic-led studios, which operate as 'design incubators' for innovation and research, along with offering students experience working on real-world projects.[10] For example Original Design Studio, which designed the award-winning Yangpu Riverside public space (see pp. 192–195) forms part of the TJAD. Established in 2001, by Ming Zhang and Zi Zhang, Original Design Studio focuses on research and practice. Ming Zhang is a Class 1 registered architect and an architecture professor who specialises in design and theory. In contrast to the vast office complex of TJAD, Original Design Studio is located in a former shoe factory, which has its own design workshop, break out spaces, and small courtyard gardens. Zhang comments that the studio operates at a much slower pace than the TJAD, providing a quiet space to think and reflect.[11] Importantly the studio can draw on the construction, administrative, and engineering expertise of the wider institute, leaving more time to focus on design.

This integration of practicing design professors into design schools shares some conceptual similarities with the 'lab' model adopted in many Japanese universities, albeit at a different scale. Final year undergraduate students along with master's and doctoral students elect to join the laboratory of an academic advisor, many of which are esteemed Japanese architects. With its own culture and style of instruction, students engage in seminars, research, and design projects with academic advisors and fellow lab members. Weekly meetings offer the chance for students to share their work and receive constructive critique from teachers and other lab members. Like Original Design Studio, the labs aim to bring together 'real' life projects, education, and research. ▶

▶ The Japanese labs (研究室 *kenkyushitsu*, meaning lab, seminar room, or professor's office) are often named directly after the lead designer. For example the Kuma Lab was established in 2009 at the University of Tokyo's Department of Architecture under the direction of award-winning architect Kengo Kuma. Lineage plays an important role in Japanese education with a strong focus on the master. The Kuma Lab is one of three labs, including Chiba and Obuchi labs, that trace back to Tadao Ando's involvement at the university. Manabu Chiba was a teaching assistant in Ando's Lab from 1998 until he established Chiba Manabu Architects in 2001.

The labs participate in architecture and design competitions and explore methodologies for sustainable and physical design, along with disseminating research through publication such as *Patterns and Layering, Japanese Spatial Culture, Nature and Architecture*, which was published by Kuma Lab in 2012.[12] Importantly, the lab structure allows the flexibility to undertake commercial projects along with responding to important community-based work such as recovery plans addressing the devasting 2011 Tohoku earthquake and tsunami. In a further example, The Urban Design Lab was founded at the University of Tokyo's Department of Urban Engineering under renowned Japanese architect Kenzo Tange, who designed the Hiroshima Peace Memorial (1955), the Tokyo Bay Plan (1960), and the master plan for the Expo Osaka '70 (1970). [13] With a fifty-year history, the Urban Design Lab continues to explore diverse understandings and methodologies for urban space and, aided by its considerable alumni network, contributes to international collaborations and capacity building across Asia including China, Korea, Vietnam, Bangladesh, Malaysia, and Singapore.

Increasingly, design schools in Western universities are developing labs as a means for merging practice and academia. However, they face constant pressure to secure funding and struggle to create productive relationships between research, industry, and academia, often leading to the separation of researchers from design schools. These Chinese and Japanese examples demonstrate alternative models shaped by cultural and political characteristics such as the importance of lineage as well as elements of more traditional apprentice models, along with an emphasis on practical application of knowledge. Guanghui Ding and Charlie Q. L. Xue comment that in the case of China, the focus on applied research 'closely relates to the Confucian idea of *jingshi zhiyong* and is reflective of an utilitarian framing of education where study is not for personal academic gain but instead for 'cultivating oneself, administering state affairs and ensuring national security (*xiushen qijia zhiguo pingtianxia*).'[14] They highlight how 'the pursuit of practical scholarship' is also aligned with the Chinese state's agenda to apply research as 'a tool for problem solving' to further a knowledge-based economy and industrial competitiveness.[15] While this government agenda is not unique to China, it does explain the relative weakness of design-directed theoretical inquiries in Chinese scholarly work. That said, the smaller design studios embedded within university-run design institutes such as Original Design Studio and the Japanese labs do provide the opportunity to work on slower more reflective projects, merging research, innovation, and design to produce outcomes which address wider cultural, social, and environmental concerns. ■

Deep Asian Ecology

Alban Mannisi

Many Asian societies share a deep understanding of the centuries-old balance between human and natural systems. For the last decades, the effects of globalisation have threatened this local knowledge, leading to the disappearance of cohesive environmental ethics. Recent political developments such as RIO+20 and the Nagoya Convention (2012) suggest that revisiting traditional ecological philosophies can provide new possibilities to approach current environmental crises.

The endeavour to defend local ecological philosophies and competencies is not a new phenomenon in the Asian context. First attempts can be traced back to the end of the industrial revolution, which overturned centuries of nature-and-culture adjustments, giving rise to the idea of political ecology. Theories discussing concepts such as 'citizen disobedience' (Thoreau, 1849), 'mutual aid' (Kropotkin, 1901), and 'universal geography' (Reclus, 1891) emerged alongside the ideas of ecological conservation and civil society resistance in the Asia-Pacific region. For instance, politician and social activist Shozo Tanaka, considered to be the first Japanese environmentalist, engaged in the advocacy for rural resistance following the Ashio mines pollution in 1890. Recent years have seen a resurgence of local political philosophies and a renewed focus on Asian ontologies lost since the nineteenth century.

To decipher current dynamics of Asian landscape, it is essential to understand and appreciate what is happening at a local level through analysing contemporary projects. Impacted by the environmental crises, Japan and Singapore have each demonstrated their capacity for resilience through the ecological philosophies deeply rooted in their ontologies. This represents a legitimate resistance to the current intellectual orthodoxy infused by various international congresses, which try to reassess each culture on generic models. Notably, two cases are examined here: the ecological philosophy approach of a landscape architecture firm in Japan dealing with social injustice, and the political ecology approach of urban farmers in Singapore addressing regional spatial injustice.

Restoring Japanese Social Cohesion

Except for the short period between the Meiji Restoration (1868) and the Second World War capitulation, Japan has brought little change to its ecological philosophy, largely due to its insularity and seismic activity. The lack of conflicts on Japan's own soil since the country renounced any imperialist inclination has led the heteronomy of Japan to what has been called a 'network society',[1] sometimes claimed as 'homogeneous society'[2] by Western counterparts. The network society in which everyone is involved in the construction of the common good suggests a heterogeneous facet of the Japanese heteronomy.

Such reciprocity between community members was mismanaged by the introduction of a centralised authoritarian state regime, as well as the nature/culture divide. Local practices such as community planning (*machizukuri*) in the 1950s, rural revitalisation (*chiiki okoshi*) in the 1960s, and era of provinces (*chiho no jidai*) in the 1970s illustrate their commitment to an autonomous management of the neighbourhood and environment of traditional Japanese civil society. After Japan's 'bubble economy' of the 1980s, the government proved itself incapable of managing the commons. At the same time, there was a growing need of Japanese grassroots self-sufficiency. This resulted in the privatisation of public spaces and the 1998 NPO Law allowing civilian communities to become legal partners of public realm management.[3] It precipitated the emergence of Japan's social-ecological designers.

177

In 2018, the Osaka-based landscape architecture firm Studio L. was approached by the Ministry of Health and Labour to address the growing issue of an aging population. Condemning the current tangible landscape planning management for failing to provide adequate solutions to the Japanese environmental crisis, Studio L. has been specialising in the intangible aspects of landscape design dealing with social links as a key factor to sustain social cohesion.[4] Such a position refers to a process of administering societal inputs as the principal agent beyond designers and stakeholders. The project, named Korekara,[5] meaning 'from now on', represents a unique case of the social-ecological investigation of the public health sector by landscape architecture experts. It illustrates the attention of Studio L. to the intangible structures of the superficial landscape. The project resonates to the philosophy of deep ecology very often associated with Japanese environmentalism that relates the cultural landscape to its physical appearance.[6]

Studio L. first organised a series of forums with various care industry stakeholders, civil society, and diverse panels of creators and designers between August 2018 and March 2019. It aimed, specifically, to bring together the people concerned in one place for open discussion, while raising awareness of the crucial issue of the growing elderly population in Japan. New approaches and techniques of social engineering (*shakai kogaku*) are being redeveloped based upon former local models such as the *dangisho* (place of discussion).[7] Studio L. intervened through consensus building (*goi-keisei*) to revive communities enfeebled by the absence of a social link (*kizuna*) following the environmental crisis caused by the Tohoku earthquake and tsunami on 11 March 2011. Attention is being redirected from a merely end-product standpoint to the custom and societal practices. This can be described as the transparency of a space observed through the flow and interaction of people within their physical and symbolic environment. An integration of society and environment in Japanese environmental ethics illustrates what the philosopher Nishida Kitaro depicts as 'the place in which things are' (*oite aru basho*).[8]

The Korekara project, above all, demonstrates how specificities and issues of a space are better identified by its users. It testifies that designing landscape is not just the leader's work, but also everybody's task. Through the multilateral forums, traditional practices are reenacted on the very sites retaining their own historical records. It highlights a process of spatial curriculum (*kukan no rireki*), which appraises not only physical, but also psychological relations to the environment.[9] Studio L. envisions landscape design beyond a tangible project, as an exercise of self-understanding in its environment.

Another major dynamic of the project is its focus on the debates among all concerned in managing the common good. The public desire to participate in the design of the commons is a worldwide momentum, as the 'globalisation from the grassroots' phenomenon articulates.[10] The task of the landscape architect as a mediator is to consider all agents of economic activity as a whole, inseparable from ecology, for everybody has an equal share of ecological responsibility. The participants fully utilised the knowledge exchange platform to restore a sense of the Japanese network society through specific debates, each as an interchangeable cog of the environmental mechanism.

The Korekara project is of great significance in offering a return to a holistic vision of the environment, a modelling of a philosophy of action in which everyone is the changing agent for a shared future. Instead of 'fitting out a vessel' where a community is invited to spread its culture and economy, the holistic inquiry expressed by Studio L. recalls how much the social links leading to the formation of the common spaces are inseparable from the landscape. Rather than placing landscape architects before a self-contradiction, it revisits the primary sense of this applied ethics of nature. Landscape is fundamentally linked to a society perceived from the place where it evolves.

Singapore, for its part, without rejecting foreign ecological and political philosophy but integrating them into its environmental approach, has innovated considerably in revitalising local culture in one of the most stimulating economies of the twenty-first century.

Singapore's Edible Landscape

The internationally prominent position of the island nation illustrates the unique journey of one of the most advanced approaches to environmental planning in Asia, beginning with Singapore's independence in 1965. Put forward by its renowned leader, Lee Kuan Yew, it applied biophilic parameters in the local urban fabric, mitigating the harsh concrete urban environment and improving the quality of life in the city.[11] The human, nature, and economic capital management of the future Garden City took the risk of deviating from the tabula rasa style of urban planning common in Asia since the 1960s.[12] The Housing and Development Board of Singapore managed to defend nature and achieve remarkable economic growth within the social and natural environment.[13] It set an exemplary model of Asian environmental design.

However, following the transfer of Hong Kong from British to Chinese sovereignty in 1997, the massive migration of international labour forces has made Singapore a new Asian economic hub, threatening its biodiversity. Large tracts of agricultural and grazing land have been erased, and green spaces have been reduced to the status of horticultural and ornamental props. Consequently, whereas the island was self-sufficient in food production in 1959, today 90 per cent of its food is imported.[14]

A major part of Singapore's food is cultivated in the Malaysian regions of the Cameron and Lojing Highlands known for their constant tropical climate. The increasingly rare food forest biotope of agriculture seen in the Green Circle Eco-Farm[15] in north Singapore, however, is now giving way to greenhouses and intensive crop farming which are devastating the region's ecosystem.[16] Vast areas of vinyl greenhouses and over-intensive use of pesticides and other chemical fertilisers are having a devastating effect on the lands.[17]

Over the years, the political ecology of Singapore has redefined and broadened its scope to include not only watershed and arable land networks but also the responsibility for the economy. The ambiguity of such an orientation has seen not only the destruction of the ecosystem but also the detrimental effects on the well-being of the inhabitants. The impact on the regions and the concern about food security has alarmed the government, as well as the citizens. As a result, the government created a statuary board of the Agri-Food and Veterinary Authority of Singapore (AVA) to regulate food safety and facilitate food production and, also, to encourage new entrepreneurial and civil initiatives.[18] It is in this context that the platform Edible Garden City (EGC) was created with the vision of revitalising local practices and customs through urban agriculture.[19]

Initially, EGC developed from an urban farming concept, focusing on underutilised spaces such as schools, hotels, and restaurants. It is based in Citizen Farm, a sustainable and socially driven urban farm in the centre of Singapore's Queenstown (Jalan Penjara) district. To reintroduce sustainable urban agriculture on its own land, EGC developed a circular economy strategy by promoting citizen empowerment. It established what has been called an 'ethical network' of locally grown produce, interacting through sensitisation workshops on urban agriculture, regional culinary, school environmental education, and regional food markets. Associating food regeneration with awareness of native foods, it produced high-quality harvests via integrated farming systems, in which people could see land and climate limitations. The social dimension of passing on the knowledge has become a growing function of the philosophy of the projects led by EGC. Schools and organisations have benefited from their farming curriculum and workshops to spread knowledge, philosophies, and a passion for growing.

The activities of EGC have made a considerable impact on local communities and have revitalised the fundamentals of local customs and traditional practices. Revealing 'what's ungreen about the green plan' advocated along with Singapore's growth, awareness was raised of ecological issues and everyday actions were repoliticised. Until then, these matters had been little known to the civil society of the region[20] due to the global rise of eco-chic consumption[21] in the ultra-global economy. The food security crisis provided EGC an opportunity to rethink the complex convergence of regional ecology and cultural sustainability through the study of the resilience of urban agriculture.

In line with the vision of 'bringing the community together through urban agriculture', care-farming projects pursuing environmental psychology are becoming increasingly important especially within the aging population. The lack of understanding of the elderly, to whom the question of food security is vital, has caused a wide gap between environmental policy and the people's concerns. Since 2020, EGC has been engaging in elderly rehabilitative services via care-farming programmes and proposing the therapeutic use of farming practices for health and social care benefits. Access to food production and its visibility reveals more than a sense of belonging to a regional ecology, producing a distinct culinary custom. It represents the fundamental aspect of ecological biopolitics where the soil contains all man's vital needs.[22]

The strength of EGC lies in its ability to insinuate ethical priorities within offshore governance of which ecological stakes tend to lose sight of its social capital. Fundamental environmental ethics, such as physical movement, social synergy, psychological well-being, mental engagement, and nutrition are reconsidered as triggers for a responsible and ethical environmental dynamic. The applied human sciences approach, including environmental psychology, allows EGC to better understand the components of cultural landscapes and their limits. The practice of EGC illustrates the necessity of participation of citizens, environmental entrepreneurs, and planners in setting out ethical future governances.

Palimpsest of Environmental Ethics

The rapid and growing exchange of cultural and technical knowledge is undoubtedly one of the most significant legacies of the twentieth century. Having deeply transformed the cultures of Japan and Singapore, it has generated new ecosystems and lifestyles, which are the envy of the world but which at the same time cause ruptures and conflicts.

The period of disruptive transition in Japan from 1868 to 1945 legitimised the idea of the resilience of ancient culture during this era. The sophistication of Japanese ecological philosophy lies in the way natural and social ecologies are not dissociated.[23] The Japanese ontology justifies the continuous attention to the commons and also the eagerness of people to engage in discussions with social link experts. The political ecology of Singapore, on the other hand, presents an alternative to agricultural trends appearing in Southeast Asia and a revitalising of community participation in the face of ecological distress caused by speculative markets. Independent environmental ethics in Asia enables a reconsideration of the patterns and models of environmental humanities from the standpoint of an appropriate and genuinely sustainable awareness. It allows an understanding that goes beyond sustainable development, which focuses only on neoliberal issues. The projects carried out by Studio L. and Edible Garden City show promises of genuine environmental resilience when the landscape is revalued from a deep ecological knowledge. The peculiarity of Japan and Singapore regarding their spatial curriculum enlightens us about their modern transformation.

As an embodiment of the environmental palimpsest, the recognition of tangible and intangible societal actions is a vital part of ecological philosophy and political ecology, to re-evaluate the validity of landscape design. Pre- and post-modern generations sceptical about the legitimacy of ideals, which undermined centuries of customs and practices, coexist today.[24] With the interests of the Asian regions in mind, the review of the cases in Japan and Singapore provides a vivid panorama of our controversial environmental history and equips landscape architects with the necessary knowledge to administer environmental justice via landscape design.[25] ■

179

China Now

A Global Landscape Laboratory

Zhifang Wang
Zhongwei Zhu

Intertwining relationships between politics and landscapes are prominent in contemporary China, where political strategies originating from the central government directly shape development trajectories. After decades of rapid urbanisation focusing on economic development, the 17th National Congress of the Communist Party of China (CPC) in 2007 declared the move towards an 'ecological civilisation', while the 18th National Congress established the two overarching visions of 'promoting ecological progress' and 'building a beautiful country' for guiding China's future development. This significant political shift makes this an opportune time to explore a decade's worth of innovative ecological and social solutions that have evolved since this new mandate. The top-down political agenda of 'ecological civilisation' seeking harmonious coexistence with natural systems has effectively recast China as a global landscape laboratory of international significance. This essay focuses on this powerful alignment between politics and landscape practices, discussing the emergence and success of globally relevant design and planning concepts used by the Chinese government to promote more balanced development approaches and improve liveability.

Adopting political strategies to recalibrate development trajectories and landscape practices is not unique in China. For centuries, politics and landscapes have been observed intertwining across the world. In the late nineteenth century, Olmstead (considered the father of American landscape architecture) promoted the establishment of public landscapes in cities across the United States in order to create democratic places for middle classes. Later J. B. Jackson in the 1970s described the 'mega-structure' of the American environment created by various American political strategies as a skeleton composed of boundaries, highways, meeting places, and monuments.[1] A more recent exploration of the multi-faceted connections between politics and landscapes is offered by Adam T. Smith in his provocative 2003 book, *The Political Landscape: Constellations of Authority in Early Complex Polities*.[2] Smith defines landscapes in the broadest sense to incorporate the physical contours of the built environment and spatial representations of design ideas and aesthetics. Politics are considered to encompass every dimension of our lives, including governmental authority, regulations, and social procedures, as well as social relationships rooted in specific horizons of power and legitimacy. Exploring landscape cases from early complex societies, ranging from the classic-period Maya and the kingdom of Urartu to the contemporary landscape design experiences in Western countries, Smith proposes three ways that political forces influence landscape: creating the physical ordering of the physical landscapes, shaping our sense of place, and embedding civic values.

Compared to Western societies, the alignments of politics and landscape practices in contemporary China are more prominent, most clearly evident in the development of 'socialism with Chinese characteristics',[3] and particularly in the top-down governance that dominates decision-making with only marginal input from public citizens and private parties. China's land-use changes and urbanisation processes are inherently political.[4] Government agencies and bureaus consistently perceive and utilise politics as a strategy to recalibrate the trajectories of land use and development for various purposes, adjusted by the development plans proposed by the central government.

Over the last four decades from 1949 to 2012, landscape has played at least three different roles in China's urbanisation and land use development, transformed by fundamental political shifts and new regulations.[5] First, in the period of the planned economy (1949–1992), landscape played a subordinate role in China's urbanisation. Land use was determined by administrative allocation with no consideration of fees, time limitations, or market needs. Second, after the establishment of market mechanisms in 1992, landscape served as an infrastructure to shape the image of cities in order to attract investment for economic growth and to enhance citizens' sense of belonging by building city landmarks. Third, in the twenty-first century, land urbanisation has been shaped by a new course as China became more open to the world and society was viewed as important within liberal market demands and rules. Beyond its ability to promote the image of cities and attract investment, landscape began to function as an engine for increasing the retail price of land and real estate. This worked in tandem with an expectation to spur regional economic development amidst the urban sprawl. The iconic landscape practice of this period is the park movement, a new phenomenon in China's urbanisation, in which parks and green spaces were designed to enhance land finance revenues and fuel real estate and commercial development.

More recently, the pronouncement of an 'ecological civilisation' has provoked a significant shift. This was an official response to the unfolding serious environmental issues emerging in China as a by-product of extreme economic growth and rapid landscape changes—including high emission of pollutants, water shortages, unsafe drinking water, carbon pollution contributing to global warming, and natural disasters such as drought, floods, haze, pollution, and sandstorms—that have significant effects on the well-being of residents.[6] The 18th National Congress's twin declarations of 'promoting ecological progress' and 'building a beautiful country' have had a profound influence in shifting the focus of China's landscape architecture in order to achieve long-lasting and sustainable development. Landscapes are no longer conceived as economic engines or represented through object-based forms but are instead critical to establishing an eco-systematic development response balancing the needs of urban and organic conditions.

These declarations, driven by the negative experiences of rapid urbanisation, have shaped twenty-first-century Chinese landscape practices into a laboratory for ecological innovation. Numerous projects at various scales and in differing contexts have been financed and promoted by both the central and local governments in order to achieve more sustainable liveability. While it is too early to assess the success of these ecologically and socially ambitious developments, these government-driven opportunities have heightened the role of contemporary Chinese landscape practice in achieving a more balanced approach to economic growth and urban development.

Advancing the Concept of Ecological Civilisation through Practice

First proposed in 2013, at the Third Plenum, the idea of the 'ecological redline' (ERL) is one of the most dominant ideologies for conceiving of an ecological civilisation. Developed as a device for environmental protection, ERL's aim is to balance and differentiate economic development and the ecological protection of different regions. In 2014, the Ministry of Environmental Protection issued the 'National Ecological Protection Red Line: Technical Guide for Ecological Function Baseline Delimitation (Trial)'. Since then, ERLs have been rolled out across Chinese cities, applying concepts and decision procedures such as ecological control lines, ecological protection lines, and urban growth boundaries across multiple scales.

In most cases, ERLs are incorporated into urban planning procedures, which require cities to set aside over 25 per cent of land as ecological redlines. For instance, Beijing's ERL covers an area of 4,290 square kilometres, accounting for 26.1 per cent of the total city area. Included are four types: water conservation, soil and water conservation, biodiversity maintenance, and essential river wetlands. The ERL forbids all development activities and any changes of land use that do not conform to the primary function orientation, to ensure that the ecological function does not decrease and that nature does not change. Most importantly, after the ERL has been delineated it can only be increased, not decreased.

Even though landscape architects are seldom directly involved in the delineation of ERLs, the redline itself shapes landscape practices through the balancing of landscape development and ecological protection, particularly in tourism projects located in natural areas with high ecological and recreation values. Before the delineation of ERLs, most landscape practices focused more attention on development and beautification, rather than engaging with ecology. Consequently, ERLs can be considered as the first top-down strategy that forces Chinese landscape practices to consider ecology. This shift in practice direction was reinforced further with the introduction of the 'sponge city' concept in 2014.

The concept emerged as a nation-wide city strategy to better resolve stormwater issues and manage interdependent natural systems that intersect urban areas. Serious flooding issues across the country partially prompted the establishment of this movement. Sponge city also draws inspiration from water-related development guidelines such as low impact development (LID), sustainable urban drainage system (SUDS), and water sensitive urban design (WSUD), which began to emerge in Western societies in the late 1970s.[7] In 2015, China's central authorities nominated sixteen sponge

181

cities and another fourteen were approved in 2016 to establish trial models for stormwater management. An ambitious timetable aims to build modern sewer systems and infrastructure for efficient stormwater solutions in 20 per cent of Chinese cities by 2020, rising to 80 per cent by 2030. So far, over 130 cities have outlined their ambitions to become sponge cities.

Sponge city development directly provides many opportunities for landscape practices. Trillions of RMB continue to be invested, involving multiple disciplines, particularly in hydrology, urban planning, and landscape architecture. The sponge city movement encourages and to some extent obliges landscape practices to consider ecological factors, particularly stormwater, in all designs. Although the trial-city programme stopped in 2016, stormwater concerns are now well established in planning and design, guided by the Technical Guide for Sponge City Construction published in 2014.

China's rapid urbanisation growth over the past two decades has also led to negative impacts on rural economies—a direct consequence of China's urban-biased policy allocating far more resources to urban areas. This has contributed to depopulation in rural China. In 2012, the concept of 'rural vitalisation' was initiated by the central government to deal with this distorted urban-rural relationship. The core objective of rural vitalisation is to address rural decline systemically by re-establishing a harmonious development of population, land, and industry in rural areas.[8] A wide variety of disciplines are actively involved in this process including artists, planners, geographers, sociologists, and designers.

Landscape practices have been actively involved in the construction of the 'beautiful village'.[9] Through the reorganisation of landscape patterns and the beautifying of rural environments, the scenic and hygienic conditions of many villages have been greatly enhanced, including some emerging as famous tourist spots.[10] However, it has become clear that a more beautiful rural environment does not necessarily equate to sustainable development, with many rural places continuing to experience depopulation and economic decline. Instead, the real challenge for landscape practice is to move beyond the comfort zone of the material landscape to systematically address the sustainable development of rural areas in terms of economic development, ecological issues, and social relationships.

Returning to urban issues: the economic attractiveness of the Chinese city has also generated many urban problems, ecologically, functionally, and socially. China's urbanisation rate reached 53 per cent in 2013, and cities entered a new period of transformation, which emphasised the achievement of healthy and sustainable development.[11] In 2015, the Ministry of Housing and Urban-Rural Development proposed the planning concept of 'ecological restoration and urban repair' (also referred to as urban double repair) using Sanya as the pilot city. Similar to urban renewal experiences in Western societies, the goal of urban double repair is to adopt micro and gradual repair, rather than massive-scale demolition and construction, to achieve social and economic benefits and maximise social wealth in urban renewal projects.[12] With a focus on improving urban function, road traffic improvement, infrastructure transformation, and urban context continuation, in tandem with social network construction, urban double repair creates many opportunities for landscape practices to develop green urban landscape systems and green infrastructure.[13] Sponge city design principles are incorporated into this new programme, together with an increased concern for residents' social behaviours and well-being. Across the country, many great new urban green spaces have emerged under this combined social and ecological focus.

Furthermore, the most recent political recalibration of ecological civilisation, 'territorial ecological restoration' (TER), represents the most radical innovation in sustainable development, aiming for the implementation of the strictest ecological environment protection system for China's natural resources. In 2017, the first pilot projects nominated for TER (also called 'system restorations of mountain-water-forest-agriculture-lake-grassland') were launched, and at present, there are twenty-five large-scale pilots cross China. In 2018, the Ministry of Natural Resources was established to lead the land planning system and the ecological protection and restoration of the land. The goals of TER are to explore more systematic and holistic management solutions for efficient use of natural resources on a regional scale. This coupling of social-ecological systems relies on multidisciplinary collaborations that include landscape architecture. Now a national strategic project in this new era of ecological civilisation, TER is considered essential to achieve the goal of a beautiful China. In this process, landscape practices are required to consider a wide variety of ecological and social factors to achieve ecological restoration across scales, while working with other disciplines collaboratively.

Determining Success

This essay has highlighted the direct correlation between Chinese political agendas and landscape architecture practices. 'Ecological redline' is the first top-down strategy that forces Chinese landscape practices to take ecological constraints seriously while 'sponge city' encourages and, to some extent, obliges landscape practices to consider stormwater relevant factors in all designs. 'Rural vitalisation' and 'urban double repair' stimulate the role of landscape practices in advancing better well-being in both rural and urban areas. 'Territorial ecological restoration' further challenges landscape practice to systematically and holistically address multifunctional landscapes across scales with collaborations from other disciplines.

It is still too early to predict how these new political strategies and landscape approaches will achieve ecological and social ambitions. There are many challenges in reinforcing these top-down strategies in local practice. First, the balance between the economy and the environment is always contentious. Many local governments remain excited about the pilot projects, not because of any potential ecological future, but because there are millions of state-based investment schemes bundled within the policy that offer the potential for improved political status. Each pilot receives several trillion RMB each year, across several consecutive years, and investments from other sources are a likely by-product of the construction process. China's economic growth rate is set at around 7 per cent, meaning that the GDP in China will double in one decade. Environmental expectations are likely be overwhelmed by continuing relentless development until such times as a growing ecological emergency is acknowledged at all levels in China.

The second challenge is how to bridge the gaps between ecological science and landscape practices, which is a global challenge.[14] However, its effects in China are more intensive, given the unprecedented speed of urbanisation, combined with the independent and separated vertical governance structure that prohibit communication across disciplines.[15] Research in urban ecology and environment conducted in China since the 1980s has been extensive and impressive. However, poor communication between ecological science and landscape practice has hindered the accessibility and relevance of science to landscape-based decision making. Numerous poor design outcomes across the country display a common phenomenon known as 'planning/designing without ecology'.[16] With the establishment of the Ministry of Natural Resources in 2018 and the promotion of territorial ecological restoration for systematic and holistic solutions toward ecological civilisation, the boundaries between different disciplines are gradually being broken down. However, there is still a bumpy road for sustainable urbanisation, given the novelty of multidisciplinary communication and practice in China.

Despite these challenges, Chinese landscape practices are gradually building the capacity to simultaneously take on multifunctional roles in maintaining ecological security patterns as well as serving as stimulators for urban renewal and rural vitalisation. In parallel, China's vertical governance and power structure is becoming more efficient in motivating and regulating agencies and stakeholders to take action towards defined goals. All of these recent landscape-focused development strategies and their long-term impacts require the attention of practitioners and academics alike to understand and evaluate their short- and long-term contributions. As a test-bed for more ecological and socially responsive development, China's evolving landscape projects should be scrutinised, offering experience, knowledge, and models of global relevance. ∎

183

Roof Sentiment

Seoul

The high spatial volumes of the wrinkle roof.

Project Name: **Roof Sentiment**
Project Location: **Seoul, Korea**
Architects: **Society of Architecture**
Landscape Architect: **Lab D+H**
Client: **National Museum of Modern and Contemporary Art (Korea), Hyundai Capital**
Completion Year: **2015**
Text: based on information from SoA and Lab D+H

**Borrowed views framed by
the wrinkles and holes.**

**A family business from Shandong
province, China, provided the
reed screens for the wrinkle roof.**

185

In 2015 Lab D+H were invited to join the Society of Architecture (SoA) team to design a temporary installation for the public courtyard of Seoul's National Museum of Modern and Contemporary Art (MMCA) as part of the Young Architects Programme. Their design Roof Sentiment references the traditional *han-ok* roof form of Korean architecture, which is highly visible and symbolic. Internally, the roof structure is exposed, offering a deep atmospheric space, while the lines of the roof compose a view, referencing a mountain behind. Technological advancements have led to thinner and lighter roofs, which have diminished the roof's symbolic and atmospheric qualities.

Roof Sentiment introduces a wrinkle roof into the courtyard. Made out of reeds, the wrinkle roof sways in the breeze and becomes a window to borrow scenery experienced through holes and the in-between wrinkles. The combination of this undulating reed roof and the landscape design acts to uncover people's senses and feelings. A ground surface of shredded pine tree bark and a series of small undulating landforms, which embrace the bundles of structural columns, enrich the tactility and spatiality of the experience. The largest landform allows people to climb up and look through the wrinkled roof to a symbolic visual axis aligned with the nearby Gyeongbokgung Palace and the symbolic mountain Inwangsan. The landforms are planted with diverse plant palettes that are the same botanical family as the roof's material.

Initially SoA looked to retail products to construct the reed roof; however, none were large enough to produce the desired 'wrinkle'. Lab D+H explored makers in China online and located a reed maker in the Shandong province, close to an extensive wetland area. This three-generation family of craftspeople provided this important design material.

Phoibos 11
Singapore

Project Name: **Phoibos 11**
Project Location: **Singapore**
Landscape Architect: **Salad Dressing**
Softscape Installer (Native Plant Hunter):
Plantwerkz
Client: **Singapore Garden Show**
Completion Year: **2018**
Text: based on information from Salad Dressing

**Encountering Phoibos 11
in a pop-up tropical jungle.**

Carnivorous pitcher plants.

187

On the 20 July 2018, a pop-up jungle sprouted overnight from a 9 x 9-metre square on the manicured lawn of Singapore Garden Show. This confined geometric space contained an implosion of the undomesticated native floras. It is not a garden, nor an environment. Instead Salad Dressing consider this insertion as a philosophical entity. Actions are happening in the pop-up jungle: creatures are fornicating, asphyxiating, agitating, and fighting for survival. They grow and mature till death sweeps by, decay, returning to ground. After squeezing though a sinuous primordial path, a space shuttle known as Phoibos 11, a replica of the Apollo 11 lunar module, gilded like deities with glittering foils of gold, appears. It resembles our worship of the Apollonian ideals of structures and systems, the rules and regulations of our society. It also signals our unquenchable quest for gold and fortune, a drive for exploration into wild and unknown, like the tales of El Dorado.

The opening of Phoibos 11 coincided with the exact day forty-nine years earlier where human first landed on the moon, gazing back to the blue marble we call home. Inside Phoibos 11 is a refuge away from the hot humid air, but it is a paradoxical place of comfort and peril, where carnivorous pitcher plants are caged inside a terrarium. Delicate glass mosquitoes created by the Japanese artist Yuki Tsunoda are lurking and waiting to feed. Saturnine virus-impregnated mosquitos swell up with warm fertile blood, giving new birth, but also causing many deaths. That's not the end to the savage world of the tropics. In the sanctum, people succumb under the irritating smell of a rotting jackfruit, blinded by the flashing fluorescent light simulating the eternal equatorial sunshine, baffled by the electronic buzzing sound of the mosquitos and the storm Super Yugen, which is triggered by the mosquito-exterminating zapping machine.

A bewildering three minutes in the vessel resembles twenty-four hours in the tropics. It is a machine that encapsulates the timelessness of the tropical jungle. Overall, it is a curation, where one moves through congested spaces within a botanical frenzy. People are forced to manoeuvre within tightness of space, confronting their internal tightness with the wild. A finite space, yet infinite possibilities. After a condensed concoction of the tropics, a puffing pink portal of candy cattleya orchids appears, sending people back to reality.

Yellowhorn Farm Park

**Augmented reality technology
presents a chronology of stories
significant in the battle against
desertification.**

Project Name: **Yellowhorn Farm Park**
Project Location: **Aohan County, Inner Mongolia, China**
Landscape Architects: **China Construction Design Group**
Client: **Yellowhorn Exhibition Centre Inner Mongolia
Yellowhorn Agricultural Technology**
Completed: **2014**
Text: based on information from the China Construction
Design Group

Aohan County

The geometry of the design was inspired by the leaf structure of the yellowhorn tree, a plant species that has been instrumental in reversing the area's desertification and promoting local economic prosperity.

Constructed in 2014, the Yellowhorn Farm Park project consists of over sixty hectares of hilltop farmland located in Aohan County in Inner Mongolia. Yellowhorn refers to a native species that thrives in harsh desert climates, stabilising soil, retaining moisture, and providing oil-rich seeds. For over a century, over-grazing, logging, expanding agriculture, population pressure, wind, and drought have turned this once-fertile grassland into a sandy plain. Through enormous local and national effort, this has been substantially reversed in the last twenty years, with approximately 1.2 million hectares of desert rehabilitated.

Initiated by the Yellowhorn Exhibition Centre and Aohan County government, this project celebrates the environmental rehabilitation of the Mongolian plateau. A series of public meetings with local governments, communities, village residents, farm employees, and scientists in the agriculture, geology, ecology, and humanities fields offered guidance for incorporating the heritage, spirit, and attitude of those battling desertification into the design strategy.

The viewing platforms overlooking the park are located on the site of the temporary office, which served as a hub for observation, organisation, and rest, for the thousands of workers involved in addressing the environmental damage. The platforms are constructed in a radial concentric shape and feature three semi-open viewing pavilions and one open overlook.

The semi-open pavilions address the three historical campaigns waged against desertification on the Mongolian plateau: Hulunbuir grassland (to the north), Xilingol grassland (to the west), and Horqin grassland (to the south). Onsite augmented reality devices, held by visitors, digitally chronicle stories and practices that have been significant in the battle against desertification.

The design aims for minimal environmental intervention and integrates site material, plants, technology, and traditional construction methods with the contemporary uses of education and recreation. The six-month landscape construction process involved no professional construction teams, but rather used only local resources and village residents. Excavated rocks and soil, abandoned agricultural machinery, and local natural plants were repurposed into the new landscape structure and pavement. Local construction methods such as cyclopean masonry with rammed mud and natural stones, and planted native species (seabuckthorn, *Miscanthus*, and yellowhorn), were used around or in the structures.

This educational park and observation platform offers open spaces, public stages, social places, and amenities to host cultural and educational events, along with an understanding and celebration of the environmental rehabilitation of the Mongolian plateau.

Medical Herbman
Café Project

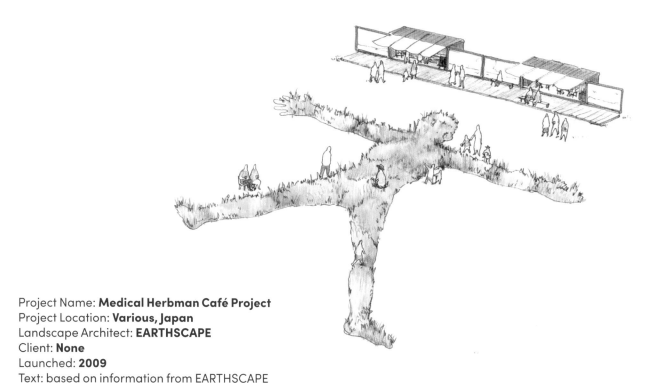

Project Name: **Medical Herbman Café Project**
Project Location: **Various, Japan**
Landscape Architect: **EARTHSCAPE**
Client: **None**
Launched: **2009**
Text: based on information from EARTHSCAPE

The travelling container transformed into the Herbman Café.

191

The Medical Herbman Café Project is a social enterprise that travels to teach people the value and use of herbs. It has two parts: the herb garden, and the café which sells tea and food dishes using the herbs harvested from the garden.

Herbman is a person-shaped herb garden. Herbs are planted on Herbman's body according to their effects: for example, herbs that aid digestion are planted in the stomach area, and herbs that work to relieve shoulder stiffness are planted in the shoulder area. In this way, Herbman acts as a kind of herb dictionary. Just by looking at Herbman, people can learn which herbs work for their trouble spots. Herbs that grow naturally in the locale are also planted so that a site-specific Herbman is born in each place.

Launched at the Echigo-Tsumari Art Triennale in 2009, the sea-ready container used to transport the project transforms into the Herbman Café, which allows people to explore the effects of herbs on their own bodies. Drinks and food made with the herbs harvested are served. The space is also used to hold various workshops relating to herbs. The line drawing on the inside of the container door, which continues to the back of the container, depicts the Echigo-Tsumari region in Niigata Prefecture, Japan. EARTHSCAPE hope that this drawing will encourage people to take the time to notice and deeply observe the local landscape. The landscapes of all of Herbman's destinations are layered on top of the base drawing wherever Herbman goes.

The interior of the container was made from recycled material from an old abandoned folk house in Echigo-Tsumari and features antique materials and objects, as well as *fusuma* (sliding wood doors) and *shoji* (sliding paper doors). As the container travels it acquires new materials and gifts from the locales to which it travels, and it evolves with each place it visits, turning into a gallery space where memories of its travels are exhibited. The proceeds from the café are used to construct playgrounds through the Herbman Fund. Herbman keeps travelling, believing in a world where people and nature are healthy, and children are happy and have enough space to play.

Yangpu Riverside Public Space

193

Project Name: **Demonstration section of Yangpu Riverside Public Space**
Project Location: **Huangpu River, Shanghai, China**
Landscape Architects: **Original Design Studio**
Architects: **Original Design Studio**
Client: **Yangpu Riverside Investment and Development Company**
Completed: **2016** Demonstration section of Yangpu Riverside Public Space
2019 Green Hill and Shanghai Shipyard double dock exhibition area

The 'liquid' aluminium wharf continues the walkway past the Yangshupu water treatment plant.

The monumental dry docks of the Shanghai Shipyards.

The transformation of the former tobacco warehouse into a 'green hill'.

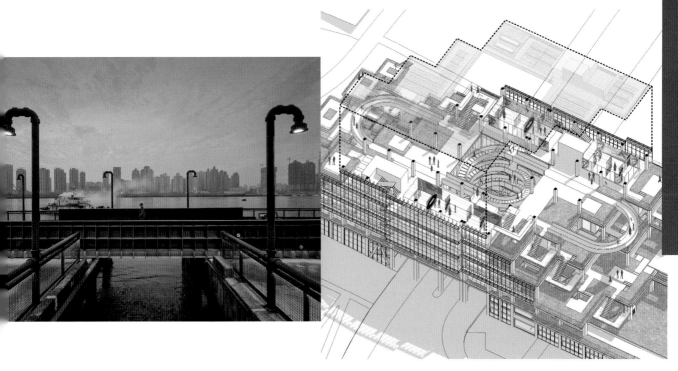

Huangpu River is considered the birthplace of China's modern industries, the site of the nation's first water, electricity, shipbuilding, and textile companies. Over time the industrial development along the river severed connections to the city and its citizens. In 2002, the Shanghai government began plans to transform forty-five kilometres of the Huangpu River's shorelines into Shanghai's longest public open space. This work has been carried out in stages by multiple designers.

This section of the Yangpu riverside designed by Shanghai-based Original Design Studio involved the extensive renovation of industrial heritage including a former tobacco warehouse, shipyards, and a water plant. Their design response explores ideas of openness and publicness and reconfigures land use to establish a stronger connection between the riverside open space and the urban hinterland. Working closely with the industrial heritage, Original Design Studio has heightened the dramatic spatial and material qualities while restoring water ecology and introducing a continuous pedestrian and cycle path along the foreshore.

The transformation of the former tobacco warehouse into a 'green hill' is a particularly striking feature. Aspects of landscape and architecture merge into a permeable public infrastructure, which connects the city with the riverbank. This renovation includes extending a road through the lower level of the warehouse to establish continuous transport networks. The adaptive reuse of the Shanghai Shipyards into a series of public spaces to house public art exhibition

and cultural events provides a unique experience for audience and performers. The monumental dry docks offer spaces for artists from around the world to stage concerts and performances, contrasting contemporary expression against the unique sense of history of the industrial zone. This culturally programmed space is supported by the hundred-year-old Maoma Warehouse (formerly a British textile company) which is the major indoor exhibition space of SUSAS (Shanghai Urban Space Art Season).

Threaded around these significant industrial legacies is the restoration of the ecological environment, which includes the design of a wetland in a depression behind the original floodwall. Establishing continuous circulation along the waterfront for cycling, jogging, and strolling was challenging, given in some cases factories and plant were constructed to the water's edge. Strategies included bridging across wharf blocks and designing passageways beyond the 'blueline' to navigate the Yangshupu water treatment plant.

With a focus on maintaining industrial heritage and limiting the extent of design intervention, Original Design Studio avoids 'building' an urban public waterfront which interrupts the continuity in time. Instead through the revitalisation of the industrial infrastructure and the poetic interpretation of memories, they have maintained the site's cultural legacy while providing a valuable public space for Shanghai.

195

Jintai Village Reconstruction

Sichuan

A new stepped housing prototype,
which accommodates site level changes,
maximises thermal comfort, and
minimises construction waste.

Jintai Village is a rural mountainous community located in northern Sichuan Province and was devasted during the 2008 Wenchuan earthquake. Post-earthquake recovery was swift and the village was promptly rebuilt on its original site. However, heavy rains in 2011 caused a landslide and the majority of the village was destroyed once again. In response, the local government began construction to stabilise the slopes with a series of concrete piles approximately 150 metres deep across a steep terrain. The design team worked closely with the villagers, local government, NGOs, and external donors throughout the reconstruction process to maximise limited financial resources. The plan extends beyond simply reconstructing the devasted homes and includes landscape infrastructural features and economic development strategies for new livelihoods instead of relying solely on remittances or subsistence agriculture.

197

The landscape master plan negotiates a ten-metre elevation difference through a series of small retaining walls, terraces, and ramps rather than one large retaining wall. The landscape team worked closely with the architects to develop a house prototype that absorbed some of the level changes within the architecture while creating an interconnected network of sloped pathways to accommodate the villagers' small vehicles and continuous village commons to foster social cohesion. Kitchen gardens are relocated to stepped roof terraces to maximise sun exposure and reserve ground space for community activities. At the foot of the hill, an open-air community centre uses steps and terraces to create a flexible program space, but more importantly provides a framework for future village enterprises such as a shared restaurant.

The design team worked with local construction methods and materials to develop replicable and sustainable construction techniques that could be used in other village communities in the region. For example, the new village homes utilise higher quality materials to maximise thermal comfort while minimising construction waste. The landscape is designed to accommodate gravity flow of both stormwater and household wastewater. Grey water and sewage are treated centrally and its effluent is polished in a series of treatment wetlands before discharge. Future phases of the project take advantage of local government incentives for collective biogas facilities to complement the waste and resource cycles of the village. Collectively, these landscape and architectural strategies challenge the norms of rural development projects and advocate for greater collaboration between the design disciplines, the community, and other stakeholders.

Project Name: **Jintai Village Reconstruction**
Location: **Jintai Village, Sichuan Province, China**
Landscape Architect: **Dorothy Tang**
Architects: **Rural Urban Framework**
Funding: **Nan Fung Group**
Completion Year: **2014**
Text: Dorothy Tang

Tokachi Millennium Forest

Shimizu

Project Name: **Tokachi Millennium Forest**
Location: **Shimizu, Hokkaido, Japan**
Landscape Architect: **Takano Landscape Planning**
Garden Designer: **Dan Pearson**
Architect: **Atelier Zo**
Client: **Tokachi Mainichi Shinbun**
Completion Year: **2008**
Text: based on information from Takano Landscape Planning
and Dan Pearson Studio

199

In 1996, Mitsushige Hayashi, the owner of the Tokachi Mainichi newspaper, approached Fumiaki Takano to develop a master plan for a 400-hectare site framed by meadows and abandoned forests located in Shimizu, Hokkaido. The 'bubble economy' had just ended, and as a reaction to the speed, efficiency, and large-scale investment that characterised this period, people began to talk about slow life and slow food; but slow design was not mentioned. Although the banks were still trying to lend more money for high-investment resort development projects, Takano convinced the client to approach the project slowly. The project began with a careful observation of the existing landscape qualities and materials. Takano describes this concept as a 'slow dialogue with the forest'. Instead of the ski and golf resort developments so prominent in Hokkaido, this project rests on the four pillars of 'forest, ecotourism, education, and agriculture'. In 2000, Dan Pearson was invited to add a more intimate layer to the original master plan. This so-called Garden Masterplan was an exercise in place-making creating new destinations to welcome and entertain a wider range of visitors to the project and explore the long-term vision of living in harmony with nature.

▶

Nothing is brought into Forest. Nothing is taken out from Forest. The design aims to connect the garden spaces with 'wilderness' by refining the attractiveness of the forests and unveiling its spirituality. It symbolises the slow 'design method of deletion' that underpins this project. Following the cutting of the thick *sasa* (broad leaf bamboo), which dominated the forest floor in the first two years of the project, over thirty annual plant and wildflower species started to bloom, allowing the return of a rich and diverse environment. Trees were thinned out to invite sunlight. The timber was reused to make furniture such as a big table and bar counters, and water channels were found in the various resting spaces throughout the forest.

201

Aside from the name-giving Forest Garden, the project includes additional extents (the Earth Garden, the Meadow Garden, the Kitchen Garden, and the Rose Garden) designed by Dan Pearson. The intimate spaces of the Earth Garden welcome visitors and provide a sense of discovery and connection. Playing with the concept of *shakkei* – the principle of incorporating a borrowed view – the landforms create a new fore-ground that draws the surrounding Hidaka Mountain ranges closer into the site. The Meadow Garden introduces naturalistic planting design with the celebration of endemic species. Over the course of a growing season, there is an almost unbroken opportunity for pollination and interest for wildlife as plants come to seed.

Rice Garden

The 'autumn wave' Rice Garden in Shuiku Village.

The Rice Garden on Chongming Island.

Project Name: **Rice Garden**
Project Location: **Chongming Island, Shanghai (2016–2017), Shuiku Village, Shanghai (2018)**
Landscape Architect: **College of Architecture and Urban Planning at Tongji University. (Initiated by Professor Dong Nannan)**
Completion Year: **2016–2019**

The Rice Gardens are a series of temporary design interventions, which work with framing and harvesting methods, along with local construction techniques, to provide spaces for cultural, education, and art activities. A collaboration between Tongji University and rural communities, the projects aim to contribute to the socio-economic development of villages, strengthen family interactions, and develop children's skills and communication, along with promoting exchange and interaction between urban and rural populations.

In 2016, the first Rice Garden was constructed on Chongming Island and was developed with the local Farming Club on rented farmland to celebrate the autumn rice harvest. With limited resources, a 'subtractive design' strategy was applied to 'harvest' a temporary space from a golden rice field. Thick layers of rice straw were used to 'pave' the ground, with the entire space ploughed into field at the end of the autumn harvest. Activities centred on teaching and included a 'rice maze' for children to help construct, visit, and play. This experience reinforced the importance of using local construction techniques and materials with a low environmental impact such as bamboo pole, rice straw, straw rope, and cloth. In 2017, the second Rice Garden offered a simpler space and placed more emphasis on rural family interactions including promoting parent-child communication and collaboration through picnics, fruit and vegetable painting, and other recreational and educational activities.

In 2018, the site for the Rice Garden shifted to Shuiku Village, Jinshan District, and the project evolved into a more comprehensive collaboration between university staff and students, local government, the village, NGOs, and public artists. The idea of 'water' and 'rice field' was combined to propose an 'autumn wave in the countryside'. Three strips were cut to create the rolling feeling of a wave, while bamboo, net rope, and the harvested ears of wheat were bound together to develop an 'autumn wave' effect. This space formed the main area for a range of events and gathering for children, parents, and volunteers such as calligraphy teaching, painting, catching fish with bare hands, and other activities that allowed children to return to nature and the countryside. A long table banquet was held in Caojing town to celebrate the Chinese Farmers' Harvest Festival.

By working with the seasonal characteristic of agricultural landscape the interim Rice Garden creates important cooperative links between universities, villages, and towns and a wide range of social resources to construct, communicate, and interact with an agricultural environment. In 2019, an exhibition Rice Garden was included as part of the Shanghai Urban Space Art Season.

203

Landscape Architects as Urbanists of our Age

Jeong-Hann Pae

Abandoned sites and redundant infrastructures of post-industrial cities around the world are posing challenges to landscape architects and urban designers. In Korea, modernisation and urbanisation were carried out rapidly and continue with numerous new cities under construction. However, with the changing economic structure over the past two decades, some cities have suffered from shrinkage and depopulation. In large metropolitan cities like Seoul, changes in industrial structure have caused modern industrial facilities and infrastructure to become derelict and abandoned. Post-industrial redundant sites are no longer strangers to Seoulites.

Redevelopment projects involving the complete demolition of older areas have been carried out on many of these derelict sites. These large-scale transformations come with many side effects, which include the market-led tendency to place value on property rather than on people, the loss of local character due to the destruction of communities, and damage to the natural environment. While the profits from such developments are returned to developers and speculative investors, the socially vulnerable and destitute, who are unable to pay the high prices of new housing, are driven to the city outskirts. The rise in property value and rent prices due to redevelopment also contributes to gentrification and other social issues.[1]

To overcome the negative effects of this 'demolish-rebuild' development approach, in the early 2000s the Ministry of Land and Transportation launched a series of urban regeneration projects to revitalise the moribund cities. Similarly, the Seoul Metropolitan Government sought an alternative approach for urban regeneration, which led to the Urban Regeneration Act of 13 April 2013. Urban regeneration projects are increasing across the country and remain a core urban policy of the present government. In this contemporary Korean urban context, landscape serves as a significant medium for urban regeneration. Abandoned transportation infrastructures, post-industrial lands, landfills, and relocation sites for military camps are now being re-appropriated as innovative parks and open spaces. The following discussion of three influential projects constructed post-2000s highlights landscape architecture's important role in achieving Seoul's impressive urban regeneration. Rediscovering these forgotten places, these design approaches demonstrate the landscape architect's role as urbanists of our age.

Post-industrial Ruin to Sublime Park

Seonyudo Park is an internationally significant exemplar for transforming a post-industrial ruin into a park of sublime and synesthetic qualities. Earliest records show that Seonyudo (Seonyu Island) was not an island but instead a humble yet elegant forty-metre-high peak which offered magnificent views of the western side of the Han River. To enjoy this scenery around Seonyu Peak, literary figures during the Joseon era gladly climbed this landscape or walked around it

The great flood of 1925, which was an unprecedented natural disaster in the history of Seoul, had an enormous effect on the geography and history of the Han River. Banks were built on both sides of the river using rocks gathered from Seonyu Peak. The construction of the second Han River Bridge (now Yanghwa Bridge) in 1962 and the subsequent Han River Development Project in 1968 ultimately changed Seonyu Peak into an island. No longer accessible, this now flat island in the middle of the river was surrounded by concrete retaining walls.

Seoul's rapid urbanisation changed the fate of Seonyu Island once again in 1978 when a water purification plant was constructed. However, changes to Seoul's water supply system meant that the Seonyu Water Purification Plant was no longer necessary. In 1999, the Seoul Metropolitan Government decided to make Seonyu Island (at over 10,900 square metres) into a park and selected a proposal by Seoahn Total Landscape Architects (STL) through a design competition. In April 2002, the park was opened to the public.

The design of Seonyudo Park reflects masterful incorporation of industrial facilities, including reusing water systems and processes, in a park design. With its redundant water purification plant, Seonyudo had become a *terrain vague*. Yet, in a post-industrial society, *terrain vague* presents a landscape of new possibilities; while uncertain and unproductive, the landscape offers the potential to be transformed into a place of memory experienced through traces of time.[2]

Accordingly, the landscape architects did not pursue a traditional design approach of filling an empty space with new objects, nor did STL intend to represent natural landscapes or idealised images of nature. Instead, they designed a park through an archaeological approach to design, rediscovering and preserving what was seemingly useless and reorganising existing structures, spaces and systems. New uses and meaning were added through the morphing of traces such as the water purification plant into a place where people could encounter the past. In other words, the design sought to make *time* a part of this place rather than simply designing a space.

Underground spaces, building columns, and walls were retained, while the existing buildings were renovated into a visitor centre, the Han River History Museum, a cafeteria, and a theatre. The underground site of the water purification plant was transformed into a water purification basin. New themed gardens were developed including the Garden of Green Pillars, the Aquatic Botanical Garden, and the Garden of Time, and a playground was added.

Seonyudo Park has been described variously as an 'alternative experiment in resolving the crisis of traditional urban parks', 'a recycling strategy for post-industrial sites', and offering 'respect for time and memory beyond form-oriented design'.[3] Seonyudo Park can be considered a 'palace of senses', replacing traditional landscape aesthetics of the beautiful and the picturesque with the aesthetics of the sublime. The raw power of the materiality of the site—whether of the broken concrete, rough cement columns, or rusty and corroded steel pipes—heighten the structural logic of the design and the sensory characteristics unique to this park. These fragments of time establish an aesthetic experience based not on the characteristics of order and harmony, but instead by feelings evoked by the disorderly, formlessness, and the uncertainty of objects.[4]

If one stands atop a wooden deck attached to the Seonyugyo Bridge, the lonely wind from the river blowing towards the deck feels brittle; the sights and the smells of Seoul are experienced all at once through and across the Han River; the mesmerising montage of the naked concrete, the cold metal, and the life of plants can be felt; long contemplative paths that require solemn steps of introspection rather than stressful physical movement are aesthetically significant.

Seonyudo Park represents a breakthrough for Korean landscape architecture and urban park design, which had been characterised by pseudo-ecological design approaches and the incorporation of elements that imply Korean cultural traditions. The discovery-based design approach has greatly influenced the design direction of several post-industrial parks and urban regeneration projects in Korea, including Seoul Forest Park and West Seoul Lake Park. By embracing the dilapidation of the purification plant, a poignant remnant of modernisation, it serves as a significant precedent for a recycling strategy for post-industrial sites which we shall see much more of in the future.

Elevated Highway to Urban River Promenade

The Cheonggyecheon Restoration and Renewal project is a significant step towards transforming Seoul into a global green city. Providing a water-filled north-south green axis, arguably a new backbone for Seoul, Cheonggyecheon creates a natural yet human-oriented urban space for an increasingly dense city. Despite the fact that water flowing through the stream is pumped from the Han River, the project is considered an immense success, restoring the city's lost landscape vitality.

205

The origin of the project is the Gaecheon (meaning open stream), which was transformed during the Joseon dynasty (1392–1910) into a drainage system crossed by bridges. Under the reign of Taejong, the third king of the Joseon dynasty, dredging and bolstering of the banks of the stream was carried out every two to three years. King Yeongjo expanded the refurbishment of the stream into a national project.

Gaecheon was renamed to Cheonggyecheon after Japanese imperialists colonised the Korean peninsula. During the Japanese colonial period, financial difficulties prevented the Imperial Japanese forces from covering the stream despite several attempts. After the Korean War (1950–1953), many people migrated to Seoul to make their living and eventually settled along this stream in shabby makeshift houses. The accompanying trash, sand, waste, and deteriorating conditions resulted in an eyesore for the city. Starting in 1958, the stream was covered with concrete, followed by the construction of a 5.6-kilometre-long and ▶

Seonyudo Park
Seoul

On the site of a former water purification plant, Seonyudo Park is considered a milestone for Korean landscape architecture, offering a significant precedent for the recycling post-industrial sites and engaging with the aesthetics of the sublime.

Project Name: **Seonyudo Park**
Location: **Yeongdeungpo-gu, Seoul, Korea**
Landscape Architects: **Seoahn Total Landscape**
Architects: **Sungyong Joh Architecture & Urbanism**
Client: **Seoul Metropolitan Government**
Completed: **2002**

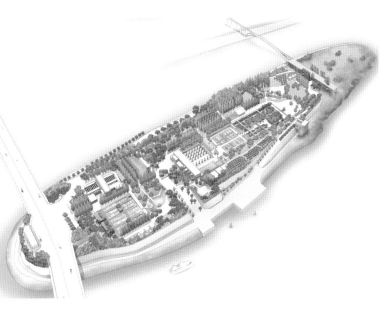

207

Maintaining the raw power
of the industrial materiality.

One of Asia's best known and ambitious contemporary landscape projects, the Cheonggyecheon Restoration and Renewal Project replaces a covered stream and elevated motorway with a new type of urban park that connects and infiltrates the city.

The Cheonggyecheon Restoration and Renewal Project

209

New open space near Sinpyeonghwa
Fashion Town.

The Cheonggyecheon Overpass
Retention Monument.

Project Name: **The Cheonggyecheon Restoration
and Renewal project**
Location: **Central District, Seoul, Korea**
Landscape Architects: **Three landscape teams of CA
Landscape Design, Seoahn Total Landscape, and
Mikyoung Kim Design**
Client: **Seoul Metropolitan Government**
Completed: **2005**

▶ 16-metre-wide elevated highway over the stream in 1976. This elevated motorway was a perfect emblem of functionalist urban planning and a prime example of the successful industrialisation and modernisation of Korea.[5]

After the 1990s, the Korean urban and landscape design paradigm shifted from high-density development into a more environmentally friendly regeneration. Combined with new sewage treatment technologies, this shift prompted the Seoul Metropolitan Government to reinstate the stream. The Cheonggyecheon Restoration and Renewal project became a major political issue supported by Mayor Myung-Bak Lee, who was elected in 2002.

In July 2003, Mayor Lee initiated a project to remove the elevated highway and to restore the stream. The project faced two critical objections. First, many transportation experts claimed that everyday life in northern Seoul would become even more chaotic, should the highway be removed. However, as the residents found out years later, this prediction was never fulfilled. Second, the stream remained dry throughout the year, except during the summer rainy season. To solve this problem, 120,000 tons of water from the Han River was pumped to the starting point of Cheonggyecheon using electric power, resulting in an average stream depth of forty centimetres. Despite the use of a non-renewable energy source, the restoration and renewal of the stream was deemed important as it reinforced the narrative of reintroducing nature into the city and promoted a more eco-friendly approach to landscape design.[6]

The regeneration project also engages with the historic stream, which had been lost for over thirty years. The *pal gyeong* (eight sceneries) approach, a historic landscape organisation method from ancient Korea, was used to guide the urban renewal. Yangkyo Chin, one of the landscape architects leading the project, highlights how 'the "Eight Cheonggyecheon Sceneries" are located at eight strategic points, beginning with the Cheonggye Plaza. ... Each of the eight scenes has its own specific characteristics with viewing decks, magnificent artworks, water fountains, and sculptures.'[7]

Another purpose of this project was to revitalise Sooul's economy and to reinforce the surrounding business area with information technology, international affairs, and digital industries. The plan encouraged the return of a pedestrian-friendly road network connecting the stream to traditional resources. The purpose of this network system, the Cheonggyecheon Culture Belt, was to build the cultural and environmental basis for the city to guide development.

The project was implemented in three sections, each guided by a different design team. The Master Landscape Architect (MLA) system was applied to ensure the development of a unified Cheonggyecheon area. Chin observes that 'the MLA not only organized three different landscape design teams but also con-trolled and coordinated other teams, such as the civil engineering team, the bridge design team, the lighting design team.'[8]

In October 2005, Cheonggyechon was opened to the public, and many praised the design. The reason why the public cheered for the project is very simple: people could now walk through the city along the water. In short, the new Cheonggyecheon is successful not because the stream was restored, but because it was transformed into an urban park which offers a framework for new possibilities.[9]

To appreciate the design, it is not necessary to walk the full six kilometres. Instead, it is a park that embraces and produces the daily life and the culture of the city. The park can be accessed from a nearby office to spend a peaceful lunchtime. With a little more time, people can walk along the waterfront and experience seasonal changes before returning to street level. Occasionally, it hosts special exhibitions or performances. Or it may function as a pedestrian street linking to the subway.

Due to its location and linear characteristics, Cheonggyecheon contributes to Seoul's urban development, intersecting with over twelve kilometres of urban fabric. It is often recognised as a novel attraction in Seoul, but it is more significant than that, presenting an alternative type of park that connects and infiltrates the city. Neither a refuge for isolation, nor a romantic green island, this park is flexible and dynamic, guiding the transformation and evolution of the city, like a blood vessel that flows through the city.

Military Base to Large Park

211

The Yongsan U.S. military base in the centre of Seoul has been transitioning over the past thirty years into a large urban park. Having been used as a military base during the Japanese colonial period and the U.S. Army occupation, the site was for over a century cut off from the rest of the city by a secured wall. Owing to its geographical advantages adjacent to the Han River, foreign troops have been stationed in Yongsan since 1882, starting with the Qing troops, and followed in 1894 by the Japanese army. The construction of the railroad and Yongsan Station in 1900 led to the area's urbanisation. After the Russo-Japanese War in 1904, the Japanese army expropriated 376 hectares as an army base. In 1945, after the Japanese army was defeated in the Second World War, ownership changed once again with the U.S. military occupying the district. After the Korean War, the Yongsan base of the U.S. Armed Forces gradually became a barracks city, continuing its disconnection from its surrounding neighbourhoods.

Plans for a park on the Yongsan base surfaced in 1990 when Korea and the United States signed an

MOU for the relocation of the military base. However, this discussion came to a halt due to costs, only to resume again in May 2003. Two years later, the Yongsan Park Planning Initiative, the first state-led park project, was established. This vision greatly influenced the subsequent plans, emphasising the need for 'a park that communicates with the city' away from urban isolation, and 'a growing park' that focuses on leading the evolution of the city.

The Special Act on the Creation of Yongsan Park was formalised in 2007, which included the establishment of a government task force team for the development, management and operation of Yongsan Park, under the Ministry of Land, Infrastructure, and Transport.[10] In 2011, the General Basic Plan for the creation and zoning of Yongsan Park was established.[11] Based on this plan, an international design competition for a master plan was held the following year. West 8 consortium grabbed the first prize with the proposal 'Healing: The Future Park'. The essence of this design is the restoration and the dramatisation of the original topographic ridgeline connecting the Yongsan Park northward to the Namsan Mountain.[12] Since winning the proposal, the West 8 consortium has further developed its master plan, which will transform the 243-hectare site into a super-scale urban park. The Yongsan Park Basic Design (YPBD) was completed at the end of 2018.

The master plan and YPBD were developed through an interactive process guided by the fundamental concept of healing nature, history, and culture.[13] As a process, the act of healing transforms the existing site, through an awareness of its history, into a significant park that offers an experience of nature, ecological restoration, and a wide range of urban park culture.

Why does Yongsan Park convey the potential to change the future of Seoul? First, the park is world-class, at least in terms of its size. The combined area of Yongsan Park, the National Museum of Korea, and the War Memorial of Korea is larger than the celebrated Central Park in New York. Being large does not only mean being rich in quantity. Large parks can create an identity and resilience for a city and serve as the basis for complex cultural creations. A green axis between the Namsan Mountain and the Han River, which will be connected through Yongsan Park, will evolve Seoul's resilient ecosystem. A variety of art galleries and cultural facilities designed inside the park will function as cultural power plants of Seoul.

Second, the site encompasses countless stories and histories. Yongsan Park is filled with layers of time and meaning in Korean history, and can act as a reminder of the past for future generations. YPBD proposes more than simply preserving historical traces. Major buildings preserved will be used as educational spaces and cultural facilities, while other buildings will be deconstructed and reconstructed to serve as social platforms that accommodate various activities in the park.

Lastly, the park contains elements from both rich nature and the dynamic urban life. It is not easy to find dialectical places where nature and cities communicate as dynamically as Yongsan Park. The ecological-scenic axis connecting Mountain Namsan, Yongsan Park, and the Han River spreads into the urban fabric through flexible boundaries of park and city. Evolving alongside the natural and urban environment, Yongsan Park could open a new chapter in the history of urban parks.

However, while this open-ended park has many opportunities and high hopes, guiding the change and growth over the next decade will be challenging. The roadmap for creating the park remains unclear, open to unforeseeable changes due to unfolding political, military, and diplomatic situations. It is important to carefully design processes that can respond wisely to changes and allow for greater participation in the park's creation-process bringing the state, citizens, and experts to work together. In this way, the new park will transform the adjacent urban fabric and work as a magnetic field for urban regeneration.

Over the last two decades, many urban projects for the transformation of post-industrial landscapes and derelict sites into urban parks have been carried out in Seoul. In these projects, landscape has served as a significant medium for urban regeneration. As discussed above, Seonyudo Park is the first Korean project to recycle industrial ruins into an ecological park, embodying the sublime and synesthetic sensibilities. It has influenced the discovery-based design strategies of several post-industrial parks and urban regeneration projects in Korea. The Cheonggyecheon Restoration and Renewal project has transformed the urban structure and pedestrian network by revitalising downtown Seoul. In addition, it has sparked a trend to renaturalise many riversides across the country. Transforming a 243-hectare military base into an X-large urban park, the Yongsan Park has been carried out by a phasing approach, not by the traditional master plan method. In the future, Yongsan Park will serve as a medium for revising and reorganising Seoul's distorted urban form and structure, offering a significant model for urban regeneration through landscape design. ∎

213

Everyday Landscapes

For design to have an impact it does not need to have a large budget or an extensive site. Sometimes just a simple seat, a strategically located connection, or the insertion of a whimsical element can make a difference in people's everyday lives.

The Health Line

Shanghai

The Bridgelife Neighbourhood is a new community centre in Shanghai's Baoshan District that integrates commercial, cultural, creative, and sports uses on the site of a former Japanese thermos bottle factory. Due to the original factory layout, only leftover narrow corridors could be used for public space. Lab D+H designed a 600-metre Health Line, which features a long linear playground sited between the commercial buildings and the car park. Ranging in width from 2.5 to 1 metres, this playground allows families to gather and enjoy some time with their children when they arrive or before they leave by car.

Project Name: **Bridgelife Neighbourhood Park**
Project Location: **Shanghai, China**
Clients: **Shanghai Qibao Enterprise Management**
Landscape Architects: **Lab D+H**
Completion Year: **2019**
Text: based on information from Lab D+H

No Longer Drowning— Waving

In 2008, BAU won a competition for the design of a landscape associated with the widening of Changning Road along Suzhou Creek, Shanghai's second largest river. A concrete flood barrier constructed along the river had squeezed a sidewalk between seven lanes of traffic, while a concrete wall blocked all river views. By raising the riverside sidewalk to the top of the flood barrier, BAU provided a new pedestrian experience, which offered river views and separation from the heavy traffic. Cleverly, the iconic waveform of the riverside balustrade comprises three modules, which supports different programs: indents for seating, folds for leaning perches, and bulges for viewing down into the flowers at the river's edge. Viewed at speed from the road or from the river on boats, the balustrade produces kinetic wave patterns in numerous dimensions.

Project Name: **No Longer Drowning—Waving**
Location: **Shanghai, China**
Landscape Architects: **Brearley Architects +**
Urbanists BAU
Client: **Changning District Construction and**
Transportation Committee
Project completion: **2010**
Text: based on information from BAU

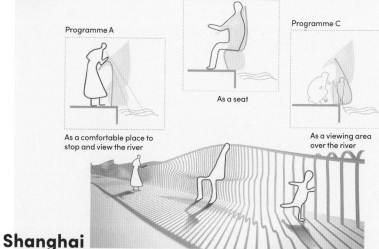

Programme A

As a comfortable place to
stop and view the river

Programme B

As a seat

Programme C

As a viewing area
over the river

Shanghai

The Jingumae Residence

Tokyo

Located in the heart of Tokyo, the Jingumae residence is situated on top of a hill. Part of the site is open to the public for cultural events and community gatherings. The private side of the park was designed like an outdoor 'living room' in which the residents can relax and appreciate seasonal changes in landscape. The design aims to pass on the memory of the forest which previously existed on site. Leaves from the former forest were pressed onto the floor tiles, tree shadows were depicted on concrete blocks, and tables and chairs were carved from the cut trees. There are ten outdoor rugs, each with a unique theme of sky, water, light, shadow, wind, tree, soil, harvest, colour, and smell. These rugs reintroduce urban residents to ways of appreciating nature in the middle of Tokyo.

Project Name: **The Jingumae Residence**
Project Location: **Tokyo, Japan**
Landscape Architect: **EARTHSCAPE**
Client: **Nippon Steel Kowa Real Estate, Mitsui, NTT Urban Development Corporation**
Completion Year: **2013**
Text: based on information from EARTHSCAPE

215

A ground surface of ten outdoor rugs.

Shangzhou

Re-establishing vital connections for communities through infrastructure such as bridges can greatly improve people's lives. Rural Urban Framework's bridge in Shaanxi Province offers an unapologetic contemporary insertion into the rural countryside. Designed to reconnect a nearby walnut orchard to a village, the Lingzidi Bridge was conceived as a 'singular loop' linking two levels of river banks, along with providing an arm that connects down to the river. The bridge operates as a community space, offering a meeting place for trade and commerce and incorporates shaded areas and seating. In an important design detail, black pigment was added to the concrete to distinguish it from the adjacent grey highway viaduct. This simple adjustment to the use of ubiquitous concrete, combined with an understanding of light and form, results in a simple but striking insertion into the Chinese rural landscape.

Project Name: **Lingzidi Bridge**
Location: **Shangzhou, Shaanxi Province, China**
Architects: **Rural Urban Framework**
Client: **World Vision, Luke Him Sau Charitable Trust**
Completion Year: **2012**
Text: based on information from RUF

Landscapes
in the Sky

Jillian Walliss While many cities around the world aspire to green urbanism, it is difficult to identify any that have matched Singapore's investment in green infrastructure. Increasingly, Singapore's airports, hotels, shopping malls, commercial buildings, and high-rise housing developments incorporate community gardens, recreational spaces, lush gardens, vertical green walls, planted balconies, and urban farms. So why is Singapore so successful integrating nature into the city? Arguably, designing living systems in a steady equatorial tropical environment is an easier proposition than in cities that experience more extreme climatic shifts. A shortage of land for development also encourages integrated vertical urbanism, giving rise to numerous 'landscapes in the sky'. However, what best explains Singapore's success is its holistic government approach. The strong alignment between public agencies and statutory authorities facilitates the coordination of policy, research, and financial incentives, effectively guiding Singapore's transition into a biophilic 'city in a garden'.

Singapore's National Parks Board (NPB) has been central to achieving this vision. The Board's work involves conducting and disseminating extensive research into the potentials of green walls and green roofs. This includes publishing the Bringing *Greenery Skywards: A Handbook on Developing Sustainable Highrise Garden* in 2017, along with implementing the Landscape Excellence Assessment Framework (LEAF), which certifies outstanding projects. In addtion, their contribution extends to providing generous financial incentives through the Sky Rise Greenery Incentive scheme. Under this scheme the NPB provides up to 50 per cent of the installation costs for rooftop greenery and vertical green walls (capped at SGD 200 and SGD 500 per square metre for rooftops and walls, respectively).[1]

The introduction of the Green Mark scheme in 2005 by the Buildings and Construction Authority (BCA) has been equally influential in greening the construction industry. In 2008, it became mandatory for all new buildings to be certified.[2] The scheme has had impact in other Asian nations, with developers in Vietnam, Thailand, Indonesia, Malaysia, China, and the Philippines applying for Green Mark certification. In 2015, Green Mark was refined further to include biophilic elements within its assessment, including a stronger focus on climatically responsive design, smart technology, embedded carbon and resources, and well-being and health.[3]

Similarly, Singapore's Urban Redevelopment Authority development codes have become progressively more innovative in their metrics. Starting in 2009 the Landscaping for Urban Spaces and High-Rises (LUSH) code required developers to 'replace greenery lost from the site' either on the ground, roof gardens, sky terraces, or planter boxes.[4] Revisions to the LUSH code in 2017 reconceived the role of landscape from a general replacement value to more expansive goals such as contributing to food resilience, enhancing community bonding and generating renewable energy. For example urban rooftop farms, critical to supplementing Singapore's food supply, can now be counted as part of the landscape replacement areas under the hardscape component.[5] The influence of the LUSH code partly explains the decision to incorporate an urban farm on top of the new Funan (discussed in Repositioning the Private Realm).

Through this combination of policy, regulations, and incentives Singapore is on track to achieve its ambition of 200 hectares of skyrise greenery (the equivalent of 200 football fields) by 2030.[6] These 'landscapes in the sky' have evolved into an innovative mix of ecological and social infrastructure, which contribute to diverse new urban typologies. Other Asian cities are beginning to explore ambitious green infrastructure. For example, Thailand has recently completed two monumental projects associated with universities. Chulalongkorn University Centenary Park (discussed in Artifical Nature) is considered Bangkok's first major piece of green infrastructure, while Thammasat University Green Roof (see pp. 236–237) is currently recognised as the largest urban rooftop farm in Asia. Measuring over 22,000 square metres, this roofscape draws on traditional rice terrace farming to offer an urban open space, which operates as a water management system, generates energy production, and provides an organic food source.[7] However for the time being, Singapore's state-driven commitment to a biophilic urbanism will continue to set a high benchmark, not just for Asia but worldwide.

The Living Skin

Nirmal Kishnani

Vegetation in/on high-rise buildings was first explored in tropical Asia in the last quarter of the twentieth century, initially as a means to an environmental end. The oil crises of the 1970s had piqued interest in energy use, which in turn led to a critique of the growing dependence on air conditioning. The humid-wet climate, coupled with local planting palettes, made it easy to grow landscapes on walls and roofs. At this stage, it was enough for flora to act as mediator between indoor and outdoor, to be envelope-affixed and function as a thermal barrier.

The rationale for vertical greening changed in the 1990s when the liberalisation of national economies transformed cities Asia-wide. To cope with changes, buildings would have to counter, sometimes offset, disruption and fragmentation. Roof gardens, for instance, were seen as ways to mitigate urban heat island effect; they were also positioned as community spaces in areas with high built-up densities. By the turn of the century, the conversation expanded to include climate change and biodiversity losses, and the same landscapes took on the mantle of regeneration. *The living skin* doubled up as habitat and farm, now performing ecosystem services. No longer a bolt-on feature, it was enmeshed into the form of a building and tied back to socio-ecological systems on the ground and within the neighbourhood.

From Bioclimatic to Biological

Credit for championing building-integrated vegetation must go to Malaysian architect Ken Yeang. He was responsible for several 'hairy skyscrapers' in the 1980s. Hairiness, a reference to sporadic vertical greening, was one of several strategies in Yeang's bioclimatic model that set out to improve indoor comfort and reduce energy use. The model was pivotal to the environmental discourse in Malaysia and Singapore and a harbinger of the Green movement that was yet to come.

By the time Green buildings made inroads into the construction sector in Asia, Yeang's argument had already shifted from bioclimatic to biological, which signalled a higher order of ecological thinking. Post 2000, he would bring several strands of science to the drawing board, notably biophilic design (human well-being), ecosystem services (mimicry of natural flows and processes), and habitat formation (pathways and patches for other species). The edge condition was no longer indoor and outdoor; it was human-made and natural. The goal was a synthesis of organic and inorganic; what Yeang termed 'biointegration'.[1] Ecology, once confined to the ground, would be drawn up vertically, becoming part of the fabric of architecture.

Solaris (Singapore, 2011) exemplifies this approach. The 17-storey office development has multiple stepped landscape decks that are connected by a 1.5-kilometre spiral garden, 3 to 6 metres wide. It coils around the facade, connecting the roof to the basement. No biodiversity audit has ever been carried out, but there are anecdotal sightings of squirrels, snakes, and hornbills.[2] What's noteworthy about Solaris, and Yeang's ecological model in general, is the idea that buildings ought not to be viewed as standalone objects: they should connect to wider systems. The living skin does more than reduce heat transmission into a building. It can cool the neighbourhood and offer a human-made proxy of nature, i.e., constructed nature, that attracts species from the neighbourhood.

The linking of scales is echoed by other practitioners in Asia. Vo Trong Nghia, the highly regarded Vietnamese architect, sees buildings as surrogates for what the city lacks.[3] For example, the House for Trees (Tan

Binh District, Ho Chi Minh City, 2014) is a private home set in a garden wherein each room is a free-standing cube that holds a full-sized tree on its roof. Were this idea to be replicated, the argument goes, House for Trees might lead to a 'City of Trees'.[4]

The degradation of blue-green systems, to which Nghia is reacting, pervades Asia. Metropolitan areas that have expanded and densified over the past few decades have eaten into natural and agricultural regions and stripped their own cores of parks and waterways. Ho Chi Minh City lost 50 per cent of its green cover in the first decade of the new millennium.[5] In Mumbai, India, 36 per cent of forests and green cover has been cut down since the 1990s; water bodies have shrunk by 12 per cent; wetlands, by 31 per cent; open spaces and croplands, by 40 per cent.[6] This systematic denaturalisation is set to get worse as Asia urbanises further.[7]

In crafting a response to the problem, Nghia and Yeang rethink known forms and typologies. House for Trees is modelled after a traditional Vietnamese courtyard home, but without its formality. Its roofscape is unlike anything seen in the past. There is no documented evidence of its impact, yet it is one of Nghia's most emblematic projects to date. Yeang's bioclimatic skyscraper was an intentional subversion of the International Style. His two best-known buildings of the era, Menara Mesiniaga (Kuala Lumpur, Malaysia, 1992) and Menara UMNO (Penang, Malaysia, 1998), were profoundly influential, not because of how they actually performed but for how they looked. The assemblage of protuberances and voids, interspersed with plants, is remembered as an environmentalist's take on deconstructivism, a design trend that was very much in vogue at the time.

The notion that style might emerge from an approach on performance was never an oxymoron to Yeang. On the contrary, he has sought to actively bridge the science/design divide. At the time that the bioclimatic model was published, many architects were making a case for regionalism; meanwhile, engineers were focused on thermal transmittance and solar coefficients. Yeang strived to simultaneously address both concerns. In the bioclimatic model and, later, its ecological successor, Yeang tapped scientific principles but also pushed for 'aesthetic exploration', the expression of elements and processes that speak to users.[8] He posited that a new design vocabulary was needed to make manifest what the components do, and how they interconnect. Form shapes performance *and* offers a perspective on process.

This position was formulated against a wider architectural discourse. By the early 1980s, postmodernism had rejected functionalistic leanings of the modern movement and brought back the idea of *relational* function.[9] Architects were given creative license to reference context and history, even if this was sometimes nothing more than an exercise in visual styling. The freedom from modernist constraints, coupled with a quest for connectivity, would resonate in Yeang's reasoning. Green roofs and vegetated walls linked people to their environment and became understandable as a set of syntactic rules.

From Biophilic to Socio-ecological

Singapore-based design firm WOHA is another important voice within the Asian architecture scene. Over the years, and through a series on ambitious and high-profile projects, it has raised the bar on how much vegetation is brought to form-making and why. For instance, Newton Suites (Singapore, 2007), a 36-storey private residential development, boasted a Green Plot Ratio (GnPR) of 130 per cent (i.e., its total landscape area is 1.3 times the size of the site), an unprecedented feat in Singapore at the time that the condominium was completed.[10] A few years later, the hotel Parkroyal on Pickering (Singapore, 2013) achieved 240 per cent, followed by Oasia Hotel Downtown (Singapore, 2016), a 27-storey mixed-use development, with 1,110 per cent.[11]

The green wall of Newton Suites was said to primarily target the experience of residents. The verdant terraces of Parkroyal on Pickering were designed to match the vegetation found in a park across the street, tying the development to its neighbourhood. The envelope of Oasia Hotel Downtown was conceived as a habitat for other species and a biophilic trigger for the community at large.

Not unlike Yeang's early work, the landscapes of WOHA start out as strategies for shaping performance. Form is contoured to draw in wind and light and create shade and shelter. Planted surfaces act as moderators of temperature and humidity. This bioclimatic imperative generates many variants of 'breathable' architecture, buildings that are porous and ventilated, and creates semi-outdoor spaces that project social affordance.[12] The School of the Arts (Singapore, 2010) comprises three linear blocks separated by atria that accelerate airflow through an otherwise deep plan. These breezeway atria are also the social enclaves where students gather. In SkyVille@Dawson (Singapore, 2015) a public housing estate, five landscaped decks connect six towers vertically, bringing plants into voids that facilitate the movement of air. The same decks offer space that fosters community interactions. The overlay of passive design and social space is a hallmark of the firm's work.

What makes WOHA's approach noteworthy is how it transitions to an ecological raison d'etre. Cofounder Wong Mun Summ says that the façade of Oasia Hotel Downtown was designed for climbing animals such as squirrels.[13] A 2018 audit found that the tower was home to a variety of fauna, accounting for some half of the species living in nearby green patches. It was also a stepping stone for the biodiversity movement. ▶

221

House for Trees

Ho Chi Minh City

Project Name: **House for Trees**
Location: **Ho Chi Minh City, Vietnam**
Architect: **Vo Trong Nghia Architects**
Client: **Private client**
Completion Year: **2014**
Text: based on information from Vo Trong Nghia Architects

External walls of in-situ concrete textured by bamboo formwork are punctuated by windows to provide cross ventilation, while locally sourced bricks are exposed on the internal walls as finishing. A ventilated cavity separates the concrete and brick walls to protect interior space from heat transfer, while the soil and trees on the roof offer additional insulation and shade.

0 1 2   5m

223

This prototype house constructed to a tight budget of USD 156,000 brings green space back into Ho Chi Minh City by combining high-density dwellings with large tropical trees. Five concrete boxes are designed as 'pots' for trees. Fitting into the informal shape of the site, the five 'pots' are positioned to create a central courtyard and small gardens in between. They open onto a central courtyard with large glass doors and operable windows enhancing natural lighting and ventilation. Living spaces such as the dining room and library are located on the ground floor. Upper floors accommodate private bedrooms and bathrooms, which are connected through bridge-cum-eaves made of steel. The courtyard and gardens, shaded by the trees above, become part of the ground floor living space. With a thick soil layer, the pots also function as storm-water basins for detention and retention, offering the potential with the multiplication of housing units to contribute to the reduction of flooding in the city.

Oasia Hotel Downtown

Singapore

Project Name: **Oasia Hotel Downtown**
Project Location: **Central Business District, Singapore**
Architects: **WOHA**
Landscape Architect: **STX Landscape Architects**
Client: **Far East SOHO**
Completion Year: **2016**
Text: based on information from WOHA and STX Land-
scape Architects

Each sky garden is treated as an open urban scale verandah, which allows breezes to pass through the building to create functional public areas with natural light and fresh air.

A verdant tower of green in the heart of Singapore's dense Central Business District (CBD), Oasia Hotel Downtown is a prototype of land use intensification for the urban tropics. Unlike the shiny and sealed skyscrapers that dot down town Singapore, this tropical 'living tower' offers an alternative image to the sleek technology of the genre. A slender silhouette wrapped in a 'living cloak' of climbing plants, Oasia occupies its entire site. It is made up of horizontal stratums comprised of different programs of SOHO (small office home office), hotel and hotel club, with generous sky gardens inserted at levels 6, 12, 21, and 27.

A close collaboration between the architect and the landscape architect established techniques and systems to make the living system viable. Initially, WOHA preferred a single species of vines but STX Landscape Architects argued for biodiversity with eventually more than twenty-one different species of creepers being used, which attract birds and insects. The tower's red aluminium mesh cladding offers a strong visual contrast to the green creepers, adding a striking presence to the Singapore skyline. Importantly this green system provides relief from reflection and glare and contributes to the amelioration of urban heat island effects.

225

Good maintenance and watering is essential to maintaining the living façade. Species were carefully mapped out, with auto-irrigation stations at each level based on water demand—in broad groups of 'lots, moderate and little'. Species positioning on each façade was determined by sunlight access, informed by shadow analysis of surrounding towers, along with consideration of the growth rate of each climber, to develop a random but calibrated coverage of the building. STX Landscape Architects had stressed the necessity of easy maintenance access via lifts, but ultimately, access to each planter was provided by a series of 'cat ladders' instead, while a minimum soil depth of one metre was achieved in the façade planters.

Thus, the 'living cloak' of climbers becomes a giant organic mosaic of different species, textures, and patterns, painted on a canvas in the sky. In time, Nature herself becomes the artist, for this living mosaic is expected to change over time, as plants find their own environmental equilibrium in space.

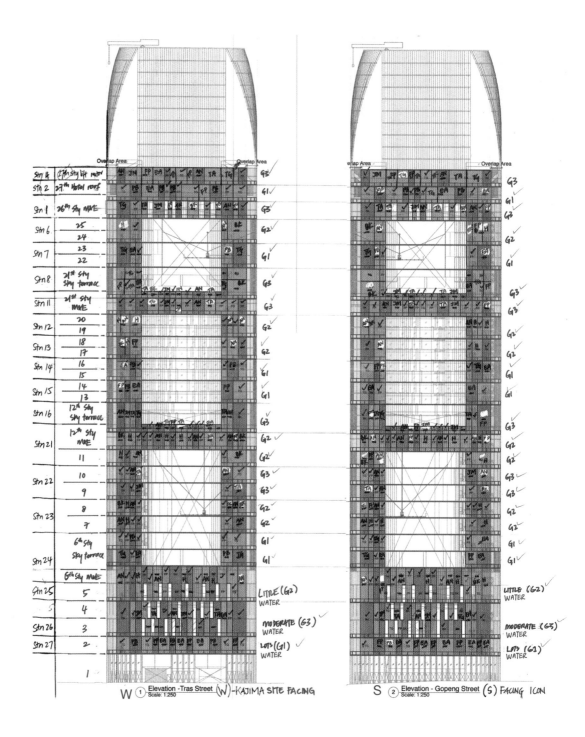

Stn 4	27th sty lift motor		G3
Stn 2	27th Hotel roof		G1
Stn 1	26th sty MME		G3
Stn 6	25		G2
	24		
Stn 7	23		G1
	22		
Stn 8	21st sty sky terrace		G3
Stn 11	21st sty MME		G3
Stn 12	20		G2
	19		
Stn 13	18		G2
	17		
Stn 14	16		G1
	15		
Stn 15	14		G1
	13		
Stn 16	12th sty sky terrace		G3
Stn 21	12th sty MME		G2
	11		G2
Stn 22	10		G3
	9		G3
Stn 23	8		G2
	7		G2
	6th sty sky terrace		G1
Stn 24			G1
Stn 25	6th sty MME		
	5		LITTLE (G2) WATER
	4		
Stn 26	3		MODERATE (G3) WATER
Stn 27	2		LOTS (G1) WATER
	1		

W ① Elevation - Tras Street (W) - KAJIMA SITE FACING
Scale: 1:250

S ② Elevation - Gopeng Street (S) FACING ICON
Scale: 1:250

Overlap Area

LITTLE (G2) WATER
MODERATE (G3) WATER
LOTS (G1) WATER

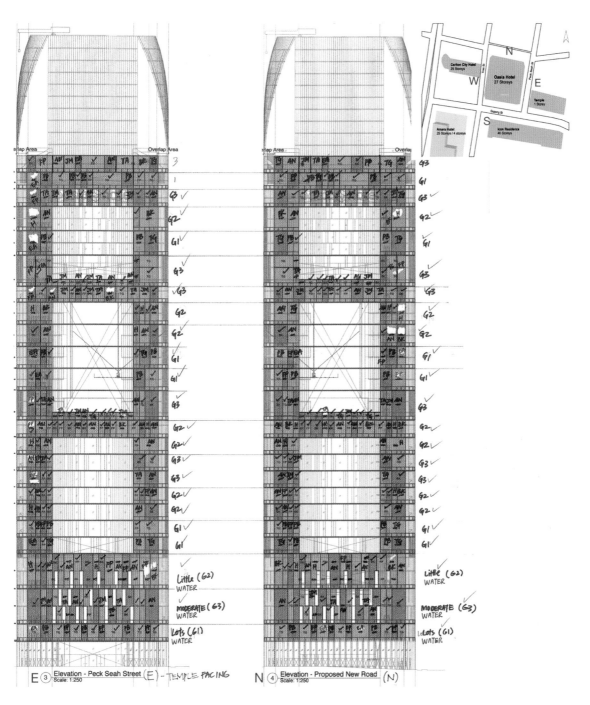

E ③ Elevation - Peck Seah Street (E) - TEMPLE FACING
Scale: 1:250

N ④ Elevation - Proposed New Road (N)
Scale: 1:250

227

The twenty-one species of
climbers on the four façades
of the tower were planted
according to their water
demand, sunlight availability,
and speed of growth.

Kampung Admiralty

Project Title: **Kampung Admiralty**
Project Location: **Woodlands, Singapore**
Architect: **WOHA**
Client: **Housing & Development Board**
Landscape Architect: **Ramboll Studio Dreiseitl Singapore**
Text: based on information from WOHA and Ramboll Studio Dreiseitl

An urban *kampung* emphasising outdoor and communal living.

Kampung Admiralty is Singapore's first integrated public development that brings together a mix of public facilities and services under one roof. Located on a tight 0.9-hectare site with a height limit of 45 metres, the scheme builds upon a layered 'club sandwich' approach. Drawing inspiration from the self-sufficiency of traditional *kampung* villages, it stacks retail amenities and a medical centre with apartments and social spaces within a single site. These diverse programs are woven together through shared landscapes, from outdoor recreational spaces, rain gardens, and the retention pond to the community farm. It is a prototype for integrating blue-green infrastructure with built form, while interpreting local Singaporean *kampung* culture and traditions to redefine active aging for the twenty-first century.

Life in the *kampung* was lived outdoors—on the front porch, in the garden and the forest. This communal living fostered community spirit, as neighbours interacted daily and supported each other in times of need. As Singaporeans moved from villages to high-rises in the 1960s, void decks were used to replace these shared spaces; but the scale had shifted, and the connection to nature and food production was lost.

Kampung Admiralty restores these shared spaces in a modern context. Throughout their day, residents are immersed in nature. This improves mental health and encourages physical activity, while reducing the risk of social isolation. Benches along common corridors enable informal interactions; residents can also work together in the community farm, exercise in the lush rooftop gardens, or gather for events in the public plaza. There is space for residents to host friends and family, and the community farm enables residents to reconnect with their culinary heritage, and to pass on knowledge of local produce and traditional dishes to the next generation.

Kampung Admiralty has become a biodiversity hotspot, transforming the ecological value of the neighbourhood. A biodiversity audit conducted from July to September 2018 found a total of fifty different species, including nineteen bird species and twenty-two insect species. Singapore is small, and densely populated. The island has transformed its urban landscape within a single generation through far-sighted urban planning and design, continually developing and testing innovative urban models. As such, Kampung Admiralty is a project driven by its context, a crucial leap forward in the journey towards the sustainable, ecological cities of the future.

229

Level 9
Community Garden

Community Decks   Sky Terraces

Studio Apartment

Level 6
Fitness Corner
& Playground

L8

Level 4
Outdoor
Living Room

Childcare Centre   L7

Active Aging Hub   L6

Medical Centre   L4

Medical Centre

Rain Garden

Medical Centre   L3

Eco pond

Food Centre   L2

People's Plaza

Retail / Food & Beverage   L1

Basement 1 Carpark

Supermarket

Basement 2 Carpark

**A 'club sandwich' approach, which
integrates blue-green infrastructure.**

▶ Birds were seen at low- to mid-heights, with a few also spotted in the upper gardens.[14]

Of the WOHA designs that embody the socio-ecological paradigm, Kampung Admiralty (Singapore, 2017) stands out. The project has a mixed-use program with a public plaza, shops and a food court on the lower levels, a medical centre in the middle, homes for elderly and a childcare facility on top. The roof is an accessible pocket park where a small farm has become a draw for residents. Vegetated terraces clean rainwater, which is collected in a central rain garden, pumped up for rooftop irrigation, or filtered down to the biotope and eco-pond. Since it opened, the development has become a nexus for planned events and informal visits. A biodiversity audit found more insects, mammals, amphibians, reptiles, and fish, including the second largest variety of birds, than elsewhere in the neighbourhood.

To get these outcomes, WOHA architects collaborate early in the design process with like-minded landscape architects such as Cicada (Newton Suites), Tierra Design Singapore (Parkroyal on Pickering), ICN Design International (SkyVille@Dawson), STX Landscape Architects (Oasia Hotel Downtown) and Ramboll Studio Dreiseitl Singapore (Kampung Admiralty). Notwithstanding a global portfolio, the firm's most experimental ideas are realised in Singapore. It has both benefitted from and influenced policies that reward the integration of architecture and landscapes.

Bridging Scales

Singapore has done much to elevate the role of green infrastructure. Green cover on the island has increased steadily over the last few decades, despite a parallel increase in population. By 2018, it was equivalent to half of the surface area of its territory.[15] The Draft Masterplan 2019 shows an additional 1,000 hectares of parks and green corridors on the way. In time, over 90 per cent of households will be within walking distance of a park.[16]

Singapore's garden city vision guided its development for over four decades until it was reframed in 2012 as a 'city in a garden'. This announcement spoke to the accrued importance of nature and a desire for coherence and contiguity of blue-green systems. Policy would be key to realising the new vision.

In 2015, National Parks Board (NParks) unveiled the Nature Conservation Masterplan (NCMP), targeting the city's natural assets for the first time.[17] The NCMP maps out what's left and in need of protection, aiming also to integrate these important reserves with ongoing urban transformations. The latter includes, for instance, a park connector network (PCN) that links green patches with pedestrian and cycling tracks island-wide and doubles up as pathways for species movement. Initiated in 1995, the PCN had a cumulative length of 330 kilometres by 2017, and this is expected to reach 700 kilometres by 2030.[18] Also part of the master plan are nature ways: roads that, through selective planting, mimic the structure of a forest and connect areas of high biodiversity. In 2018, there were some 80 kilometres of these, to be expanded to 260 kilometres by 2020.[19]

At the building scale, the Green Plot Ratio is a metric used by planning authorities in Singapore to stipulate targets for the quantum of vegetation that is to be embedded in a project. The GnPR accounts for ground-based *and* vertical landscapes, giving designers leeway when working on tight sites, and is a requirement under the Green Mark, Singapore's Green building standard, which is mandatory for all new construction. Augmenting this regulatory stick is a carrot: the Skyrise Greening Incentive Scheme is a voluntary programme that promotes green roofs and walls, offering financial subsidies and guidance to developers. The aim is to have 200 hectares of vertical landscapes by 2030.[20] By 2017, NParks also began to make recommendations on the type and structure of landscape. It issued guidelines on attracting biodiversity to roof gardens, integrating biological knowledge with design decisions at the drawing board.[21]

A nature-centric approach to urbanism is by no means unique to Singapore. In the late 1990s, Seoul introduced policies on nature conservation. Seventeen sites of ecological value have since been protected, and almost fifty species of fauna and flora listed.[22] Cheonggyecheon River Restoration is one of its most successful urban regeneration projects and an illustration of social and ecological aspirations. Since it opened in 2005, the area in and around the park has witnessed a resurgence of life. It draws large crowds: some 60,000 visitors daily. Audits show a proliferation of fauna drawn to the greenery and clean water.[23] Pollution levels are down, and urban heat island has been lowered by some 3 degrees Celsius. Yet despite this and other noteworthy projects, there has been no concerted effort in Seoul to link landscapes in buildings to bigger green initiatives in the city.

Fragmentation of scales is particularly conspicuous in Mumbai. Since economic liberalisation in the 1990s, the city has witnessed massive ecological losses. The Mithi River, one of its most important waterways, flooded in 2005, a consequence of changes to its hydrology and the loss of wetlands.[24] More than 1,000 people perished in the calamity. Notwithstanding, the city has been labelled the greenest city in India because it has the highest number of green-certified buildings, many built at a time that blue-green layers were being actively compromised.[25] Architect Rahul Mehrotra, a prominent voice on the Mumbai scene, argues that eco-logical concerns in Indian cities is often eclipsed by social and economic concerns, leading to, for instance, the reclamation of land from rivers and water bodies for real-estate development. The role of the design profession, he says, is to counter fragmentation by reimagining spatial contiguity, and break down barriers between layers and groups.[26]

It is evident that the future resilience of the Asian city will be contingent on a deeper understanding of ecology: how this informs planning and urban design, and how it integrates into an existing socio-cultural landscape, how it trickles down to decisions at the scale of the building. The challenge of contiguity that Yeang, Nghia, WOHA, and Mehrotra advocate can be addressed only if there are policies that counter or reverse fragmentation. Living skins are a part of the solution, acting as nodes within a wider system-of-systems. The replication of nodes, propelled and guided by codes and incentives, can impact urban systems, generating human and social capital. It can also lead to hybrids of human-made and ecological, producing new forms of natural capital. ∎

231

Toshima Ecomusée Town

Tokyo

Project Name: **Toshima Ecomusée Town**
Location: **Tokyo, Japan**
Landscape Architects: **Landscape Plus**
Architect: **Nihon Sekkei**
Exterior, Parts of Interior & Design Supervision: **Kengo Kuma & Associates**
Client: **Minami Ikebukuro 2-chome A District Category Urban Redevelopment Consortium**
Completion: **2015**
Text: based on information from Landscape Plus

**The project area with Ikebukuro
station in the background.**

233

The project site is located the heart of Ikebukuro in Tokyo's inner north-west. Home to Tokyo's second-busiest station and historical neighbour-hoods where old shrine groves can still be found, the district is marked by diverse land use that blends the old with the new. Toshima Ecomusée Town is a mixed-use development that includes the Toshima City government as well as shopping, entertainment, medical institutions, and private residents. The forty-nine-floor complex was conceived as 'tree-like architecture' and built on the concept of 'co-existence with nature and building', where the government building would contribute to the regeneration of the urban environment and local community.

Inspired by Ikebukuro's rich topography, the height difference of the base (1F-10F) reflects the natural terrain variation in the area. It is surrounded by what the designers call an 'eco-veil' curtain wall, which includes green walls, sun-shading devices, and solar panels to save energy and maximise a comfortable work environment in the building. The Toshima Forest on the tenth floor recreates the former natural environment of the city. It includes a small stream where local medaka fish swim, an aquarium, and an outdoor classroom for chil-dren. Most importantly for the design team, the roof landscape with ▶

its panoramic views over the city allows both visitors and government officials to reflect on the directions and needs for Toshima's future urban developments. Allowing visitors to experience low-carbon yet comfortable ways of working and living that harmonise with a diverse natural environment, the project is envisaged as an inspiration or 'seed' for positive change to be brought back into the community.

Just before Toshima Ecomusée Town was completed, UNESCO registered the surrounding historical district as one of Japan's 'Heritage for the Future' sites. The relocation of the Toshima City government office into the district reflects a new momentum for urban development, demonstrating how a carefully conceived mixed-use complex can operate as a regional asset, providing a legacy for the century to come.

The accessible green duct and 'eco-veil' curtain wall surround the complex between the 1F–10F.

235

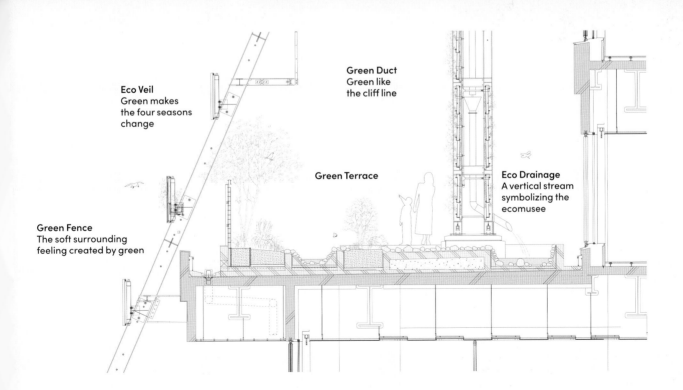

Eco Veil
Green makes
the four seasons
change

Green Duct
Green like
the cliff line

Green Terrace

Eco Drainage
A vertical stream
symbolizing the
ecomusee

Green Fence
The soft surrounding
feeling created by green

Thammasat University Green Roof

Bangkok

Project Name: **Thammasat University Green Roof**
Location: **Rangsit Campus Bangkok, Thailand**
Landscape Architects: **LANDPROCESS**
Architects: **Arsom Silp Institute of the Arts**
Engineers: **Degree System, TPM Consultants**
Client: **Thammasat University**
Completion Year: **2019**
Text: based on information from LANDPROCESS

The project is managed by university staff and students.

237

A century ago, the Rangsit field was filled with paddy fields and swamps, envisioned by King Rama V to be the most productive rice-farming area in the world. But after years of unstoppable urban sprawl, the marshlands have been absorbed into Bangkok's peri-urban area, no longer able to absorb water or produce food. To revive the land on which it stands, Thammasat University, one of Thailand's leading universities, has constructed (at the time of writing) the largest urban rooftop farm in Asia.

At 22,000 square metres, the Thammasat University Green Roof (TUGR) merges the resourcefulness of farmers on mountainous terrains across Southeast Asia with landscape architecture to produce a green roof, urban farm, renewable energy, and green public space. The roof mimics the form and functions of cascading rice terraces to achieve maximum food productivity while collecting and storing over 11,000 cubic metres of rainwater for irrigation.

Thailand is one of world's largest importers of pesticide. Cutting the use of all pesticide and fertiliser, the TUGR demonstrates a sustainable organic farming model. Growing a variety of indigenous plant species

and a naturally bred strain of rice tolerant to floods and droughts, the TUGR can grow up to approximate 135,000 rice meals each year, served through the on-site organic canteen. Any edible food is distributed to the local community, while other waste is composted for the farm. With the organic food source and destination in such close proximity, emissions and waste produced during production, processing, packaging, transportation, and disposal are reduced. The mountain-shaped TUGR also incorporates a renewable photovoltaic system, producing 500,000 watts (equivalent to 25,000 electric lights) per hour to pump water for irrigation and for use in the building beneath it. In addition, the green roof contributes to the cooling of air both inside and outside of the building, reducing the need for air-conditioning.

Thammasat University Urban Farming Green Roof has become an all-in-one solution—offering a public green space, an urban organic food source, water management system, energy house, and outdoor classroom—which serves as an adaptation model for anticipated climate impacts that can be implemented and developed across Thailand and Southeast Asia.

Designing Thermal Delight in the Asian City

Jillian Walliss

Rising humidity, pollution, and urban densities have made it increasingly more difficult to be comfortable in the streets and parks of many Asian cities. Combined with the rise of the middle class and more recreational time, these factors have contributed to the air-conditioned shopping mall assuming a major role as leisure space. Across Bangkok, Kuala Lumpur, Jakarta, Hong Kong, Tokyo, Seoul, Singapore, and Shanghai, the cool air and internalised nature of the shopping mall operates as places of refuge and recreation. The design of a 'conditioned' nature extends to airports and botanic gardens, with Singapore offering two particularly impressive examples: the award-winning biome conservatories of the Gardens by the Bay (2012) and Jewel Changi Airport (2019) which features a forty-metre-tall rain vortex. The location of these engineering marvels in Singapore is not surprising, given that the modification of the tropical atmosphere through air-conditioning has been central to its development as a modern nation-state. As stated by former prime minister Lee Kuan Yew:

> Before air-con, mental concentration and with it the quality of work deteriorated as the day got hotter and more humid. Historically, advanced civilizations have flourished in the cooler climates. Now, lifestyles have become comparable to those in temperate zones and civilizations in the tropical zones need no longer lag behind.[1]

Lee's position highlights the colonising effect of air-conditioning where the taming of Singapore's tropical environment was considered essential for progress and modernity. Air conditioning was first introduced in the late 1930s, initially for cinemas and hotels, before its adoption in more prestigious office buildings after the Second World War. Following Singapore's independence in 1965, air-conditioning became integral to the state's extensive urban renewal projects, which among other advancements included the replacement of traditional shop housing with the air-conditioned typology of the podium tower. Throughout the 1970s the podium tower transformed into mixed-use developments incorporating residential apartments, hotels, offices, and shopping arcades. In this model, the traditional street form was reconfigured within an air-conditioned 'atrium and corridor' typology quarantined from the tropical environment.

Jiat-Hwee Chang and Tim Winter observe that while not unique to Singapore, 'it was a typology driven by and deeply entangled with the post-independence Singapore state's development agenda of modernising, sanitising and rationalising the built environment.'[2] An increasing reliance on air-conditioning (accounting for 28 per cent of all electricity use by 1976) led to a focus on efficiency, encouraging the further insulation of building envelopes to minimise heat transfer.[3] Jewel Changi Airport offers the latest evolution of the atria typology, which was first explored in Singapore with the construction of Marina Square (1986) and Suntec City (1995). These multi-storey atria spaces 'sealed against the real' produce an interior urbanism of plazas, internal streets, fountains, and gardens, with light (but not air) provided by vertical glazing and skylights. The adoption of district cooling systems in the millennium provided the state with desirable energy efficiencies, thereby reducing the energy consumption of these developments by 15 to 20 per cent.[4]

Generations of inhabitants have become increasingly attuned to conditioned air. Russell Hitchings and Shu Jun Lee comment on the potential for Singaporeans to 'no longer care about an external environment upon which they have largely turned their backs.'[5] Their interviews with young Singaporeans revealed the increasing prevalence of physically sensitive people (which is growing stronger with each generation) with a shrinking tolerance towards heat and humidity. Fewer and fewer social spaces are of a 'non-conditioned state', leading Hitchings and Lee to conclude that this technology 'will inexorably come to be seen as the only tool for achieving the appropriate thermal regulation of their bodies.'[6]

Fortunately, it seems that Hitchings and Lees' dystopian observation may not eventuate. Instead across many Asian cities, new design approaches are challenging 'sealed' architecture typologies to instead reconnect inhabitants with the thermal delight of the tropics and subtropics and introduce a relative notion of thermal comfort.

Recalibrating to the External

Before the introduction of air-conditioning and notions of universal comfort standards, vernacular Asian architecture in tropical environments was designed to maximise airflow. Cultural practices such as carrying personal fans and umbrellas, walking slowly, and wearing loose light clothing offered further relief, along with the modification of external environments through vegetation, shade, and water. For example, the Japanese practice of uchimizu (打ち水, literally: to hit with water), which has origins in the Edo period, encouraged the sprinkling of water onto streets, gardens, and temples to cool the surface, dampen dust, and encourage contemplation.[7] Rising temperatures and humidity in Japanese cities are leading local government to encourage a return to uchimizu through initiatives such as Uchimizu 2019, which features a community Instagram campaign.[8] The use of furin (bell-like wind chimes) is a further example of a Japanese cultural practice which offers relief during the humid summer. Traditionally it was believed that a strong breeze would spread epidemics.[9] During the summer, furin were hung to alert people to these conditions. A piece of paper hanging from the bowl-shaped bell catches the wind and moves a clapper to emit a gentle sound, while the movement of the paper visually signifies the presence of wind. Today the relaxing sound of the furin is used in Japanese housing to offer relief from heat and humidity.

With increased urbanisation heightening thermal discomfort in Asian cities, many governments and designers are exploring the potentials of technology to improve the human experience of external spaces. The upgrading of Singapore's Clarke Quay redevelopment (2006) led to the insertion of large environmental canopies, known as 'the Angels', to encourage a more comfortable pedestrian experience. Developed by Alsop Architects and Arup, this ethylene tetra fluoroethylene (ETFE) canopy is designed to maintain external temperatures at a constant 28 degrees Celsius.[10] Constructed high above the existing buildings, the structures channel breezes from the river, with large air blowers positioned strategically at the pedestrian level to achieve an average of 1.2 m/s wind speed along the street.[11] Water fountains introduce evaporative cooling, spilling chilled water over pavement slabs for a cooling effect, and trees offer additional visual and thermal amenity. The design strategies combine to achieve the equivalent performance of an air-conditioned glass-covered atrium, however with up to ten times more energy efficiency.[12] Most importantly, the scheme has led to an almost doubling of the hours considered to be thermally comfortable according to the equatorial comfort index, increasing from 41 per cent to 80 per cent of the time. This combination of ETFE canopy and external fans is now commonly used in the outdoor eating streets of Singapore, for example, a regular experience in Chinatown.

In Tokyo, concerns over the urban heat island effect have produced innovative architectural responses such as The Sony City Osaki Building. Designed by Nikken Sekkei, the building incorporates an innovative system called Bioskin, which acts as an urban scale environmental radiator.[13] Completed in 2011, the architecture is conceived as a thin rectangle, aligned against the prevailing winds. Requiring no internal columns, the façade of the buildings operates as a structural environmental system. On the eastern side, Bioskin tubes incorporating water-retentive terracotta shells circulate rainwater collected on the roof down the face of the building. As the water permeates through the porous ceramics, it evaporates and cools the adjacent air, leading to a 12-degree Celsius temperature reduction in the building surface and up to 2 degrees Celsius in the surrounding microclimate.[14]

239

Moving to a larger scale, Taichung Central Park in Taiwan (2018) explores the potentials of technological insertions and biological performance to modify the external environment. Designed by landscape architect Catherine Mosbach and architect Philippe Rahm, the park aims to return the outdoor experience to the public by developing exterior spaces that diminish the discomfort of Taichung's subtropical warm and humid climate. This designed outdoor environment combines the effect of two overlapping strata; a lithosphere of soils, topography, and rainwater, and atmosphere comprised of the effects of heat, humidity, and pollution.

Mapping the climatic variations of the site through CFD modelling informed the conceptualisation of the atmospheric strata. Three climatic maps, documenting the intensity of heat, air humidity, and atmospheric pollution, were overlaid to create a diversity of conditions, conceived as a series of Coolia, Dryia, and

Clearia 'climatic lands'. Rahm stresses that this approach is not a functional response that simply modulate conditions, for instance by making the hotter areas cooler.[15] Instead, the design extends the graduation of conditions, by increasing qualities where areas are naturally cooler, less polluted, and less humid. A polarity of conditions emerges, with hot spaces necessary to establish cool ones, thereby 'creating spaces by acting on difference'.[16] Space develops through the transformative boundaries of atmospheres and conditions, not as hard spatial delineations.

Climatic devices inserted at strategic points are used to augment the climatic lands: ultrasonic speakers keep mosquitos away; artificial water devices such as rain fountains offer evaporative cooling; dry clouds remove humidity from the air; and passive cooling techniques improve thermal comfort. Considered 'a contemporary extension of traditional furniture of parks', these devices operate like the pavilions, grottos, and trellises found in older parks, and offer a texture of sensory experiences of refuge, delight, and interest.[17] Detailed planting regimes, featuring plants with particular performative qualities, offer further support to these technological insertions. Whether this merging of technological and biological performance will realise the climatic ambitions of the designers is yet to be seen, requiring the maturing of the carefully selected plant species before the combined effects can be felt. However, the design approach offers a valuable precedent for increasing the climatic performance of parks in dense Asian cities.

Returning to Singapore: it is possible to see many architectural examples that reject air-conditioning and embrace the environmental knowledge underpinning vernacular tropical architecture in the Southeast Asian region. Singapore designers WOHA and Malaysian-based Ken Yeang, amongst others, are internationally acclaimed for their extensive portfolios of cultural buildings, apartments, and housing, which respond to the tropical environment through passive cooling techniques and innovative use of materials. What is new is the application of these concepts within larger urban design strategies.

Thermodynamic Urban Typologies

In 2009, developers CapitaLand opened Singapore's first passively cooled shopping mall.[18] Designed by Aedas Architects in collaboration with Arup, the Star Vista mall passively cools all common areas including a large central atrium space. Unlike the internal conditioned corridors and atria spaces that dominate the luxury shopping malls of Orchard Road, this mall presents as a monumental architectural headland with the southern elevation open to an adjoining park. Reaching fifteen storeys, the design minimises the east-west exposure (to reduce solar heat gain) while orientating the circulation corridors to maximise the cooling northern and southern prevailing winds.

Significantly the central atrium space is designed with the largest possible opening to the south. A 40-metre high roof provides shelter to the stepped amphitheatre and large semi-outdoor central space, while a 5000-seat auditorium forms the highest point of the building. Located throughout the mid-levels are a variety of public spaces and over 100 shops. Architect Andrew Bromberg explains further:

> The building is an organic object opening to public discovery. One can crawl under, move through, transverse around and climb onto the complex via a series of ramps, escalators, terraces, and public gardens. All circulations, movements and internal forms are so sinuous as if the civic activities have shaped the inside of the complex.[19]

While the shops are air-conditioned, the circulation and common gathering spaces are cooled passively with ceiling fans. On extremely hot days, these spaces are expected to be uncomfortable, and during big rain events, water penetrates the building envelope. Unusual for a mall, the design offers some unique public open space experiences. Moving higher into the building, generous open-decked spaces project into the air, opening up spectacular views and accessing the cooling breezes. For the majority of the year, the scheme achieves the projected thermal comfort levels, along with significantly reduced energy consumption.[20]

As might be expected in the context of air-conditioned dependent Singapore, reactions to the design have been mixed. A 2013 review observed that 'while some visitors instantly like the idea of openness and connectivity to the surrounding, some visitors readily declared their dismay for the absence of air-conditioned atrium.'[21] Commercially the mall is successful, and the risk is tempered by the collaboration with the New Creation Church who uses the auditorium space intensively over the weekend.[22] For a developer to so radically challenge the accepted norm of a shopping mall is a bold move. However, Asian developers have been particularly adventurous in exploring alternatives to the 'sealed' urban typologies. The mixed-use projects of the South Beach development (2016) and Tanjong Pager (2017) offer further innovative Singaporean examples. Designed at the scale of the city block, these schemes feature permeable green corridors that challenge the dominance of conditioned interior corridors and, most importantly, present an urban form responsive to the tropical environment.

The South Beach development, designed by Foster + Partners in collaboration with Aedas Architects, ARUP, and landscape architects ICN Design International, introduces a thermodynamic typology at the scale of the urban precinct. Encompassing a city block and incorporating four heritage buildings and established trees, the scheme features a metro station, high rise hotel and office towers, retail shopping, and eating establishments. The design is notable for its highly permeable urban form incorporating significant public space and a dramatic roof canopy conceived as an environmental modulator.[23]

As discussed earlier in relation to Clarke Quay, the roofing of external space has emerged as a go-to solution for creating more thermally comfortable streets in Singapore. However, the dynamic canopy of South Beach and its relationship to civic space and pedestrian movement offers a far more complex way to consider the performance and experience of an external roof.

Outside of the air-conditioned commercial towers, the dominant feel of South Beach is of a tropical environment with extensive planting, green walls, and water features interwoven throughout the multiple levels of plazas and pedestrian walkways. At times, the canopy is monumental in height—offering a framing of War Memorial Park located across the road, while other times it swoops down to a human scale. Open to the prevailing winds, and in some places the rain, the design presents a major shift from the static interior associated with the sealed atria.

Working with the computational power of parametric modelling, the dynamic roofing system is designed as a multi-factor environmental system.[24] Optimally angled louvres and solar panels harness sunlight, deflect heat gain, and offer shade. Rainwater collects at the bottom of the canopy and is used to irrigate planting. And the sweeping form encourages air circulation into the lower civic spaces, reducing the need for air-conditioning, while solid panels provide protection from the rain—strategically located to offer a dry circulation area at all times

Post construction analysis confirms the environmental performance of the canopy. A 'felt temperature' up to 13-degrees Celsius lower than other canopied spaces in Singapore (and up to 17-degrees Celsius lower than unsheltered spaces) has been achieved.[25] And most importantly for a tropical urban environment, the wind speed beneath the canopy is on average 1.5 m/s. It must be noted, that the decreased light levels associated with the canopy created challenges for the landscape architects in developing a successful planting design. Extensive light studies, careful interrogation of species selection, and the integration of grow lights in the lower spaces were necessary to guarantee the health of the planting.[26] Given that the scheme delivers a higher level of thermal comfort than what was initially projected during the design phase, it would be possible to allow more light through the roof without detrimentally affecting thermal comfort levels.

What is a particularly refreshing experience of this urban-scale mixed-use development is that the light and air conditions fluctuate with the external environment. This is in contrast to the 'thermal monotony' of atria urbanism where air and light qualities remain constant.[27] The Tanjong Pager (2017) redevelopment offers a further interpretation of a tropical urbanism, focused on the idea of a 'city room'. A collaboration between developers GuocoLand and Singapore Urban Development Authority, Tanjong Pager features a sixty-four-storey tower which, at the time of construction, was the highest tower in Singapore. The tower, designed by Skidmore, Owings, and Merrill, was strategically pushed back to the eastern side of the site to allow for the continuation of the Tanjong Pager park corridor along the site's western edge. While technically a podium and tower development, the strong relationships established between the commercial spaces and the park create an extremely different climatic and spatial experience to those developed in the first iterations of this typology during the 1970s and 1980s. At the human scale, the park takes centre stage of the development. The basement layers of car parking, retail, and a metro stop make room for significant areas of ground-level public space. ▶

241

The South Beach Development

Singapore

Project Name: **The South Beach Development**
Location: **Downtown Core, Singapore**
Architects: **Foster + Partners**
Landscape Architects: **ICN Design International**
Sustainability Analysis: **Ove ARUP + Partners Hong Kong**
Client: **South Beach Consortium**
Completed: **2016**
Text: based on information from Foster + Partners

Constructed over an entire city block in the heart of downtown Singapore, South Beach combines the restoration of existing buildings with a mixed-use, energy efficient new urban quarter featuring two hotel and office towers, shops, cafes, restaurants, and public spaces. A wide landscaped pedestrian avenue—a green spine—weaves through the site and is protected by an extensive environmental canopy, which shelters the light-filled public spaces beneath from the fluctuating tropical climate.

A dramatic roof canopy operates as an environmental modulator.

Extensive green walls, water features,
and planting are interwoven through
multiple levels of walkways and plazas.

▶ The 'city room' introduces a novel climatic interface between the park and the adjacent retail premises. This flat-roofed infrastructure floats thirty metres above, modulating thermal comfort and framing a large gathering space. The experience is light and airy. Louvres on the western side offer additional shade, while large high-volume low-speed fans attached to the roof increase air circulation. The roof also contains extensive PV cells. People circulate between densely planted garden spaces, urban plazas, and open lawns with options of moving into the food and retail services and the metro located in the adjacent podium. In contrast to the South Beach development, where the permeable corridors are interwoven into the mixed-use development, this approach unambiguously maintains the open space as public, allowing for the continuation of the park independently from commercial activities.

A Return to Thermal Delight

The introduction of modern building typologies into Asian cities has led to the rejection of vernacular architecture techniques and cultural practices that had evolved to modulate environmental conditions. Increased urban density has been accompanied by a reliance on air-conditioning, driven by a technocratic idea of universal comfort. While much publicised projects such as Jewel Changi Airport are marvels of technology they continue to construct spaces segregated from the environmental realities of Singapore's tropical environment.

We are now in a period where designers must work increasingly hard to ensure external urban spaces retain their commercial, cultural, and recreational importance in the Asian city—to ensure the public remains acclimatised to their microclimates. This can be addressed in two ways: first, by revisiting Asian cultural practices which temper the effects of the external environment on the body, along with reintroducing ritual and thermal delight; and second, by returning to spatial and architectonic design principles which respond to, rather than deny, atmospheric conditions.

The Singaporean thermodynamic typologies discussed in this essay demonstrate the applicability of these principles at the scale of the urban precinct. Significantly, these design typologies 'decentre' the role of air-conditioning, limiting its use to strategic points such as commercial areas.[28] Working across a range of design strategies, these responses introduce a relative notion of thermal comfort, reconnecting the public with dynamic weather patterns and encouraging the inhabitation of the exterior. Over time these schemes will not only reduce the extensive energy consumption required by air-conditioning but more importantly will contribute to the 'conditioning' of the public to environmental attributes such as humidity and heat. ∎

245

Retreat

EXIT

Heike Rahmann   Asia has long been a source of fascination for travellers seeking to explore exotic cultures, food, and places. The travel and tourism industry contributes significantly to the region's economy, generating over USD 1.593 billion revenue for China in 2018,[1] while the tourism industry in Thailand is currently around 21 per cent of the GDP.[2] The tropical and subtropical regions of South and Southeast Asia, with their lush rainforests and turquoise waters, are often associated with the idea of paradise and exert a particular appeal not only for resort tourists and backpackers but also numerous artists and designers.

One of the most renowned expatriate landscape designers working in the tropical region is Made Wijaya (born Michael White), who built over 600 gardens across Indonesia, Singapore, India, and his native Australia. Wijaya's creations are understood as celebrations of the rainforest landscape and have informed the typology of the tropical garden. Designers such as Wijaya are highly influential in the emergence of resort architecture. Travelling to Bali in 1973, after finishing his architecture degree in Sydney, Wijaya came to garden design by chance following the invitation to 'create a garden for a house in the Batu Jimbar residential complex designed by [Sri Lankan architect] Geoffrey Bawa.'[3] This experience sparked his fascination with tropical planting design and led to further work in resort design, including the commission of Bali Hyatt hotel in Sanur, designed by Peter Mueller.

Wijaya, who set up offices in Bali, Java, and Singapore, is part of first wave of Australian architects who came to Southeast Asia in the 1970s and began specialising in hotel design, such as Adelaide-born Mueller and Kerry Hill from Perth. Influenced by Bawa, the father of 'tropical modernism', this group of expatriates significantly defined tropical resort architecture. Beyond shaping an understanding of the Bali Style,[4] Mueller, Hill, and Wijaya contributed to the embracement of regional approaches to tropical architecture and landscape, influencing a new generation of designers currently working across Southeast Asia, especially in Singapore. For example, Wong Mun Summ and Richard Hassell, founders of WOHA, both started their architectural careers under Kerry Hill's guidance. Similarly, Wijaya's comprehensive knowledge of tropical planting and his fight 'against a tsunami of indifference to nature'[5] has inspired Huai-yan Chang of Singapore-based landscape practice Salad Dressing (discussed in Designing for Consiousness in a Time of Flux), to rediscover the importance and beauty of tropical ecology.

The motivation to travel is driven by the desire to explore new places as much as it is by the desire to escape. Across Asia, this is fuelled by the stark contrast between dense urban centres and sparsely populated rural areas. In Japan, the idea of the country retreat has therefore a long tradition dating back to the Tokugawa period in the seventeenth century.[6] From the early twentieth century, the 'industrial elite' as well as 'missionaries and foreign nationals' established country villas, known as Besso,[7] as summer retreats in areas such as Hakone and Karuizawa[8] to escape the heat and humidity in the cities. While Japan's declining economy and aging population has left many Besso abandoned,[9] the popularity of resort villages close to metropolitan areas has not diminished. This has given rise to the reconceptualisation of luxury resorts, such as Hoshinoya Karuizawa, to contribute to overall village life and the economy by including communal spaces and amenities open to the general public.

In contrast, the population growth in the small island state of Singapore has dissolved the boundaries between the urban and the rural. With the departure from vernacular architecture, the shift from village to high-rise living has resulted in the loss of connections to the tropical environment. Despite strong philosophical links, the cultural relationship to nature in the tropics is complex. As this hot and humid environment is very conducive for plants, where everything grows everywhere at enormous speed, the maintenance of buildings and infrastructures requires constant attention. Therefore, preferring clean and open spaces, locals have often fought against nature, and literally battled 'against the banyan tree in the drain pipe'.[10]

While tourists are mesmerised by the lushness and disorder of the rainforest as illustrated in Henri Rousseau's paintings of the jungle, clients can associate these same conditions as a breeding ground for mould, mosquitos, and disease. Aware of this conundrum, Wijaya claims that the 'resort movement is a bit of a fad' and that the 'Rousseau-esque fecundity is a romantic notion of the symbolist'.[11] Planting design in the tropics therefore has to move between the image and performance of messiness, carefully navigating the 'fine line between messiness and mess'.[12]

Over the past decade, a series of projects in Singapore have begun to rediscover the potential of living in the tropical forest through an urban interpretation of resort and vernacular architecture. For example, the Parkroyal on Pickering, designed by WOHA and landscape architects Tierra Design (see pp. 252–253) explores the possibilities of the lush resort garden and natural ventilation in the downtown vertical hotel. Bringing the rural and the regional back into the city, these projects restore communal spaces and a deeper connection with the natural environment through the use of artful, natural planting and careful attention to the qualities of solace and restoration.

Slow Living within the Limits of Growth

Heike Rahmann

By the end of the 1980s, Japan's strong economic growth ended abruptly with the burst of the 'bubble economy'. The collapse of the speculative banking sector and inflated real estate market led to a downturn that affected all parts of the Japanese economy. Within a few month massive investments in public infrastructure and amenities evaporated. While the construction sector survived, project procurement continued at a significantly slower pace. The Great East Japan Earthquake in March 2011 further shattered society, highlighting Japan's unsustainable preoccupation with economic growth, which caused a significant imbalance between rural and urban communities. Prominent environmental journalist Junko Edahiro argues that today Japan's 'biggest pressure comes from the obsession for growth on the part of economists, industry and the government, in spite of the expected population decrease.'[1]

The architecture profession emerged from these challenges with a renewed direction to build on its pre-bubble legacy of creative design experimentation.[2] Yet, little is known about contemporary landscape practice in Japan. What is driving the profession today? And how have these events influenced landscape practice? This essay explores how Japan's dynamic economic condition and subsequent social and environmental challenges have influenced the understanding and practice of contemporary landscape architecture.[3] It highlights how practitioners, in the quest for new meaning for the profession, are revisiting traditional cultural knowledge to explore new ideas that embrace principles of slow life and promote sustainable growth to bring positive change.

In Search of Identity

In contrast to the architectural profession, which established a prolific global presence during the second half of twentieth-century, the landscape architecture profession in Japan is still in the process of shaping its own identity. Contributing factors are the linguistic intricacies of terminologies, which provide multiple meanings of landscape and nature (as discussed in *Continuum*). Further complexities arise with the profession's relationship to traditional garden design, as landscape architect Hiko Mitani outlines:

> 'Teien (garden-making) and Zoen (landscape gardening)' in general are understood in depth due to the very fact of them being historically recognized Japanese terms. On the other hand, the foreign terminology of 'landscape,' [sic] includes a variety of fields from natural scenery and cultural scenes conceived through means of human agency, to spaces designed by designers on a scale of 0 to 100.[4]

This problematic distinction between landscape gardening and landscape architecture is reflected in the two governing bodies representing the profession today. The Japanese Institute of Landscape Architecture (Nihon Zoen Gakkai), established in 1925, represents the traditional occupation of landscaping and focuses on historic and scientific evaluation of work as represented in its membership, which ranges from 'university researchers to government officials, to practitioners working for private consultants and design firms'.[5] In contrast, the Japan Landscape Architects Union (JLAU), an organisation founded by registered landscape architects in 2013, represents landscape design practices tracing their linage back to the amendments of the Construction Industry Law in 1971.[6] These amendments incorporated landscape works as one of the specialised areas within the civil engineering sector, which gave rise to the contemporary landscape architecture profession. Since 2016, JLAU has been affiliated with the International Federation of Landscape Architects (IFLA), which positions the profession within a global design context.

In this environment, landscape architects today are still subsumed in large architecture and engineering companies such as Nikken Sekkei, Taisei Corporation, and Takenaka Corporation, who were founded in the spirit of the 'master builder', which include all aspects of project design, construction, and procurement under one roof. Working within this corporate environment and the scope of projects often leaves little room for creative endeavour or experimentation. The economic downturn and the desire to identify professional impact have resulted in a number of designers leaving the corporate world and establishing their own practice, such as Tatsuya Hiraga, who left Nikken Sekkei in 2008 to establish Landscape Plus. While Hiraga claims that his approach to design has not changed, the independence now allows him to voice his opinions and values through his projects.[7] Also, having to establish a profitable business has required him to engage more critically in public life and consider how to make valuable contributions to society. Similarly, Hiko Mitani founded MLS in 2009. Combining the master builder principles gained at Nikken Sekkei with the knowledge of traditional Japanese garden design he gained during an earlier apprenticeship, Mitani now focuses on the intricate relationships between details, materials, and construction to achieve projects, which contribute to bigger urban issues.

Mitani's work involves projects around Asia including Thailand, Indonesia, Taiwan, and Hong Kong, places which, according to Mitani, have discovered the value of landscape to address significant environmental issues such as pollution and urban heat island phenomenon. Mitani states that in comparison to Japan, while working in these other Asian contexts he has also witnessed a greater pride in cities and a positive attitude to landscape, which is seen as a 'kind of illusion of the wonderful paradise', in addition to providing ways to create healthier and 'more fascinating cities' through increased biodiversity.[8] By seeing opportunities in Japan, he claims that a change in attitude is required to appreciate the value of green and ecology to achieve healthier and more liveable cities. Importantly, this demands a shift from quantifying green spaces to including quality measures for design and maintenance.

This view is shared among many designers in Japan, considered a legacy of the excessive growth during the post-Second-World-War period and bubble economy. While local and national governments heavily invested in the production of public infrastructure such as buildings, parks, plazas, and other open spaces supported by national policies that promoted an urban park system, this has generally not produced quality spaces that contribute to the community and ecology. Instead, as Hiroki Hasegawa of studio on site reflects, this 'age of public construction' allowed architects to build 'a lot of useless trash, which nobody needs.'[9] This conundrum has left contemporary landscape designers, especially the younger generation, paralysed and 'guilty, without confidence to design anything'.[10]

Critical of spatial and physical design, many practitioners have moved into place-making—most famously Ryo Yamazaki, who has since become the figurehead of community design in Japan. Hasegawa shares many of the same concerns as Yamazaki and contemplated leaving the profession for a couple of years in the early stages of his career. Yet, he continued in landscape design establishing studio on site with Toru Mitani after both returned from their education and practice experience in the United States. The shared concerns and interests between Hasegawa and Yamazaki have since led to a joint discussion forum with invited guests, published as a series in the professional journal *Landscape Design*. In 2017, Hasegawa published the book 風景にさわる ランドスケープデザインの思考法 (How to think about landscape design that touches the landscape). Arguing that landscape designers need to evidence the impact of their designs through work that creates experience and evokes feelings, he declares:

My biggest rival is just a vacant lot, because if people come to the place that we design and if the same people go to just a vacant lot and say 'this is much more fun' then we have lost.[11]

249

In this respect the larger argument is that physical space can facilitate societal change through creating positive experiences, which lead to community actions. The economic downturn and collapse of public investment in open space has left a vacuum in city making. As private developers are slowly discovering the value of landscape architecture for their projects, they have an increased power to change cities beyond the boundary of the development. This includes a shift from projects that solely focus on appearance and aesthetics to instead offer an understanding of how people use the space, acknowledging the different needs in the rapidly changing society.

Significantly, this also applies to ecological concerns and a move away from 'fake green' to environmental performance in order to address the increasing heat stress and loss of biodiversity. As Hiraga states 'what is essentially required is not an artificially controlled landscape where flowers bloom all year around, but instead is a landscape in which various life forms can co-exist as a result of the natural forces of the land.'[12]

If studied through the issues of energy and thermal performance relevant today, traditional Japanese garden designs offer a valuable insight into sustainable low-key solutions and how to live in nature through the typical interplay between topography, water, vegetation, and built forms that influence wind movements. Further, projects start to embrace a more holistic approach to ecology and ecological education. For example, the Toshima Ecomusée Town (see pp. 232–235) involved collaboration with the Board of Education of Toshima City to produce a video called *Toshima-no-Mori Monogatari* (The tale of the Toshima Forest) targeting young children. Additionally, the project encourages company staff to acquire a government-certified ecological educational license to guide visitors through the educational programmes on-site.

Slow Experiments

Numerous designers have foregrounded ecological designs beyond the notion of environmental science. Instead, projects also include cultural experiences based on the intrinsic understanding of humans' relationship to nature.[13] Fundamental to this is a stronger advocacy for a revised approach to management and maintenance. This ranges from simply proposing skilled contractors and maintenance companies as a means of quality control and educating clients, to contractual arrangements that include long-term management plans.

Michio Tase of Plamtago is undoubtedly one of the leading figures promoting an alternative maintenance regime grounded in a profound understanding of local ecology and links to Japanese lifestyle in co-existence with nature. Renowned for his signature planting design of the 1995 ACROS Fukuoka project (in collaboration with Emilio Abasz), Tase positions maintenance as a slow experiment and actively constructs projects over time. The roof gardens encompass an intricate planting schedule as well as watering and soil solutions that allow the gardens to function as a completely self-sustaining system. Based on the initial planting of 80 tree and scrub species, the project now encompasses more than 200 species and features a complex undergrowth resembling the mountain ecology of the Fukuoka region.[14]

One project that best exemplifies Tase's approach to slow experimentation is the Queen's Meadow Country House 100 Horses Project. Located in Tono, Iwate Prefecture, in northern Japan, the project engages with the consequences of the economic decline, ecological degradation, and the re-evaluation of social values in rural communities. The project started in 1992, emerging from the private interest of a group of individuals living and working in Tokyo. Looking for a lifestyle change from the corporate business world, they purchased an abandoned property in the Tohoku region. On a basic level, the project can be understood as an experiment to explore organic farming practice and forest revitalising, responding to the declining forest industry, which introduced a monoculture that led to significant ecological degradation.

The project began by successively cutting the forest to re-establish the native plant communities. Importantly, the designers reintroduced the traditional practice of working horses, suitable to the climate and work in mountainous terrain, which was lost with the introduction of beef farming in the region. Starting with just five horses, the broader vision of this project is to sequentially increase the stock to develop tourism based around the experience of the slow country life. Although originating as a private project, Queen's Meadow soon attracted the interest of the local government and subsequently grew from the farm into the development of a comprehensive master plan for Tono City. Since the Great East Japan Earthquake, the project includes a strong social advocacy to counter the long-term population decline in Tohoku by providing local education and employment opportunities for younger people.

Tase conceives this experiment as an initiative to bring back to Tokyo, as a way to 'infiltrate' other places in a response to the weak planning system in Japan in general and Tokyo in particular, arguing that the traditional 'Tokyo village' is dying due to aging population, infrastructure, and lack of community.[15] Working with university students, Tase claims that the younger generation of landscape architects is interested in his approach, leading him to developing unconventional teaching methods. In the field, learning activities for example involve students weeding as a means to study ecology. In 2019, Tase collaborated with students in the Gedai Hedge project, replacing the campus wall with thickened greenery and offering more transparency, biodiversity, and green for the community—a rare opportunity in Tokyo's dense urban environment.

Practicing in the Age of Slow Life

Over the past decade, a series of other innovative design experiments have emerged that share similar sentiments of process and retreat such as studio on site's engagement with Hoshinoya Resorts (see pp. 58–59, pp. 254–255, and pp. 258–261) and Takano Landscape Planning's scheme for the Tokachi Millennium Forest (designed with Dan Pearson and discussed on pp. 198–201). Critical about the economic pressures at the height of the bubble economy, Fumiaki Takano has also reflected about the impact of the loss of values on his personal lifestyle. Working intensely in community-participation and playground design in the 1980s, Takano grew increasingly frustrated with the life in Tokyo, the orientation toward profit, and the construction boom, which eventually required the practice to vacate their 660-square-metres office in 1990. Contemplating the balance between increasing work hours to afford Tokyo's high rent and maintaining the pleasures of life, the practice took the extreme measure to relocate into an abandoned elementary school in Tokachi, a rural village in the pastoral landscapes on the northern island of Hokkaido. Reflecting on the past thirty years, Takano explains that the move got them to 'go back to primal things and small things [that] take time to proceed. Keep in mind to live flexibly with nature. Going to Hokkaido is not just going north, it was a choice of another life value.'[16] Takano is also a dedicated equestrian whose move to Hokkaido further allowed him to pursue his dream of riding; he explains that horses also broaden his work.[17]

As in many other places around the word, the landscape architecture profession faces challenges in demonstrating an independent contribution to the built environment. In Japan, the main challenge is the positioning and recognition of the discipline, which led JLAU to promote an internationally recognised qualification system (RLA system). First introduced in 2003 and administered by the corporate body Consultants of Landscape Architecture in Japan (CLA), there are around 350 registered landscape architects as of June 2020.[18] Although the numbers stand in stark contrast to developments in other places around Asia, the RLA system currently only operates as a 'private or voluntary system'.[19] Since the landscape profession is not officially recognised and protected, the RLA systems is conceived as a first step to establish professional accreditation in Japan.

Acknowledging that landscape architecture is a diverse profession, the division between the historic, scientific, and design perspectives is not conducive for creating an environment for discourse and dissemination that can strengthen the position of landscape architecture in the built and natural environment. Similarly, the division between traditional landscape design (zoen) and landscape architecture has caused confusion not only for the public. The common reflection among design practitioners is that without a definition of landscape architecture in Japan the young generation of students is caught between the appeal of community design, a focus on garden styles, and a lack of understanding of design techniques. In this context Hiko Mitani argues:

that the root of landscaping in Japan can be found none other than in our nation's 'garden culture' with its long history that we pride to the world. On the contrary, now that the backdrop of our economy, society, and culture are beginning to undergo a significant change, I accept the reality that a culture that had once been prized for its luxury and extravagance is no longer that which can be presented as it is. However, my understanding is that it is perhaps not possible to exercise new 'creativity' unless we simultaneously try to learn from history. In this respect it is important to confront these solemn facts from head on.[20]

Over the past decades, Japan has faced significant challenges that have left negative impressions on the mood and outlook in today's society. As Edahiro expresses, 'If you come to Japan nowadays, you might not see as many happy, cheerful people. You might think they look like they are in some difficulty.'[21] Yet, as the chief executive of the NGO Japan for Sustainability and founder of the Institute of Studies in Happiness, Economy and Society, Edahiro remains hopeful that a realigned relationship between economic and societal interests through a 'new lifestyle that stays within the limits of growth' can lead to 'an alternative path to survival and well-being'.[22]

Japan's landscape architects have embraced the socio-economic and environmental challenges by realigning their practices to reflect on and promote a slow lifestyle that accepts growth. This is evident in process-based projects and new business models. Connecting traditional practices with modern values and techniques provides a basis for experimentation and positive change that can only strengthen the confidence and future impact of the profession over time. ∎

251

Parkroyal
on Pickering

Singapore

The contoured tropical sky terraces
allow light into lower gardens and
offers wider planting areas.

Project Name: **Parkroyal on Pickering**
Project Location: **Chinatown, Singapore**
Architects: **WOHA**
Landscape Architect: **Tierra Design**
Client: **UOL Group**
Completion Year: **2013**
Text: based on information from WOHA and Tierra Design

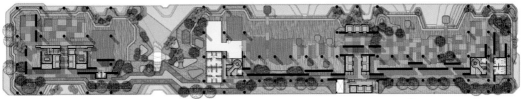

The 'new ground plane' podium on level five contains extensive gardens, swimming pools and lush landscapes.

Fronting Singapore's Hong Lim Park, at the junction of the CBD, Chinatown, and the entertainment district Clarke Quay, this hotel and office development offers over 15,000 square metres (equivalent to 215 per cent of the site area) of sky gardens, reflecting pools, waterfalls, planter terraces, and green walls. The iconic building contrasts modernist orthogonal forms with an abstracted contoured landscape designed on every fifth floor of the building's façade. Proposed by the landscape architects, these serpentine green contours are critical to achieving the lush vegetated appearance of the Parkroyal, allowing light into lower levels and creating deeper cave-like spaces for larger plant species.

On level five is a 'new ground plane' podium that separates public areas from the hotel and office space. Covering the entire site, this podium offers swimming pools, terraces, gullies, valleys, waterfalls, knolls, and plateaus, formed by sculpting selective bays of the carpark slabs below. A 300-metre-long walking trail winds through the landscape. Small pavilions, inspired by traditional local fish traps, hang out over the street. The room blocks, organised as an E-shape, support hanging gardens between them, giving foreground interest to the views over the park. Finally, at the top of the building, planted roof terraces give great views over the city.

Around fifty different plant species native to Singapore were chosen to thrive in the varying light levels and strong wind conditions. Across the long façade, large-leaved ferns and broad shrubs act as accent plants while tall *Euterpe* palms interrupt the horizontal lines and screen the car parks behind. Trailing plants (*Phyllanthus cochinchinensis*, *Vernonia elliptica*) form a green cascade of 'hanging gardens' against the earthy brown corbelled façade. The incorporation of extensive gardens has helped to minimise the use of air-conditioning and provided added insulation. For example, 51 per cent of guestroom corridors and 100 per cent of office tower lobbies have become attractive garden spaces with fresh air, shaded by tropical trees, and flanked by water features.

To achieve these extensive landscape areas within a standard development budget required careful trade-offs. Initially costed with a large basement and stone cladding, the architects proposed an above-ground, naturally ventilated carpark above the public areas, which saved both cost and time in excavation, lighting, and ventilation, while the cladding was changed to precast concrete with a paint finish. Garden areas, which are exempt from floor area calculations, extend the hotel's event facilities at minimal cost and create unique tropical environments.

253

Harunire Terrace

Hoshino

Project Name: **Harunire Terrace**
Landscape Architects: **studio on site**
Location: **Karuizawa, Nagano Prefecture, Japan**
Architects: **Azuma Architect & Associates**
Client: **Hoshino Resorts**
Completion Year: **2009**
Text: based on information from studio on site

Terraces thread around the *harunire* trees.

255

Harunire Terrace is a new commercial complex in the Hoshino resort, Karuizawa, located seventy minutes by Shinkansen from Tokyo. This riverside site features a forest of over one hundred *harunire* trees (Japanese elm trees), which grow naturally alongside the Yukawa (Yu River). Studio on site's design studies explored a variety of scenarios for developing a publicly accessible external space linking the sixteen shops and restaurants, while also offering an entrance for the resort visitors and protecting the important *harunire* trees.

Just like a little urban plaza floating on the rich natural environment of Karuizawa, Harunire Terrace attracts people to a community place to spend time with their friends and find their own way to enjoy their vacation. The buildings follow the flow of Yukawa and the existing elm trees, creating a pathway, which weaves through a series of unique spaces. They are not simply in-between spaces left among the buildings, nor monotonous streetscape. Each space is designed with its own character; while walking on the terrace, visitors might find themselves on a lively open plaza, or in a cosy enclosed space. Plazas closer to the stream invite visitors to enjoy the scenic view. Importantly in order to avoid damaging the tree root system, the deck sits on the steel frame with posts spanning between four to six metres.

Working with the new buildings, magnificent elm trees, the winding river, and rich topography of the site, studio on site's new terrace orchestrates these landscape elements of both new and existing and offers a pleasant stay in the indigenous landscape of Karuizawa.

Okutama Forest Therapy Trail

Hikawa

The trail provides opportunities for the elderly population to engage in exercise and social activities.

Project Name: **Okutama Forest Therapy Trail**
Location: **Hikawa, Okutama Town, Tokyo Prefecture, Japan**
Landscape Architects: **studio on site**
Architects: **Mitsumasa Sanpei (infield architects)**
Structure engineer: **Yasunori Kirino**
Client: **Okutama town**
Completion Year: **2010**
Text: based on information from studio on site

The long, continuous retaining wall along the trail is reinterpreted as furniture, combining landscape, engineering, and architectural construction details.

The Okutama Forest Therapy Trail is located in Okutama Town, a mountainous area in the western outskirts of the Tokyo Metropolitan region. Conceptualisation for the trail commenced in 2005 when Okutama Council applied to become one of Japan's government-certified forest therapy bases, issued by the Forest Research and Management Organization (FRMO). Studio on site developed the trail, designated exclusively for therapy programmes, in collaboration with the Faculty of Horticulture at Chiba University and the FRMO who assisted in analysing the physical, therapeutic qualities and appropriate programs for the site.

Instead of a simple walking track, the 1,295-metre-long trail is interpreted as a linear living room along the hillside forest. A series of seating areas, follies, and decks provide the chance to spend more time in the forest. Designed to rest the body in various positions, these areas focus attention on the sounds and the changing light conditions of the forest.

Constructing the trail on the steep hillside proved challenging for finding an appropriate design language. The designers applied the timesaver standards of forest civil engineering and translated these infrastructural details into a design form for the furniture. Timber logs are used as an efficient and budget saving building material, which provide a rough and bold appearance suitable to the site. The tilted retaining wall was conceived as a timber-clad backrest for seats; decks and other furniture are made of polyhedron logs. The stone masonry, applied in parts of the retaining wall, offers an architectural backdrop for the three building facilities.

257

During the design process, studio on site realised that the project had the potential to reflect on other issues concerning Japanese society today. One matter involved the revitalisation of the degraded forest. Planted around Japan in the early twentieth century, the monoculture conifer forests have been abandoned for decades due to the declining timber industry. The designers have used the large volume of wood chips produced under the new forest management as footpath ground cover. Another concern is the improvement of quality of life (or QOL) especially of elderly residents in the depopulated mountain area. Under the guidance of Okutama hospital the trail was designed to make the mountainous terrain more accessible to the elderly population. Appreciated as a unique place in the abandoned forest, the trail has become a popular destination for visitors to enjoy the benefits of forest therapy.

Hoshinoya
Resorts

Hoshinoya Bali—the café gazebo
floats like a bird cage above the
sacred canyon below.

Project Name: **Hoshinoya Resorts**
Location: **Karuizawa, Nagano Prefecture, Japan**
Ubud, Bali, Indonesia
Fujikawaguchiko, Yamanashi Prefecture,
Japan
Landscape Architects: **studio on site**
Architects: **Azuma Architect & Associates**
Client: **Hoshino Resorts**
Text: based on information from studio on site
and Hoshino Resort

Hoshinoya Bali—all villas face the swimming pool, as a spring that purifies the soul.

259

Operating their century-old hot spring resort business out of Nagano Prefecture, Japan, the Hoshino family developed a new luxury resort brand in 2005, beginning with the opening of Hoshinoya Karuizawa. Designed in collaboration with architect Rie Azuma and landscape architects studio on site, six Hoshinoya resorts are now operating in multiple locations across Japan, Indonesia, and Taiwan. Each resort is conceived with the simple aspiration to reveal the hidden characteristics, distinct experiences, and specific culture of the respective location. The design team thus carefully draws out the essence of the site by heightening the existing qualities instead of introducing new features.

For example, Hoshinoya Karuizawa (2005) is located in a secluded valley in Nagano Prefecture. Without access to panoramic views, the design instead draws attention to the lush forest and abundance of water on site through careful consideration of view lines. Working with a thirty-metre level change and forest clearings, a sequence of internal and external spaces is created that reveals the water flow through the landscape. Water is also at the heart of Hoshinoya Bali (2017). The site is located next to an eighty-metre-deep canyon, and a *subac* (traditional Balinese irrigation system) runs through the site. Public spaces and walkways are designed along the canyon and forest, while elevated gazebos provide spaces to relax above the jungle. Hoshinoya Fuji (2015) is designed in two sections: each guest cabin in the lower residential quarter overlooks the iconographic landscape of Mt Fuji and Lake Kawaguchi. The upper area instead focuses on communal spaces in the forest. Forests are ubiquitous in Japan and are neither dynamic nor wild. However, through a series of floating decks the unassuming landscape is turned into a special experience.

**Hoshinoya Fuji—the cloud terrace provides
various places to stay in the forest.**

Hoshinoya Karuizawa—water drawn from the Yu River feeds the resort's hydro power plant, which has operated on site since 1929.

261

Muh Shoou Xixi

Hangzhou

A series of water features guide
visitors through the hotel spaces.

Project Name: **Muh Shoou Xixi**
Project Location: **Hangzhou, Zhejiang Province, China**
Landscape Architects: **Z+T Studio**
Architects: **GOA**
Client: **Muh Shoou Shiye Hotel Company**
Completion Year: **2018**
Text: based on information from Z+T Studio and GOA architects

The architecture is carefully sited amongst the existing trees, with minimal site intervention.

This boutique hotel lies at the southwest corner of the Xixi natural conservation wetland in Hangzhou, the capital city of Zhejiang Province. A cluster of four existing buildings was transformed into a modern hotel, which responds to the natural beauty and qualities of the wetland—coldness, quietness, uniqueness, wildness, and seclusion. The term *muh shoou* refers to the last fruit left on the tree by farmers, which is intended to be shared with animals in nature as a prayer for the harvest of the coming year. This philosophy is evident in the siting of the architecture and landscape, which responds carefully to the forest and wetland ecology with minimal site intervention. This includes maintaining many existing plants such as persimmon trees, some of which are over one hundred years old. In a direct reference, an existing persimmon tree was 'saved' in the centre of the entry courtyard, symbolising the last fruit on the tree and memorialising the native persimmon found in the area.

263

Water is very important to the designed experience of the hotel. The wetland offers an ancient waterway access, allowing visitors to appreciate the beauty of the Xixi wetland from a different perspective. The original landform and water system based on fishing agriculture informs the design of the stormwater and runoff treatment. A eutrophic lake near the guest rooms was purified through ecological design. Aquatic plants in and around the lake offer bioremediation, while a corten steel runnel oxygenates the lake's water. A series of water features mark important dates in the Chinese lunar calendar, such as the equinox date, the first day of spring, and the big raining day for grain. This process of renovation demonstrates the power of a creative landscape language in reconnecting people to the natural world by offering spaces and views of serenity and harmony.

Treetop Cinema

Project Name: **Treetop Cinema**
Project Location: **Sabah, Borneo, Indonesia**
Landscape Architect: **Salad Dressing**
Client: **Rimba Wildlife Festival**
Completion Year: **2015**
Text: based on information from Salad Dressing

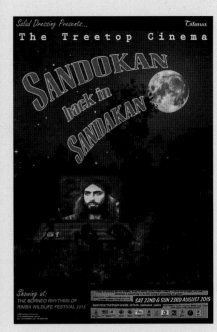

In 2015, Salad Dressing took part in the Borneo Rhythms of Rimba Wildlife Festival, which was held in the Rainforest Discovery Centre (RDC) on the forest fringes of Sepilok and Sandakan, Sabah. They constructed a temporary scaffolding structure for a treetop cinema located twenty-six metres high in the rainforest canopy. The top of the platform was conceived as a mechanical bud, with contraptions unfolding into screens and cantilevered hammock, cradled among the emergent *Dipterocarpaceae*, a dominant family of trees that covered up to 90 per cent of the lowland forest in Sabah.

265

During the day, curious long-tailed macaques and the playful orangutan would drop by the treetop cinema when nobody was there. At sunset, murmuration of birds and many pairs of the great hornbills returned to the emergent trees. Right before the movie started, flying insects gathered on the illuminated screen. There were swallowtail moths, lantern bugs, ghost praying mantises, and other insects, bewildering the team with a spectacle of buzzling dance and plays of shadows.

On the treetop cinema, Salad Dressing screened an old Italian film called *Sandokan*, made by Emilio Salgari. It is a fictional tale of hero pirates set during the post-colonial period in Malaysia. Many Italians grew up with this film; however, few know it fictionally took place in the jungles of Sabah called Sandakan. Nor were the local Sandakans familiar with this film. For the designers, this became an opportunity to dissolve this unfamiliarity and post-colonial dissonance between these two distant lands, the East and West, revealing a shared fantasy of the wild rainforest of Borneo.

After a week, the festival was over, and the tower was dismantled to leave behind no footprint on the forest floor. However, traces of memories continued to resonate within those who were involved. For Salad Dressing, this was an intimate contact with the beauty and menace of Borneo's rainforest. They also hope that the Treetop Cinema would inspire change in our bioethics as we face a post-human epoch.

Designing for Consciousness in a Time of Flux

Yazid Ninsalam
Jillian Walliss

As we weave through the rabbit warren of staircases and corridors that comprise Singapore's old Grandstand (a disused race course) in search of the Salad Dressing's studio, it soon becomes clear that this is no ordinary landscape architecture firm. It is a relief to enter their calm white space filled with desks, artefact, terrariums, fish tanks, and many, many plants. Salad Dressing was founded in 2002, by Malaysian born Huai-yan Chang, and employs around thirty-seven people, working across Singapore, Malaysia, and Indonesia. In his early career Huai-yan was mentored by Made Wijaya (Michael White), an Australian landscape architect who moved to Bali in 1973. Wijaya developed an expertise in Hindu Bali culture and ritual and the design of tropical landscapes, and inspired Huai-yan 'to love the tropics and see my Asian roots.'

Huai-yan and his colleagues have shaped a unique design studio, which merges philosophical explorations of time, meaning, and the natural world with the business demands of a contemporary landscape practice. This mix of slow and fast thinking was evident in our discussion, which transformed into more of a salon atmosphere.[1] Dishes of fish head curry and roti prata arrived from various food stalls within the Grandstand as we attempt to follow Huai-yan on a journey of ideas, frustrations, and inspiration. After lunch, the staff moved to the 'living lab' of tropical plants stacked on the grandstand steps outside their office, to celebrate the release of a gecko grown in Salad Dressing's terrarium. Staff return to their desks to work the demanding hours required of Asian landscape architecture firms but are rewarded annually by an office trip to different parts of the world. Last year, staff went on a safari to Tanzania and Ethiopia, the year before on a pilgrimage across the landscapes of Leh, Kashmir, and Amritsar.

For Huai-yan, landscape architecture has two roles. The first is to work with government and authorities to solve social issues. He states that it is the role of politicians (rather than designers) to implement societal vision, citing the success of Ng Sek San in encouraging the establishment of edible landscape everywhere in Kuala Lumpur. The second role, and the most important to Huai-yan, is the need to be creative and 'express the current period of time'. He highlights how many landscape architects are focused on problem solving, for example applying technical solutions for the capturing and cleansing of water. While solving problems is not in- herently a bad thing, it is the replication of solutions that is a major issue for him. He exclaims 'What is the role for landscape architects if we just copy and replicate solutions? Being a designer is becoming a rare thing.'

Instead Huai-yan argues that it is the role of the landscape architect to 'represent the flux of humanity' and 'to engage with consciousness.' These are aspects which technology and the machine cannot replace and it is the role of the designer 'to recognise the truth in the now.' Design director, Yukio Hasegawa states that their aim is 'not to solve problems' but to instead 'express problems', which aligns their practice with artists.

For Salad Dressing their expression of problems much concerns the environmental state of the planet. The practice is very interested in ideas of biophilia and is inspired by observations made from the tropics. Since 2012, Salad Dressing have been venturing into the rainforests of Borneo in Sabah which are being deforested at an alarming rate of 1.3 million hectares per year. Huai-yan cites German film director Werner Herzog who describes the rainforest as a place 'full of miseries and murdering'—a place that God did not finish. But for Salad Dressing, this savageness is a place of unrequited beauty and a complex web of life and a rich ecosystem.

The slow experiments within their office terrariums and fish tanks, combined with their office jungle, provide opportunities to observe and record tropical phenomena. Projects such as Phoibos 11, inspired by the Apollo 11 vessel (see pp. 186–187), offer a provocation on the influence of space travel that allowed us to 'look back' at Earth. Huai-yan suggests that this moment may have given us the 'epiphany to have the urge to nurture her. This significant technological folly of ours has brought forward another wisdom.'[2] These ideas are explored further in the 'Nature, Nurture, Future' Singapore pavilion proposed for the Expo 2020 Dubai, which in collaboration with WOHA pays tribute to Singapore's relationship with nature and technology.

Many of Salad Dressing's projects explore ideas of a hybrid nature, which Huai-yan argues offers a bioethics reflective of a post-anthropogenic era. One project focuses on the durian tree, which is infamous for its strong-smelling fruit. They propose to graft six less palatable dura species for humans and other primates onto the tree to produce a 'biodiversified

Inside the office: a fresh water aquarium for studying native fish sits below the treetop cinema poster created for the Borneo rainforest event. On the table is a tribute to Made Wijaya's mentorship of Salad Dressing and a photo of Huai-yan sitting below a Meru during his days in Bali. The transparent umbrella inspired by Yogyakarta Kraton was made in Japan.

hybrid.' These species are attractive to hornbill and other birds, which do not depend on their olfactory sense. He considers tropical biodiversity 'a metaphor for the challenge of altruism' reflecting 'a struggle of competition but equally a balancing act of many species.' The durian hybrid is therefore a new tree of life that expresses altruism offering 'a plurality within a singularity, without being ambivalent.'

So how does this expression of consciousness work for commercial projects? Huai-yan comments that he can easily submit a project which meets the aims of a client, without declaring that he is also choosing to explore other ideas such as biophilia or the feeling for light in the tropics. He states 'We are made out of so many layers, the decision to express ourselves as either the artist or the designer to the client is ours—that is our skill.'

This interview continued a couple of months later, as we tried to delve deeper into Salad Dressing's practice. This time we turned to a very Asian way of communicating—via text. Unsurprisingly for anyone who has met Huai-yan, this shift in media did not change the tenor of the discussion.

Considering how Buddhism influences his thinking provides greater clarity for how Huai-yan works with ideas of consciousness and awareness. He signals the importance of *satori* (悟り), a Japanese Buddhist concept for awakening or *lingwu* (领悟) in Chinese in guiding his practice. Through the work of Japanese Buddhist scholar D. T. Suzuki (1870–1966), *satori* inspired 'the Zen boom in the US' which led to minimalism art practice, along with the Fluxus movement which values artistic process over the finished product. Huai-yan considers himself more aligned with the practices of Nam June Paik (a Korean-American who is considered the founder of video art) than minimalism. 'If you look at Nam June Paik's projects, they do not look minimal but the spirit is *satori*. It is less of a style. He accepts changes.'

Accordingly, Salad Dressing has no style or specialisation; instead it responds to 'the flux' meaning that they work with contemporary influences such as the digital, robotics, or dataism, alongside climatic or biophilic concerns. Looking at the work of Wijaya, Huai-yan recognises a certain romanticising of the past. Instead he aspires for a practice which has a freedom of thought to accept and respond to flow, rather than being guided by any overarching ideology. This includes challenging the boundaries of thought such as the East and the West and the artist and designer.

Our final question focused on this relationship between landscape architect and artist. Huai-yan considers himself 'an artist' who is working in a distinct

moment of expression. In this way he is 'just one of 7.7 billion humans with cognitive power in this current flux of humanity.' When asked about how the name Salad Dressing came about, Huai-yan laughed self-deprecatingly. He was only twenty-three when he set up the company, and acknowledges the influence of then famous Japanese firm, Takashi Sugimoto's Super Potato and UK graphic design group Tomato. He said 'I thought well, why not give them a dressing ... but in a very literal way, it is also about dressing up the green, which is our profession'. In an ironic twist, the first big developer that hired the firm was particularly interested in this name and who was behind it. Now, in the context of landscape architecture in both Asia and internationally, it is clear that Salad Dressing offers far more than this modest reflection. Huai-yan and his colleagues are demonstrating that it is not necessary to make a choice between a contemporary design practice and commercial viability, or between sound environmental outcome and artistic processes. In his words, it was a practice that initially sought to be 'synchronic' and later became 'diachronic'. ∎

269

The office garden is perched on the seventh-floor cantilevered spectator platform of the old turf club. There is no niche left unused in this floating garden, which is filled with over 500 native plant species including the biggest canopy flower—*Fragraea auriculata*—and carnivorous pitcher plants, along with native fauna such as stick insects, tree frogs, and mourning gecko released from Salad Dressing's terrariums. A wind turbine creates electricity to support the garden. Salad Dressing is keen on rewilding the sky with an aspiration to rewild one's mind.

Closing Remarks

I am very pleased to write the closing remarks for this book, following Damian Tang's optimistic Preface. It is particularly fitting given in December 2019 I took over from Damian as president of IFLA APR (International Federation of Landscape Architects, Asia-Pacific Region).

In a very short period of time, the earth has faced many fluctuations. Australia's forest fires have burnt at an unprecedented scale, and even before they subsided, the coronavirus outbreak began to spread rapidly around the world and remains an uncertain danger. The damage of grasshoppers in Africa and the Middle East has been overwhelming, having a major impact on the food situation in African countries. And in contrast to the dry weather conditions that contributed to the Australian forest fires, heavy flood damage from unprecedented rainfall in India, Bangladesh, China, and Japan is far beyond the scale of the past. It is evident that abnormal weather caused by global warming and the imbalance between nature and human society are causing these situations. This calamity has been apparent for a long time, but now its scale is just one step below crisis. These problems can no longer be dealt with by the power of one country or particular disciplines. The need for more countries, disciplines, organisations, and generations to work together is urgently needed to build a consolidated approach.

Against this background, the publication of *The Big Asian Book of Landscape Architecture* is timely. I would like to express my greatest respect to the efforts of Dr Jillian Walliss and Dr Heike Rahmann for developing this book. After studying floriculture and gardening in Japan and some practical experience, I gained an MLA from the School of Environmental Design at the University of Georgia in the United States. Following my Western-style landscape education I worked under Jhone Omsbee Simonds and returned to Japan to establish Takano Landscape Planning. Since then I have worked in many countries such as Korea, Malaysia, France, China, and the Middle East and had the opportunity to lecture and experience a variety of cultures around the world.

As part of this process, I have spent many hours wondering about the uniqueness of landscape design in each country. Globalism has created exposure to a wide range of information, and the landscape world has undergone major changes. But on the other hand, homogenisation of design has spread, and the identity of each culture has tended to be lost. Each country has its own view of nature rooted in the climate, religion, and culture and has fostered a rich relationship between nature and people.

Now in Asia, a young generation is growing up with the 'scent' of a Western-style landscape. But many are trying to develop landscape design rooted in their own culture, and I think this next generation of Asian designers are going to learn a lot from each other. I am pleased to see this book developed from the active exchange of views between landscape architects in Asia. In particular, its novel editorial policy, which emerged from a two-day workshop involving twenty-four designers and scholars, transcends regions and generations and has created a valuable collaborative platform.

As chairman of IFLA APR, I am now calling for the participation of the eighteen countries that have not joined IFLA, along with expansion of the Internship Programme, as a way of furthering our learning from Asia. These collaborations and networks are important for the next generation of landscape architects and will open up new horizons for responding to the global warming and abnormal weather that we are all facing. I am very impressed by the flexibility and passion of Jillian and Heike, and hope that the wide network and strong connections established between the academics and designers who appear in this book will spread further in the future.

25 June 2020

Fumiaki Takano
IFLA APR President

Editors

Jillian Walliss is an Associate Professor in landscape architecture at the University of Melbourne. Her research explores the relationship between theory, culture, and contemporary design practice. She has published widely, including the book *Landscape Architecture and Digital Technologies: Re-conceptualising Design and Making* (2016) with Heike Rahmann.

Heike Rahmann is a Senior Lecturer in landscape architecture at RMIT University. Her research focuses on the intersection of landscape architecture and contemporary urbanism with a special interest in design practice, theory, and urban ecology. She has practiced in Europe, Asia, and Australia and has co-authored two books, including *Tokyo Void: Possibilities in Absence* (Jovis, 2014) with Marieluise Jonas.

Authors

Charles Anderson is an Associate Professor in landscape architecture at RMIT University. A landscape architect, artist, and critical thinker, Charles has over thirty years of experience making, publishing, and exhibiting work around the world. Charles is founding director of CAStudios / SAALA, an award-winning art and design practice based in Melbourne.

Eiki Danzuka is the CEO and head of design of EARTH-SCAPE. Born on a small island in Oita Prefecture, Japan, Danzuka was raised surrounded by the ocean and deep forests, scenery which profoundly influenced his appreciation of the natural environment. After graduating from Kuwasawa Design School, Danzuka started his career as an assistant in the Environment Art Studio, headed by artist Nobuo Sekine. He founded EARTH-SCAPE in 1999.

Bruno De Meulder is a Professor of Urbanism at the University of Leuven. His teaching and research travels between practices of urban design and theory and the history of urbanism. His work combines design with research in his own post-industrial European context and within a number of post-colonial situations that are characterised by fast and dynamic development.

Jeffrey Hou is Professor of Landscape Architecture and director of the Urban Commons Lab at the University of Washington, Seattle. Hou is recognised for his pioneering writings on public space, guerrilla urbanism, and bottom-up placemaking, with collaborative publications including *Messy Urbanism: Understanding the 'Other' Cities of Asia* (2016).

Jungyoon Kim and **Yoon-Jin Park** founded PARKKIM in Seoul in 2004. Their work is recognised internationally for pushing the boundaries of contemporary landscape architecture practice. In 2016 they published the book *Alternative Nature*, which is a compilation of their writings on nature and landscape in the context of East Asian urbanism. Jungyoon is an Assistant Professor of Practice of Landscape Architecture at the GSD, Harvard University.

Nirmal Kishnani is an Associate Professor in architecture at the National University of Singapore. He is a driving force for sustainable architecture in Asia, advising government and industry, and acting as chief editor of *FuturArc* journal. He has published widely including *Greening Asia: Emerging Principles for Sustainable Architecture* (2012) and *Ecopuncture: Transforming Architecture and Urbanism in Asia* (2019).

Alban Mannisi is a Senior Lecturer in landscape architecture at RMIT University. His research interests lie in the areas of political ecology, social ecology, and ethical activism in landscape planning, ranging from theory to design to implementation. He is the founder and director of SCAPETHICAL, the Built Environment Practice and Research Platform. www.scapethical.org.

Yazid Ninsalam is a Singapore-born landscape architect and Lecturer at RMIT University. His research builds upon the interdisciplinary nature of landscape architecture, actively integrating collaborations with industry and teaching. He sits on the Climate Resilient Infrastructure Expert Panel for Pacific Island Countries overseen by DFAT.

Akiko Okabe is Professor of Environmental Studies, Architecture, and Urban Design at the University of Tokyo. She practiced as an architect at Arata Isozaki & Associates in Barcelona. In 2014, her work on urban upgrading in Jakarta via stakeholder participation received the Regional Holcim Award. Her books include *Further Concentration in Megacities* (2017; co-authored) and *Barcelona: A Mediterranean City* (2010).

Jeong-Hann Pae is Professor of Landscape Architecture at Seoul National University and executive editor of *Landscape Architecture Korea*. His research and teaching focus on the intersections between landscape theory and environmental aesthetics. Pae has published extensively, including translating major English landscape texts (*Large Parks and Landscape as Urbanism*) into Korean.

Ricky Ray Ricardo is a Melbourne-based landscape architect and communications manager at OCULUS, a landscape architecture and urban design practice with studios in Melbourne, Sydney, and Washington, D.C. Prior to this, Ricky worked in design publishing, with former roles as editor of *Landscape Architecture Australia* magazine and as assistant editor at *Topos* magazine.

Kelly Shannon is Professor of Urbanism at the University of Leuven. Her design research lies at the intersection of analysis, mapping and new cartographies, and design. It primarily focuses on the evolving relation of landscape, infrastructure, and urbanisation in the Asian public sector.

Sidh Sintusingha is a Senior Lecturer in landscape architecture at the University of Melbourne. Before joining academia, he practiced as an architect and landscape architect in Thailand and Australia. His research explores socio-cultural, environmental, and scalar issues relating to urbanisation, including the retrofitting for urban sustainability of Southeast Asian cities.

Fumiaki Takano is the founding director of Takano Landscape Planning and a passionate advocate for the landscape profession in Japan and globally. He is the current president of the International Federation of Landscape Architects Asia-Pacific Region. His recent book *Dream of Landscape* (2020) reflects on the design philosophy and process that underpins his extensive body of work developed around the world for over forty-five years.

Damian Tang is the senior director, Design Division at Singapore's National Parks Board, where he has been involved in the strategic planning and design of public parks, urban spaces, and conservation areas. He is also the immediate past president for IFLA Asia-Pacific Region and the Singapore Institute of Landscape Architects.

Dorothy Tang is a doctoral candidate at MIT's Department of Urban Studies and Planning. Her work is concerned with the intersection of infrastructure and everyday life, and she is currently researching the urban impacts of Chinese-funded infrastructural development overseas. Dorothy was previously an Assistant Professor of Landscape Architecture at the University of Hong Kong.

Zhifang Wang is an Associate Professor in the College of Architecture and Landscape Architecture, Peking University. Her research examines sustainable design and performance assessment, with a focus on the interface between ecological science and design practice. She has published over fifty peer-reviewed articles and the book *Hyperscape: Contemporary Landscape Architecture in China* (2016).

Dong Zhang and **Ziying Tang** founded Z+T Studio in Shanghai in 2009. The studio has gained an international reputation for its unique design approach, which explores the basic elements of nature across the scales of master planning, public parks, urban spaces, gardens, and city furniture. Z+T Studio has received numerous national and international awards, including two ASLA General Design Honour Awards in 2014 and 2017.

Zhongwei Zhu is a graduate student in the College of Architecture and Landscape, Peking University. His research focuses on ecological planning and design, landscape perception, and social data mining in landscape assessment.

Kyung-Jin Zoh is a Professor of Landscape Architecture at Seoul National University. He has served as chief advisor of Parks and Green Space in Seoul Metropolitan Government and as a master planner of Seoul Botanic Park, which opened in 2019. His more recent research explores themes of place, memory, and soundscapes related to peace tourism along the Demilitarized Zone (DMZ).

Endnotes

FRONT MATTER

1   Excepts from 'The Heart Sutra', Triratna Buddhist Community, https://thebuddhistcentre.com/system/files/groups/files/heart_sutra.pdf.

RAHMANN/WALLISS: WHERE IS THIS PLACE CALLED ASIA?

1   Gang Song, '"Re-locating the 'Middle Kingdom'": A Seventeenth-Century Chinese Adaptation of Matteo Ricci's World Ma', in Martijn Storms et al., eds., *Mapping Asia: Cartographic Encounters between East and West* (Springer International Publishing, 2018), p. 192.
2   Myongsob Kim and Horace Jeffery Hodges, 'Is the 21st Century an "Asian Century"? Raising More Reservations Than Hopes', *Pacific Focus*, 225 (2010), p. 163.
3   Song, 'Re-locating the "Middle Kingdom"', pp. 193–4.
4   Sayoko Sakakibara, 'Localizing Asia: Mapping Japan, Asia, and Europe in the Early Modern World', in Storms et al., *Mapping Asia*, p. 113.
5   Ibid.
6   Hui Wang, 'The Idea of Asia and Its Ambiguities', *The Journal of Asian Studies*, 69/4 (2010), p. 986.
7   Ibid., p. 987.
8   Sakakibara, 'Localizing Asia: Mapping Japan, Asia, and Europe in the Early Modern World', in Storms et al., *Mapping Asia*, p. 123.
9   Amitav Acharya, 'Asia is Not One', *The Journal of Asian Studies*, 69/4 (2010), p. 1001.
10 Prasenjit Duara, 'Asia Redux: Conceptualizing a Region for Our Times', *The Journal of Asian Studies*, 69/4 (2010), p. 963.
11 Acharya, 'Asia is Not One', pp. 1001–2.
12 Vietnam (1945), Cambodia (1953), and Laos (1953) gained independence from France; Indonesia (1945) from the Netherlands; and the Philippines (1945) from the United States. The United Kingdom progressively granted independence to India and Pakistan (1947), Burma (1948), Malaysia (1957), North Borneo (1963), Sarawak (1963), Singapore (1963), and lastly Hong Kong (1997).
13 Acharya, 'Asia is Not One', p. 1002.
14 Mark Beeson and Troy Lee-Brown, 'The Future of Asian Regionalism: Not What It Used to Be?', *Asia and the Pacific Policy Studies*, 4/2 (2017), p. 198.
15 Ministry of Foreign Affairs National Development and Reform Commission, and Ministry of Commerce of the People's Republic of China, 'Vision and Actions on Jointly Building Silk Road Economic Belt and 21st-Century Maritime Silk Road', http://christchurch.chineseconsulate.org/eng/zt/abc123/.
16 Craig A. Lockard, 'Chinese Migration and Settlement in Southeast Asia before 1850: Making Fields from the Sea', *History Compass*, 11 (2013), p. 765.
17 James DeShaw Rae and Xiaodan Wang, 'Placing Race, Culture and the State in Chinese National Identity: Han, Hua, or Zhongguo', *Asian Politics and Policy*, 8/3 (2016), p. 475.
18 Prasenjit Duara, 'Asia Redux: Conceptualizing a Region for Our Times', p. 978.
19 Debrah A. Yaw, 'Introduction: Migrant Workers in Pacific Asia', *Asia Pacific Business Review*, 8/4 (2002), p 4.
20 Will Kymlicka and He Baogang, 'Introduction', in Will Kymlicka and He Baogang He, eds., *Multiculturalism in Asia* (Oxford: Oxford University Press, 2005), p. 1.
21 Yeoh Seng Guan, 'In Defence of the Secular? Islamisation, Christians and (New) Politics in Urbane Malaysia', *Asian Studies Review*, 35 (2011), p. 83.
22 Gerd Langguth, 'Asian Values Revisited', *Asia Europe Journal*, 1 (2003), p. 31.
23 For more detail see Ian Reader, *Religion in Contemporary Japan* (London: Mac Millan Press, 1991).
24 Acharya, 'Asia Is Not One', p. 1004.
25 Ibid.
26 Michael Hill, '"Asian Values" as Reverse Orientalism', *Asia Pacific Viewpoint*, 41/2 (2000), p. 177.
27 Acharya, 'Asia Is Not One', p. 1010.
28 Ibid.
29 Ibid., p. 1011.
30 Adam Cohen, Shengtau Michael Wu, and Jacob Miller, 'Religion and Culture: Individualism and Collectivism in the East and West', *Journal of Cross-Cultural Psychology*, 47/9 (2016), p. 1241.
31 Jeroen de Kloet, Yiu Fai Chow, and Gladys Pak Lei Chong, *Trans-Asia as Method: Theory and Practices* (New York: Rowman & Littlefield International, 2019), p. 4.
32 Yoshimi Takeuchi, 'Asia as Method', in Richard F. Calichman, ed., *What Is Modernity? Writings of Takeuchi Yoshimi* (New York: Columbia University Press, 2005), p. 150.
33 Kuan-hsing Chen, 'Takeuchi Yoshimi's 1960 "Asia as Method" Lecture', *Inter-Asia Cultural Studies*, 13 (2012), p. 323.
34 de Kloet, Chow, and Chong, *Trans-Asia as Method*, p. 4.
35 Sun Ge, 'How Does Asia Mean?', in Kuan-Hsing Chen and Beng Huat Chua, eds., *The Inter-Asia Cultural Studies Reader* (Oxon: Routledge, 2007), p. 26.
36 Ibid.
37 Olaf Kühne, 'Landscapes: Theory, Practice and International Context', in Diedrich Bruns et al., eds., *Landscape Culture—Culturing Landscapes: The Differentiated Construction of Landscapes* (Wiesbaden: Springer, 2015), p. 35.
38 Ibid.
39 Gehring and Ryo Kohsaka, '"Landscape" in the Japanese Language: Conceptual Differences and Implications for Landscape Research', *Landscape Research*, 32 (2007), pp. 9–10.
40 Ken-ichi Sasaki, 'Perspectives East and West', *Contemporary Aesthetics*, 11 (2013), online access https://quod.lib.umich.edu/c/ca/7523862.0011.016/--perspectives-east-and-west?rgn=main;view=fulltext.
41 Gehring and Ryo Kohsaka, '"Landscape" in the Japanese Language', pp. 9–10; Hirofumi Ueda, 'Landscape Perception in Japan and Germany,' in H. Shimizu and A. Murayama, eds., *Basic and Clinical Environmental Approaches in Landscape Planning* (Japan: Springer, 2014). pp. 16–7.
42 Ueda, 'Landscape Perception in Japan and Germany', p. 17.
43 Cuttaleeya Jiraprasertkun, 'Thai Conceptualization of Space, Place and Landscape' in Diedrich Bruns et al., eds., *Landscape Culture—Culturing Landscapes*, p. 96.
44 Ibid., p. 100.
45 Ibid.
46 For a detailed understanding of Daoism in English see Livia Kohn, *Daoism and Chinese Culture* (St. Petersburg, Florida: Three Pines Press, 2001).
47 Günter Nitschke, *Japanese Gardens* (Cologne: Taschen, 1999), p. 25.
48 Kohn, *Daoism and Chinese Culture*, p. 22.
49 Cheryl Stock, 'The Interval Between … The Space Between … : Concepts of Time and Space in Asian Art and Performance', in Urmimala Sarkar Munsi, ed. *Time and Space in Asian Context: Contemporary Dance in Asia* (Kolkatta: World Dance Alliance, 2005), p. 7.
50 Ibid., p. 13.
51 Haruka Fujii, *Discover: Haruka Explains 'Ma (間)' | SILKROAD*, YouTube video, posted by "Silkroad" (25 September 2018), https://www.youtube.com/watch?v=TfgEVRYhV8U.
52 Isao Tsujimoto, *The Concept of 'Ma' in Japanese Life and Culture*, YouTube video, posted by Carnegie Hall (27 April 2011), https://www.youtube.com/watch?v=VI0xgxCOf8E.
53 Guenter Nitschke, 'Ma: Place, Space, Void', *Kyoto Journal* (16 May 2018), https://kyotojournal.org/culture-arts/ma-place-space-void/.
54 Stock, 'The Interval Between … The Space Between …', p. 13.
55 Richard B. Pilgrim, 'Intervals ("Ma") in Space and Time: Foundations for a Religio-Aesthetic Paradigm in Japan,' *History of Religions*, 25/3 (1986), p. 256.
56 Xiangqiang Chen and Jianguo Wu, 'Sustainable Landscape Architecture: Implications of the Chinese Philosophy of "Unity of Man with Nature" and Beyond', *Landscape Ecology*, 24/8 (2009), p. 1015.
57 Ibid., p. 1018.
58 Stanislaus Fung, 'Mutuality and the Cultures of Landscape Architecture', in J. Corner, ed., *Recovering Landscape: Essays in Contemporary Landscape Architecture* (New York: Princeton Architectural Press, 1999), p. 147.
59 Ibid., p. 144.
60 Ibid.
61 Stock, 'The Interval Between … The Space Between … ', p. 7.
62 Nitschke, *Japanese Gardens*, p. 32.
63 Ibid., p. 34.
64 Kelly Shannon, and Bruno De Meulder, 'The Mekong Delta: A Coastal Quagmire', in E. Mossop, ed., *Sustainable Coastal Design and Planning* (Boca Raton, FL: CRC Press, 2019), p. 11.
65 Wei Fan, 'Village Fengshui Principles', in R. G. Knapp, ed., *Chinese*

Landscapes: The Village as Place (Honolulu: University of Hawaii Press, 1992), p. 35.

66 Kongjian Yu, *Ideal Landscapes the Deep Meaning of Feng-Shui Patterns of Biological and Cultural Genes* (Oro Editions, 2020), p. 13.

67 Ibid., p. 15.

68 Yin Zhihua, 'Taoist Philosophy on Environmental Protection', in Zhongjian Mou, Junliang Pan, and Simone Normand, eds., *Taoism* (Boston: Brill, 2012), p. 279.

69 Fumiaki Takano, *Dream of Landscape* (Tokyo: Kenchikushiryokenkyusha, 2020), p. 21.

70 Ibid.

71 Kazuhiko Takeuchi, 'The Nature of Satoyama Landscapes', in Kazuhiko Takeuchi, Robert D. Brown, Izumi Washitani, Atsushi Tsunekawa, and Makoto Yokohari, eds., *Satoyama: The Traditional Rural Landscape of Japan* (Tokyo: Springer, 2003), p. 10.

72 Catherine Knight, 'The Discourse of "Encultured Nature" in Japan: The Concept of Satoyama and Its Role in 21st-Century Nature Conservation', *Asian Studies Review*, 34/4 (2010), p. 423.

73 Osamu Matsuda, 'Satoumi: The Link Between Humans and the Sea' (28 July 2010), https://ourworld.unu.edu/en/satoumi-the-link-between-humans-and-the-sea.

74 Brian McGrath, Terdsak Tachakitkachorn, and Danai Thaitakoo, 'Bangkok's Distributary Waterscape Urbanism from a Tributary to Distributary System', in Kelly Shannon and Bruno De Meulder, eds., *Water Urbanisms East* (Zurich: Park Books, 2013), pp. 52–3.

75 I Gusti Agung Ayu Rai Asmiwyatia et al., 'Recognizing Indigenous Knowledge on Agricultural Landscape in Bali for Micro Climate and Environment Control', *Procedia Environmental Sciences*, 28 (2015), p. 623 and p. 628.

76 Ibid. p. 629.

77 Watsuji Tetsuro, *A Climate: A Philosophical Study*, trans. Geoffrey Bownas (Japan: Japanese Government, 1961), p. 18.

78 Jeroen de Kloet, Chow, Chong, *Trans-Asia as Method*, p. 2.

79 Ibid., p. 4.

80 Chen, 'Takeuchi Yoshimi's 1960 "Asia as Method" Lecture', p. 323.

DE MEULDER/SHANNON: ARTIFICIAL NATURE

1 Keigo Nakamura et al., 'River and Wetland Restoration: Lessons from Japan,' *BioScience*, 56/5 (2006), pp. 419–29.

2 Ibid., p. 421.

3 Huan Liu et al., '"Sponge City" Concept Helps Solve China's Urban Water Problems', *Environmental Earth Science*, 76 (2017), p. 473.

4 H. S. Lim and X. X. Lu 'Sustainable Urban Stormwater Management in the Tropics: An Evaluation of Singapore's ABC Waters Program', *Journal of Hydrology*, 538 (2016), pp. 842–62.

5 Bruno De Meulder and Kelly Shannon, 'The Mekong Delta: A Coastal Quagmire', in E. Mossop, ed., *Sustainable Coastal Design and Planning* (CRC Press, Taylor & Francis Group, 2019), pp. 293–314.

DE MEULDER/SHANNON: DEEP FORM WATER LANDSCAPES

1 Wang Chengzu, *History of Geography in China* (Beijing: Shangwu Press, 2005), p. 33.

2 Nathan Sivin and Gari Ledyard, 'Introduction to East Asian Cartography', in J. B. Harley and David Woodward, eds., *The History of Cartography*, vol. 2, book 2, *Cartography in the Traditional East and Southeast Asian Societies* (Chicago: The University of Chicago Press, 1994), pp. 23–31.

3 Sumet Jumsai, *Naga: Cultural Origins in Siam and the West Pacific* (Singapore: Oxford University Press, 1988), pp. 16–25.

4 Barbara Watson Andaya, 'Rivers, Oceans and Spirits: Water Cosmologies, Gender and Religious Change in Southeast Asia', *TRaNS: Trans-Regional and -National Studies of Southeast Asia*, 4/2 (2016), pp. 239–63.

5 Karl Wittfogel, 'The Hydraulic Civilizations', in W. L. Thomas, ed., *Man's Role in Changing the Face of the Earth* (Chicago: The University of Chicago Press, 1956), pp. 152–64.

6 Pierre Gourou, *Man and Land in the Far East*, translated by S. H. Beaver (London: Longman, 1975), p. 29.

7 James C. Scott, *The Art of Not Being Governed: An Anarchist History of Upland Southeast Asia* (New Haven: Yale University Press, 2009), p. 23.

8 Brian McGrath et al., 'The Architecture of the Metacity: Land Use Change, Patch Dynamics and Urban Form in Chiang Mai', *Urban Planning*, 2/1 (2017), p. 57.

9 Ma Zhenglin, 'City Localities and Rivers in Ancient China', *Journal of Shaanxi Normal University* (Social Science), 28/4 (1999), p. 83.

10 Bruno De Meulder and Moravid Khorramirad, 'Persian Qanats: A Case Study into the Archeological Foundations of Water Urbanism', in Kelly Shannon and Bruno De Meulder, eds., *Water Urbanisms East* (Zurich: Park Books, 2013), pp. 164–75.

11 Kelly Shannon, 'South Asian Hydraulic Civilizations: India, Sri Lanka, Bangladesh', in K. Shannon, B. De Meulder, V. D'Auria, and J. Gosseye, eds., *Water Urbanisms* (Amsterdam: SUN Publishers, 2018), pp. 46–57.

12 Joseph Needham, *Science and Civilization in China* (London: Cambridge University Press, 1956), pp. 359–63, here p. 361.

13 Karl A. Wittfogel, *Oriental Despotism: A Comparative Study of Total Power* (New Haven: Yale University Press, 1957), p. 3.

14 Paul Schellinger and Robert Salkin, *International Dictionary of Historic Places*, vol. 5, Asia and Oceania (Chicago: Fitzroy Dearborn, 1996), p. 362.

15 Bruno De Meulder and Kelly Shannon, 'Settling with Water on and in Thua Thien Hue (Vietnam): Past, Present & Future', *Landscape Architecture Frontiers (LAF)* 40, 7/4 (2019), pp. 10–27.

16 Damian Evans et al., 'Uncovering Archeological Landscapes at Angkor Using Lidar', *Proceedings of the American Academy of Sciences of the United States of America*, 110/31 (2013), pp. 12595–600, here p. 12595.

17 Ibid., p. 12596.

18 Ibid., p. 12598.

19 Colin Rowe and Fred Koetter, *Collage City* (Cambridge, MA: MIT Press, 1979).

20 J. B. Jackson, *Discovering the Vernacular Landscape* (New Haven: Yale University Press, 1984).

21 Gerard Foster, 'The Concept of Regional Development in the Indigenous Irrigation Systems of Ceylon', *Yearbook of Association of Pacific Coast Geographers*, 31 (1969), p. 93.

22 Rohan D'Souza, 'Water in British India: The Making of a 'Colonial Hydrology', *History Compass*, 4/4 (2006), p. 625.

23 Bruno De Meulder, 'Batavia, Simon Stevin in the Tropics: A Catastrophic Displacement of a Universal Water Urbanism Prototype', in Shannon and Muelder, *Water Urbanisms East*, pp. 188–95.

24 Sun Yat-Sen was the first president of the Republic of China and was instrumental in overthrowing the Qing dynasty in 1911.

25 Sun Yat-Sen, *Complete Works*, vol. 5 (Shanghai: 1920), pp. 127–360, here 153.

26 Ibid., p. 139.

27 Ibid., p. 140.

28 Brahma Chellaney, *Water: Asia's New Battleground* (Washington D.C.: Georgetown University Press, 2011), p. 59.

29 Gourou, *Man and Land in the Far East*, p. 29.

30 Keigo Nakamura et al., 'River and Wetland Restoration: Lessons from Japan,' *BioScience*, 56/5 (2006), pp. 419–29, here p. 420.

31 Chellaney, *Water: Asia's New Battleground*, pp. 1–2.

WALLISS: FLOOD AND MUD

1 Judith Shapiro, *China's Environmental Challenges* (New York: John Wiley, 2016), p. 3.

2 Britt Crow-Miller, 'Discourses of Deflection: The Politics of Framing China's South-North Water Transfer Project', *Water Alternatives*, 8/2 (2015), pp. 173–92, here p. 180.

3 For a comprehensive discussion in English see Maurizio Marinelli, 'How to Build a "Beautiful China" in the Anthropocene: The Political Discourse and the Intellectual Debate on Ecological Civilization', *Journal of Chinese Political Science*, 23 (2018), pp. 365–86.

4 This idea was discussed by Yu at The Big Asian Book workshop in Beijing in January 2019.

5 For more detail on Yu's letters, see Kongjian Yu and Terreform, ed., *Letters to the Leaders of China: Kongjian Yu and the Future of the Chinese City* (New York: Terreform/Urban Research, 2018).

6 The letter was openly published as 'Let the Rain be a Blessing but Non-disastrous', *Wenhui Daily* (3 August 2012).

7 Anchalee Kongrut, 'Roiling on the River', *Bangkok Post* (11 October 2016).

8 Ibid.

9 Teerada Moonsiri, 'Meet the Friends of the River Trying to Save the Chao Phraya', *Bangkok Daily* (27 August 2015).

10 Shma Soen, 'Co-Create Charoenkrung', https://shmasoen.com/portfolio/co-create-charoenkrung/.

11 Email with Yossapon Boonsom (26 February 2020).

12 Shma Soen, 'Co-Create Charoenkrung'.

13 Jillian Walliss and Heike Rahmann, *Landscape Architecture and Digital Technologies: Re-conceptualising Design and Making* (Abington: Routledge, 2016), p. 22.
14 Jungyoon Kim and Yoon-Jin Park, 'Sansujeonlyag: Strategy for Mountain and Water', in this volume, pp. 66–7.
15 Walliss and Rahmann, *Landscape Architecture and Digital Technologies*, p. 23.
16 Kim and Park, 'Sansujeonlyag', p. 66.

RAHMANN/WALLISS: SCALING UP AND SCALING DOWN
1 Guenter Nitschke, *Japanese Gardens* (Cologne: Taschen, 1999), p. 34.
2 Yizhao Yang and Jie Hu, 'Sustainable Urban Design with Chinese Characteristics: Inspiration from the Shan-Shui City Idea', *Articulo: Journal of Urban Research*, 14 (2016). https://journals.openedition.org/articulo/3134.
3 Guenter Nitschke, 'Ma: Place, Space, Void', *Kyoto Journal: Hidden Japan* (16 May 2018), https://kyotojournal.org/culture-arts/ma-place-space-void/.
4 Christian Tschumi, 'Between Tradition and Modernity: The Karesansui Gardens of Mirei Shigemori', *Landscape Journal*, 25/1 (2006), p. 108.
5 Jesse Rodenbiker, 'Superscribing Sustainability: The Production of China's Urban Waterscapes', *UPLanD – Journal of Urban Planning, Landscape & environmental Design*, 2/3 (2017), p. 75.
6 Ibid.
7 Ma Yansong, 'Ma Yansong / Mad Architects: Shan Shui City at Designboom Conversation', https://www.designboom.com/architecture/mad-architects-shan-shui-city-guiyang-china/.
8 Ibid.
9 Yang and Hu, 'Sustainable Urban Design with Chinese Characteristics'.
10 Ibid.
11 Reimann Kim Dohyang, 'Testing the Waters (and Soil): The Emergence of Institutions for Regional Environmental Governance in East Asia', in Saddia M. Pekkanen, ed., *Asian Designs: Governance in the Contemporary World Order* (Ithaca, NY: Cornell University Press, 2016).
12 Yang and Hu, 'Sustainable Urban Design with Chinese Characteristics'.
13 Rodenbiker, 'Superscribing Sustainability', pp. 71–2.
14 Ibid., p. 72.

KIM/PARK: SANSUJEONLYAG STRATEGY FOR MOUNTAIN AND …
1 The term is used widely in China, Korea and Japan to refer to landscape paintings. Sansu (山水) comprises of the two characters 山 (san) meaning mountain and 水 (su) meaning water. Together they translate as 'landscape'.
2 Yoon-Jin Park and Jungyoon Kim, 'Seoul: Gangnam Alternative Nature: The Experience of Nature without Parks', in William S. W. Lim, ed., *Asian Alterity with Special Reference to Architecture + Urbanism through the Lens of Cultural Studies* (Singapore: World Scientific Publishing, 2008), pp. 58–67.
3 The relationship of 'nature vs. artefacts' in developing a new notion of wilderness as a counterpart to urbanism has been explored through a series of option studios we led at the Harvard GSD.

ANDERSON: CONTRADICTION, COMPLEMENTARITY …
1 For an introduction and discussion of the Tao Te Chi, its theory of opposites and key concepts, see Chad Hansen (trans.), *Tao Te Ching: on the Art of Harmony* (New York: Shelter Harbour Press, 2017).
2 The interview with Pang Wei was conducted in Chinese at his office in Guangzhou, China, on 15 November 2019; translation by Tianxiu Hu with assistance from Jason Ho. The interview with Kongjian Yu was held via Skype between Melbourne and Beijing on 5 November 2019.
3 When Kongjian first met Pang he recognised him as someone who was 'very creative, very artistic, very good', who was not going make a very good government officer, and so Kongjian encouraged Pang to quit the government position he held at the time and invited him to work together on the Zhongshan Shipyard Park.
4 There are literally a multitude of scholarly and populist commentaries of Taoism. There are similarly a myriad of variant translations of Laozi's 'Three Treasures'. I have used the most

common translation found in English texts. Recently it has been argued that they express the more conventional Confucian morals of 'charity, frugality, and modesty'. See, for example, Hansen, *Tao Te Ching*, p. 249.
5 The Zhongshan Shipyard Park brought Turenscape instant national and international recognition and a 'big reputation', as Pang describes it.
6 As of November 2019, there are only twenty-five employees.
7 This is a quite famous neighbourhood of Guangzhou, the Li Jiang Garden Community. Built primarily for the new middle class, it sits amidst existing villages populated with indigenous villagers and migrant workers.
8 There are, of course, resonances between what Pang is striving for in practices in other parts of the world, but Pang nuances these approaches when he speaks of a park that grows itself as a park with 'its own mind'. As he argues: if, when writing becomes a book, it has a mind, then a park as a form of writing becoming something in the world should be attributed a mind as well. Attributing mind to organisms (and distributed ones at that) other than the human is perhaps a riposte to Pascal's anthropocentric exceptionalism that defines 'Man (as) only a reed, the weakest in nature, but he is a thinking reed.' If reeds and trees are thinking, too, then we really do need to reconceive our relationships with the world/cosmos.
9 Pang has at least two volumes of poetry and a book of photographs published in China.
10 What in the West might be referred to as 'spirit-of-place'.
11 See The Memorial Park for the Local People of Futian. In Pang Wei (2013) *Landscape Practice: Selected Works of Guangzhou Turenscape*, Dalian University of Technology Press. Pang is especially fond of directing visitors to the pictures in the project that have documented the various government slogans painted on the walls—particularly the notice of demolition which uses the character 拆. Pang makes a play on this with the word China, humorously but grimly suggesting that the new China is defined by 'demolition'.
12 保守 (bao shou) can be inflected with backwardness and political conservatism, but Pang uses the word with its sense of care (忧, 服侍, 忧心), prudence (合理), and operations of maintenance (保持, 维护, 维持, 保留, 维修).
13 Poem translated by Jessica Xiu, Jason Ho, and Fang Qin.
14 For discussion of the way in which 'modern systems of production and "globalisation" through ridiculing of tradition' erases the past and any notion or possibility of ongoing connection via inheritance or revival, see Bruno Latour, *Down to Earth: Politics in the New Climatic Regime* (Cambridge, UK: Polity Press, 2018), p. 90.
15 Paul Carter, *Decolonising Governance: Archipelagic Thinking* (London: Routledge, 2019), p. 93.

WALLISS: THE ECONOMIC RETERRITORIALISATION OF ASIA
1 Felicity H. H. Chan, 'Claiming the Ordinary Space in the "Cosmopolitian Grid": The Case of Singapore', in Tridib Banerjee and Anastasia Loukaitou-Sideris, eds., *The New Companion to Urban Design* (London: Routledge, 2019), p. 110.
2 Ibid.
3 Kyung-Sup Chang, 'The Second Modern Condition? Compressed Modernity as Internalized Reflexive Cosmopolitization', *The British Journal of Sociology*, 61/3 (2010), p. 447.
4 Stephan Ortmann and Mark R. Thompson, 'China and the "Singapore Model"', *Journal of Democracy*, 27/1 (2016), p. 39.
5 Weiming Tu, 'Multiple Modernities: A Preliminary Inquiry into the Implications of the East Asian Modernity', *Globalists and Globalization Studies* (2014), pp. 2–14, here p. 105.
6 S. N. Eisenstadt, 'Multiple Modernities', *Daedalus: Journal of the American Academy of Arts and Sciences*, 129 (2000), p. 15.
7 Ibid.
8 William Siew Wai Lim, ed. *Asian Alterity: With Special Reference to Architecture and Urbanism through the Lens of Cultural Studies* (Singapore: World Scientific Publishing 2008), p. 56.
9 Ibid.
10 Ibid.
11 Weiming Tu, 'Implications of the Rise of "Confucian" East Asia', *Daedalus*, 129/1 (2000), pp. 195–6.
12 Tu, 'Multiple Modernities', p. 108.
13 Ibid., pp. 108–9.
14 Kyung-Sup Chang, 'Compressed Modernity in South Korea:

Constitutive Dimensions, Manifesting Units, and Historical Conditions', in Youna Kim, ed., *The Routledge Handbook of Korean Culture and Society* (London: New York: Routledge, 2017), p. 31.

15 Ibid., p. 33.
16 Ochiai Emiko, 'Introduction', in Emiko Ochiai and Leo Aoi Hosoya, eds., *Transformation of the Intimate and the Public in Asian Modernity* (Leiden: Brill, 2014), p. 20
17 Lim, *Asian Alterity*, p. 59.
18 Heidi Wang-Kaeding, 'What Does Xi Jinping's New Phrase "Ecological Civilization" Mean?', https://thediplomat.com/2018/03/what-does-xi-jinpings-new-phrase-ecological-civilization-mean/.
19 For more detail see Jilin Xu, 'The New Tianxia: Rebuilding China's Internal and External Order', in D. Ownby, ed., *Rethinking China's Rise: A Liberal Critique* (Cambridge: Cambridge University Press, 2018), pp. 127–54.
20 Ibid., p. 132.
21 Ibid., p. 133.
22 Ibid.
23 Horng-Luen Wang, 'The Relevance of Modernity to Contemporary East Asia: An Outline', *International Journal of Japanese Sociology*, 27 (2018), p. 49.
24 Ibid.
25 Tu, 'Multiple Modernities', pp. 2–14, here p. 105.
26 Im Sik Cho and Blaž Kriznik, *Community-Based Urban Development: Evolving Urban Paradigms in Singapore and Seoul* (Singapore Pte Ltd.: Springer, 2017), p. 11.
27 Ibid.
28 Ortmann and Thompson, 'China and the "Singapore Model"', p. 40.
29 Heejin Han, 'Singapore, a Garden City: Authoritarian Environmentalism in a Developmental State', *Journal of Environment & Development*, 26/1 (2016), p. 7.
30 Cho and Kriznik, *Community-Based Urban Development*, p. 11.
31 Ibid.
32 Eleanor Albert, 'South Korea's Chaebol Challenge', https://www.cfr.org/backgrounder/south-koreas-chaebol-challenge.
33 Ibid.
34 Ibid.
35 Cho and Kriznik, *Community-Based Urban Development*, p. 9.
36 Ibid.
37 Xiaolu Wang, 'China's Macroeconomics in the 40 Years of Reform', in Ross Garnaut, Ligang Song, and Cai Fang, eds., *China's 40 Years of Reform and Development: 1978–2018* (Canberra: ANU Press, 2018), p. 167.
38 David Dollar, 'Decentralisation, Local Innovation and Competition among Cities', in Garnaut, Song, and Fang, *China's 40 Years*, p. 156.
39 Michael Keith et al., *China Constructing Capitalism: Economic Life and Urban Change* (Oxon: Routledge, 2014), p. 72
40 Ivan Turok and Gordon McGranahan, 'Urbanization and Economic Growth: The Arguments and Evidence for Africa and Asia', *Environment & Urbanization*, 25/2 (2013), p. 466.
41 Keith et al., *China Constructing Capitalism*, p. 25.
42 Albert, 'South Korea's Chaebol Challenge'.
43 Murray Weidenbaum, 'The Bamboo Network: Asia's Family-Run Conglomerates', https://www.strategy-business.com/article/9702?gko=44b6b.
44 Parag Khana, *The Future Is Asian: Global Order in the Twenty-First Century* (London: Weidenfield & Nicolson, 2019), p. 156.
45 Peter Vanham, 'The Story of Viet Nam's Economic Miracle', https://www.weforum.org/agenda/2018/09/how-vietnam-became-an-economic-miracle/.
46 Ibid.
47 Manish Chalana and Jeffrey Hou, 'Chapter 1: Untangling the "Messy" Asian City', in Manish Chalana and Jeffrey Hou, eds., *Messy Urbanism: Understanding the 'Other' Cities of Asia* (Hong Kong: University of Hong Kong Press, 2016), p. 8.
48 International Labour Organisation, 'More Than 68 Per Cent of the Employed Population in Asia-Pacific Are in the Informal Economy', https://www.ilo.org/asia/media-centre/news/WCMS_627585/lang.
49 Ibid.
50 Ibid.
51 Khana, *The Future Is Asian*, p. 183.
52 'World Population Review', https://worldpopulationreview.com/world-cities/mumbai-population/.
53 Khana, *The Future Is Asian*, p. 183.
54 Jean-Pierre Cling, Mireille Razafindrakoto, and François Roubaud, 'The Informal Economy in Asia: Introduction to the Issue', *Journal of the Asia Pacific Economy*, 17/4 (2012), p. 554.
55 Khana, *The Future Is Asian*, p. 162.
56 United Nations, '68% of the World Population Projected to Live in Urban Areas by 2050, Says Un', https://www.un.org/development/desa/en/news/population/2018-revision-of-world-urbanization-prospects.html.
57 Pu Miao, 'Introduction' in Pu Maio, ed., *Public Places in Asia Pacific Cities: Current Issues and Strategies* (Dordrecht, the Netherlands: Kluwer Academic Publishers, 2001), p. 14.
58 Keith et al., *China Constructing Capitalism*, p. 2.
59 Ibid., p. 24.
60 Ibid., p. 18.
61 Anna Greenspan, *Shanghai Future: Modernity Remade* (Oxford: Oxford University Press, 2014), p. 47.
62 Ibid.
63 Ibid.
64 Ibid.
65 Keith et al., *China Constructing Capitalism*, p. 73.
66 Ibid., p. 99.
67 Zhifang Wang, 'Evolving Landscape-Urbanization Relationships in Contemporary China', *Landcape and Urban Planning*, 171 (2018), pp. 30–41.
68 Ibid., p. 33.
69 Ibid.
70 Ibid., p. 34.
71 Chan, 'Claiming the Ordinary Space in the "Cosmopolitian Grid: The Case of Singapore', p. 112.
72 Cho and Kriznik, *Community-Based Urban Development*, pp. 13–4.
73 Ibid.
74 Angelia Poon, 'Common Ground, Multiple Claims: Representing and Constructing Singapore's "Heartland"', *Asian Studies Review*, 37/4 (December 2013), pp. 562–3.
75 Han, 'Singapore, a Garden City', p. 19.
76 Hong Liu and Guanie Lim, 'The Political Economy of a Rising China in Southeast Asia: Malaysia's Response to the Belt and Road Initiative', *Journal of Contemporary China*, 28/116 (2019), p. 216.
77 Ibid.
78 Ibid., p. 219.
79 Ibid., p. 230.
80 Sarah Moser, 'Forest City, Malaysia, and Chinese Expansionism', *Urban Geography*, 39/6 (2018), p. 937
81 Ibid.
82 Ibid., p. 936.
83 Miao, 'Introduction', p. 26.

WALLISS: REPOSITIONING THE PRIVATE REALM

1 Email with Stephen Jones (23 January 2020).
2 Shawn Lim, 'The 'Phygital' Mall: Capitaland Explains Why Funan Represents the Future of Shopping', *The Drum* (4 August 2019). https://www.thedrum.com/news/2019/08/04/the-phygital-mall-capitaland-explains-why-funan-represents-the-future-shopping.
3 Ibid.
4 Ibid.
5 Email with Stephen Jones (23 January 2020).
6 Ibid.
7 John Jervis, 'Taikoo Li, Chengdu', *Icon Magazine* (9 November 2015). https://www.iconeye.com/architecture/news/item/12320-taikoo-li-chengdu.
8 Ibid.
9 Swire Properties SD 2030 'Places' Pillar Working Group, 'The Creative Transformation of Island East and Development of Taikoo Place' (2020).
10 Ibid. p. 1.
11 'Group Overview', https://www.vanke.com/en/about.aspx.
12 Ella Thorns, 'Aedas Latest Mixed-Use Development Creates a City Inspired by "the Cloud"' (25 March 2018). https://www.archdaily.com/890861/aedas-latest-mixed-use-development-creates-a-city-inspired-by-the-cloud.
13 Email with Huicheng Zhong (14 June 2020).

OKABE: PUBLIC, PRIVATE, COMMONS ...

1 Arch+Aid, *Arch+Aid Record Book 2011–2015 Architects' Pro Bono Outreach following 3.11* (in Japanese, Tokyo: Flick Studio, 2016).

2 issue+design project and Yusuke Kakei, *Design for Change: 30 Ideas to Reactivate Communities* (in Japanese, Tokyo: Eiji Press, 2011); Susumu Namikawa, *Social Design—Projects for Better Society* (in Japanese, Tokyo: Kirakusha, 2012).

3 Junichi Saito, *Publicness* (in Japanese, Tokyo: Iwanami-Shoten, 2000); Anri Gon, *The Public: Arendt and Post-war Japan* (in Japanese, Tokyo: Sakuhinsha, 2018).

4 Jordan Sand, *Tokyo Vernacular: Common Spaces, Local Histories, Found Objects* (Berkeley, CA: University of California Press, 2013); Akiko Okabe, 'Dynamic Spaces with Subjective Depth: The Public Space in Monsoon Asia', *Kultur* 4/7 (2017), pp. 151–64.

5 Masakazu Ishigure, Shinjuku, Shibuya and Ikebukuro Redevelopments, now, *Web Architectural Debate* (AIJ/Architectural Institute of Japan, 2014), https://www.aij.or.jp/jpn/touron/4gou/jihyou9.html; 'Shibuya Redevelopment', http://www.tokyu.co.jp/shibuya-redevelopment/index.html.

6 Francesc Muñoz, *Urbanalización: Paisajes Comunes, Lugares Globales*, (Barcelona: Editorial Gustavo Gili, 2008).

7 Hannah Arendt, *The Human Condition* (Chicago: The University of Chicago Press, 1958).

8 Hannah Arendt, *The Human Condition, Second Edition* (Chicago: The University of Chicago Press, 1998), p. 257.

9 Ibid., p. 38.

10 Naomi Klein, *The Shock Doctrine: The Rise of Disaster Capitalism* (Toronto: Knopf Canada, 2007).

ZOH: POLITICS, CITIZENSHIP, AND THE MAKING ...

1 See Michel Foucault, *Security, Territory, Population* (London: Palgrave Macmillian, 2007).

2 Homer Bezalleet Hulbert, *The Passing of Korea* (Seoul: Yonsei University, 1969), p. 249.

3 Kil-Chun Yu, *Seoyugyonmun* (Seoul: Seohae Munjib, 2004), pp. 511–84.

4 Trained as a lawyer, Sir John McLeavy Brown was the secretary to the Burlingame Mission, the first Chinese diplomatic mission to Europe and the United States. After joining the Custom Service in 1873, he was offered the position of manager of Korea's Customs Department, which brought him to the attention of King Gojong.

5 Yoo Yong Jeon, *Seoul is Deep* (Seoul: Dolbaegyae, 2008), p. 23

6 Seiroku Hondo was a forestry expert and landscape designer who trained at Tokyo University and Munich University. He designed major public spaces in Tokyo including Hibiya Park and the outer gardens of the Meiji Shrine.

7 Todd A. Henry, *Assimilating Seoul: Japanese Rule and the Politics of Public Space in Colonial Korea, 1910–1945* (Los Angeles: University of California Press, 2014), pp. 62–91.

8 Anna Klingmann, *Brandscapes: Architecture in the Experience Economy* (Cambridge, MA: The MIT Press, 2010), pp. 271–84.

9 Kyung-Jin Zoh, 'Rediscovering Memory: Reading Seonyudo Park', *Journal of Technology and Design*, 1/1 (February 2002), pp. 29–35

10 Kyung-Jin Zoh, 'Landscape Architecture in South Korea', *Topos*, 52 (2005), pp. 94–101.

11 Interview of Woonjin Park, *Domus Korea: Harmony*, 1 (Spring 2019), pp. 93–100.

12 Yun Seon Park, 'Cheongyecheon, Dongdaemun Gentrification', *Seoul, Citizen's City* (Seoul: Marti, 2017), pp. 62–71.

13 Kyung-Jin Zoh, 'Seoul Botanic Park, Looking Back at it Planning Process', *Seoul Botanic Park Archive 01* (Seoul: Seoul Metropolitan Government, 2019), pp. 66–77.

14 Seoul Metropolitan Government, *Every Citizen is a Mayor of Seoul* (Seoul: Seoul Metropolitan Government, 2012), p. 6.

15 Im Sik Cho and Blaž Križnik, *Community-Based Urban Development: Evolving Urban Paradigms in Singapore and Seoul* (Singapore: Springer, 2017), p. 89.

16 For more discussion on the relationship between politics and parks, see Kyung-Jin Zoh, 'Place Memory and Representation: Traversing across Park Politics and Design in Korea', in In-ha Chŏng, ed., *Topography of Discourse: Architecture, Urbanism and Landscape Architecture* (Seoul: Namudoshi, 2011), pp. 182–236.

WALLISS: ENSEMBLES

1 Shigeru Satoh, 'Evolution and Methodology of Japanese Machizukuri for the Improvement of Living Environments', *Japan Architectural Review*, 2/2 (2019), pp. 127–42.

2 Ibid. pp. 128–30

3 Ibid. p. 127.

4 'Our Tampines Hub', https://worldarchitecture.org/architecture-projects/hczcm/our_tampines_hub-project-pages.html.

5 Huaiyuan Kou, Sichu Zhang, and Yuelia Liu, 'Community-Engaged Research for the Promotion of Healthy Urban Environments: A Case Study of Community Garden Initiative in Shanghai, China', *International Journal of Environmental Residential Public Health*, 16/21 (2019), pp. 41–5.

6 Jillian Walliss, 'China as a Laboratory for Change', *Landscape Architecture Australia*, 157 (2018), p. 43.

7 Ibid.

8 'Pacific Rim Community Design Network', http://prcdnet.org/.

HOU: EMERGING SPACES OF CITIZENSHIP

1 Mike Douglass and Amrita Daniere, 'Urbanization and Civic Space in Asia', in Amrita Daniere and Mike Douglass, eds., *The Politics of Civic Space in Asia: Building Urban Communities* (London and New York: Routledge, 2009), pp. 1–18.

2 Yukio Nishimura, 'Public Participation in Planning in Japan: The Legal Perspective', in Randolph T. Hester, Jr. and Corrina Kweskin, eds., *Democratic Design in the Pacific Rim: Japan, Taiwan, and the United States* (Mendocino, CA: Ridge Times Press, 1999), pp. 6–13; Jeffrey Hou, Li-Ling Huang, and Tamusuke Nagahashi, 'From Exchange to Collaboration: Cross-Cultural Learning of Participatory Planning in the Pacific Rim', Paper presented at the Seventh Conference of Asian Planning Schools Association (APSA), Hanoi, Vietnam, 12–14 September 2003.

3 Hyung-Chan Ang and Sohyun Park, 'Design Tools and Three Steps in Participatory Design Processes: A Proposal for Better Communications among Residents and Experts, based on a Case Project of Neighbourhood Park in Seoul, Korea', *Proceedings of the 6th Conference of the Pacific Rim Community Design Network*, Quanzhou, Fujian, China, 18–21 June 2007; Hae-Joang Cho, 'Breathing New Life into Urban Communities Struck Down by the "Block Attack" and Apathetic Individuals', *Green Community Design: Proceedings of the 8th International Conference of the Pacific Rim Community Design Network*, Graduate School of Environmental Studies, Seoul National University, 22–24 August 2012, pp. 1–8.; Young Bum Reigh, 'Issues of Urban Community Design in Korea: Urban Redevelopment vs. Community Renewal', *Green Community Design*, pp. 67–72.

4 Mee Kam Ng, 'Property-Led Urban Renewal in Hong Kong: Any Place for the Community?', *Sustainable Development*, 10 (2002), pp. 140–6; Mee Kam Ng, 'From Government to Governance? Politics of Planning in the First Decade of the Hong Kong Special Administrative Region', *Planning Theory & Practice*, 9/2 (2008), pp. 165–85.

5 Paul Collins and Hon S. Chan, 'State Capacity-Building in China: An Introduction', *Public Administration and Development*, 29 (2009), pp. 1–8.

6 Li-Ling Huang, 'Urban Politics and Spatial Development: The Emergence of Participatory Planning', in Reginald Y-W. Kwok, ed., *Globalizing Taipei: The Political Economy of Spatial Development* (London and New York: Routledge, 2005), pp. 78–98.

7 Ahn and Park, 'Design Tools and Three Steps in Participatory Design Processes'.

8 André Sorensen, *The Making of Urban Japan: Cities and Planning from Edo to the Twenty-First Century* (London and New York: Routledge, 2002), pp. 269–72.

9 Chu-Joe Hsia, 'Theorizing Community Participatory Design in a Developing Country: The Historical Meaning of Democratic Design in Taiwan', in *Democratic Design in the Pacific Rim*, pp. 14–21; Chi-Nan Chen, 'Reflections on the Community Building and Progress of Taiwan Democracy', *Reflections, and Future of Community Empowerment in Taiwan: Proceedings of the First Community Empowerment Forum* (Taipei: Society of Community Empowerment, 2013) (in Chinese).

10 Ahn and Park, 'Design Tools and Three Steps in Participatory Design Processes'.

11 Reigh, 'Issues of Urban Community Design in Korea', p. 69.

12 Ian Chong Ip, *Nostalgia for the Present: The Past and Present State of Cultural Conservation* (Hong Kong: Hong Kong Institute of Asia-Pacific Studies, Chinese University of Hong Kong, 2010) (in Chinese).

13 Yun-Chung Chen and Mirana M. Szeto, 'Reclaiming Public Space Movement in Hong Kong: From Occupy Queen's Pier to the Umbrella Movement', in *City Unsilenced: Urban Resistance and Public Space in the Age of Shrinking Democracy*, eds. Jeffrey Hou

and Sabine Knierbein (London and New York: Routledge, 2017), pp. 69–82.

14 Hou, Huang, and Nagahashi, 'From Exchange to Collaboration', n.p.

15 Reigh, 'Issues of Urban Community Design in Korea', p. 71.

16 Xiaohua Zhong and Ho Han Leung, 'Exploring Participatory Microregeneration as Sustainable Renewal of Built Heritage Community: Two Case Studies in Shanghai', *Sustainability*, 11/1617 (2019), pp. 1–15, accessed 25 September 2019, http://dx.doi.org/10.3390/su11061617; http://dx.doi.org/10.3390/su11061617.

17 Yves Cabannes and Zhuang Ming, 'Participatory Budgeting at Scale and Bridging the Rural-Urban Divide in Chengdu', *Environment and Urbanization*, 26/1 (2013), pp. 257–75.

18 It's important that we recognise the distinct projects as each represents an intersection of issues, context, and an ensemble of actors and processes.

19 Sung-Yong Choi, 'Various Meanings behind Making Han-Pyeong Park', *Green Community Design*, pp. 265–8.

20 Yun-Keum Kim, 'Looking Back at the Development of Community Participatory Design in Korea through Hanpyeong Park Project', Presentation at Democratic Design without Borders, EDRA 46 Mobile Intensive, Los Angeles, 27 May 2015.

21 Reigh, 'Issues of Urban Community Design in Korea', p. 71.

22 ChenYu Lien and Jeffrey Hou, 'Open Green: Placemaking beyond Place-Bound Communities in Taipei', in *Public Space Design and Social Cohesion: An International Perspective*, eds. Patricia Aelbrecht and Quentin Stevens (London and New York: Routledge, 2019), pp. 178–95.

23 Urban Regeneration Office of Taipei (URO), *Way to Community: Collaboration and Placemaking* (Taipei: Urban Regeneration Office of Taipei, 2019) (in Chinese and English).

24 Jeffrey Hou, 'Bottom-up Placemaking', *Landscape Architecture Australia*, 'Embracing the Asian Century', 157 (2018), pp. 76–81.

25 Hendrik Tieben, 'Magic Carpet Sai Yin Pun', in Hendrik Tieben and Min Jay Kang, eds., *Magic Carpet: Towards Community Benefit Plans for Urban Regeneration in Taipei and Hong Kong* (Taipei: Tonsan Books, 2017), pp. 217–43.

26 Benjamin C-H. Sin, 'Two Tales of One City: Building Resilient Communities in Pokfulam Village and Sai Sin Pun', in Tieben and Kang, eds., *Magic Carpet*, pp. 399–409.

27 Quoting from Daniel Burnham, but to emphasise the power of citizens, vis-à-vis professionals.

28 Sun-Ju Choi, Won-Sil Hwang, Sun-Hee Kim, and Chang-Sug Park, 'Analysis of Social Networks in the Management Organization of Seoul Forest Park', *Journal of the Korean Institute of Landscape Architecture*, 39/2 (2011), pp. 74–82.

29 http://seoulforest.or.kr/english (accessed 25 September 2019).

30 http://www.studio-l.org/en/service/01_arimafuji.html (accessed 25 September, 2019).

31 Min Jay Kang, 'Identity Politics and Community Artivism: A strategic Arts Project of Cultural Landscape Conservation at Treasure Hill, Taipei', in Jeffrey Hou, Mark Francis, and Nathan Brightbill, eds., *(Re)constructing Communities: Design Participation in the Face of Change* (Davis, CA: Center for Design Research, University of California, Davis, 2005), pp. 153–65.

32 https://www.scmp.com/comment/letters/article/1539875/protect-pok-fu-lam-village-preserve-cultural-heritage (accessed 27 September 2019).

33 Mihye Cho and Jiyoung Kim, 'Coupling Urban Regeneration with Age-Friendliness: Neighbourhood Regeneration in Jangsu Village, Seoul', *Cities*, 58 (2016), pp. 107–14.

34 Cho and Kim, 'Coupling Urban Regeneration with Age-Friendliness'; Hak-Yong Park, 'Experiment of JangSoo Village for the Renewal of Aged Housing', *Green Community Design*, pp. 409–14.

35 K.H. Yeo, 'A Study on the Growth of Community through Maeul-mandeulgi: Focused on the Jangsu Village, Seongbuk-gu' (in Korean), *Journal of The Korean Urban Management Association*, 26/1 (2013), pp. 53–87.

36 Park, 'Experiment of JangSoo Village', p. 413.

37 Mathew Pryor, *The Edible Roof: A Guide to Productive Rooftop Gardening* (Hong Kong: Mccm, 2016), p. 36.

38 Jeffrey Hou, 'Urban Commoning, Against City Divided: Field Notes from Taipei and Hong Kong', *Perspecta 50: Urban Divides, Journal of Yale University School of Architecture* (Cambridge, MA: The MIT Press, 2017), pp. 292–301.

39 https://www.rooftoprepublic.com/impact (accessed 27 September 2019).

40 Bo-Eun Lee, 'Mullae Community Garden: Designing a New Community and Relationship', *Green Community Design*, pp. 139–44.

41 Hou, 'Bottom-up Placemaking', p. 80.

42 Lee, 'Mullae Community Garden', p. 142.

43 https://tokyogreenspace.com/2009/08/06/ginza-honey-bee-project/ (accessed September 27 2019).

44 Jeffrey Hou, 'Governing Urban Gardens for Resilient Cities: Examining the Garden City Initiative in Taipei', *Urban Studies*, 11 (July 2018), https://doi.org/10.1177%2F0042098018778671.

45 Yuelai Liu, Haoyang Fan, Min Wei, Keluan Yin, Jianwen Yan, 'From Edible Landscape to Vital Communities: Clover Nature School Community Gardens in Shanghai', *Landscape Architecture Frontiers*, 5/3 (2017), pp. 72–83.

46 https://life.tw/?app=view&no=634786 (accessed 2 October 2019).

47 Jeffrey Hou, ed., *Insurgent Public Space: Guerrilla Urbanism and the Remaking of Contemporary Cities* (London and New York: Routledge, 2010), p. 7.

SINTUSINGHA: DESIGNING INDIGENOUS MODERNITY ...

1 For more detail see Edward Said, *Orientalism* (New York: Vintage Book, 1978).

2 This is encapsulated by the self-colonising tactics the Siamese elites employed to evade direct European colonisation in the nineteenth century; see S. Sintusingha and M. Mirgholami, 'Parallel Modernization and Self-Colonization: Urban Evolution and Practices in Bangkok and Tehran', *Cities*, 30/1 (2013), pp. 122–32.

3 Bahasa Indonesia, itself a legacy of modernity, transliterates the term 'modern' (modernisation is translated as 'modernisasi').

4 Unless they are famed tourist products like street food.

5 Unless the design involves deeper biases within society, such as the undesired informality of skateboarding, homelessness etc.

6 For more detail see Maurizio Peleggi, *Lord of Things: The Fashioning of the Siamese Monarchy's Modern Image* (Honolulu: University of Hawai'i Press, 2002).

7 See Sidh Sintusingha, 'Neoliberal "Intensities" in "Most Visited" Bangkok and "Most Livable" Melbourne: A View from the Cultural Interstices', in Satoshi Honda, ed., *Mn'M Workbook 3: Future Urban Intensities* (Tokyo: Flick Studio, 2014), pp. 98–101.

8 Moreover, the image of youth practicing their dance moves, adapted from and shared through YouTube, is a global phenomenon whether in Tokyo, Bangkok, or Melbourne.

9 Or *localised* agents—a prominent example being the Italian 'father of Thai modern art', Professor Corredo Feruci, better known by his Thai name of Silp Bhirasri.

10 Endang Triningsih, 'Investigating Bandung's Cafe Cultures: Everyday Life and Morphological Analysis of Coffeehouses in Bandung, Indonesia' (PhD dissertation, The University of Melbourne, 2018).

11 Sumet Jumsai, *Naga: Cultural Origins in Siam and the West Pacific* (Bangkok: Chalernnit Press and DD Books, 1997).

12 Kitapatr Dhabhalabutr, 'The Empowerment of the Slum Inhabitant as a Primary Agent of Low-Income Housing: the case study of Slum Upgrading in Thailand between 1980 and 2011' (PhD dissertation, The University of Melbourne, 2017).

13 See http://www.nationthailand.com/national/30333825

14 As has occurred at Kampung Tamansari, just downriver from Teras Cihampelas. See https://en.tempo.co/read/1283218/police-arrest-25-during-bandungs-tamansari-eviction. See also Amanda Achmadi, J. Connor, T. Rosmarin, and S. Sintusingha, 'Contested Riverscapes In Indonesian Cities: Urban Kampungs in the Age of Design Activism and the Image Economy', in *Proceedings of The 12th Conference Of International Forum On Urbanism Beyond Resilience: Towards A More Integrated And Inclusive Urban Design Jakarta*, 24–26 June 2019, Universitas Tarumanagara.

15 See https://www.youtube.com/watch?v=u9WufNmWXmo&list=LLGzC5T8CSWOIgtKrezxoxtg&index=769&t=0s (in Thai with English subtitles).

16 See https://www.iconsiam.com/en/events&activities/the-iconic-multimedia-water-features.

17 One should note that street vending can be very lucrative, especially in central locations.

Endnotes

TANG: TACIT NEGOTIATIONS AND THE PUBLIC REALM

1   Paul N. Edwards, 'Infrastructure and Modernity: Force, Time, and Social Organization in the History of Sociotechnical Systems', in Thomas J. Misa, Philip Brey, and Andrew Feenberg, eds., *Modernity and Technology* (Cambridge, MA: The MIT Press, 2003), pp. 188–9.
2   Paul Marsden and Tim Whiteman, eds., *Top Ten Construction Achievements of the 20th Century* (HKL International, 1999).
3   *Cities without Ground: A Hong Kong Guidebook*, Hong Kong Guidebook (Rafael, CA: Oro Editions, 2012).
4   Alan Berger, 'Drosscape', in Charles Waldheim, ed., *The Landscape Urbanism Reader* (New York: Princeton Architectural Press, 2006), pp. 197–217.
5   Xiaoxuan Lu, Ivan Valin, and Susanne Trumpf, 'Interstitial Hong Kong', *Landscape Architecture Frontiers*, 5/3 (2017), 127, https://doi.org/10.15302/J-LAF-20170312, emphasis in the original.
6   Jeffrey Chow, 'Public Open Space Accessibility in Hong Kong: A Geospatial Analysis, Hong Kong Civic Exchange' (24 October 2018), https://civic-exchange.org/report/open-space-geospatial-analysis/.
7   HKPSI, 'Hong Kong Public Space Awards 2013', *Hong Kong Public Space Initiative* 拓展公共空間 (blog), 2014, http://www.hkpsi.org/projects/hong-kong-public-space-awards-2013-2/.
8   Daniel Stone and Pierfrancesco Celada, 'Welcome to Hong Kong's "Instagram Pier"', *National Geographic* (17 October 2017), https://www.nationalgeographic.com/photography/proof/2017/10/welcome-to-hong-kongs-instagram-pier/.
9   Benni Pong, 'Unfolding the Western District Public Cargo Working Area in Hong Kong', *Landscape Architecture Frontiers*, 5/6 (2017), pp. 115–25, http://journal.hep.com.cn/laf/EN/10.15302/J-LAF-20170613.
10 Hillary Leung, 'Here's How Much Domestic Workers Add to Hong Kong's Economy', *Time* (6 March 2019), https://time.com/5543633/migrant-domestic-workers-hong-kong-economy/.
11 Jonathan Solomon, 'Hong Kong-Aformal Urbanism', in Rodolphe El-Khoury and Edward Robbins, eds., *Shaping the City: Studies in History, Theory, and Urban Design* (Abingdon, Oxon: Routledge, 2013), pp. 109–31.
12 BBC, 'Protesters Launch Bangkok "Shutdown"', BBC News (13 January 2014), https://www.bbc.com/news/world-asia-25708092.
13 Suzanne Sataline, 'How Hong Kong Police Lost the City's Trust', *The Atlantic* (1 September 2019), https://www.theatlantic.com/international/archive/2019/09/hong-kong-police-lost-trust/597205/.
14 Hillary Leung, 'The Crisis Facing the MTR, Hong Kong's Subway', *Time* (25 October 2019), https://time.com/5705799/hong-kong-subway-protests-mtr/.
15 RTHK, 'Mall Stays Open for Protesters, Closed for Police', *RTHK English News* (15 August 2019), https://news.rthk.hk/rthk/en/component/k2/1474758-20190815.htm.

SINTUSINGHA: A DESIGN PRACTICE OF PUBLIC ADVOCACY

1   The interview was conducted by Sidh Sintusingha with the Shma directors Namchai Saensupha, Prapan Napawongdee, and Yossapon Boonsom on 17 January 2020 at Shma's Ekkamai office.
2   http://landezine.com/index.php/2012/05/lifeladprao-18-condominium-garden-by-shma-design/. They note that the practice of elaborate sales galleries for high-rise residential began in Singapore.
3   https://www.archdaily.com/148548/vertical-living-gallery-sansiri?ad_medium=gallery.
4   http://landezine.com/index.php/2012/11/central-plaza-chiang-rai-by-shma-company-limited/.
5   https://worldlandscapearchitect.com/bridging-the-gaps-bangkok-thailand-shma/#.Xl4CDKgzYfw.
6   https://shmadesigns.com/knowledge/tcdc13-makkasan-workshop/.
7   https://shmadesigns.com/work/2050-ultra-flood-plain/.
8   https://shmasoen.com/portfolio/luang-pracha-burana-temple/.
9   https://shmasoen.com/portfolio/sathorn-smart-eco-street/.
10 https://apolitical.co/en/solution_article/thailand-upgraded-thousands-slums-giving-residents-control.
11 The pioneer generation, led by Professor Decha Boonkham, advocated for a nascent discipline to design public parks and also private housing subdivisions. American transplant Bill Bensley has been influential in this strong design focus and establishing the

landscape as core to hospitality development.
12 Shma offer provident funds, insurance, and subsidised staff meals as the office is in an aggressively gentrifying location.

RAHMANN: TRANSFORMATIVE FORCES

1   Hartmut Rosa, *Social Acceleration: A New Theory of Modernity* (Columbia University Press: New York, 2013).
2   Thijs Lijster and Robin Celikates, 'Beyond the Echo-Chamber: An Interview with Hartmut Rosa on Resonance and Alienation', *Krisis Journal for Contemporary Philosophy*, 1 (2019), p. 63.
3   Alan R. Teo, 'A New Form of Social Withdrawal in Japan: A Review of Hikikomori', *International Journal of Social Psychiatry*, 56/2 (2010), p. 178.
4   Ibid., p. 3.
5   ESCAP, *Technical Paper Information and Communications Technology and Disaster Risk Reduction Division: Overview of Natural Disasters and their Impacts in Asia and the Pacific, 1970–2014* (2015), p. 6.
6   Ibid.
7   Ibid., p. 8.
8   Dominic Barton, 'Why Japan Must Be Reimagined', in McKinsey & Company, *Reimagining Japan: The Quest for a Future That Works* (San Francisco: VIZ Media, 2011), p. 1.
9   Dominic Funabashi, 'March 11—Japan's Zero Hour', in McKinsey & Company, *Reimagining Japan: The Quest for a Future That Works* (San Francisco: VIZ Media, 2011), p. 14.
10 Padmal de Silva, 'The Tsunami and Its Aftermath in Sri Lanka: Explorations of a Buddhist Perspective', *International Review of Psychiatry*, 18/3 (June 2006), p. 284.
11 Taku Satoh, Naoto Fukasawa, Fumie Okumura, and Noriko Kawakami, eds., *Tema Hima: The Art of Living in Tohoku* (Tokyo: 2121 Design Sight, 2012), http://www.2121designsight.jp/en/program/temahima/.
12 Ibid.

NINSALAM: EMERGING TERRITORIES IN SOUTHEAST ASIA

1   Kevin G. Cai, 'The One Belt One Road and the Asian Infrastructure Investment Bank: Beijing's New Strategy of Geoeconomics and Geopolitics', *Journal of Contemporary China*, 27/114 (2018), pp. 831–47.
2   For more detail see Geoffrey Gunn, 'China's Globalization and the Belt and Road Project: The Case of Indonesia and Malaysia', in Jean A. Berlie, ed., *China's Globalization and the Belt and Road Initiative* (Springer International Publishing, 2020), pp. 123–38.
3   Zha Daojiong, 'In Pursuit of Connectivity: China Invests in Southeast Asian Infrastructure', *ISEAS Perspective*, 62 (2018), p. 9.
4   Willian A. Stricklin, *The Prince and I: Miss Olive* (Pittsburgh: Rosedog Books, 2020), p. 48.
5   To date, the BRI involves more than sixty-five countries and constitutes over 30 per cent of the Global Gross Domestic Product and impacts on 62 per cent of the global population.
6   For more detail see Hongying Wang, 'The New Development Bank and the Asian Infrastructure Investment Bank: China's Ambiguous Approach to Global Financial Governance', *Development and Change*, 50 (2019), pp. 221–44; Hong Yu, 'Motivation Behind China's "One Belt, One Road" Initiatives and Establishment of the Asian Infrastructure Investment Bank', *Journal of Contemporary China*, 26/105 (2017), pp. 353–68.
7   Peter Cai, 'Understanding China's Belt and Road Initiative', *Lowy Institute for International Policy* (2017), accessed 3 March 2020, https://www.lowyinstitute.org/publications/understanding-belt-and-road-initiative.
8   Jeffrey Craig, 'Learning from the Rust Belt: How to Revive Northeast China', *CKGSB Knowledge* (2018), accessed 3 March 2020, https://knowledge.ckgsb.edu.cn/2018/04/17/chinese-economy/rust-belt-revive-northeast-china/; Ian Johnson, 'As Beijing Becomes a Supercity, the Rapid Growth Brings Pains', *The New York Times* (2015), accessed 3 March 2020, https://www.nytimes.com/2015/07/20/world/asia/in-china-a-supercity-rises-around beijing.html.
9   Cai, 'Understanding China's Belt and Road Initiative'.
10 Joseph Sipalan, 'China, Malaysia Restart Massive 'Belt and Road' Project after Hiccups', *Reuters* (2019), accessed 3 March 2020, https://www.reuters.com/article/us-china-silkroad-malaysia/china-malaysia-restart-massive-belt-and-road-project-after-hiccups-idUSKCN1UK0DG.
11 Tham Siew Yean, 'Chinese Investment in Malaysia: Five Years into

the Bri', *ISEAS Perspective*, 11 (2018), p. 9.

12 These projects include the Melaka Gateway (RM 43 billion) launched in 2014 by Power China International; the Carey Island Port and City Complex (RM 200 billion), with negotiations ongoing with China Merchants Group; and Kuantan Port and Malaysia-China Kuantan Industrial Park (RM19 billion), by Guangxi Beibu International Port Group to be completed in 2020.

13 Johan Saravanamuttu, 'Malaysia's East Coast Rail Link: Bane or Gain?', *S. Rajaratnam School of International Studies* (2017), p. 4.

14 Pooja Thakur Mahrotri and En Han Choong, '$100 Billion Chinese-Made City near Singapore "Scares the Hell out of Everybody"', *Bloomberg* (2016), accessed 3 March 2020. https://www.bloomberg.com/news/features/2016-11-21/-100-billion-chinese-made-city-near-singapore-scares-the-hell-out-of-everybody.

15 These projects include the upcoming Kuantan deep water port and industrial park to the east and the Melaka Gateway project to the west.

16 Aliyu Salisu Barau and Salman Qureshi, 'Using Agent-Based Modelling and Landscape Metrics to Assess Landscape Fragmentation in Iskandar Malaysia', *Ecological Processes*, 4/8 (2015).

17 Chris Milton, 'The Sand Smugglers', *Foreign Policy* (2010), accessed 3 March 2020, https://foreignpolicy.com/2010/08/04/the-sand-smugglers/.

18 Joshua Comaroff, 'Built on Sand: Singapore and the New State of Risk', *Harvard Design Magazine* (2014), p. 138.

19 Eric Oh, 'Sasaki's "Forest City" Master Plan in Iskandar Malaysia Stretches across 4 Islands', *ArchDaily* (2016), accessed 3 March 2020, https://www.archdaily.com/781247/sasakis-forest-city-master-plan-in-iskandar-malaysia-stretches-across-4-islands.

20 For more detail see Serina Rahman, 'Johor's Forest City Faces Critical Challenges', *Trends in Southeast Asia*, 3 (2017), p. 47; Sylvain Ourbis and Albert Shaw, 'Malaysia's Forest City and the Damage Done', The Diplomat (2017), accessed 3 March 2020, https://thediplomat.com/2017/08/malaysias-forest-city-and-the-damage-done/.

21 For more detail see Guanie Lim 'Resolving the Malacca Dilemma: Malaysia's Role in the Belt and Road Initiative', in Alessandro Arduino and Gong Xue, eds., *Securing the Belt and Road Initiative: Risk Assessment, Private Security and Special Insurances along the New Wave of Chinese Outbound Investments* (Singapore: Palgrave Macmillan, 2018), pp. 81–99; Hong Liu and Guanie Lim, 'The Political Economy of a Rising China in Southeast Asia: Malaysia's Response to the Belt and Road Initiative', *Journal of Contemporary China*, 28/116 (2019), pp. 216–31.

22 World Bank, 'Indonesia: Country Partnership Framework for the Period FY16–20', *World Bank Report* 1 (2015), p. 167.

23 Ibid.

24 Ibid.

25 Wilmar Salim and Dharma Negara Siwage, 'Why Is the High-Speed Rail Project So Important to Indonesia?', *ISEAS Perspective*, 16 (2016), p. 10.

26 Ibid.

27 Fanny Potkin and Tabita Diela, 'Fast Track: Indonesia, Malaysia Rail Projects May Give China More Deals', *Reuters* (2019), accessed 3 March 2020, https://www.reuters.com/article/us-china-silkroad-indonesia/fast-track-indonesia-malaysia-rail-projects-may-give-china-more-deals-idUSKCN1RZ07F.

28 CGTN, 'China-Indonesia Ties: Chinese FM: We're Natural Partners', *China Global Television Network*, 0:37, China (2018), accessed 3 March 2020, https://news.cgtn.com/news/79417a4e7a454464776c6d636a4e6e62684a4856/share_p.html.

29 Forest City, 'The Iskandar Edge', (2020), accessed 3 March 2020, https://www.forestcitycgpv.com/about-forest-city/strategic-location#:~:text=Forest%20City%20is%20at%20the,the%20Malaysian%20government%20in%202006.

30 Siwage Dharma Negara and Leo Suryadinata, 'Indonesia and China's Belt and Road Initiatives: Perspectives, Issues and Prospects', *Trends in Southeast Asia*, 11 (2018), p. 40; Leo Suryadinata, 'The Growing "Strategic Partnership" between Indonesia and China Faces Difficult Challenges', *Trends in Southeast Asia*, 15 (2017), p. 35.

RICARDO/WALLISS: DOING BUSINESS IN ASIA

1 Mee Kam Ng, 'Transformative Urbanism and Reproblematising Landscape Scarcity in Hong Kong', *Urban Studies*, 57/7 (2020), pp. 1452–68.

2 Email with Catherin Bull (9 February 2020).

3 Email with Keith French (5 September 2019).

4 'Passionate Visionary Receives Prestigious Medal of Honour', https://ramboll.com/media/rgr/passionate-visionary-receives-prestigious-medal-of-honour.

5 Email with Keith French (5 September 2019).

6 Craig Czarny, 'Building Partnerships', *Landscape Architecture Australia Embracing the Asian Century*, 157 (2018), pp. 36–9.

7 Email with Hong Zhou (14 September 2019).

8 Email with Alex Breedon (28 January 2020).

9 Ricky Ray Ricardo, 'Communicating Landscape Architecture in Asia', *Landscape Architecture Australia, Embracing the Asian Century*, 157 (2018), pp. 70–4.

10 Rowan Moore, 'A Garden Bridge that Works: How Seoul Succeeded Where London Failed', *The Guardian* (19 May 2017).

11 Email with Jungyoon Kim (19 April 2020).

12 Ibid.

13 SWA Group, 'Eight Years in China', https://www.swagroup.com/eight-years-in-china/.

14 Email with Tao Zhang, Michael Grove, and Dennis Pieprz (29 August 2018).

15 Ibid.

16 Ibid.

17 Email with Stephen Jones (23 January 2020).

18 Email with Keith French (5 September 2019).

19 Email with Hong Zhou (14 September 2019).

20 Email with Adrian McGregor (20 September 2019).

21 Email with Alex Breedon (28 January 2020).

22 Email with Stephen Jones (23 January 2020).

RAHMANN/WALLISS: URBANISM IN A STATE OF IMPERMANENCE

1 'Taming Asia's Megacities', https://www.urbangateway.org/content/news/taming-asia%E2%80%99s-megacities.

2 United Nations, *The Future of Asian & Pacific Cities: Transformative Pathways Towards Sustainable Urban Development* (Bangkok 2019), p. 30.

3 Ibid., p. 31.

4 Kisho Kurokawa, *The Philosophy of Symbiosis from the Ages of the Machine to the Age of Life* (London: Academy Editions, 1994), p. 17.

5 Ibid.

6 Fumino Nanjo, 'Metabolism's Current Significance, Contribution to Disaster Recovery, and Future', in Mami Hirose, Hitomi Sasaki, and Naotake Maeda, eds., *Metabolism, the City of the Future: Dreams and Visions of Reconstruction in Postwar and Present-Day Japan* (Tokyo: Shinkenchikusha, 2011), p. 6.

7 Ibid.

8 Ibid., p. 19.

9 Ibid.

10 William Gardner, 'Liquid Cities', in *Places* (May 2020), https://placesjournal.org/article/liquid-cities/?cn-reloaded=1.

11 Jonathan Watts, 'Japan Suffocates under a Concrete Blanket', *The Guardian* (27 July 1999), https://www.theguardian.com/world/1999/jul/27/jonathanwatts.

12 Yoji Sasaki, 'Continuous Space in the Urban Landscape', in David N. Buck, ed., *Responding to Chaos: Tradition, Technology, Society and Order in Japanese Design* (New York: Spon, 2000), p. 188.

13 Ibid.

14 Hajime Yatsuka, 'The Metabolism Nexus' Role in Overcoming Modernity', in Hirose, Sasaki, and Maeda, *Metabolism, the City of the Future*, p. 11.

15 Anne Allison, 'New-Age Fetishes, Monsters, and Friends', in Tomiko Yoda and Harry Harootunian, eds., *Japan After Japan: Social and Cultural Life from the Recessionary 1990s to the Present* (London: Duke University Press, 2006), p. 341.

16 Toyo Ito, *Ano hi kara no kenchiku* (Tokyo: Shinsho Shuesha, 2012), pp. 3–8.

17 Kurokawa, *The Philosophy of Symbiosis*, p. 29.

18 Ibid.

19 Rory Stott, 'Spotlight: Kisho Kurokawa', *ArchDaily* (8 April 2020), https://www.archdaily.com/616907/spotlight-kisho-kurokawa.

20 Xavier Guillot, 'Between "Asianization" and "New Cosmopolitanism": Housing in Twenty-First-Century Singapore', in Catherin Bull, Davisi Boontham, Claire Parin, Darko Radovic, and Guy Tapie, eds., *Cross-Cultural Urban Design: Global or Local*

Practice (Oxon: Routledge, 2007), p. 35.

21 Peter Newman, 'Singapore: Biophilic City', YouTube video, posted by Linda Blagg (7 May 2012), https://www.biophiliccities.org/singapore.

22 Ng Lang, 'A City in a Garden', in Civil Service College Singapore, *World Cities Summit Issue* (14 June 2008), https://www.csc.gov.sg/articles/a-city-in-a-garden.

23 Mun Summ Wong and Richard Hassell, 'Sustainability and Urban Design: Garden City, Mega City', *Urban Solutions*, 9 (2016), p. 54.

24 Mun Summ Wong, Richard Hassell, and Alina Yeo, 'Garden City, Megacity: Rethinking Cities for the Age of Global Warming', *CTBUH Journal*, 4 (2016), p. 46.

25 Christopher DeWolf, 'Biophilic Design: Greening the City', *CLADmag*, 2 (2016), https://www.cladglobal.com/architecture-design-features?codeid=30964.

26 Wong, Hassell, and Yeo, 'Garden City, Megacity', p. 50.

27 Wong and Hassell, 'Sustainability and Urban Design', p. 59.

28 DeWolf, 'Biophilic Design: Greening the City'.

29 Heejin Han, 'Singapore, a Garden City: Authoritarian Environmentalism in a Developmental State', *Journal of Environment & Development*, 26/1 (2016), p. 9.

30 Joshua Bolchover and John Lin, *Rural Urban Framework: Transforming the Chinese Countryside* (Basel: Birkhäuser, 2013), p. 11.

31 Chaolin Gu, Christian Kesteloot, and Ian G. Cook, 'Theorising Chinese Urbanisation: A Multi-layered Perspective', *Urban Studies*, 52/4 (2015), p. 2565.

32 Cindy C. Fan, 'Migration, Hukou and the City', in Shadid Yusuf and Tony Saich, eds., *China Urbanizes: Consequences, Strategies and Policies* (Washington, D.C.: The World Bank, 2008), p. 66.

33 Mark Yaolin Wang, 'Small City, Big Solution? China's Hukou System Reform and Its Potential Impacts', *disP—The Plannnig Review*, 151 (2002), p. 24.

34 Fan, 'Migration, Hukou and the City', pp. 70–1.

35 Ling Wu, 'Decentralization and Hukou Reforms in China', *Policy and Society*, 32/1 (2013), p. 35.

36 Ruibo Han Ruibo and Wang Linna, 'Challenges and Opportunities Facing China's Urban Development in the New Era', *China Perspectives* (2013), p. 18.

37 Ibid.

38 Ibid.

39 Ibid.

40 Yansui Liu et al., 'The Process and Driving Forces of Rural Hollowing in China under Rapid Urbanization', *Journal of Geographical Sciences*, 20/6 (2010), p. 887.

41 Kunio Igusa, 'Globalization in Asia and Local Revitalization Efforts: A View from One Village One Product (Ovop) Movement in Oita' (2006), www.iovoppa.org/files2/igusa.pdf, p. 30.

42 Valentin Noble, 'Mobilities of the One-Product Policy from Japan to Thailand: A Critical Policy Study of Ovop and Otop', *Territory, Politics, Governance*, 7/4 (2019), p. 459.

43 Ibid., 454

44 Anna-Paola Pola, 'Reframing Chinese Villages', *Modu Magazine: A Tale of Urban China*, https://www.modumag.com/focus/reframing-chinese-villages/.

45 Igusa, 'Globalization in Asia and Local Revitalization Efforts', p. 31.

46 Long Hoang Thanh et al., 'One Village One Product (Ovop)—A Rural Development Strategy and the Early Adaption in Vietnam, the Case of Quang Ninh Province', *Sustainability*, 10 (2018), p. 5.

47 Igusa, 'Globalization in Asia and Local Revitalization Efforts', p. 37.

48 Noble, 'Mobilities of the One-Product Policy', p. 461.

49 Pola, 'Reframing Chinese Villages'.

50 Ibid.

51 Junren Wan, 'The Philosophical Wisdom and Action Implications of "Beautiful China"', *Social Sciences in China*, 34/4 (2013), p. 152.

52 Junli Yang, 'Construction of "Beautiful Village" Landscapes from the Perspective of Ecological Civilization: A Case Study of Zizhulin Village in Yanshan County', *Journal of Landscape Research*, 10/4 (2018), pp. 120–2.

53 Pola, 'Reframing Chinese Villages'.

54 Ibid.

55 Bolchover and Lin, *Rural Urban Framework*, p. 12.

56 Yongqi Lou, Francesca Valsecchi, and Clarisa Diaz, 'Prologue', in *Design Harvests: An Acupunctural Design Approach Towards Sustainability* (Gothenburg, Sweden: A Mistra Urban Futures Publication, 2013).

57 See Yizhao Yang and Jie He, 'Sustainable Urban Design with Chinese Characteristics: Inspiration from the Shan-Shui City Idea', https://journals.openedition.org/articulo/3134.

58 Lou, Valsecchi, and Diaz, *Design Harvests*, p. 6.

59 Ibid., p. 4.

60 Ibid., p. 4.

61 Ibid., p. 6.

62 Ibid., p. 8.

63 Wan, 'The Philosophical Wisdom and Action Implications of "Beautiful China"', p. 144.

64 Kamala Tiyavanich, *Forest Recollections: Wandering Monks in Twentieth-Century Thailand* (Honolulu: University of Hawaii Press, 1997), p. 1.

65 Oliver Smith, 'Diving into Misogi, the Ancient Japanese Ritual of Waterfall Bathing', *National Geographic* (9 May 2020), https://www.nationalgeographic.co.uk/travel/2020/05/diving-into-misogi-the-ancient-japanese-ritual-of-waterfall-bathing.

66 Pittu Laungani, 'Hindu Spirituality and Healing Practices', in Roy Moodley and William West, *Integrating Traditional Healing Practices into Counseling and Psychotherapy* (Thousand Oaks: Sage, 2005), p. 140.

67 Pinit Ratanaku, 'Buddhism, Health, Disease, and Thai Culture', in Harold Coward, Harold G. Coward, and Pinit Ratanakul, eds., *Cross-Cultural Dialog on Health Care Ethics* (Waterloo: Wilfrid Laurier University Press, 1999), p. 19.

68 Ibid

69 Liyuan Huang and Honggang Xu, 'A Cultural Perspective of Health and Wellness Tourism in China', *Journal of Chinese Tourism Research*, 10/4 (2014), p. 496.

70 Ibid., p. 498.

71 Ibid., p. 497.

72 Christopher Key Chapple, 'Hinduism and Deep Ecology', in Roger S. Gottlieb, ed., *This Sacred Earth: Religion, Nature, Environment* (Oxon: Routledge, 2004), p. 304.

73 Ibid., p. 313.

74 Alex Kerr, *Dogs and Demons: The Fall of Modern Japan* (London: Penguin, 2001), pp. 51–77.

75 Wei Guo and Peina Zhuang, 'Ecophobia, "Hollow Ecology", and the Chinese Concept of "Tianren Heyi" (天人合一)', *ISLE: International Studies in Literature and Environment*, 26/2 (2019), p. 438.

76 Ibid., p. 440.

77 Jim Taylor, 'Buddhist Revitalization, Modernization, and Social Change in Contemporary Thailand', *Sojourn*, 8/1 (1993), p. 62.

78 Referring to communities with more than 50 per cent of the population over the age of sixty-five.

79 Eid-Ul Hasan, 'Nature-Based Tourism and Revitalization of Rural Communities in Japan: An Ethnographic Case Study of Oyama Town', *Journal of Social Science Studies*, 4/1 (2017), p. 140.

80 Ibid.

81 Ibid., p. 141.

82 Ibid.

83 Pia R. Kieninger, Marianne Penker, and Eiji Yamaji, 'Esthetic and Spiritual Values Motivating Collective Action for the Conservation of Cultural Landscape—A Case Study of Rice Terraces in Japan', *Renewable Agriculture and Food Systems*, 27/1 (2012), p. 2.

84 Pia Kieninger, Eiji Yamaji, and Marianne Penker, 'Urban People as Paddy Farmers: The Japanese Tanada Ownership System Discussed from a European Perspective', *Renewable Agriculture and Food Systems*, 26/4 (2011), p. 2.

85 Ibid.

86 Yasuo Ohe et al., 'Evaluating the Relaxation Effects of Emerging Forest-Therapy Tourism: A Multidisciplinary Approach', *Tourism Management*, 62 (2017), p. 323.

87 Forest Agency, Press release (18 April 2006), http://www.rinya.maff.go.jp/j/press/h18-4gatu/0418wagakunino.html.

88 Ohe et al., 'Evaluating the Relaxation Effects of Emerging Forest-Therapy Tourism', p. 326.

WALLISS: FAST AND SLOW

1 Feng Li, *'Critical' Practice in State-Owned Design Institutes in Post-Mao China (1976–2000s): A Case Study of Cag (China Architecture Design and Research Group)* (The University of Melbourne, 2010), p. 18.

2 Ibid., p. 19.

3 Charlie Q. L. Xue and Guanghui Ding, *A History of Design Institutes in China: From Mao to Market* (London, New York: Routledge, 2018), p. 8.

4 Li, *'Critical' Practice*, p. 1.

5   Email with Alex Breedon (28 January 2020).
6   Ibid.
7   Guanghui Ding and Charlie Q. L Xue, 'Mediating Production, Teaching, and Research: The Role of University-Run Design Institutes in Chinese Architectural Practice', *arq*, 23/4 (2018), p. 83.
8   Xue and Ding, *A History of Design Institutes in China*, p. 143.
9   'About Tjad', http://www.tjad.cn/about/tjad.
10 Ding and Xue, 'Mediating Production, Teaching, and Research', p. 161.
11 Presentation at Original Design Studio (11 December 2019).
12 'Kuma-Lab', http://kuma-lab.arch.t.u-tokyo.ac.jp/projects.html.
13 'Urban Design Lab', http://utud.sakura.ne.jp/en/about/concept/.
14 Ding and Xue, 'Mediating Production, Teaching, and Research', p. 86.
15 Ibid.

MANNISI: DEEP ASIAN ECOLOGY

1   S. Kumon, 'Japan as a Network Society', in S. Kumon and H. Rosovsky, eds., *The Political Economy of Japan*, vol. 3: *Cultural and Social Dynamics* (Stanford: Stanford University Press, 1992), pp. 109–141.
2   C. Nakane, *Japanese Society* (London: Weidenfeld & Nicolson, 1970).
3   A. Ogawa, *The Failure of Civil Society: Anthropology of NPOs and the State in Contemporary Japan* (New York: Cornell University, 2005).
4   R. Yamazaki, コミュニティデザイン一人がつながるしくみをつくる (How to lead people to community design) (Tokyo: 学芸出版社, 2011).
5   For more information see https://korekara-pj.net.
6   A. Drengson and Y. Inoue, *The Deep Ecology Movement: An Introductory Anthology* (Berkeley, CA: North Atlantic, 1995).
7   A. Mannisi, 'La méthode du Dangisho' (Dangisho method), in *L'Esprit des Villes* (Paris: Infolio, 2014), pp. 6–8.
8   K. Nishida, *Nishida Kitarō Zenshū* 5西田幾多郎全集 (Complete works of Nishida Kitarō) (Tokyo: Iwanami Shoten, 1978–1980), pp. 98–122.
9   T. Kuwako, *Kansei no tetsugaku* (Environmental philosophy) (Tokyo: NHK, 2001).
10 A. Magnaghi, *The Urban Village: A Charter for Democracy and Local Self-Sustainable Development* (London & New York: Zed Books, 2005).
11 Chua Beng Huat, 'Singapore as Model: Planning Innovations, Knowledge Experts', in Ananya Roy and Aihwa Ong, eds., *Worlding Cities: Asian Experiments and the Art of Being Global* (Chichester, West Sussex: Malden, MA: Wiley-Blackwell, 2011), pp. 29–54.
12 M. Miller and M. Douglass, *Disaster Governance in Urbanising Asia* (Singapore: Springer, 2016).
13 S. Hamnett and B. Yuen, *Planning Singapore: The Experimental City* (Singapore: Routledge, 2019).
14 C. Tortajada and H. Zhang, *Food Policy in Singapore in Reference Module in Food Science* (Amsterdam: Elsevier, 2016).
15 http://www.greencircle.com.sg/.
16 K. Jomo, Y. Chang, and K. Khoo, *Deforesting Malaysia: The Political Economy and Social Ecology of Agricultural Expansion and Commercial Logging* (London: Zed Books, 2004).
17 This set of issues led in 2019 to the author's project Hokkien Mee Diplomacy (www.scapethical.org/portfolio/hokkien-mee-diplomacy/).
18 E. Ludher, *Urban System Studies: Food and The City; Overcoming Challenges for Food Security* (Centre for Liveable Cities (CLC), Singapore, 2018).
19 https://www.ediblegardencity.com.
20 E. Rahbar, 'The Malaysian Consumer and the Environment: Purchase Behavior', *Global Business and Management Research: An International Journal* (2010), pp. 323–36.
21 B. Barendregt and R. Jaffe, *Green Consumption: The Global Rise of Eco-chic* (London: Bloomsbury, 2014).
22 C. J. Cavanagh, 'Biopolitics, Environmental Change, and Development Studies', *Forum for Development Studies*, 41/2 (2014), pp. 273–94.
23 M. Bookchin, *Our Synthetic Environment* (New York: Knopf, 1962).
24 V. Shiva, *The Violence of the Green Revolution* (London: Zed Books, 1991).
25 R. Grove and D. Vinita, 'Imperialism, Intellectual Networks, and Environmental Change: Origins and Evolution of Global Environmental History 1676–2000; Part I', *Economic and Political Weekly*, 41 (2006), pp. 4345–54.

WANG/ZHU: CHINA NOW

1   J. B. Jackson, *Landscapes: Selected Writings of J. B. Jackson* (Amhurst: University of Massachusetts Press, 1970), pp. 153–4.
2   A. T. Smith, *The Political Landscape: Constellations of Authority in Early Complex Polities* (Oakland, CA: University of California Press, 2003).
3   For further discussion, see Kamwing Chan, 'Fundamentals of China's Urbanization and Policy', *China Review*, 10/1 (2010), pp. 63–93; Zhifang Wang et al., 'Perspectives on Narrowing the Action Gap between Landscape Science and Metropolitan Governance: Practice in the US and China', *Landscape and Urban Planning*, 125 (2014), pp. 329–34.
4   For further discussion, see Zhiji Huang et al., 'Urban Land Expansion under Economic Transition in China: A Multi-Level Modeling Analysis', *Habitat International*, 47 (2015), pp. 69–82; L. J. C. Ma, 'Urban Transformation in China, 1949–2000: A Review and Research Agenda', *Environment and Planning A*, 34/9 (2002), pp. 1545–69; Han Li et al., 'Administrative Hierarchy and Urban Land Expansion in Transitional China', *Applied Geography*, 56 (2015), pp. 177–86.
5   Zhifang Wang, 'Evolving Landscape-Urbanization Relationships in Contemporary China', *Landscape and Urban Planning*, 171 (2018), pp. 30–41.
6   For further discussion, see Jianguo Liu and P. H. Raven, 'China's Environmental Challenges and Implications for the World', *Critical Reviews in Environmental Science and Technology*, 4/9–10 (2010), pp. 823–51; Chunyan Luo et al., 'Challenges Facing Socio-economic Development as a Result of China's Environmental Problems, and Future Prospects', *Ecological Engineering*, 60 (2013), pp. 199–203.
7   T. D. Fletcher et al., 'SUDS, LID, BMPs, WSUD and More: The Evolution and Application of Terminology Surrounding Urban Drainage', *Urban Water Journal*, 12/7 (2015), pp. 525–42.
8   Hualou Long et al., 'Rural Vitalization in China: A Perspective of Land Consolidation', *Journal of Geographical Sciences*, 29 (2019), pp. 517–30.
9   Junli Yang, 'Construction of "Beautiful Village" Landscapes from the Perspective of Ecological Civilization: A Case Study of Zizhulin Village in Yanshan County', *Journal of Landscape Research*, 10/4 (2018), pp. 120–2.
10 Jing Gao and Bihu Wu, 'Revitalizing Traditional Villages through Rural Tourism: A Case Study of Yuanjia Village, Shaanxi Province, China', *Tourism Management*, 63 (2017), pp. 223–33.
11 *China Statistical Year Book* (2014), p. 8.
12 Naomi Carmon, 'Three Generation of Urban Renewal Policies: Analysis and Policy Implications', *Geoforum*, 30 (1999), pp. 145–58.
13 Luqi Gu et al., 'The Theory and Practice of City Betterment and Ecological Restoration', *Urban Planning*, 3 (2017), pp. 18–25.
14 For further discussion, see L. R. Musacchio, 'The Ecology and Culture of Landscape Sustainability: Emerging Knowledge and Innovation in Landscape Research and Practice', *Landscape Ecology*, 24/8 (2009), pp. 989–92; J. I. Nassauer and P. Opdam. 'Design in Science: Extending the Landscape Ecology Paradigm', *Landscape Ecology*, 23/6 (2008), pp. 633–44.
15 Zhifang Wang et al., 'Perspectives on Narrowing the Action Gap between Landscape Science and Metropolitan Governance: Practice in the US and China', *Landscape and Urban Planning*, 125 (2014), pp. 329–34.
16 Jianguo Wu et al., 'Urban Ecology in China: Historical Developments and Future Directions', *Landscape and Urban Planning*, 125 (2014), pp. 222–33.

PAE: LANDSCAPE ARCHITECTS AS URBANISTS OF OUR AGE

1   Mintaek Oh, 'Seoul's Urban Regeneration Model' *Seoul Solution* (17 October 2017), https://seoulsolution.kr/en/content/6875.
2   On the place memory of Seonyudo Park, see So-Young Han and Kyung-Jin Zoh, 'Urban Parks in Seoul as Place Representation', *Journal of the Korean Institute of Landscape Architecture*, 38/2 (2010), pp. 46–52.
3   Myung-Jun Lee, 'Transforming Post-industrial Landscapes into Urban Parks: Design Strategies and Theory in Seoul, 1998–Present', *Habitat International*, 91 (2019), https://doi.org/10.1016/j.habitatint.2019.102023.
4   For a more detailed discussion of the aesthetic experience at Seonyudo Park, see Jeong-Hann Pae, 'The Garden of Time, Design as a Discovery: What Seonyudo Park Criticizes', in Jeong-Hann

Pae, ed., *Beyond the Landscape Architecture* (Seoul: Jokyung, 2007), pp. 56–73.
5   Landscape Division in Green Seoul Bureau, 'Cheonggyecheon Stream', in *Landscape Architecture of Seoul* (Seoul: Seoul Metropolitan Government, 2019), pp. 162–7.
6   Regarding the policy on this restoration, see Green Seoul Bureau, 'Restoring Cheonggyecheon', in Green Seoul Bureau, ed., *From Cheonggyecheon to Seoul Forest* (Seoul: Seoul Metropolitan Government, 2006), pp. 152–81.
7   Yangkyo Chin, 'Cheonggyechon: Revitalizing of an Urban River', *Topos*, 55 (2006), p. 44.
8   Ibid.
9   For a more detailed discussion, see Jeong-Hann Pae, 'Cheonggyecheon as an Urban Park', *POAR*, 115 (November 2005), pp. 145–7; 'Cheonggyecheon as a Synaesthetic Urban Landscape', *Space*, 456 (November 2005), pp. 244–5.
10 For further detail on this process, see Hyeyoung Choi and Young-Ai Seo, 'The Process of Creating Yongsan Park from the Urban Resilience Perspective', *Sustainability*, 11/5 (2019), https://doi.org/10.3390/su11051225.
11 Ministry of Land, Transport and Maritime Affairs, *General Basic Plan for the Creation and Zoning of the Yongsan Park, Korea* (2011). I participated in this plan as a senior researcher in charge of park planning.
12 Jeong-Hann Pae, ed., *Yongsan Park: A Critical Review of the International Competition for the Master Plan of the Yongsan Park, Korea* (Seoul: Namudosi, 2013).
13 Ministry of Land, Infrastructure and Transport, *The Yongsan Park Basic Design* (2018).

WALLISS: LANDSCAPES IN THE SKY

1   'Skyrise Greenery Incentive Scheme 2.0', National Parks, https://www.nparks.gov.sg/skyrisegreenery/incentive-scheme.
2   Nirmal Kishnani, *Greening Asia: Emerging Principles for Sustainable Architecture* (Singapore: BCI Asia, 2012), p. 14.
3   Devina Mahendriyani, 'Singapore: Bca Introduces a New Green Mark 2015', http://www.asiagreenbuildings.com/10759/singapore-bca-introduces-a-new-green-mark-2015/.
4   Urban Redevelopment Authority, 'Circular Package: Lush Programme—Landscaping for Urban Spaces and High Rises', https://www.ura.gov.sg/Corporate/Guidelines/Circulars/lushprogramme.
5   Urban Redevelopment Authority, 'Updates to the Landscaping for Urban Spaces and High-Rises (Lush) Programme: Lush 3.0', https://www.ura.gov.sg/Corporate/Guidelines/Circulars/dc17-06.
6   *Bringing Greenery Skywards: A Handbook on Developing Sustainable Highrise Gardens* (National Parks Board, 2017), p. 2.
7   Mooool, 'Thammasat Urban Rooftop Farm', LANDPROCESS, http://www.landprocess.co.th/.

KISHNANI: THE LIVING SKIN

1   Ken Yeang et al., *Constructed Ecosystems: Ideas and Subsystems in the Work of Ken Yeang* (Novato: Applied Research + Design Publishing, 2016), pp. 152–9.
2   Kuan Chee Yung, Senior Vice President, CPG Consultants, Interview with Nirmal Kishnani (15 March 2018).
3   Vo Trong Nghia, Skype interview with Nirmal Kishnani and Heather Marshall Banerd (18 June 2018).
4   Nirmal Kishnani, *Ecopuncture: Transforming Architecture and Urbanism* (Singapore: FuturArc, 2019), p. 116.
5   'Ho Chi Minh City Loses 50% of Green Space in 11 Years', *Tokyo Green Space* (3 January 2010), https://tokyogreenspace.com/2010/01/03/ho-chi-minh-city-loses-50-of-green-space-in-11-years/.
6   Hossein Shafizadeh Moghadam and Marco Helbich, 'Spatiotemporal Urbanization Processes in the Megacity of Mumbai, India: A Markov Chains-Cellular Automata Urban Growth Model', *Applied Geography*, 40 (June 2013), pp. 140–9.
7   'Vietnam: Green Construction Opens up Opportunities for Building Materials Suppliers', *Asia Green Buildings* (18 September 2013), http://www.asiagreenbuildings.com/7093/vietnam-green-construction-opens-up-opportunities-for-building-materials-suppliers/.
8   Yeang et al., *Constructed Ecosystems*, p. 13 and p. 16.
9   Kishnani, *Ecopuncture*, p. 78.
10 Patrick Bingham-Hall, *Garden City Mega City: Rethinking Cities for the Age of Global Warming* (Oxford: Pesaro Publishing, 2016), pp. 220–3.
11 Ibid.
12 Ibid, pp. 232–5, pp. 244–7.
13 Philip Oldfield, 'What Would a Heat-Proof City Look Like?' *The Guardian* (15 August 2018), https://www.theguardian.com/cities/2018/aug/15/what-heat-proofcity-look-like.
14 Anuj Jain, *Final Report: OASIA Downtown Biodiversity & Social Audit* (26 April 2018).
15 Meera Senthilingam, 'How Did Singapore Become Such a Green City?', *CNN* (21 July 2016), https://edition.cnn.com/travel/article/singapore-greenest-city/index.html. As Singapore's population and economy grew, so did its green cover: it was about 36 per cent in the 1980s, and it now stands at 47 per cent, according to the Center for Liveable Cities.
16 Urban Redevelopment Authority, 'Draft Master Plan 2019: Proposals for an Inclusive, Sustainable and Resilient City' (27 March 2019), https://www.ura.gov.sg/Corporate/Media-Room/Media-Releases/pr19-13.
17 National Parks Board, *Nature Conservation Masterplan* (Singapore, 2017), https://www.nparks.gov.sg/~/media/nparks-real-content/news/2017/fob/factsheet-e-nature-conservation-masterplan.pdf.
18 Stephanie Yeow, 'A Garden City's Green Veins', *The Straits Times* (27 November 2017), http://www.straitstimes.com/singapore/a-garden-citys-green-veins.
19 'Greening Singapore So Wildlife Can Return', *The Straits Times* (7 June 2018), http://www.straitstimes.com/sites/default/files/attachments/2018/06/07/st_20180607_nature07_4041868.pdf.
20 Ministry of Environment and Water Resources, Ministry of National Development, and the Centre for Liveable Cities, *Sustainable Singapore Blueprint* (Singapore, 2014), https://www.mewr.gov.sg/docs/default-source/module/ssb-publications/41f1d882-73f6-4a4a-964b-6c67091a0fe2.pdf.
21 Centre for Urban Greenery & Ecology, National Parks Board, *Design Guides to Promote Biodiversity on Roof Gardens: CS E12:2017* (Singapore, 2017), https://www.nparks.gov.sg/skyrisegreenery/news-and-resources/guidelines.
22 Ki-Yeong Yu, 'Urban Environment of Seoul', *Seoul Solution*, last modified 12 June 2018, https://www.seoulsolution.kr/en/node/6343.
23 'Cheonggyecheon Stream Restoration', *Landscape Performance Series*, accessed 24 May 2019, https://landscapeperformance.org/case-study-briefs/cheonggyecheon-stream-restoration.
24 'Mumbai Floods: What Happens When Cities Sacrifice Ecology for Development,' *The Conversation* (2 September 2017), http://theconversation.com/mumbai-floods-what-happens-when-cities-sacrifice-ecology-for-development-83328.
25 Sonia Minz, 'With 753 Green Buildings, Mumbai Tops the Chart, Delhi Follows', *MakaanIQ* (8 November 2016), https://www.makaan.com/iq/living/with-753-green-buildings-mumbai-tops-the-chart-delhi-follows.
26 Rahul Mehrotra, Skype interview with Nirmal Kishnani and Heather Marshall Banerd (16 May 2018).

WALLISS: DESIGNING THERMAL DELIGHT IN THE ASIAN CITY

1   Sophia Siddique Harvey, 'Mapping Spectral Tropicality in the Maid and Return to Pontianak', *Singapore Journal of Tropical Geography*, 29 (2008), p. 28.
2   Jiat-Hwee Chang and Tim Winter, 'Thermal Modernity and Architecture', *The Journal of Architecture*, 20/1 (2017), p. 107.
3   Ibid. p. 111.
4   Ibid., p. 116.
5   Russell Hitchings and Shu Jun Lee, 'Air Conditioning and the Material Culture of Routine Human Encasement: The Case of Young People in Contemporary Singapore', *Journal of Material Culture*, 13 (2008), p. 254.
6   Ibid., p. 261.
7   Anna Solcerova et al., 'Uchimizu: A Cool(ing) Tradition to Locally Decrease Air Temperature', *Water*, 10/6 (2018), pp. 1–2.
8   'Uchimizu', http://uchimizu.jp/.
9   'Furin' (wind chimes), https://matcha-jp.com/en/2487.
10 Alsop Architects, 'Clarke Quay', www.arcspace.com/features/alsop-architects/clarke-quay.
11 Evyatar Erell, David Pearlmutter, and Terry Williamson, *Urban Microclimate: Designing the Spaces between Buildings* (London/Washington, D.C.: Earthscan, 2011), pp. 246–7.

12 Ibid.
13 Andrew Galloway, 'Building Skin Developed That Could Cool Our Cities', https://www.archdaily.com/529486/building-skin-developed-that-could-cool-our-cities.
14 Ibid.
15 Jillian Walliss and Heike Rahmann, *Landscape Architecture and Digital Technologies: Re-conceptualising Design and Making* (UK: Routledge, 2016), p. 51.
16 Interview with Philippe Rahm (20 December 2014).
17 Paysagistes Mosbach, Philippe Rahm Architects, and Ricky Liu & Associates, 'Taichung Gateway Park International Competition Overview of the Winning Project' (2013), unpublished.
18 'Singapore's First Naturally-Cooled Mall.' https://www.across-magazine.com/singapores-first-naturally-cooled-mall/.
19 Andrew Bromberg, 'The Star', http://www.archdaily.com/510587/the-star-andrew-bromberg-of-aedas.
20 Interview with Dion Anandityo (21 June 2017).
21 D. Tunas, 'Shopping Malls as Town Squares in the Tropics: How Sustainable Are They?', http://www.greenasiaforce.com/shopping-malls-as-town-squares-how-sustainable-are-they/.
22 In 2019 the New Creation Church acquired The Star Vista mall for SDG 296 million.
23 Fosters+Partners, 'Beach Road, Singapore', http://www.fosterandpartners.com/projects/beach-road/.
24 Roland Schnizer et al., 'South Beach Towers, Singapore: Canting Towers and a Cooling Canopy', *Council on Tall Buildings and Urban Habitat*, 2 (2017), p. 16.
25 Ibid.
26 Narelle Yabuka, 'South Beach: Building and Planting a Green City Block', *CityGreen*, 7, 'Stepping up with Green' (2013), p. 94.
27 Tim Winter, 'An Uncomfortable Truth: Air-Conditioning and Sustainability in Asia', *Environment and Planning A*, 45 (2013), p. 518.
28 Ibid., p. 528.

RAHMANN: RETREAT

1 Statista, 'Total Contribution of Travel and Tourism to GDP in the Asia Pacific Region in 2019, by Country or Region', https://www.statista.com/statistics/313589/travel-and-tourisms-direct-contribution-to-gdp-in-asia-pacific-countries/.
2 Knoema, 'Thailand: Contribution of Travel and Tourism to GDP as a Share of GDP', https://knoema.com/atlas/Thailand/topics/Tourism/Travel-and-Tourism-Total-Contribution-to-GDP/Contribution-of-travel-and-tourism-to-GDP-percent-of-GDP.
3 Jamie James, 'Made Wijaya, Landscape Architect, Author and Stranger in paradise', *Sydney Morning Herald* (8 September 2016), https://www.smh.com.au/national/made-wijaya-landscape-architect-author-and-stranger-in-paradise-20160831-gr58qs.html.
4 Anthony Dennis, 'How Balinese Style Was Born: The Architects Who Shaped "Bali style"', *Traveller* (20 June 2018), https://www.traveller.com.au/how-balinese-style-was-born-the-architects-who-shaped-bali-style-h11jw8.
5 Rüdiger Kortz, 'The Tropical Paradise of Made Wijaya', YouTube video, posted by madewijaya3 (29 January 2010), http://www.youtube.com/watch?v=makDyycHvmw&feature=fvhl.https://www.youtube.com/watch?v=sf24g1Yx0cY.
6 Akihiko Seki and Elizabeth Heilman Brooke, *Japanese Spa: A Guide to Japan's Finest Ryokan and Onsen* (Tokyo: Tuttle, 2005), p. 13.
7 Walk Japan, 'Besso (Country Villas)', *Nakasendo-Way: A Journey to the Heart of Japan* (2020), https://www.nakasendoway.com/besso-country-villas/.
8 Hiromu Tsuchiya, 'Residents Launch Campaign to Save Historic Karuizawa villa', *The Asahi Shimubun* (19 August 2019), http://www.asahi.com/ajw/articles/AJ201908190047.html.
9 Ibid.
10 Kortz 'The Tropical Paradise of Made Wijaya'.
11 Ibid.
12 Ibid.

RAHMANN: SLOW LIVING WITHIN THE LIMITS OF GROWTH

1 Junko Edahiro, 'Toward a Sustainable Japan: Challenges and Changes in Society and Population', in *United Nations University Our World* (24 January 2015), https://ourworld.unu.edu/en/toward-a-sustainable-japan-challenges-and-changes-in-society-and-population.

2 Thomas Daniell, *After the Crash: Architecture in Post-bubble Japan* (New York: Princeton Architectural Press, 2008).
3 The research for this essay was kindly funded by a Japan Foundation Visiting Research Fellowship.
4 Hiko Mitani, 'New Creation with History in Mind and Heart', *The Japan Architect: Landscape in Japanese Architecture 2015*, 98 (Summer 2015), p. 53.
5 Nihon Zoen Gakkai, https://www.jila-zouen.org/koukoku.
6 Japan Landscape Architecture Union, 'About Us', http://jlau.or.jp/about_us/.
7 Tatsuya Hiraga, interview by author, Tokyo (5 July 2012).
8 Hiroki Hasegawa, interview by author, Tokyo (27 June 2012).
9 Hiroki Hasegawa, interview by author, Tokyo (20 June 2014).
10 Ibid.
11 Ibid.
12 Tatsuya Hiraga, 'Thinking about City Reproduction of Tokyo from a Form Principle of Nature', *The Japan Architect: Landscape in Japanese Architecture 2015*, 98 (Summer 2015), p. 85.
13 Toru Mitani, 'The Modernist Listening to the Earth', in David Buck, *Responding to Chaos: Tradition, Technology, Society and Order in Japanese Design* (London: Spon Press, 2000), p. 58.
14 Sayuri Kobayashi, 'Shaping the Regional Landscape through Everyday Life: A How-To of "Total Landscape"', *Ueno Park Studies Lecture 02*, Ueno Cultural Park (21 December 2017), https://ueno-bunka.jp/uenostudies/321/.
15 Michio Tase, interview by author, Tokyo (6 July 2012).
16 Fumiaki Takano, *Dream of Landscape* (Tokyo: Kenchikushiryokenkyusha, 2020), p. 133.
17 Ibid., p. 181.
18 See Consultants of Landscape Architecture in Japan, https://www.cla.or.jp/rla/outline/.
19 Hiko Mitani, interview by author, Tokyo (5 July 2012).
20 Hiko Mitani, 'New Creation with History in Mind and Heart', p. 53.
21 Junko Edahiro, 'Toward a Sustainable Japan: Challenges and Changes in Society and Population', in *United Nations University Our World* (24 January 2015), https://ourworld.unu.edu/en/toward-a-sustainable-japan-challenges-and-changes-in-society-and-population.
22 Ibid.

NINSALAM/WALLISS: DESIGNING FOR CONSCIOUSNESS ...

1 This essay is based on an interview conducted at Salad Dressing's office on 11 July 2019 and further text discussions occurring on 23 and 25 June 2020.
2 Salad Dressing, Phoibos 11 pamphlet (23 July 2018). https://issuu.com/saladdressing/docs/phoibos_11_pamphlet.

P.24 Turenscape P.25 Turenscape P.28 V.C.Nguyen P.29 V.C.Nguyen P.30 RUA, KU Leuven, 2016 P.31 RUA, KU Leuven, 2016 P.36 Ramboll Studio Dreiseitl P.37 Top: Ramboll Studio Dreiseitl; Bottom: Finbarr Fallon P.38 Turenscape P.39 Turenscape P.40 Wison Tungthunya P.41 Shma P.42 LANDPROCESS P.43 LANDPROCESS P.44 LANDPROCESS P.46 Turenscape P.47 Friends of the River P.48 PARKKIM P.49 PARKKIM P.50 Golden Park Landscape Architecture, Environmental Planning & Design P.51 Golden Park Landscape Architecture, Environmental Planning & Design P.52 Shuang Pan P.53 Shuang Pan P.54 Top: Edward Hendricks; Bottom: Fabian Ong P.55 Fabian Ong P.56 Arch-Exist P.57 Arch-Exist P.58 Makoto Yoshida P.59 Makoto Yoshida P.60 Arch-Exist P.61 Arch-Exist P.62 Arch-Exist P.63 Conggang Yu P.64 Xi Tang P.65 Xi Tang P.68 Kyungsub Shin P.69 Yoon-Jin Park P.70 Top: Jong Oh Kim, Middle: Jong Oh Kim; Bottom: PARKKIM P.71 Jong Oh Kim P.74 Dong Zhang P.75 Hai Zhang P.76 Hai Zhang P.77 Hai Zhang P.80 Yusuke Komatsu P.81 Yusuke Komatsu P.82 Yusuke Komatsu P.96 Darren Soh for Woods Bagot P.97 Darren Soh for Woods Bagot P.99 Top: MIR; Bottom Right: Gustafson Porter + Bowman; Bottom Left: Dscribe P.100 Top: Darren Soh for Woods Bagot; Bottom: Jillian Walliss P.101 Darren Soh for Woods Bagot P.102 Kawasumi—Kobayashi Kenji Photograph Office P.103 Kawasumi—Kobayashi Kenji Photograph Office P.104 Jong Oh Kim P.105 Jong Oh Kim P.106 Hai Zhang P.107 Hai Zhang P.108 Zhewei Su P.109 Zhewei Su P.116 Edible Way P.117 Edible Way P.121 Plan b P.122 Magic Carpet, Chinese University of Hong Kong (CUHK) P.125 Jeffrey Hou P.126 Top and Middle: Liu Yuelai; Bottom: Jillian Walliss P.130 Top: Martha Schwartz Partners; Middle: Martha Schwartz Partners; Bottom: Sidh Sintusingha P.132 Sidh Sintusingha P.133 Sidh Sintusingha P.137 Adam Frampton, Jonathan Solomon, and Clara Wong P.139 Lu Xiaoxuan, Ivan Valin, and Susane Trumpf P.140 Benni Pong P.142 Pierfrancesco Celada P.143 Pierfrancesco Celada P.147 Shma P.149 Shma and Shma Soen P.150 Heike Rahmann P.151 Heike Rahmann P.158 Sky X Terrain—Marieluise Jonas, Heike Rahmann, Yazid Ninsalam, Chris Bellman, and Scott Mason P.159 Sky X Terrain—Marieluise Jonas, Heike Rahmann, Yazid Ninsalam, Chris Bellman, and Scott Mason P.174 Fabian Ong P.175 Fabian Ong P.184 Ian Kim P.185 Ian Kim; Bottom left: Yerin Kang P.186 Fabian Ong P.187 Fabian Ong P.188 Wenzhong Gao P.189 Wenzhong Gao P.190 Top: Shin Suzuki; Bottom: EARTHSCAPE P.191 Shin Suzuki; Bottom right: EARTHSCAPE P.192 Top: Yong Zhang; Bottom: Original Design Studio P.193 Top: Yong Zhang; Bottom: Original Design Studio P.194 Top: Yong Zhang; Bottom: Provided by Shanghai Urban Public Space Design Promotion Centre: Fangfang Tian P.195 Left: Yong Zhang; Right: Original Design Studio P.196 Rural Urban Framework P.197 Rural Urban Framework P.198 Shogo Oizumi for Dan Pearson and Tokachi Millennium Forest P.199 Shogo Oizumi for Dan Pearson and Tokachi Millennium Forest P.200 Shogo Oizumi P.201 Top: Shogo Oizumi for Dan Pearson and Tokachi Millennium Forest; Bottom: Kiichi Noro for Dan Pearson and Tokachi Millennium Forest P.202 Qi Zhan P.203 Qi Zhan P.206 Seoahn Total Landscape P.207 Seoahn Total Landscape P.208 CA Design P.209 CA Design P.210 Top: CA Design; Bottom: Seoul Metropolitan Government P.213 Tadamasa Iguchi P.214 Top left: Bing Lu; Top right: Bing Lu; Bottom Left: Tony Metaxas for BAU; Bottom right: BAU P.215 Tadamasa Iguchi P.216 Rural Urban Framework P.217 Rural Urban Framework P.218 Jonathon McFeat P.219 Jonathon McFeat P.222 Hiroyuki Oki; Bottom Right: Vo Trong Nghia Architects P.223 Hiroyuki Oki P.224 Patrick Bingham-Hall P.225 Left: K. Kopter; Right: Patrick Bingham-Hall P.226 STX Landscape Architects P.227 STX Landscape Architects P.228 Top: Patrick Bingham-Hall; Bottom: K. Kopter P.229 Patrick Bingham-Hall P.230 Ramboll Studio Dreiseitl P.232 Kawasumi—Kobayashi Kenji Photograph Office P.233 Kawasumi—Kobayashi Kenji Photograph Office P.234 Kawasumi—Kobayashi Kenji Photograph Office P.235 Top: Kawasumi—Kobayashi Kenji Photograph Office, Bottom: Landscape Plus P.236 LANDPROCESS P.237 LANDPROCESS/ Panoramic Studio P.242 Nigel Young/Foster + Partners P.243 Foster + Partners P.244 Nigel Young/Foster + Partners P.246 Fabian Ong P.247 Fabian Ong P.252 Patrick Bingham-Hall P.253 Top: Skyshot Pte Ltd; Bottom: Tierra Design P.254 Makoto Yoshida P.255 Makoto Yoshida P.256 Makoto Yoshida P.257 Makoto Yoshida P.258 Makoto Yoshida P.259 Makoto Yoshida P.260 Makoto Yoshida P.261 Top: Hoshino Resorts; Bottom: Makoto Yoshida P.262 Z+T Studio P.263 Z+T Studio P.264 Salad Dressing P.265 Salad Dressing P.267 Fabian Ong P.268 Left: Jillian Walliss; Right: Fabian Ong

Imprint

© 2020 by jovis Verlag GmbH
Texts by kind permission of the author.
Pictures by kind permission of the photographers/
holders of the picture rights.

Design and setting: Felix Holler—Stoffers Graphik-Design
Cover: Felix Holler—Stoffers Graphik-Design
Lithography: Stefan Rolle—Stoffers Graphik-Design
Printed in the European Union.

Bibliographic information published by the Deutsche
Nationalbibliothek.
The Deutsche Nationalbibliothek lists this publication
in the Deutsche Nationalbibliografie. Detailed bibliographic data are available on the Internet at
http://dnb.d-nb.de.

jovis Verlag GmbH
Lützowstraße 33
10785 Berlin

www.jovis.de

jovis books are available worldwide in select book-
stores. Please contact your nearest bookseller or visit
www.jovis.de for information concerning your local
distribution.

ISBN 978-3-86859-612-0